CORPUS CHRISTI

Books by Geddes MacGregor
Published by The Westminster Press

Corpus Christi
The Thundering Scot

CORPUS CHRISTI

The Nature of the Church According to the Reformed Tradition

by

GEDDES MacGREGOR

Wipf & Stock
PUBLISHERS
Eugene, Oregon

Wipf and Stock Publishers
199 West 8th Avenue, Suite 3
Eugene, Oregon 97401

Corpus Christi
The Nature of the Church according to the Reformed Tradition
By MacGregor, Geddes

ISBN: 1-59244-706-6
Publication date 5/19/2004
Previously published by Westminster, 1958

VENERABILI

ECCLESIÆ SCOTIÆ

CONVENTVI GENERALI

HOC OPVS QVANTVLVMCVMQVE

HVMILLIME

DEDICO

CONTENTS

PREFACE

To SAY that High Churchmen are those who think highly of the Church and lowly of themselves, while Low Churchmen are those who think lowly of the Church and highly of themselves, may be too clever to be true. Experience proves, however, that the quickest way of getting a correct answer, in a particular case, to the very theological question, ' What think ye of Christ? ' is by not asking it at all, but by ascertaining, rather, what your audience thinks of the Church. If, on the one hand, their answer makes it clear that they think the Church is an amalgamation of clubs ' for religious purposes ' (side shows notwithstanding) , you may stake your library, if not your life, on the conclusion that the riches of their Christology will be exhausted in the proclamation of ' Jesus our Guide, our Hero, and our Friend '. If, on the other hand, it is less dogmatic, beware: you may be dealing with people of such Chalcedonian orthodoxy that they are to be suspected of having been caught reading the New Testament without commentary from their grandfather's modern prejudices. It may even be that they stand in no need of a reminder that though the first amendment to the Constitution provides for ' the right of the people peaceably to assemble,' its other phrase, designed for the safeguard of religious liberties, is for Christians not on that account a tautology.

The questions raised in what Christian theologians call ' the doctrine of the Church ' are questions that would not have occurred to our forefathers, as did questions about the Person of Christ. They are modern questions; indeed, for Christians, the modern questions *par excellence*. This book is intended as a contribution to the discussion that has already become, by the grace of God, vivacious.

My debt to other scholars is great; too great to make adequate acknowledgement possible. I cannot forbear, however, to thank Professor George Johnston of the University of Toronto, who generously provided me with some useful materials which I have freely plundered in writing Chapter VI and in compiling the Bibliography. The literature relevant to the latter, even in the past hundred years or so, is too varied and indefinitely vast to permit either completeness or any entirely defensible principle of selection. It is hoped that the list provided, which comprises nearly five hundred books and articles, will be of use to those engaged in similar studies.

I wish also to express my thanks to the following persons for their courtesy in answering questions: the Rev. John Wilson Baird, St. Machar's Cathedral, Aberdeen; the Rev. Professor J. H. Baxter, St. Andrews; Professor T. R. S. Broughton, Bryn Mawr; the Rev. Dr. Nevile Davidson, Glasgow Cathedral; Professor Richard Lattimore, Bryn Mawr; Professor Milton Charles Nahm, Bryn Mawr; Lady Philip, Edinburgh; the Rev. James Mackintosh, Trinity College, Glasgow; the Rev. Professor Norman Pittenger, General Theological Seminary, New York City; the Rev. J. A. T. Robinson, Clare College, Cambridge; the Rev. Dr. John Sinclair, Glasgow; the Very Rev. Dr. Charles L. Warr, Edinburgh; Professor Emeritus H. A. Wolfson, Harvard.

To my friend and former Oxford tutor, the Rev. Dr. Austin Farrer, who has for long borne with my questions, I owe gratitude such that it would be ungracious merely to include him in a list. It is a special pleasure for me to take the opportunity of rendering him my thanks.

Finally, my thanks are due to Miss Sarah Ann Caner, one of my graduate students, for valuable suggestions and extensive help with the proofs.

GEDDES MACGREGOR

PART ONE

CHAPTER I

THE PROBLEM

During the first three centuries, the period of persecution, Christians were confronted with important theological problems. These were discussed so extensively that by the time of Constantine's death in 337, they had already been so formulated that, though controversy about them was far from being over, the lines on which further argument would proceed were in large measure already determined. When, for example, Basil and the Gregories were opposing the redemptive theory of Apollinaris, much still remained to be said about the nature of Christ; but the framework in which it would be said had taken shape. Yet a thousand years later, when Wyclif was writing, and a papacy at Avignon had begun to make conciliarism a fashionable topic among scholars, discussions about the nature of the Church, though they had much canonistic learning behind them, had no theological framework such as the christological controversies had had a millenium earlier. Indeed, it was not till after the Reformation that discussion of the nature of the Church began to take as theological a form as discussion of the nature of Christ had taken before St Augustine was born.

Why the nature of the Church did not present itself as a problem till so comparatively late in Christian history is a question that it is better to postpone. But let it be stated at the outset that its neglect was due to anything other than lack of church-consciousness among Christians of the earlier period. Early Christian consciousness of the Church was, however, akin to the consciousness that a healthy man has of his enjoyment of energy and life. Such a man does not give much thought to the workings of his digestive system; he is not likely to inquire about his metabolism or to ascertain whether there is too much cholesterol in his blood. So when St Paul rejoices at being 'in Christ' he is at the same time expressing his joy as a member of 'the Body of Christ'.[1] The New Israel consists of those who have been incorporated (σύμφυτοι) into Christ by Baptism. It would not have occurred to any New Testament writer to suppose that a man might be 'in Christ' yet not 'in the Church': it would have seemed a logical impossibility, somewhat like saying of a man that he has parents, yet is not a member of a family. On all this much more must be said later on.

How different from this is the theological climate today may be seen from any competent review of the doctrines of the Church that are held in various communions in modern Christendom. From the Report of the second World Conference on Faith and Order held at Edinburgh in 1937, it seemed to many that probably the most divisive features in the theological controversies of modern Christendom were rooted in differences about the nature of the Church. In contrast to the fourth and fifth centuries, when the differences were christological, the disputes of today were seen to be at heart ecclesiological.[2] Various papers were therefore written and circulated by members of three theological commissions whose reports, with a selection of some of the papers that had been circulated, were published[3] as a basis for discussion at the third World Conference at Lund in 1952. So when over two hundred and fifty delegates from various communions met at Lund, they all knew where everyone stood; the question was only whither they might be able to go. Lund did indeed disclose how fundamental were the ecclesiological differences in twentieth-century Christendom, and perhaps this conference more than any other was pervaded by what Pierre Maury has called 'the ecumenical sadness'. The dis-

[1] Cf. A. Nygren, *Christ and His Church* (Eng. tr. A. Carlsten, London, 1957), pp. 93 ff. To say that being ἐν Χριστῷ is the same for Paul as being a member τοῦ σώματος τοῦ Χριστοῦ does not imply an identification of Christ and the Church. *Infra*, c. viii.

[2] 'Ecclesiology' is used throughout the present work to denote discussion of the nature of the Church; the term has another sense with which we are not at all concerned.

[3] *The Nature of the Church*, edited by R. Newton Flew, D.D., Chairman of the International Theological Commission on the Church (London, SCM Press, 1951).

cussions at Lund can hardly be said to have been a landmark in contemporary theology. There was much truth in the complaint of Professor A. M. Ramsey (now Archbishop of York) that any competent theologian giving an account of the various current views on the nature of the Church could have done the task as well. This was not for lack of plain speaking. When Bishop Gulin of Finland spoke as one having the apostolic succession against those who held it to be essential, he evoked bluntness in plenty, and when an American representative of the Churches of Christ was speaking on the nature of the Church, a German Lutheran was heard to murmur, '*Montanisten!*' Yet for all the frustrations there was to many at the Lund conference a curious sense of 'waiting on God': after the Swedish Archbishop Brilioth had, at the closing service, pronounced the benediction, the delegates remained for at least three minutes in spontaneous meditation in which many thought, no doubt, of the East German delegates returning to conditions that other Christians did not at present have to face. Such a sense of unity in Christ did not, however, diminish the force of the ecclesiological differences; it sharpened rather, the 'ecumenical anguish'.

Since the Roman Church was not officially represented, the delegates at Lund belonged to communions which, except for the Greek Orthodox and the Old Catholic, are in one way or another the heirs of the Reformation. Though this sixteenth-century movement was from every ecclesiological point of view the most seismic in the history of Christendom, the Reformation Fathers exhibited, for the most part, remarkable unity on the christological questions that had in the fourth and fifth centuries caused the most acrimonious disputes all over Christendom at a time when east and west were nominally undivided by the schism that separated them in the eleventh century. Various theological issues were indeed raised at the Reformation; but there is, to say the least, a *prima facie* case for saying that they were all rooted in ecclesiological questions. It is a defensible thesis that the Reformation was about the nature of the Church more than it was about justification or grace. According to this thesis, it is to the Reformation that we must constantly turn in any modern discussion on the nature of the Church, just as it is Nicaea and Chalcedon that a Christian theologian must use as a point of reference in any modern discussion about the Person of Christ. This is recognized by Roman theologians no less than by others; not least by one of the most distinguished contemporary thinkers in the Roman Church, the French Dominican, Père Yves Congar, whose important book on the nature of the Church, one which exhibits great erudition and profound historical and theological insight, is a study of the ecclesiological question from a modern Roman Catholic point of view and having the Reformation as its principal point of reference.[1]

A study of the Reformation documents reveals on all sides the nascent ecclesiological concern of the sixteenth century. The delight of the Reformers in the recovery of Scripture as the norm for all theological discussion has often obscured the fact of their ecclesiological preoccupation. Yet the essential meaning of the Reformation is lost when it is interpreted apart from this. The late Dom Gregory Dix, in his justly celebrated *opus maximum*,[2] drew the attention of many besides members of his own Anglican communion, to the folly of trying to interpret the history of Christianity without constant reference to the eucharistic action that is central to the life of the Church. It is no less misleading to attempt to render an account of any theological development within the Christian Church without constantly calling to mind the fact that all Christian theology that is not mere trivial abstraction springs from the living reality of corporate awareness of being within the Family of God. The historic phrase, 'the Body of Christ' (*corpus Christi*), with which we shall be much concerned in the present study, is applied in Scripture and the Fathers to both the Church and the Eucharist or Supper. How close was the connection between Eucharist and

[1] Yves M.-J. Congar, O.P., *Vraie et fausse Réforme dans l'Eglise* (Paris, Editions du Cerf, 1950, 648 pp.). This work, bearing the *nihil obstat* and *imprimi potest* of his religious superiors and the *imprimatur* of the Vicar-General of Paris, was published as Cahier IV of Père Congar's *Essais sur la communion catholique*, and withdrawn shortly after publication, so that copies of it are not ordinarily obtainable.

[2] Gregory Dix, *The Shape of the Liturgy* (London, Dacre Press, 1945).

and Church in the mind of St Augustine is dramatically presented in passages quoted from his sermons by Dix.[1] 'So the Lord willed to impart His Body and His Blood which He shed for the remission of sins. If you have received well, you *are* that which you have received.'[2] And again: 'Your mystery is laid on the Lord's table; your mystery you receive. To that which you *are* you answer "amen", and in answering you assent. For you hear the words "the Body of Christ"[3] and you answer "amen". Be a member of the Body of Christ that the amen may be true.'[4] When the leaders of the Reformation and the multitude of preachers they trained or inspired addressed themselves to the common man in Germany and Switzerland, in France and England, in Scotland and the Netherlands, the impression of their appeal was not fundamentally dissimilar from that received by the Africans who had the good fortune to have Augustine for their preacher. In the sixteenth century, wherever the presence of Christ was believed to be rediscovered, there a doctrine of the Church was already in process of development.

Such was the complexity of the Reformation background that the ecclesiology took many forms, some wayward, some perhaps half-hearted. It is the purpose of the present study to inquire into one of them. The tradition that is to be considered, which may make at least a plausible claim to be central, is the special, though by no means the exclusive, inheritance of that family of Churches now commonly called 'Reformed' in contradistinction to other ecclesiastical families, groups or communions, such as the Anglican, Lutheran, Congregationalist and Baptist.

In order that this purpose may be more fully exhibited, it will be convenient to consider briefly at this point the various ecclesiological traditions, and to survey conceptions of the Church to be found at the present time in Christendom. This survey is not intended to be in any sense complete; it is meant,

[1] *Op. cit.* (5th impression, 1952), p. 247.

[2] St Augustine, '*Serm.* ccxxvii. See Appendix I, 13'.

[3] I.e., the words applied to the Eucharist in the liturgy, in the administration of the Sacrament,

[4] St Augustine, '*Serm.* cclxxii. See Appendix 1, 12.' Cf. St Thomas, *Summa Theol.*, III, q. 73, a. 3.

rather, briefly to indicate the significance of the enterprise in hand.[1]

(*a*) *Lutheran:* The Augsburg Confession (*Confessio Augustana*) provides a doctrinal norm for all Lutherans, and it expresses its doctrine of the Church in view of Luther's essential attitude towards his reforming work. There was no thought in his mind of 'founding' a 'new Church'; his intention was to serve the Church that was there, and which was, he believed, *una sancta ecclesia*. This attitude was due not merely to Luther's personal, temperamental inclination to conservatism; it was due, rather, as we shall see later, to the essential nature of the Reformation itself. The Church is 'the congregation of saints in which the Gospel is purely taught, and the Sacraments rightly administered'.[2] The Word and the Sacraments are the two and only basic marks of the Church (*notae ecclesiae*), and so the only essential ministry is the ministry of Word and Sacrament. Questions of ecclesiastical order are regarded as external and incidental; they are concerned only with the 'clothes' of the Church, not with its fundamental nature. So the constitution of Lutheran Churches may and do vary considerably. The Church, as the *congregatio fidelium*, is hidden,[3] in the sense that only God can know precisely who are its constituent members; nevertheless the *fideles* can recognize it by the presence of the marks, for the Church is an actuality in the world, not an ideal Zion. Only in later Lutheran theology is the Calvinistic distinction drawn between the visible and the invisible Church.

In view of the strong emphasis on Scripture that is so characteristic of Luther, it is noteworthy that in the Augsburg Confession the Church is defined without mention of the Bible. There is, indeed, no article on the Scriptures as such, not even a list of the canonical books of the Bible. The reason is simple. The importance of the Scriptures lies in the witness they bear to the

[1] For current ecclesiologies I am considerably indebted to *The Nature of the Church* (London, S.C.M., 1952; ed. R. N. Flew).

[2] *Confessio Augustana*, art. 7.

[3] Luther favoured the word 'hidden' (*abscondita*), perhaps even preferring it to *invisibilis*, which he is the first to apply to the Church. See *Ad librum Ex. Mag. Nostri Mag. Ambrosii Catharini . . . Responsio* (1521), ed. Weimar, VII, p. 722.

Gospel of Christ; as the final standard for testing theological doctrine, no ecclesiastical tradition, however valuable or venerable, can ever compete with them. But the Scriptures do not constitute the Church. The Church is constituted by Christ Himself, acting through and present in what happens (*das Ereignis*) when the Gospel is preached and the Sacraments administered. As the Ignatian formula has it, *ubi Christus, ibi ecclesia.*[1]

On the other hand, while all this belongs to Lutheran Orthodoxy, grounded as this is on the Augsburg Confession, Luther's own utterances about the Church are by no means always clear. His rendering into the vernacular of the classic phrase *una sancta ecclesia catholica* by *eine Versammlung aller Christglaubigen auf Erden*[2] leads one to question what, precisely, Luther meant by the Church. He used ideas that were already familiar, not least to the conciliarists, in whose practical failure lay the justification of his reformatory movement; but it is arguable that in the translation of terms such as *societas fidelium, congregatio fidelium, communio, aggregatio*, and the like, into the vernacular, Luther lost sight of their full significance. He did not like the term *Kirche*[3]; his use of it is sometimes vague, and his use of *Christenheit* is such as to suggest that he has in mind the word *ecclesia* and is giving it a special sense, 'society of believers,' which is alien to neither New Testament nor tradition, yet can be wrenched out of context in such a way as to enfeeble and distort the Greek.

Though every believer is a priest, the priesthood is exercised in a special way by those who are called to the ministry. The ministry is considered as a gift to the Church, for the sake of good order, yet it is God's gift, not a mere human convenience. It receives its authority from Christ in His living Church. There is no place for self-righteousness either in the ministry or else-

[1] Ignatius, *ad Smyrn.*, viii, 2. Cf. Gustaf Aulén, *The Universal Church in God's Design* (London, 1948), p. 20, where this formula is inverted: *ubi ecclesia, ibi Christus.*

[2] *Von dem Papsttum zu Rom* (1520), vi, p. 292; *Von den Konziliis und Kirchen* (1539), III, I, p. 624 f.; also in both the large and the small catechism.

[3] *Infra*, p. 247, n. 1.

where, for the Church consists of redeemed sinners who know that apart from Christ they are sinners, dependent always on justification; hence the believer never ceases to be *simul justus et peccator*. Nor is the Church in its outward form a *congregatio sanctorum* only; Lutheran Orthodoxy fully recognizes that the Church must contain both the *sancti* and the *hypocritae*.[1] This is a consequence of what is perhaps most central in Luther's own ecclesiology, the inward-outward polarity, which is also behind the well-known eschatological emphasis that critics such as Dr Karl Barth have considered to be a grave weakness of Lutheranism in its relations with the State.

(*b*) *Anglican:* Though the result of the theological dialectic that finds a locus in Anglicanism is complex, a few observations may be made in this brief note, sufficient to indicate in a very general way both the fundamental presuppositions underlying Anglican teaching on the nature of the Church and the relevance to these of the present study.

The Anglican communion comprises several Churches which, while maintaining much independence from each other in action, cherish their bond with the See of Canterbury. For the very limited purposes of the present note, what is said of the Church of England may be applied to the Anglican communion generally, except that no other Church in that communion is so closely associated with the Crown; some are not associated with it at all.

'The Religion of the Church of England, by Law established,' wrote a seventeenth-century Anglican divine, 'is the true Primitive Christianity; in nothing new, unless it be in rejecting all that novelty which hath been brought into the Church. But they[2] are the cause of that. For if they had not introduced new Articles, we should not have had occasion for such Articles of Religion[3] as condemn them. Which cannot indeed be old be-

[1] *Confessio Augustana*, art. 8.

[2] I.e., those who adhered to Rome.

[3] The XXXIX Articles of Religion (1571), which, with the Book of Common Prayer and the Canons Ecclesiastical, set forth the corpus of doctrine in the Church of England.

cause the doctrines they condemn are new, though the principle upon which we condemn them is as old as Christianity,—we esteeming all to be new, which was not from the beginning.'[1] The English Reformation, though it had both Lutheran and Calvinistic elements in it, sought to preserve as much of the old structure of the medieval Church as seemed to be compatible with the elimination of medieval abuses. Though the fresh attitude to scholarship in the sixteenth century that everywhere fostered a return to the sources of Christian doctrine—the Bible and the Fathers—played at least as important a role in England as elsewhere, English churchmen were on the whole less inclined to rigorous theological formulation than to a moderate pruning, in the light of the new learning, of the theological tradition they felt they already had. This attitude towards scholarship has much helped to mitigate the excesses of two wings in English Church life, a conservative wing of which modern Anglo-Catholicism is the successor and a more radical wing that foreshadowed the Evangelical churchmanship that has also played an important role in the life of the Anglican communion. But Church unity could never have scholarship as its sole ground. It is the presence of a common heritage of liturgy and order that provides the best safeguard against schism within a Church that is so much the locus of theological dialectic. Indeed, the liturgy may be said to be a theological confession in the second person singular, and it would accord with the *ethos* of Anglicanism to say that this dramatized form is a much safer medium for the expression of theological ideas than dogmatic propositions ever are. The immense significance of liturgical change is, on this presupposition, not difficult to understand. Order is equally important: the bishop, whether he be, as some hold, of the *esse* of the Church, or else, as others believe, only of the Church's *bene esse*, is peculiarly important. It is not only, as it is in Lutheranism and elsewhere, a focus of discipline: for all Anglicans it is more than this, and for some the bishop's function as the guarantor of the purity and validity of

[1] Simon Patrick, *The Second Note of the Church Examined*, p. 55.

the Sacraments is by far the most important function that he has.

The Church is one: national or particular Churches, in which the apostolic doctrine and practice are guarded by the episcopate, form parts or branches of the One Holy Catholic and Apostolic Church. The several Churches in communion with the See of Canterbury are held to be such parts or branches. Neither impurity of doctrine nor laxity in practice are fatal to the life of any branch of the Church, though they may seriously impair its well-being. For instance, the Roman Church is held to belong to the Catholic Church, though some of its doctrines are accounted novel and corrupt. In like manner, though eighteenth-century deism is said to have resulted in such neglect of the Sacraments in the Church of England that on Easter Day 1800 the number of communicants in St Paul's Cathedral was six,[1] the English Church could later feel that it had survived such baneful influences, having also continued to be, even in such dark times, a branch of the indivisible Church of God. In Anglicanism the notion of visible unity is important; the unity is there even when unrecognized by one or more of the constituent Churches. The formularies say nothing about the invisible Church, a conception of great importance, as we shall see, in the Reformed tradition; but the fact that they do speak of the visible Church reflects awareness of the distinction made by Calvin between the invisible and the visible Church. The traditional phrase, *congregatio fidelium*, used by both Luther and Calvin, is adopted, and the Church is defined in Reformation terms: 'The visible Church of Christ is a congregation of faithful men, in the which the pure Word of God is preached, and the Sacraments be duly ministered according to Christ's ordinance in all those things that of necessity are requisite to the same.'[2] But the characteristic reticence in the definition is such as to lead one, for a fuller understanding of the Anglican tradition concerning the nature of the Church, to the Book of Common Prayer itself, which is of greater authority than the Articles.

[1] This is only partly accounted for by the explanation that many persons would make their communions in their own parishes.

[2] *Articles of Religion*, art. xix.

Such is, indeed, the nature of the Church that no norm or standard is to be regarded as absolute when considered independently of all else. The Church is the guardian of Scripture, yet 'it ought not to decree anything against the same, so besides the same ought it not to enforce anything to be believed for necessity of Salvation'.[1] Apart from the episcopate the Sacraments are invalid; apart from the Sacraments the episcopate would be empty. The Eucharist, however interpreted, is central to the life of the Church, and it seems fitting to Anglicans that the phrase 'the Body of Christ' should be applied to both the Eucharist and the Church: 'By grace,' wrote Hooker, 'we are every one of us in Christ and in His Church, as by nature we are in those our first parents. God made Eve out of the rib of Adam. And His Church He frameth out of the very flesh, the very wounded and bleeding side of the Son of man. His body crucified and His blood shed for the life of the world, are the true elements of that heavenly being, which maketh us such as Himself is of whom we come. For which cause the words of Adam may be fitly the words of Christ concerning His Church, "flesh of my flesh, and bone of my bones,"[2] a true native extract out of mine own body. So that in Him even according to His manhood we according to our heavenly being are as branches in that root out of which they grow.'[3]

(*c*) *Separatist:* Any full account of the ecclesiological doctrines that are held in the various Christian denominations would treat bodies of Christians such as the Congregationalists and the Baptists individually; it would also include an attempt to trace these ecclesiologies to their source or sources. Between the two bodies just mentioned, the theological differences that exist are very notable, and though these denominations and others share certain common ancestries, their historical roots are plainly distinguishable and in some respects they have developed

[1] *Articles of Religion*, art. xx.

[2] Cf. Methodius, *Banquet of the Ten Virgins*, III, viii.

[3] Richard Hooker, *Ecclesiastical Polity*, V, lvi, 7; quoted by Dr E. L. Mascall in *Report of the Sixth Anglo-Catholic Congress: The Church* (London, Dacre Press, 1948), p. 143.

along very divergent lines. In their ecclesiological attitudes and pre-suppositions there is, however, a common element that makes it convenient, in a survey designed only to exhibit the broad attitudes and general traditions relevant to our principal enterprise, to treat together all groups whose ecclesiology is predominantly of what may be called the Separatist type. We shall note special emphases occasionally as we proceed.

In its baldest form the Separatist type of ecclesiology may be illustrated as follows. A Quaker, mentioning by name, in conversation with the present writer, an extremely small 'Christian denomination', added the opinion that there was much to be said for belonging to a *small* Church. The implication is plain. There is much to be said for belonging to a small Church, as there is much to be said for going to a small College, because it is presupposed that a Church is structurally similar to a College, though their functions are different. So one seeks admission to a Church and joins it, as one seeks admission to and joins a College. Colleges may be large or small; they may be closely associated with other Colleges or remain more isolated. In the Separatist view, the same may be said of Churches. Though most Colleges include teaching as a major part of their work, there are institutions that are devoted exclusively to research. So with Churches: they are generally organized for the instruction and spiritual awakening of a group desirous of obtaining such spiritual benefits; but a Church may usefully exist for other Christian purposes, such as the exchange of meditations upon the Gospel and the recounting of experiences that witness to and may provoke livelier faith.

The outlook just delineated is indeed an extreme one, and probably not even the most 'radical' sects in Reformation times would have recognized it even as a caricature of their own attitudes. But some denominations whose roots are in these 'radical' sects find it unnatural to speak of the Church at all; for instance, in America, the Southern Baptists. Baptist theologians may speak of belonging to 'the Holy Catholic Church';

but not only is such language rare among Baptists, it connotes a very different conception of the Church from that which is common among, say, Anglicans. By the term 'Church' the Baptists mean either the whole number of 'regenerate believers' on earth, or else one of the organized local gatherings or communities of Christian believers to be found scattered throughout the world. By 'churchmanship' would be intended the worship and service of Christ in an essentially local Christian community. Each of these communities comes into being by the will of Christ, receiving its vitality from the indwelling of the Holy Spirit; but though it has been gathered by Christ, such a community may be dispersed. Membership is not, however, a matter of choice: believers are bound to join a community as opportunity occurs. Yet the obligation to join a community of believers springs from a personal encounter with Christ. Full membership always implies a background of such individual experience. According to the practice of 'close membership' Churches, this is sealed by 'believers' baptism'; but the rite is not essential, since 'open membership' Churches receive some who profess Christian faith without submitting to the rite.

The conception of the Church among Baptists, though affected in various ways by their special traditions, is principally determined by a theological presupposition that they hold in common with Separatists generally. It was this presupposition that made separation seem right and even good to all those who, in Reformation times, took the Separatist way, and the same presupposition underlies the ecclesiology of many denominations today. It is this: individual conviction of the revelation of God in Christ through the Scriptures is and remains antecedent to full participation in the fellowship of believers, and this fellowship constitutes the Church. The *ethos* of Congregationalism is very different from that of the Baptists; but it exhibits the same ecclesiological presupposition. The early Congregationalists in England looked upon the Brownists somewhat as modern Congregationalists look upon the Pentecostal sects; that is, they respected their Separatist principles though they disliked their particular kind of Separatism.[1]

Those puritans who in seventeenth-century England felt impelled to leave 'the Ignorant, the Vile, and the Profane' regarded their separation from the Church of England as being no different in principle from what they took to be the separation of their forefathers from Rome. So, in 1615, Dr Hull could write of 'The Blamelesse Separatist', meaning one who left Rome for the Church of England. Such were the ecclesiological presuppositions of the Puritans that their own action in leaving the English Church seemed to them to be in principle the same as that of their forefathers. Whenever a Christian finds that the standards of the group to which he belongs are seriously defective, he may find that his witness to Christ can become more effective outside the group than it is within it, so that it is his plain duty to separate from the group and make the witness, joining himself, as he will naturally do, to others who are of a like mind. So, according to this view, the saints are 'gathered'. Separation is justified only when it is necessary to preserve 'the fitness of the Church' for Christ.[2] Churches are fellowships of believers who are *gathered* for Christ, and they order their polity accordingly, ordaining and calling pastors *ad hoc*. This view, we shall see, was regarded by the seventeenth-century Scottish divines as one of the greatest errors of the Separatists. It is certainly alien to the view of Calvin, who affirms that the 'stability' of the Church is 'the stability of Christ' (*firmitudine Christi*),[3] and argues, after the manner of Augustine, that we must not only believe 'in' the Church but must 'believe the Church' (*ecclesiam credere, non in ecclesiam*).[4]

[1] Robert Browne has been commonly accounted the father of modern Congregationalists (cf. Williston Walker, *Creeds and Platforms of Congregationalism*, p. 17; R. W. Dale, *History of English Congregationalism*, p. 120); but recent historians of the movement regard him as only one of the influences that contributed to its beginnings. See Geoffrey F. Nuttall, *Visible Saints: the Congregational Way* (Oxford, Blackwell, 1957).

[2] Dr Nuttall (*op. cit.*) distinguishes four principles animating early Congregationalism: separation, fellowship, freedom and fitness.

[3] *Corpus Reformatorum* (Brunswick, 1863–1900), xxx, 748.

[4] *Loc. cit.*, 746.

To a Catholic observer, the action of a Separatist in 'joining a Church' recalls reception into a religious order or congregation rather than what takes place at Baptism or Confirmation. Membership of such an order or congregation, according to the Catholic view, confers immense benefits on those who, having a religious vocation, seek perfection. But it is not essential: perfection is theoretically possible by following the eremitical way or by sanctifying one's soul in the world. For the vast majority, however, entry into a religious order or congregation is a practical necessity for the attainment of Christian perfection. So, to our hypothetical observer, the Separatist seems to view his relationship towards the 'society of believers' to which he attaches himself. As religious communities and houses vary in antiquity, mobility and the kind of work they do, so the Separatist may prefer one Church to another without implying more than a Catholic would imply by a preference for the Benedictines over the Redemptorists. When a Separatist calls his Church 'the Body of Christ', as he may sometimes do, he uses the figure in a radically different way from that in which a Catholic would use it of the Church. We shall see that it is also radically different from what is implied in the ecclesiology of the Reformed tradition.

It may be of historical importance, but it is of little ecclesiological significance that the Puritans of the Massachusetts Bay Colony were intolerant, or that Congregationalism became the State Church there. When Roger Williams was banished from the colony as an 'irritating non-conformist', he founded at Providence, Rhode Island, a new Church based on the principle of separation of Church from State and on general Baptist principles; but he and his persecutors both held the same ecclesiological presuppositions, and these are basically irreconcilable to all other doctrines of the Church that we are now surveying. The widespread influence of the Separatist ecclesiology must be taken into account, however; not so much because of its importance in the development of a very large number of sects as because of the effect that such presuppositions have had when imported into the Reformed tradition to which they are fundamentally alien.

(*d*) *Reformed:* Technically, the phrase 'Reformed Church' is applied to that group or family of Churches owing their origin, directly or indirectly, to the Reformation in France and Switzerland rather than to the Reformation in Germany or England. Historically, this statement would have to be slightly qualified because of the fact that Reformation ideas sprang from many sources and there was an interplay of these ideas before Churches of the group we are now considering came into being. For example, Scotland, where a national Church was eventually established that may be taken as characteristic of the group, was already affected by Lollardy before Knox was born; its first native martyr, Patrick Hamilton, was burned for teaching Lutheran ideas several years before Calvin's conversion; the teachings of George Wishart, the next martyr, owed much to Zwingli; and Knox himself served his apprenticeship as a preacher of the Reformed Faith in England where he was chaplain to Edward VI and declined the bishopric of Rochester. The Reformed Church is, however, predominantly indebted to Swiss and French forms of the Reformation, and its government is usually though not necessarily Presbyterian. While it has been held within the Reformed tradition that *only* this form of government is entirely consistent with Scripture and so willed by God for his Church, this view is not representative of the tradition as a whole and is not common today. Much more characteristic is the view implicit in the question asked in Scotland of ordinands, 'Do you acknowledge the Presbyterian government of this Church to be agreeable to the Word of God?'[1] The Presbyterian Church in the United States of America takes a similar view, while in continental Europe several Churches in this tradition have permanent officers with functions not unlike those of a Lutheran bishop. What theory of the ministry is implied by a Presbyterian polity is a question

[1] James T. Cox, *Practice and Procedure in the Church of Scotland* (Edinburgh, Blackwood, 2nd edit., 1939), p. 344.

to be fully considered later on. It is too technical to be raised a this point.

Though the Reformed Church has never had a common confessional bond such as the Lutherans have had in the Augsburg Confession, it has a very strong historical tradition about doctrine. Not only is there a universal emphasis on the uniqueness of the Bible as the 'rule' of faith; the early confessional statements that have played a very influential part in the development of the Reformed tradition were composed with the so-called 'Apostles' Creed' in view, and this Creed, accepted without question by Calvin and Knox, was widely used in Scotland both before and after the Reformation,[1] though during the eighteenth and early nineteenth centuries vulgar prejudice caused it to fall into disuse because of an association with a disliked polity that it had unfortunately acquired in the minds of the people. A knowledge of the Creed was required in Scotland of all seeking admission to Communion, and the Creed, recited in ordinary services in many churches in this tradition throughout the world, was a normal part of regular worship at Geneva under Calvin, and finds a place in the official liturgy of several of the Reformed Churches.[2] Several of the early confessional statements were regarded as expositions of the Creed, including the Westminster Confession, which is still the principal confessional standard of the Church of Scotland. The *Shorter Catechism*, which summarized its doctrines, was for long taught in Scottish schools. The Reformed Churches on the continent of Europe hold various confessional documents in varying degrees of esteem: the French Church adheres to the *Confessio Gallicana*, as modified by the Synod of La Rochelle, while in Holland the documents held in special honour are the *Confessio Belgica*, the Geneva Catechism, the Heidelberg Catechism, and the Canons of Dort. Both in Europe

[1] It appears in both prose and a metrical form in the popular collection of 'Gude and Godlie Ballates' published at Edinburgh in 1578 under the title, *Ane Cōpendious buik of godlie Psalmes and spirituall Sangis*. See David Laing's reprint (Edinburgh, 1868), p. 3 f (prose version) and 9 f (metrical version).

[2] See, for example, *Liturgie des Eglises réformées de France* (Paris, Nancy, Berger-Levrault, 1897), p. 27.

and in America the authority of accepted standards varies; but it is always rigorously subordinate to that of Scripture.

Two special considerations must be taken into account in estimating the importance of the doctrine of the Church in the Reformed tradition. Within this tradition, both in continental Europe and Britain, whence American and other Presbyterian Churches derived their origin, there has always been a marked historical sense of belonging to the Holy Catholic Church. Where this sense has been attenuated in certain Churches it has been due to influences from without. All Reformed Churches on the continent of Europe claim to belong to the Holy Catholic Church and acknowledge the sinfulness of schism. The Church of Scotland has always emphasized this claim, regarding itself also as having continuity with the Scottish Church before the Reformation.[1] It was not least this sense of continuity and catholicity that motivated the Scottish divines in the seventeenth century in their uncompromising opposition to all forms of sectarianism and separatism. The other consideration is that, to the extent that the Reformed Churches owe their inspiration to Calvin, they are much affected by the Calvinistic emphasis on the sovereign majesty of God (*soli Deo gloria*), and his insistence on the divine nature of the Church and its importance in the divine plan of salvation. 'Whosoever departs from the Church denies God and Jesus Christ.'[2] For 'the fatherly mercies of God and the special witness of the spiritual life are so bound up with the people of God that separation from the Church always entails destruction'.[3] In contrast to the Lutheran emphasis on justification by faith, Calvinism stresses, rather, a co-ordination of faith and obedience, justification and sanctification.

The Calvinistic distinction between the visible and the invisible Church, adapted from Augustine, implies no real separation between two aspects of the Church. The Church is

[1] 'The fact that the Church of Scotland existed before the Reformation is of great importance in relation to its Constitution.' (James T. Cox, *op. cit.*, p. 1.)

[2] Calvin, *Institutio*, IV, i, 10.

[3] *Op. cit.*, IV, i, 4.

one: visible in that it can be recognized in faith, in the preaching of the Word, the administration of the Sacraments, and the exercise of discipline[1]; invisible in that when it is considered *sub specie aeternitatis* it is seen to be 'the total number of the elect, whether angels or men, and whether living men or dead'.[2] It was very characteristic of the Scottish divines to think of the Church as the True Israel and to speak of the holy men of the Old Testament and of the New as belonging to the same 'Family of God'[3]; yet nothing is more characteristic of the Reformed tradition than to regard the Church as the Body of Christ, so that in its visible ordering everything must be made to serve this, its true nature. There is a marked distrust in the Reformed tradition of anything that seems to be capable of injuring this conception of the Church, especially any view that would, in docetic fashion, remove the Church into timelessness. The Church is Christ's Body, renewed and nourished by His 'vivifying flesh'. In the ecclesiology of the Reformed tradition the Sacrament of Christ's Body and Blood is central, whether there be in practice, as Calvin himself desired, a weekly celebration, or, as has been more common, a less frequent one. The fundamental ecclesiology of the Reformed Church has sometimes been endangered by this infrequency. The infrequent celebrations that became customary in Scotland were, however, attended by solemn fastings and surrounded by observances so time-consuming that greater frequency would have been impracticable except at the cost of reducing the impressive solemnity. The emphasis on preaching that is commonly associated with this tradition, and the ideal of a learned ministry that the Reformed Churches sought to realize, sprang from the great importance attached to the Church's duty of proclaiming the 'Word' that is contained in the Scriptures.

[1] The Genevan Confession specifies three marks: Word, Sacraments, and 'Ecclesiastical Discipline, which standeth in admonition and correction of faults'.

[2] *I. Calvini Opera Selecta* (ed. Barth and Niesel, vol. I–V; Munich, 1926–52), I, 86.

[3] Cf. *Confessio Scoticana* (1560), art. 5: 'We maist constantly beleeve, that God preserved, instructed, multiplied, honoured, decored, and from death called to life, his Kirk in all ages fra Adam, till the cumming of Christ Jesus in the flesh.'

When papal jurisdiction in Scotland was abolished by the Scottish Parliament in 1560, there was no thought of the Reformed Church as other than the Church purified of error and corruption; nor was any particular designation adopted to indicate an allegiance to one sort of reformation rather than another. All such designations were resented when, in the seventeenth century, they came to be applied by ecclesiastical adversaries. A seventeenth-century tract[1] exhibits this: 'To call us *Calvinians*, and the Reformed Churches *Calvinian Reformed Churches*, is to disgrace the true Churches of Christ, and to symbolize with the Papists, who call themselves the Catholic Church. . . . They who apprehend any danger in names (as there is a great deal of danger in them) ought not . . . to join with Papists in giving names of sects unto the Reformed Churches.' However drastic the reforms might be, they were reforms of the Catholic Church, and that which they were intended to establish was simply the Catholic Church Reformed. Since this point is important in, as well as relevant to, the main subject of the inquiry before us, evidences for it will be provided in the course of the main investigation.

In the Reformed tradition, ecclesiology is closely linked to christology, because when the divines argued about the Church they felt they were arguing about that which is closest to Christ and inseparable from Him. It was their concern for the glory of Christ that made them wish to vindicate their conception of the Church of which they accounted Him the Head. It was not only that Christ and the Church were two correlative ideas; it was, rather, that they were, in the eyes of these divines, one living reality.

[1] *Reformation of Church Government in Scotland cleared from some Mistakes and Prejudices, by the Commissioners of the General Assembly of the Church of Scotland, now in London* (1644).

CHAPTER II

THE MEDIEVAL BACKGROUND

The historical association of the renaissance of learning with the Reformation has often obscured the fact that the Reformers, Calvin not least, were thoroughly schooled in medieval ways of thought. However much they returned to the primitive sources, as the new learning taught them to do, they still thought in medieval categories, in terms of the scholasticism and canon law in which they had been trained. Even in their repudiation of certain medieval notions in the light of their reading of Scripture, their arguments presuppose the background with which they and their contemporaries were familiar, and it is especially impossible to understand the doctrine of the Church in the Reformed tradition without taking that complex medieval background into account. The conciliarist theories that had been so fashionable in intellectual circles on the eve of the Reformation were not novelties invented out of desperation at the prevailing ecclesiastical anarchy; they had very ancient roots. Ecclesiological questions had been raised in the Middle Ages, it is true, in a canonistic rather than in a theological context, and they were often, if not generally, raised without any conscious recognition of their being ecclesiological questions in the sense in which a modern scholar would understand this phrase. Yet they carried echoes from Scripture and the Fathers—echoes that Calvin and others, approaching the Bible in a manner very different from that of a modern Biblical scholar, were able to pick up and relate to the canonistic discussions with which they were familiar.

The conciliarists had approached the problem of the seat of authority in the Church from many different points of view, so that there is no body of conciliarist doctrine that might be set down as common to them all. But the notion of the Church as the *congregatio fidelium*, having authority over the papacy and the papal curia,[1] was a central feature of all the conciliarist theories. These theories were in opposition to another medieval view, which we may call papalist, whose more extreme protagonists had contended that the Pope personified the Church, so as to embody in himself whatever authority the Church possessed. Against this papalist view, Conrad of Gelnhausen, whose *Epistola Concordiae* was the first important work on the conciliarist side to appear after the outbreak of the Schism, insisted that the Church that enjoyed Christ's promise of divine guidance and protection could not be the *Ecclesia Romana* in the narrower sense in which this phrase was used to signify 'the Pope and the cardinals'; for if this were so, argued Conrad, that body of men would be the recipients of a grace not bestowed even on the apostles, whose faith had wavered in face of the Crucifixion. The promise of Christ must then be not to any particular body of men but to the whole Church, the *congregatio fidelium*.[2]

According to the conciliarists, the authority that resides in the *congregatio fidelium* might be given to a representative; but it could not be irrevocably alienated from the *congregatio* to whom alone it belonged.[3] The Pope therefore enjoyed the *plenitudo potestatis* only so long as he did not abuse it. When he did abuse it he was subject to correction by a council, to whom belonged an authority superior to that of the Pope.[4] The superiority of a council over a pope sprang from the greater

[1] Dislike of the Roman curia was widespread. Luther's false etymology of the German word *Kirche*, which he thought was derived from *curia* (see his *Larger Catechism*, ii, 3), probably had much to do with his aversion to the word. In his translation of the Bible he used the word only once in the New Testament (John x. 22) and in the Old Testament only of heathen shrines. The revised text of his translation abandoned it altogether. He apparently thought the word a vague one and so when he did use it he used it in a vague way. *Infra*, c. vi.

[2] Conrad of Gelnhausen, *Epistolae Concordiae* in Martène and Durand, *Thesaurus Novus Anecdotorum*, ii, cols. 1208–10.

[3] Francis Zabarella, *Tractatus de Schismate* in Schardius, *De Iurisdictione, Auctoritate et Praeeminentia Imperiali* (Basel, 1566), p. 708. Zabarella (c. 1335–1417), the most distinguished canonist of his time, was created a cardinal by Pope John XXIII. He died during the Council of Constance, at which he was papal legate.

[4] *Op. cit.*, p. 703: 'potestatis plenitudo est in papa ita tamen quod non errat, sed cum errat habet corrigere concilium.'

authority delegated to the more representative body. Peter D'Ailly applied this representative theory not only to the special case of the papacy but to all ranks of the hierarchy.[1] Authority is delegated for the edification of the Church, whence alone springs the immense power of the General Council. This is, according to the famous definition of the Council of Constance, a body which, being representative of the whole Church, has its power immediately from Christ.[2] The principle of the withdrawal of authority from a representative who abuses it was very carefully defined and well established among the conciliarists before the collapse of their practical efforts.[3]

Gratian, whose *Decretum* appeared in 1140, had been the first canonist to undertake, in an academic and systematic fashion, the integration of the various existing compilations of the growing body of canon law.[4] So important was Gratian's work that it quickly received universal recognition in the schools as the basis of all further canonistic study, and during the next fifty years the decretists[5] occupied themselves in writing glosses, *summae* and *quaestiones* on various points that Gratian had left open. About 1190, the *Summa* of Huguccio, Bishop of Pisa, reviewed the work of all these writers on the *Decretum* of Gratian. The tendency of all this early decretist literature would seem to be towards a papalist interpretation of authority; nevertheless, ambiguities existed, as they do in even the best codifications. The decretists were lawyers; as such they were not concerned with the more profound ecclesiological questions that their theories raised. Nevertheless, ecclesiological presuppositions can be detected, and these are of great interest because they reveal that there were two sharply conflicting ideas that were

[1] Peter D'Ailly in Gerson, *Opera* (ed. du Pin, Antwerp, 1706), ii, col. 942. Cf. his *De Ecclesiae et Cardinalium Auctoritate*, *loc. cit.*, col. 949 ff.

[2] Decree *Sacrosancto*. Cf. Conrad of Gelnhausen, *op. cit.*, col. 1217.

[3] Cf. Nicholas of Cusa, *De Concordantia Catholica*, in *Opera Omnia* (Basel, 1565), xviii, p. 741.

[4] Gratian's work was originally entitled *Concordia Discordantium Canonum*. Cf. R. Koestler, 'Zum Titel des Gratianischen Dekrets' in *Zeitschrift der Savigny-Stiftung für Rechtsgeschichte* (*Kanonistische Abteilung*), lii (1932), pp. 370 ff.; S. Kuttner, 'The Father of the Science of Canon Law' in *The Jurist*, i (1941), p. 15, n. 29.

[5] Of these early decretists, two succeeded to the papal throne, Rolandus as Alexander III and Albertus as Gregory VIII.

not reconciled in the work of the decretists, and this conflict is the source of interesting ambiguities. On the one hand, there is the notion that the Church is a system of clerical offices ultimately deriving their authority from the Pope; on the other hand, the idea of the Church as a *societas*, the heir of Christ's promise, is evidently no less in the mind of the decretists. It is the presence of these two underlying ecclesiological notions that makes the decretists' work so relevant to our present purpose.

With ample use of the text, 'tu es Petrus,'[1] Gratian attributed to the Pope a legislative and judicial authority over the whole Church, and he affirmed that papal decretals were of the same authority as the decrees of oecumenical councils.[2] Nevertheless, the decretists exercised some caution on this point. No local church was to resist the *Ecclesia Romana* without just cause (*sine discretione justitiae*).[3] This naturally raised the question: what would constitute a just cause?[4] There was confusion, too, in the interpretation of the binding and loosing power attributed to the Pope: sometimes it was understood to be a sacramental power; sometimes it was given out as a judicial and administrative one. But in the notion that the Pope was the successor of Peter, who symbolized the Church, the decretists generally felt able to pass over such important distinctions. This very notion of the Pope standing *in figura ecclesiae* was, however, crucial: it left open the question whether, for instance, he was responsible to the Church, or directly to God. There was also the question: if the Pope stands *in figura*, how does the General Council stand? According to Nicholas of Cusa, the last great conciliarist, writing three centuries after the decretists, the Pope symbolizes the Church less perfectly than does the Council.[5]

The interpretation of Scripture was treated by Gratian as a special case. Even in this the Pope's judgment was worthy of

[1] Matthew xvi. 18.

[2] Gratian, *ad Dist.* 20 *ante* c. 1: 'Decretales itaque epistolae canonibus conciliorum pari iure exequantur.'

[3] *Dist.* 12, c. 1.

[4] Guido de Baysio, *Rosarium seu in Decretorum Volumen Commentaria* (Venice, 1577), *ad Dist.* 12, c. 1, c. 2.

[5] *De Concordantia Catholica* in *Opera omnia* (*ed. cit.*), xviii, p. 741.

high respect; nevertheless, if it were to conflict with, say, the judgment of one of the great Fathers of the Church, the latter was to be preferred.[1] The *Summa Parisiensis*, in considering papal authority in theological questions, draws a significant distinction: in deciding upon a disputed article of faith the Pope's authority is greater than that of such a Church Father; nevertheless, if the Pope and the Church Father, each in his own private room, were to write a theological treatise, the Church Father's would be the one to be preferred.[2] The significance of the distinction lies in the fact that in this case the papal authority was derived from the Pope's judicial supremacy, so that the question of the precise nature of this supremacy became all the more important, especially since Gratian had made it abundantly plain that a pope could be guilty of heresy. Not only were Marcellinus and Anastasius II acknowledged to have erred; Peter himself was accounted by Gratian to have been in error in his judaizing tendencies.[3] The decretists, in their endeavour to clarify the difficulties, distinguished between two senses of the word *Romana* in the phrase *Romana ecclesia*: it was, on the one hand, the See of Rome; it was also, on the other hand, the *universitas fidelium*. But there was a more perplexing ambiguity remaining in the other word *ecclesia*. Huguccio, taking up this question, concluded that it was the *universitas fidelium* that had received the divine promise of preservation from error, not the *Romana ecclesia* in the narrower sense.[4] Huguccio was very influential, and in the circumstances in which canonistic development took place, this last distinction was of incalculable importance. The canonists of the next century widely recognized the principle that whatever authority the Pope has it cannot be used to injure the Church, and though there was by no means agreement on the relation of Pope and Council, the opinion that the Pope was bound by the decrees of oecumenical councils

[1] *ad Dist.* 20, c. 1.

[2] *Summa Parisiensis, ad Dist.* 20 *ante* c. 1: 'sed si alias in camera librum expositionis suae componat dominus papa, componat et Augustinus, praecellit et Augustini.'

[3] C. 2 q. 7 *post* c. 39.

[4] *Summa ad Dist.* 19 c. 9 (MS 72 in Pembroke College, Cambridge, fol. 129 r*b*).

in all matters affecting the *status ecclesiae* was very widely held. It was recognized that it was always the interests of the whole Church that mattered, and these were assumed to be more safely guarded by the Council than by the Pope, however great the latter's authority might be in the whole Church. That which gave the Council its weight of authority was that it was assumed that its decrees were supported by universal consent, and in order that they might be supposed to be so supported, the Council had to be seen as representing the whole Church, while the Pope, on the contrary, had his authority from the fact that he symbolized the whole Church.

That the decretists both perceived the confusion in all this and were unable to provide a satisfactory solution is not surprising. From Gratian onwards they had always seen their task as a laborious attempt to harmonize discordant ecclesiastical canons, in the interests of unity, for in their day, when the long reign of pre-Carolingian anarchy was still painfully recollected, unification seemed always wholly good. Moreover, they were, it must not be forgotten, lawyers. Yet though they thought in legalistic terms they were confronted with theological and ecclesiological ideas. With the rise of the movement towards papal monarchy that was so strong in the first half of the thirteenth century, the legalistic mould of the decretists' work seemed to fit ecclesiastical needs. In spite of problems that arose, the difficulties were seen as canonistic rather than theological. It is noteworthy that St Thomas, who neglected little that pertained to 'sacred doctrine', devotes less space to the doctrine of the Church, in the course of all his vast theological writings, than almost any modern theologian would give this subject within the compass of a single book covering major theological issues of the day. Moreover, approaching ecclesiological questions only in the most general, not to say superficial, manner, he is content to describe the Church as a *corpus mysticum* having Christ as its Head,[1] and to liken the Holy Spirit to the heart of

[1] *Summa Theologica*, III, q. 8, a. 1. But on the phrase *corpus mysticum*, cf. G. Dix, *op. cit.*, p. 246 f.

the Church, invisibly quickening and unifying it.[1] In the *Summa Theologica*, St Thomas takes up this subject in connection with christological problems, attending to it under the question of how the grace of Christ operates, where he considers the headship of Christ in relation to men and to angels as well as to the Church.[2] Other references to the Church in St Thomas's writings are often casual, as when he brings the subject into a discussion about bigamy, in the course of which he discountenances an opinion held by some that as the Church was Christ's Spouse, so the old Israel (*synagoga*) had been His concubine. This could not be, said St Thomas, for the Church is one, before and after the Incarnation.[3] Yet Christ only is the Founder of the Church, which He has committed to Peter and Peter's successors.[4] There are many offices—prophets, evangelists, pastors, doctors—but all are for one end; all are for the one Body of Christ.[5] But the predominant thought of St Thomas on the nature of the Church is that it is a mystical body, comprising both the faithful on earth, who as the *ecclesia secundum statum viae* constitute the *congregatio fidelium*, and the beatified in heaven, the *ecclesia secundum statum patriae*, which he calls the *congregatio comprehendentium*.[6] So for all his immense importance in the shaping of medieval thought, St Thomas throws little light on the problems that were facing the ecclesiastical lawyers, and which they were trying to solve in their own, much less theological, fashion. As lawyers, these were bound to give a legalistic cast to all they touched; yet they were a special kind of

[1] *Loc. cit.*, ad. 3. For a modern Roman Catholic account of the ecclesiology of St Thomas, see A. Darquennes, S.J., *La Définition de l'Eglise d'après saint Thomas d'Aquin*, in *L'Organisation corporative du Moyen-Age à la fin de l'Ancien Régime* (Louvain, 1943), pp. 1–53.

[2] It is noteworthy that in the same context (*S. Theol.* III, q. 8) St Thomas considers the question of the headship of Antichrist and the Devil over the forces of evil. For the Reformers, writing three centuries later, were steeped in Thomistic theology, and it is not improbable that their identification of the papacy with Antichrist may have been suggested by their familiarity with this passage as much as by their interest in Biblical apocalyptic.

[3] *4 Sent.*, Dist. 27, q. 3, a. 1, solutio 3: 'sicut est una fides antiquorum et modernorum, ita una ecclesia: unde illi qui tempore synagogae Deo serviebant, ad unitatem Ecclesiae in qua Deo servimus, pertinebant.'

[4] *De Regim. Princ.*, lib. 3, cap. 10.

[5] 'in aedificationem corporis Christi.' See *In Epist. ad Ephes.*, cap. 4, lect. 4.

[6] *S. Theol.* III, q. 8, a. 4 ad 2.

lawyers, working on special materials. Scripture and the writings of Fathers such as Augustine and Jerome were woven into these materials and could not be ignored. Nor could the canonists forget the principle that was so brought into the weave: all ecclesiastical authority is for the good of the Church. They could not escape the ecclesiological problems. Nevertheless, they could scarcely avoid colouring the Scriptural and patristic phrases in such a way as to obscure their original meaning. St Thomas's ecclesiology, on the other hand, was of as little use to the fourteenth-century canonists as it is to us for our present, very different study, for even apart from the paucity of his references to the subject, he made no considerable advance on the ecclesiology of Augustine. So in our effort to delineate the medieval background of the Reformation we are compelled to return to the lawyers themselves.

As these lawyers developed the legalistic notion of the Church as a corporation, they tried to take account of the ecclesiological principle that everywhere confronted them in their sources, that it is only in the interest of the whole Church that there is any authority committed to any part of it. In the thirteenth century, while Pope Innocent IV, who was probably the greatest lawyer ever to occupy the papal throne, was propounding the most extravagant claims for the papacy,[1] his contemporary, Hostiensis, Cardinal-bishop of Ostia, was developing the theory that the authority in a corporation is diffused throughout all the members and not confined to its head. This was in sharp contrast to Innocent's theory on the subject; but it was supported in the canons as Innocent's was not. Hostiensis, a careful thinker, was dealing with a highly technical concept, the nature of a corporation. So important was this concept at that stage of the development of medieval institutions, and so penetrating was that writer's analysis that his theory had incalculable influence on later thought about the now baffling question of the seat of authority in the Church. Much of the influence of

[1] For instance, that the Pope could dispense from the letter of the Gospel though not from its spirit. See his *Commentaria in V libros Decretalium* (Venice, 1578), I, ix, 11, fol. 95.

Hostiensis was due to the fact that the questions raised in his treatment of the corporation theory were often very practical, topical questions about the rights and duties of bishops and chapters in regard to ecclesiastical property and the like. If it were to be said that the ownership (*dominium*) resided in the bishop alone, it would mean that he could dispose of it as if it were his own, and this appeared to be wrong; but even if it were said that it was the bishop and chapter together, as a corporate unity, that had the *dominium*, there was still a serious difficulty, for it was by no means impossible that, for one reason or another, this body might consist of one survivor, which again would not do. But since it had been already established by Huguccio that the *dominium* over ecclesiastical property resided in the *congregatio fidelium*, such property could be vested in one person only in the capacity of a proctor (*procurator*). This notion of proctorship gradually acquired great importance and was much discussed. It enabled the clergy to put a brake, for instance, on the administrative activities of selfish or irresponsible prelates. A bishop's administrative authority was strictly limited by its being derived from the members of the chapter that elected him.

It was plain enough that the bishop was elected by the members of his chapter. Was it possible to apply the proctorial principle to the *corpus mysticum*? If the *corpus* could be taken from its theological context and shown to be a legal corporation, the proctorial principle could be applied. Indeed, if the *corpus mysticum* could be shown to be a legal corporation, the principle might be applied not only to matters such as ecclesiastical property but much more extensively. Lawyers could not be expected to handle purely theological ideas; but if these could be translated into their language, they could do so. Medieval lawyers could effect the translation more easily than their modern counterparts would be prepared to do, for in the Middle Ages figures of speech tended to be pressed far beyond the purpose for which they were originally intended. We have already noticed, for example, that it was under the head of bigamy that St Thomas discussed the continuity of the old and the new Israel. That was because in the Middle Ages one could put forward the notion that as the Church was the Spouse of Christ, the synagogue might be regarded as a divine concubine, and could then go on to ask questions such as: then is not premarital concubinage permitted? St Thomas, though he repudiated this conclusion, does not reject the argument for the reason that a modern philosopher would reject it: he seriously pursues the metaphor. So the medieval writers, by pursuing the metaphors of a Paul or a Cyprian far beyond what we could permit ourselves to do, succeeded in effecting remarkable translations of ancient theological ideas into medieval legal theory. Likewise, on the one hand it could be argued that the Pope, being the earthly Head of the Church, was the earthly Head of the *corpus mysticum*, in whom, therefore, resided the authority of Christ Himself; yet, on the other hand, it could be pointed out that since the *corpus mysticum* was a legal corporation, the proctorial principle could be fully applied. For various historical reasons that need not concern us here, everything in the latter part of the thirteenth century pointed to the victory of the papalist over the conciliarist implications. The conciliarist implications were, however, gradually drawn out, and the ancient theological ideas, now increasingly hidden within the phrases the lawyers adopted, were eventually extricated from their canonistic bondage.

Two principles were defended by the fourteenth-century canonists: (*a*) the full authority (*plenitudo potestatis*) that resides in the Pope as *caput ecclesiae* is given him directly by God, and (*b*) this same *plentitudo potestatis* is diffused throughout the whole Church, which is a corporation, so that in an emergency, at any rate, the Pope may be restrained in the exercise of his authority on the ground that it is proctorial power only that he possesses. The analogy with the well-known medieval doctrine of popular sovereignty in the State is easily seen: the prince receives power from God, but so also do the people receive power which they may exercise in the event of a prince's defection from justice (*aequitas*), which John of Salisbury had defined as 'giving to each his own' (*tribuens unicuique quod suum est*). The tension between the two principles defended by the fourteenth-century canonists presented at first only an academic problem; the Schism made it a very practical matter. But the conciliarists did not need to resort to the analogy from the State: there was enough pabulum in the canonistic literature, and from John of Paris onwards they made abundant use of it.

But the imagination of the conciliarists was also caught by the theological ideas embedded in the canonistic language. When a thoroughgoing papalist such as Zenzelinus de Cassanis could admit that, strictly speaking, the Church consisted of the *congregatio fidelium*,[1] a conciliarist could not only use the same idea in another cause, but see more theological content in it. Yet he dared not probe too deeply into theological questions. His cause was essentially that of the unity of Christendom, now rent by the Schism and spiritually sapped by the most far-reaching abuses. It served the conciliarist purpose very well to be able to look behind the conventional phraseology of the jurists; it would have ill suited it to inspect more closely how the *corpus mysticum*, for instance, could be identifiable with a corporation in the lawyers' sense.

The phrases that the conciliarists exploited in the interest of unifying and purifying Christendom were no less in the thought of the more theologically-minded Wyclif and Hus. Both of these wrote treatises *De Ecclesia*, Hus's work on this subject owed much to Wyclif, and upon it were based the charges made against him at the Council of Constance which led to his martyrdom. Though Hus is generally more conservative than Wyclif, both refer constantly to the canonistic literature as well as to Scriptural and patristic sources. Wyclif identified the *corpus mysticum* with the whole number of the

[1] *Glossa Ordinaria ad Extravagantes in Constitutiones Ioannis Papae XXII* (Paris, 1601), I, i, 2 s.v. *ecclesiis:* 'proprie dicitur ecclesia congregatio fidelium.' Cf. Zabarella, *Super Quinque Libris Decretalium Commentaria* (Venice 1602), Gloss on I, i, 1, fol. 11 *va*: 'ecclesia nihil est aliud quam congregatio fidelium.'

elect.[1] In the divine election lies the ground of the Church. The Church has, indeed, a visible manifestation in the world; but its origin and its home is in an invisible world. So Wyclif gives to the phrase *corpus mysticum* an essentially different interpretation from that of the corporation theorists. He treats the *corpus mysticum* as belonging to an invisible realm, where all transactions between God and man take place. Far from being the corporation with which the lawyers identified it, the *corpus mysticum* is not a visible body at all. Neither the figure 'Body of Christ' nor the figure 'Spouse of Christ' could be applied to the Church as this term was used by the vulgar (*simplices christiani*), the Church of 'prelatis and prestis, monkis and chanouns and freris and alle men that han crownes, though thei lyven nevere so cursedly agenst Goddis lawe'. The Pope, who is the Head of this 'Church' is, in Wyclif's later writings, called Antichrist.

It would, however, be anachronistic to affirm that Wyclif held this view as a carefully worked out ecclesiology. It is vain to pretend that he was on this side or that in terms of later ecclesiological controversies. What he says about the invisibility of the *corpus mysticum* as a *societas perfecta* of God's elect, a spiritual entity having no important relationship with the Church of 'prelatis and prestis', makes him sound like one of the Separatists of a later age. But Wyclif had no such ecclesiology to offer. Theologically he was in many ways conservative; for instance, though he repudiated transubstantiation, his attitude towards Mary was typical of his age: 'worship we Jesus and Mary,' he says. After all, the days of Berengar and Lanfranc were not very remote in his time, and transubstantiation had been officially affirmed by the Fourth Lateran Council only in the century before Wyclif lived. In christology he maintained a Chalcedonian orthodoxy. Docetic views were not unknown in the

[1] *Trialogus*, iv, 22: 'Vere dicitur ecclesia corpus Christi mysticum, quod verbis praedestinationis aeternis est cum Christo sponso ecclesiae copulatum.' Cf. *De Ecclesia et membris ejus* (not to be confused with the *De Ecclesia*, which forms part of Wyclif's *Summa Theologiae*), i: 'And this chirche is moder to eche man that shal be saved, and conteyneth no membre but only men that shulen be saved.'

Middle Ages; indeed neo-docetism took curious and insidious forms.[1] Because of what Wyclif says about the nature of the Church it might be tempting to wonder whether he had a docetic element in his christology that would account for an ecclesiology that has in some ways a 'docetic sound'; but there is no evidence for this and much against it. For instance, in a criticism of the Thomist view about the headship of Christ, already referred to in the present chapter, Wyclif argued that Thomas was in error in saying that Christ is the Head of all men: he tries, by a subtle distinction, to provide a better answer, suggesting that while Christ is, according to His deity the extrinsic Head of all men, the life-giving principle of the Church is Christ's humanity. There is not a hint in Wyclif's writings of views in the least resembling those docetic ones against which Ignatius of Antioch had preached.

It would seem, rather, that Wyclif does not relate his doctrine of the Church as the *universitas fidelium predestinatorum*[2] to his campaign for the purification of the Church of 'prelatis and prestis'. He never really departs, in principle, from what he says in the opening chapters of the *De Ecclesia,* to the effect that the Church, though a reality that can be known by those who belong to it, is essentially spiritual in nature. He did adopt, it is true, a distinction that Augustine had made in controversy with the Donatists, the distinction between the true Body of Christ and the simulated (*permixtum, simulatum*) Body.[3] The wheat and the chaff are mixed on the threshing-floor. The *congregatio fidelium* is mixed, for the present, in this evil world, with Satan's *ecclesia malignantium.*[4] But he does not work out ecclesiologically how the *corpus mysticum* is related to the *corpus*

[1] For instance, in the museum of the ancient Premonstratensian Abbey of Tongerloo, near Antwerp, is preserved a piece apparently cut out of a fifteenth-century English reredos and depicting God as a bearded man bearing in His hand the Dove carrying the Sacred Host in its beak to the lap of the Virgin. The implied docetism had presumably been detected and disallowed.

[2] *De Ecclesia,* ii: 'Et satis est sibi pro fide articuli de ecclesia catholica, ut credat fide formata quod sit una universitas fidelium predestinatorum, salvanda virtute meriti Christi. . . .'

[3] St Augustine, *De Doctrina Christ.*, iii, 32.

[4] This phrase is borrowed from Ps. lxiv. 2 (Vulg.).

permixtum, which is almost the first question a modern theologian would be likely to ask.

Wyclif's predilection for Augustine has inclined some writers to represent him as seeking a way back from Thomas and all the later medieval tradition to a 'pure' Augustinianism.[1] This is, however, misleading. Wyclif abundantly uses Augustine, as also does Hus;[2] but he looks to Thomas as well, not least for support for his own predestinarian theology[3]. Nor is he by any means uninfluenced by the juristic tradition delineated in the present chapter. Though he seems less inclined, perhaps, than was Hus to seek corroboration of his views in that quarter, much of what he says in his attacks on ecclesiastical corruption has a direct reference to the canonistic discussions. It was Wyclif's *De Dominio* that chiefly brought him to fame, and the concept of *dominium* was, of course, central in the jurists' writings. When Wyclif insists that the spiritual office of the clergy is a *ministerium*, not a *dominium*, he is implying what we have seen to be implied in the corporation theory: the clergy are not masters (*domini*); they are proctors (*procuratores*).

On Wyclif's view of the *corpus mysticum*, it would seem that the *corpus permixtum* ought to have little theological or practical importance. Yet he constantly treats it as if it had. He toys, for example, with the possibility that a time may come when the Church (the *ecclesia militantium*) may consist only of poor believers scattered in many lands.[4] In the conditions that prevailed in western Europe in the fourteenth century, it was difficult, however, to envisage such a possibility, since every man, practically, belonged to the Church of 'prelatis and prestis', as also he belonged to his country. Wyclif's reforms are to take place within the existing corporation; but to the question whether

[1] Cf. A. Gwynn, S.J., *The English Austin Friars in the time of Wyclif* (Oxford, 1940), p. 59 ff.

[2] Cf. P. de Vooght, *La part de saint Augustin dans le 'De Ecclesia' de Jean Hus* (*Rech. Théol. Anc. et Méd.*, XIII, 1946), pp. 304–36.

[3] *De Ecclesia*, iii: 'Non enim vidi in S. Thoma vel alio doctore probabili, quod totum genus sed pars ejus predestinata sit sancta mater ecclesia. . . .'

[4] *Cruciata* (Wyclif Soc., 1883), ii, p. 619 f.

it is important that they should be within the Church rather than without the Church, we must expect no answer from Wyclif, for he apparently has not given serious attention to problems of this kind. Nor may we expect an answer to the question whether the *corpus permixtum* is in any sense the *corpus Christi*.[1] Today we should be disposed to argue that if, as Wyclif tells us, it is Christ's humanity that is the life-giving principle of the True Church, then surely that Church must be something else besides the purely spiritual society he indicates it to be. It is difficult to resist the conclusion that the reason why Wyclif can give neither an affirmative nor a negative response to such a suggestion is that he simply does not have an ecclesiology. The same is true of Hus. When Hus appeals to the canonistic literature, it is generally to the proctorial principle that he appeals. For instance, in his complaint against the worldly pomp of the papacy, he observes that it ought to follow from the *Decretum* that the Pope is charged with serving the people, not ruling them for his own ends.[2] Both he and Wyclif, besides setting before us the concept of the Church as the *societas perfecta*, called to its perfection by Christ with whom it is mystically united, present us with visions of what a thoroughly purified 'institutional' Church would look like. But one is tempted to ask what a Church pure enough to meet their requirements would do in the world; whether indeed it could ever be said to be in the world at all. When Wyclif and Hus talk about the Church as it ought to be, they never specify precisely what it is they are talking about.

It is significant that, in the documents of the groups commonly accounted forerunners of the Reformation, the only one that makes any attempt at all to answer the sort of question that would first occur to a modern theologian is a Waldensian one which critical research has shown to be of a much later date than was at one time supposed, for it is based on the works of

[1] Luther, on the other hand, maintained that Rome, though under the rule of Antichrist, was nevertheless *within* the Church, since it had Word and Sacrament. Cf. his commentary on Galatians, i. 2.

[2] Hus, *De Ecclesia*, xv.

the sixteenth-century Martin Bucer.[1] The Waldensians indubitably anticipated certain aspects of Reformation doctrine as early as the twelfth century, and after the Reformation they were naturally the subject of special interest to Protestants. Extravagant claims were made for their antiquity: they were even said to be the descendants of a primitive Church founded by St Paul himself on his way to Spain. It was suggested that, partly due to the independence of the See of Milan and the vigour of the See of Turin in its resistance to Rome in the ninth century, the inhabitants of the inaccessible regions of Piemonte, with which the Waldensians are chiefly associated, had been able to preserve their primitive purity. These claims are now discarded by the Waldensians themselves. Not only is there no evidence for the antiquity they once claimed; it has been demonstrated that the date of a document given out as 1130, before the time of Peter Waldo's preaching, is spurious, and that the true date, 1430, had been fraudulently altered to support the claim to an existence of this community before Waldo exercised his ministry.[2]

So we cannot look to the Waldensians any more than to the Lollards or Taborites for an ecclesiology. What they say about the *corpus mysticum* is indeed important, though not novel; but they do not relate it to their programmes of reform. The conciliarists, who like the cathedral builders of the Middle Ages may have been building better than they knew, throw more light on the ecclesiological problem, though, being lawyers, they do not speak ecclesiological or theological language. In the work of men such as Nicholas of Cusa and Marsilius of Padua we get closer to the heart of the ecclesiological problem than we do in Wyclif, for all the latter's immense importance as a precursor of the Reformation. But conciliarism, after the Council of Basel, failed as a practical movement to meet the urgent need for reform.

[1] The distinction between the visible and invisible Church is formulated in the following terms: the Church is to be considered under two aspects, (*a*) substantially, as the elect of God, (*b*) ministerially, as 'the company of the ministers of Christ together with the people committed to their charge'.

[2] Leighton Pullan, *From Justinian to Luther* (Oxford, 1930), p. 136.

The work of the most notable exponent, before the Reformation, of a papalist doctrine of the Church must now be considered, for he describes the position the Reformers were especially concerned to refute. In his *Summa de Ecclesia*, Johannes de Turrecremata (Juan de Torquemada), a Spanish Dominican writing in mid-fifteenth century, after the failure of the conciliar movement, expounds the view maintained by Innocent III, that the Pope is not only superior in jurisdiction to other prelates, but the source of their jurisdiction.[1] He begins by asking how the Church and the synagogue may be said to differ, and he concludes, citing Bede, that they are not conterminous. He then goes on to discover in the term *ecclesia* no fewer than fifteen meanings. According to him, while it may mean the predestinate, or the *congregatio fidelium*, it may also mean the clergy; sometimes it means a group of people gathered for prayer, sometimes it means the ecclesiastical hierarchy. Turrecremata observes that it is impossible to distinguish the good from the bad in the Church on earth, and he discusses the bonds of the Church's unity, which include the Pope—bonds which heretics and schismatics lack.[2] While he teaches that it is in Christ that one must put one's faith, as the foundation of the Church, there is no salvation outside the visible Church of Christ.[3] This Church, he maintains, shall endure in holiness, teaching, hierarchy and sacraments.[4] Turrecremata's discussion of the manner in which members of the *corpus mysticum* are united with each other and with Christ owes much to Augustine and perhaps even to the Augustinian psychology. Christ is the unifying principle, and members of His Body are joined to Him in unity of will. By the indwelling of the Holy Spirit, the faithful are one with Christ in the unity of will; but Turrecremata avoids the

[1] Cf. Prieras, *Dialogus de potestate Papae*, in B. J. Kidd, *Documents illustrative of the Continental Reformation* (Oxford, 1911), No. 15, p. 31 f: 'Ecclesia universalis essentialiter est convocatio in divinum cultum omnium credentium in Christum. Ecclesia vero universalis virtualiter est ecclesia Romana, ecclesiarum omnium caput, et Pontifex maximus. Ecclesia Romana repraesentative est collegium Cardinalium, virtualiter autem est Pontifex summus, qui est ecclesiae caput, aliter tamen quam Christus. . . . Qui circa indulgentias dicit ecclesiam Romanam non posse facere id quod de facto facit haereticus est. . . .'

[2] *Summa de ecclesia*, vi.

[3] *Op. cit.*, xxi.

[4] *Op. cit.*, xxviii, xxxi.

charge of pantheism to which the medieval mystics often exposed themselves when they forgot their theology in the excitement of their description of mystical union, by pointing out that unity of will does not imply unity of substance.[1]

Though Turrecremata recognizes so many meanings in the term *ecclesia*, he does not explain how they are related to each other. He treats them as aspects of the same thing. He finds himself able to consider the aspect of the Church as the company of Christ's faithful side by side with the aspect of the Church as the hierarchically organized institution whose head is the Pope. The various ranks in that institution really belong to the Body of Christ.[2] Hus had ventured the opinion that in the primitive Church bishop and presbyter were the same office. 'What,' he asked, 'does the bishop do, except ordain, that the presbyter does not do?' In the primitive Church there had been indeed a distinction between deacons and presbyter-bishops; but this, Hus suggested, was in view of the fact that then 'the harvest was larger'.[3] Turrecremata maintains that the distinction between bishops and presbyters is, on the contrary, a Biblical distinction and intended by Christ Himself. He likewise holds that the papacy was so intended. The institutional body as it had developed in the fifteenth century is therefore to be accounted, on this view, structurally according to Christ's will, though abuses of power within it are, of course, against His will. But Turrecremata never explains what, in view of the conflicts in the canonistic tradition, constitutes an abuse.

Though there is no medieval ecclesiology outside of the canonistic writings to compare in quality or subtlety or thoroughness with the theological systems of Thomas and Scotus, there are, however, strong and influential currents or tendencies in ecclesiological thinking. One of these inclined towards an extremely 'interior' view. When Luther's own superior, Staupitz, could expound, as he is said to have done,[4]

[1] *Op. cit.*, lxvii, lxviii. [2] *Op. cit.*, lxxix, lxxx, xcvi. [3] Hus, *De Ecclesia*, xv.

[4] Cf. Friedrich Huck, *Die Entwicklung der Christologie Luthers von der Psalmen zur Römervorlesung* in *Theologische Studien und Kritiken*, CII, (1930), p. 83: 'Der heilige Geist wirt von oben herab in dich kommen.'

the mystical view that God speaks directly to the soul, requiring no intermediary, it was natural to raise the question: then what has the Church, whose constitution the canonists are discussing, to do with the spiritual perfection we have come to the cloister to attain? The Church, it could be answered, provides the means of grace; but without an ecclesiology to match the theological framework in which all such thinking had to take place, it must have been very difficult to relate the teaching of the German mystics to what the canonists were saying. The fact that some much earlier medieval writers had identified the Church quite simply with the *respublica christiana*, associating with this identification a strongly predestinarian theology, as did Honorius of Autun[1] early in the twelfth century, did nothing to mitigate the difficulty. This Honorius was a prolific writer, perhaps poet rather than scholar, a *scholasticus* at Autun who later followed the eremitical life. He was not uninfluential: his method, combining Biblical exegesis with independent philosophical inquiry, anticipated that of the great schoolmen, and his *Speculum Ecclesiae* is said to be one of the sources of inspiration of cathedral sculpture in the Middle Ages.[2] By the time of the Reformation, the Cain-Abel[3] antinomy that Augustine had bequeathed to the medieval Church in the *De Civitate Dei* had moulded western thought sufficiently to prepare those who were now reading the Scriptures with new eyes to find ample corroboration of this notion in the sacred pages. All Scripture, it seemed, was full of examples, supporting an already venerable patristic notion which, though to be found in the writings of men as different in outlook and circumstance as Wyclif and Honorius of Autun, had been too long neglected.

It was a notion very much in the mind of Luther when, in 1520, he published *Von dem Papsttum zu Rom*. The Church is essentially invisible and pure. It is built upon faith in Christ. It consists of the faithful: where they are, there it is. It is the Com-

[1] Cf. W. Schwer, *Stände und Standeordnung im Weltbild des Mittelalters* (Paderborn, 1934), p. 38; p. 78 f.

[2] Cf. E. Mâle, *L'Art religieux du XIIIe siècle*.

[3] Cf. H. Preuss, *Martin Luther. Der Prophet* (Gütersloh, 1933), p. 216.

munion of Saints. Were it otherwise, why should not we say of the Church in the Creed, not 'I believe', but 'I perceive'?[1] A man's membership of the Church is not achieved by means of any external situation whatsoever. Still, as a soul needs a body and finds expression in one, so the Church that is essentially invisible needs and finds visible expression. Christendom (*die Christenheit*) must have a formal structure. There are seven signs by which it may be known: the preaching of the Word of God, the administration of the Sacrament of Baptism, the Eucharist, Discipline, the ordination of ministers of the Word, prayer and thanksgiving, and the bearing of one's cross according to the spirit of Christ.[2] Luther is here confronted with a genuinely ecclesiological problem, which he tries to solve in terms of the existential situation as he finds this. It cannot be said that the Pope's Church, the *corporatio* of the decretalist literature, lacks all the signs. On the contrary, it seems to have them all. But having legs might be taken as a sign that a man is able to walk, yet the strongest and straightest legs would be of no avail to a man if he were dead. Those who have a lively faith in Christ constitute the living Church; the rest are dead members (dead to Christ), and unless by faith they wake to life they are the enemy of the living body, the True Church. The figure that springs most readily to mind today is that of a cancerous organ which must be excised if it is not to spread. This figure seems apposite nowadays, when it is observed that certain types of cancer *simulate* the healthy cell formation. So it would seem that on Luther's view, at this stage of his thought at any rate, the dead members may exhibit the signs, in a formal way, yet so long as they resist faith and oppose the Word of God they are members, not of Christ, but of Satan. Within the *corporatio*, Cain and Abel continue their struggle.

[1] Luther, *Von dem Papsttum zu Rom* (1520), ed. Weimar, VI, p. 295 ff. 300 f.
[2] *Von den Konziliis und Kirchen*, ed. Weimar, L., pp. 628–43.

CHAPTER III

CALVIN

The influence of Calvin's ecclesiology on the structure of the Reformed Church is well known. To scholars, its influence on theology elsewhere, not least among the seventeenth-century Anglican divines, is hardly less of a commonplace. It has been widely recognized that, in contrast to the vagueness of Luther's and Zwingli's notions about the relation of the invisible Church to the external ecclesiastical institution, Calvin appears to have developed a definite theory on this subject.[1] That some of his ideas were fostered by Bucer's influence, as well as by his own experience of the ministry and his genius for organization, is generally admitted. That even in his earlier days he attached special importance to the concept of the Church is incontestable, and the general character of his ecclesiology has often been described. Sufficient attention has not always been paid, however, to the historical context of its formulation, without which its full significance cannot be properly understood.

In his youth, Calvin[2] read law both at Orléans, under the leading French jurist of his day, Pierre de l'Estoile, and at Bourges, under the brilliant Italian jurist, Andrea Alciati.[3] The canonistic literature on the constitution of the medieval Church, described in the preceding chapter, would therefore have been very familiar to him before his attention was turned to Biblical and theological studies. His work at Geneva was arduous and successful. He encountered many difficulties and met with

[1] Cf. A. C. Headlam, *The Doctrine of the Church and Reunion* (Bampton Lectures, 1920; London, John Murray, 2nd ed., 1921), p. 199.

[2] Born in 1509, Calvin had entered the University of Paris when he was fourteen; he went to Orléans in 1528 and to Bourges in 1529.

[3] Emile Doumergue, *Jean Calvin: les hommes et les choses de son temps* (17 vols., Lausanne 1899–1927), vol. i, p. 141 ff.

opposition; but by 1553 the result of his labours, by whatever means he achieved it, was such as to command the admiration of visitors to the city he had transformed into what seemed to many of them to be, as Knox said it was, 'the most perfect school of Christ that ever was in the earth since the days of the Apostles.' Knox did not mean, of course, that it had become a great theological centre; as a seat of learning it could not have compared with Basel or Lausanne. But it seemed to him, as to others, that it was a cosmopolis where Christians from all over Europe could be seen gathered together in visible communion, demonstrating the fruits of the Holy Spirit and the presence of the Risen Christ. By 1559, the year the French King Henry II died, Calvin, with but a few years more to live, had practically finished his life's work. It was estimated that at that time there were 400,000 of his adherents in France.[1]

Calvin would have preferred, of course, to have seen greater victories for the Protestant cause throughout the world. In March 1552, Cranmer had proposed to him the convocation of a council of learned men from all over Europe who were committed to the cause of the Reform and would promote the unity of all who, however they might differ on points of doctrine, were in general sympathy with Reformation aims. This proposal was made with an eye to what the Roman Church was endeavouring to do in its nineteen-year long deliberations in the Council of Trent. Calvin had welcomed the proposal; but nothing had come of it. Still, the failure of imaginative schemes of this kind must have been offset, in his mind, by the quality of the success he saw it was possible to achieve in organizing the Reformed Church. The refugees that flocked to Geneva were an exceptional company. They were naturally men of courage and character who left their native lands for conscience' sake, and they were often also men of learning and social position. 'There was perhaps in the Protestant world,' writes Kampschulte from his point of view as an 'Old' Catholic, 'no other community that

[1] The estimate was that of the Venetian ambassador, Soranzo. Cf. L. von Pastor, *History of the Popes* (English tr., ed. R. F. Kerr; London, Kegan Paul), vol. xiv (1924), p. 326.

could show so many noble, distinguished, and aristocratic names.'[1] Predominantly French, they included also distinguished refugees from Mary Tudor's England, and continental noblemen such as Galeazzo Caraccioli of Naples. Disappointments notwithstanding, Calvin had far more reason than Luther had had to cherish the hope that, if only the forces of Reform could be well organized, the unity of the visible Church, for long obscured, would be seen clearly again by the light of purified doctrine and practice. He did not underestimate what he took to be the power of superstition and idolatry; but he could not but have been profoundly impressed by the vision of a glorious future that his own experience, despite much bitterness, encouraged him to hope for. And if this may be said of the older Calvin, it may be safely affirmed that when, at the age of twenty-seven, he had completed the first edition of the *Institutes*, he is not likely to have been less optimistic. The doctrine of predestination did not have the central place in that edition that it acquired later on, yet the doctrine of the Church was there in its essentials. To Calvin, God's will for His Church seemed plain. The unity of the visible Church, so dear to Augustine, had been preserved, after a fashion, even in the dark days of papal oppression, and in God's time, by God's mercy, it would emerge in greater clarity to gladden the hearts of the faithful from whom it had been for long more than half hidden by the tyranny of Rome.

'The secret choice of God is the foundation of the Church,' wrote Calvin, whose doctrine on this subject is inseparable from his predestinarian theology. Intrinsically, the Church of God is indeed invisible; it is invisible even to the angels. But this same Church is also the instrument in which God offers Himself to His people, so that 'there arises an integrated structure of the *congregatio fidelium*'.[2] The familiar medieval phrase, so

[1] F. W. Kampschulte, *Johann Calvin, seine Kirche und sein Staat in Genf* (Leipzig), vol. II (1899), p. 247.

[2] *Institutio*, IV, iii, 3. The standard collection of Calvin's works is the one constituting vols. xxix–lxxxvii of the *Corpus Reformatorum*. The French translation published in 1541 is reproduced, showing the variation between the Latin editions of 1536 and 1539, in a text edited by Jacques Pannier: *Institution de la religion chrestienne*, 4 vols., Paris, Société les belles lettres, 1936.

prominent in the canonistic discussions, is now being used by Calvin in a sense close to that given it by the conciliarists, from the ashes of whose failure the Reformation had sprung. It is a living body which, being organized by Christ, its only Head, exhibits structure. It is *corpus Christi*, the living instrument on earth of God's loving purpose and sovereign will. There is no place in it for any human self-glorification, for in the Church man is confronted with the absolute sovereignty of God. The distinction between the invisible Church and the visible Church, lightly sketched in the first edition of the *Institutes*, receives more careful attention in the revision of 1539. It is by certain signs and symbols that the visible Church is recognized.[1] These are divinely imprinted upon it, so that, in so far as it belongs to us to recognize it, we may do so.[2] In the first edition, Calvin had already stated that in regard to the question of the Church as visible, our judgments do not require to have the certitude of faith; they are to be judgments of charity. We ought to recognize as members of the Church all who by confession of faith, good example in life and participation in the Sacraments, acknowledge 'the same God and the same Christ as do we'.[3] In the revision of 1539 he enlarged on this notion, pointing out that 'under this Universal Church, the Churches which are distributed through towns and villages are included so that each has the title and authority of the Church'.[4] We may have to treat as brothers and as Christ's faithful those whom we personally doubt to belong to the company of the elect. Though in our private judgment[5] we do not approve of a certain individual, we must give him the place he has been accorded by the Church so long as he is 'suffered in the Body of Christ', and until he is expelled from it in a legitimate way.[6] Our judgments about a group are in a different case, for there we must be even more

[1] 'symbolis': the French translation of 1541 (*ed. cit.*, vol. ii, c. iv, p. 127) has 'enseignes '.

[2] *Loc. cit.*: 'en tant qu'il nous appartient de la congnoistre.'

[3] *Loc. cit.*, p. 128.

[4] *Loc. cit.*

[5] 'suffragio nostro.'

[6] 'jure': *loc. cit.*, p. 129.

cautious, bearing in mind that the Word, so long as it is preached and honoured, and the Sacraments, so long as they are rightly administered, cannot but bear fruit. We ought not, therefore, to seek to take away the authority that belongs to the ecclesiastical assemblies scattered throughout the world: we ought to uphold it in the interest of the unity of the Universal Church, which the Devil is eager to impair.[1]

From this insistence on the unity of the Church as visible, together with his recognition elsewhere that even under the tyranny of Rome the visibility of the True Church had not been entirely destroyed, it is plain that from the time of his earliest formulation of an ecclesiology, Calvin never thought of the organization of the Reformed Church as involving a separation from the medieval institution; it was, rather, a vivification of the Body of Christ that had become oppressed and encumbered by a diabolical cancer that sought to destroy it. So in his fully developed doctrine of the Church he follows and restates the fundamental Cyprianic doctrine that outside the Church there is no salvation. Like Cyprian, he teaches that he cannot have God for his Father who has not the Church for his Mother,[2] and it is the figure of Mother that best pleases Calvin. 'But as our present design is to treat of the *visible* Church, we may learn even from the title of *Mother*, how useful and even necessary it is for us to know her; since there is no other way of entry into life, except that we be conceived by her, born of her, nourished at her breast, and continually preserved in her care and under her government till we are divested of this mortal flesh and "become as the angels".[3] For our infirmity will not admit of our being dismissed from her school; we must continue under her instruction and discipline to our lives' end. It is also to be noticed that out of her bosom there can be no hope of remission of sins, or any salvation, according to the testimony of Joel and Isaiah,[4]

[1] *Loc. cit.*

[2] Cyprian, *De Unitate*, vi: 'Habere non potest Deum patrem qui ecclesiam non habet matrem.' Cf. *Ep.* LXXIV, vii, 2; also Augustine, *De Symb. ad Catech.*, 13 (*Migne*, P.L. xl, 668): 'Nec habebit Deum patrem qui Ecclesiam noluerit habere matrem.'

[3] Matt. xxii. 30.

[4] Joel ii. 32; Isaiah xxxvii. 35.

which is confirmed by Ezekiel,[1] when he says that those whom God excludes from the heavenly life shall not be enrolled among His people.'[2]

The precise significance that Calvin attaches to the notion of the Church as Mother has been questioned. It has been suggested that Calvin associated the Church with the idea that God first gives His priceless gift to individuals directly and then makes them all share in the joy thay have each received. In this case, it might be argued, the visible Church is no more than a visible sign concomitant with the direct action of God upon the individual.[3] So the Church in Calvinist ecclesiology would mean something radically different from what it means to a Cyprian, not to say a Zarabella. In the thought of the Fathers, the Church had been supposed necessary for salvation in the sense that the Incarnation was necessary for salvation: as God 'needed' a human body to accomplish man's redemption in Christ, so he might be said to 'need' the Church, and it is in this sense that the Church becomes the Mother of the faithful. If Calvin were to be interpreted after this fashion, the Church, with all its ministry, would be at most a foster-mother.

There is no doubt that Calvin was methodologically in error when he so closely tied his doctrine of the Church to his predestinarian doctrines. The reason why he did so is not far to seek: the doctrine of the invisible Church had, as we saw in the last chapter, important precedents, and it had been associated with the predestinarian doctrine that is to be found in St Paul. This predestinarian doctrine had been given a place of fundamental importance among the schoolmen: in a sense, it had been accorded, from the time of Albert the Great,[4] a higher place of honour than it was given by Calvin, for these older medieval theologians had dealt with it under the heading, *De*

[1] Ezek. xiii. 9.
[2] *Institutio*, IV, i, 1. Cf. Calvin's *Commentary on 1 Tim.*, iii, 15.
[3] Cf. H. Strohl, *La notion d'Eglise chez les Réformateurs* in the *Revue d'Histoire et de Philosophie religieuse*, XVI (1936), pp. 265–319, esp. p. 305 and p. 312.
[4] H. Doms, *Die Gnadenlehre des sel. Albertus Magnus* (Breslau, 1929), p. 245 f.

Deo, while Calvin treated it under the head of salvation.[1] Calvin's methodological error lay, curious though it may seem, in his giving predestination a less exalted *locus* in his theological system than St Thomas had given it in his. By bringing predestination into the definition of the Church one falls inevitably into a great error. Predestination is outside the temporal order; the Church is within this. In the last resort it will be seen, as it may now be seen *sub specie aeternitatis*, that beyond the Church, as beyond the whole process of redemption, there is a principle hidden even from the angels and known only to God. But in terms of the redemptive process the Church must be considered apart from any such principle. The danger of treating the Church in terms of the eternal decrees of God, instead of in terms of the redemptive process, is analogous to the danger, very obvious in later Calvinism, of treating the atonement in terms of those eternal decrees that are made by God in His inscrutable wisdom.[2] 'The Word,' writes Athanasius, 'took a body in order to die for all.'[3] That Christ in His unrestricted generosity shed His Blood for all men was affirmed by Calvin himself on the eve of his own death:[4] Calvin did not account this incompatible with his own 'double predestination' theory. In the *Institutes*, in his doctrine of the Church, he ought, no doubt, to have more clearly distinguished the eternal and temporal orders instead of linking his ecclesiology with predestination. But the mistake was a methodological one; it was not due to any real failure to

[1] In the final edition of the *Institutes* he treats of God and knowledge of God in Book I, while in Book III, in which he considers the action of the Holy Ghost and of salvation by faith, he deals with predestination. Cf. St Thomas, *Summa Theologica*, I, q. 23.

[2] There is an example of the confusion in the successful prosecution, in the Scottish ecclesiastical courts, of John MacLeod Campbell, who was deposed from the ministry as a heretic, in 1831, for affirming that Christ died for all men, not for the elect only. Such was, however, Calvin's own belief (*infra*, n. 4). The theological climate underwent such a rapid change that in Campbell's own lifetime his book, *The Nature of the Atonement*, which expounded the views for which he had been deposed was used as a text-book in the Scottish theological colleges while its author was still under sentence of deposition from the holy ministry. *Infra*, p. 91, n. 5.

[3] Athanasius, *De Incarnatione Verbi*, ix.

[4] Calvin wrote in his will: 'Testor etiam ac profiteor me suppliciter ab eo petere, ut ita me ablutum et mundatum velit sanguine summi redemptoris effuso pro humani generis peccatis ut mihi liceat apud tribunal ipsius consistere sub ipsius redemptoris imagine.'

appreciate the nature of the living Church that is the instrument of our salvation. Calvin, in calling the Church our Mother, recognizes that the visible Church belongs to this temporal order of our redemption.[1]

As soon as predestination is brought into any discussion of the Church or of our salvation, there is a puzzle to be solved. But it is a puzzle that no ecclesiology could conceivably solve, for ecclesiology, like soteriology, is not capable of being equipped to give even the most fumbling answer to questions of this kind. These questions, if they are to be raised at all, must be raised in a wider theological frame of reference. It might seem that there was an aggravation of the predestinarian puzzle in the fact that the *corpus Christi* is encumbered with the reprobate who adhere to it as a cancer 'adheres' to a body from within and in its own malevolent way endeavours to 'feed upon' it. Yet the fundamental mystery lies not here, but in the existence of the reprobate. Once this existence is granted, it is hardly remarkable that they should seek access to the Body of Christ in order to attack and destroy it. Indeed, the case might even be argued that it is difficult to understand why some of them neglect to do so. These are not, however, ecclesiological questions, properly speaking. They treat of the invisible Church, the *terminus a quo* and *ad quem* of the visible Church. They are, at most, ecclesiological questions only in the sense that the Beatific Vision is a question relating to faith: strictly, as the Beatific Vision is beyond the realm of faith, so the invisible Church is beyond the visible Church, and therefore beyond ecclesiology, which is capable of discussing it only in the limited and cautious way in which it is proper for dogmatic theology to deal with the nature of an ineffable experience.

There is no question of regarding the invisible Church as a 'soul of the Church' that can be detached from the visible Church and carry on an independent existence on its own, in a Platonistic fashion, Lecerf, in an important article on Calvin's

[1] Whoever separates himself from the visible Church must be held *pro transfuga et desertore religionis*, guilty of *abnegatio Dei et Christi* (*Institutio*, IV, i, 10).

ecclesiology,[1] offered an explanation why such an interpretation of Calvin ever gained currency. Calvin, in his dedication of his work to Francis I, affirmed that the Church can subsist without visible appearance, and objected to those who demand a visible and apparent form of the Church.[2] Likewise, the Rochelle Confession says that 'in our time . . . the constitution[3] of the Church has been interrupted'.[4] But, Lecerf points out, this form, this constitution, consists of the distinctive marks that enable one to recognize the True Church and discern it from the 'synagogues of Satan'. Because of 'abnormal conditions' it may become impossible to recognize the True Church in certain circumstances: the distinctive marks may be temporarily lacking. Nevertheless, the True Church is there though its visible features are temporarily obscured. A man's face may be so covered with sores that I may not notice that he is my old friend and so pass him by on the street; but this is not to say he is invisible or that he is dead. Lecerf quotes Calvin: 'd'autant qu'il [Dieu] a mis une fois son alliance en France, en Italie, en l'Allemagne et autres pays, combien que tout ait été après oppressé par la tyrannie de l'Antéchrist, néanmoins afin que son alliance y demeurât inviolable, il a voulut que le Baptême y soit demeuré pour témoignage d'icelle alliance.'[5] The rest may be in ruins; still, the ruins attest that 'not everything is destroyed'. Some marks of the Church remain among the ruins, though not the 'distinctive marks' of the Church.[6] So Calvin does not deny to a corrupt Church the title of Church; he distinguishes, rather, between the right and the wrong *state* of the Church.[7] Lecerf distinguishes this view of the Church from both the Roman conception of the Church that reduces the individual to nothingness and the 'radical Protestant' conception in which the Church is 'dégradée au rang de *debating club*'.[8]

[1] Auguste Lecerf, *La Doctrine de l'Eglise dans Calvin* in *Revue de Théologie e de Philosophie* (vol. xvi, new series, 1928, pp. 256–70).

[2] It is to be noted that the visibility is referred to the form, not to the Church: 'nulla apparente forma' and 'ecclesiae formam semper apparere et spectabilem esse contendunt'.

[3] *constitutio*. [4] Art. xxxi. [5] *Institutio*, IV, ii, 11. [6] *Op. cit.*, IV, ii, 12 *in fin.*

[7] *Op. cit.*, IV, ii, 11 *in fin.* and 12. [8] Lecerf, *op. cit.*, p. 268.

Calvin notices that it is not only the godless who are exposed to the temptation of pride: believers are tempted to despise the Church,[1] and they must surrender their pride, for 'not otherwise than if He were Himself speaking doth God searchingly try our obedience'.[2] Were God to speak to us directly, we should be terrified: even Moses was afraid to look upon God.[3] So He mercifully chooses to speak to us through the Church. The Church is therefore, according to Calvin, a divinely ordained institution, whose purpose it to accomplish among us the work of the risen and exalted Christ, who, having instituted certain ordinances, wills that we recognize in them His divine presence.[4] Those who disdain the fare the Church provides when the Gospel is preached and the Sacraments rightly administered deserve 'to perish from terrible hunger'.[5] In keeping with his patristic and medieval heritage, Calvin treats such people as children who despise their own mother's milk.

The proclamation of the Word gives the Church a peculiar position, quite different from that of any merely human institution, and invests it with a mysterious character. God, being Lord of His Gospel, wills that that Word which nourishes His people and also slays the wicked shall be preached in and through the Church. 'God wills to make bare His sovereign power by means of the spiritual sword of His Word whenever it is preached by the pastor.'[6] Christ lives in His Word proclaimed by His ministers. Yet in spite of Calvin's emphasis on the Word, which he held to have been wickedly neglected for centuries in the Church, he also considered the Church to be essentially a eucharistic fellowship. It is the objective reality of the Eucharist that is peculiar to the Church's corporate worship, for while the proclamation of the Word is made, in the course of the pastor's admonitions to the people, to individuals as well as to congregations, corporate worship in the full sense is eucharis-

[1] *Institutio*, IV, i, 5.
[2] *Loc. cit.*
[3] Exodus, iii. 6.
[4] *Institutio*, IV, i, 5; cf. *Corpus Reformatorum*, xlviii, 204.
[5] *Corpus Reformatorum*, lxxxiv, 14.
[6] *Corpus Reformatorum*, xiii, 72.

tic.[1] On the other hand, the Eucharist depends on the Word in the sense that it is by His Word that Christ lifts the eucharistic elements out of their earthiness, investing with His presence the Sacrament in which they are used. Hence the importance of preaching in the life of the Church: it is by preaching that faith is born,[2] and without the preaching of the Word that leads us to the sacred Feast, the latter is vain.[3] For while the Eucharist is the focus of corporate worship in the Church, it is, apart from the Word, mere magic.

When Calvin speaks, as he regularly does, of the Church as the Body of Christ, he invests the Scriptural figure with immense significance. When he insists on the Headship of Christ in His Church—a central doctrine in Calvin—he is not merely protesting against corruption in ecclesiastical government or obliquely reminding his hearers of the tyranny of Rome; nor is

[1] There is abundant evidence that Calvin desired a weekly celebration of the Eucharist, though interference by the Geneva magistrates frustrated his plans. Daily communion in the Middle Ages was a monastic devotion in the West: the people, for the most part, communicated only once a year at Easter. Attributing the origin of this custom to Zepherinus, bishop of Rome in the third century, Calvin held that the arrangement had been in the first instance well meant, to meet the needs of the Church under persecution, but that it had become an excuse for lethargy, a custom that was 'an invention of the devil'. 'A very different practice ought to have been pursued. Once every week at least the table of the Lord ought to have been spread before each congregation of Christians, and the promises declared for their spiritual nourishment; no one ought to have been compelled to partake, but all ought to have been exhorted and encouraged, and those who were negligent, to have been reproved. Then all, like ravenous persons, would have assembled in crowds to such a feast.' (*Institutio*, IV, xvii, 46.) Even in the first edition of the *Institutes* he had expressed himself accordingly, and as early as 1537 he submitted, in the *Ordonnances Ecclesiastiques*, his desire to the Geneva magistrates that 'la communication de la saincte Cene de Iesuchrist fust tous les dimenches pour le moins en usage'. (*Opera*, x, i, 7 in *C.R.*). There was, indeed, a quarrel between the clergy and magistrates on the subject, as a result of which Calvin was banished for a time from Geneva, whence in 1538 he went to Strassburg. That he should have been, while still in his twenties, so firm upon the question, indicates the centrality of the Eucharist in Calvin's conception of the Church. To the magistrates of Berne he wrote in 1555, referring to the infrequency of eucharistic celebration there and at Geneva: 'Or plust a Dieu, Messieurs, que vous et nous eussions lusaige plus frequent. Car on voit par S. Luc, au livre des Actes, quen lEglise primitive on lavoit bien plus souvent. Et cela a continue par longue espace de temps en lEglise ancienne, iusque a ce que ceste abomination de messe a este dressee par Sathan, qui a estee cause quon ne recevoit la cene quune fois ou deux lannee.' (*Opera*, xv, 538.) By 1561 he was still unhappy with the arrangements at Geneva, 'sed quum minime persuaderem, satius visum est populi infirmitati ignoscere, quam pertinacius contendere.' (*Opera*, x, i, 213.)

[2] *Institutio*, IV, xiv, 5–6.

[3] *Corpus Reformatorum*, ix, 21.

he using the figure in a general, mythopoeic fashion. The Headship of Christ is a reality without which the notion of the Church would be deprived of all the importance he attaches to it. The language, though Biblical, is figurative; nevertheless, Calvin used it with an eye to the ontological fact of the relation of being that exists between Christ and the Church. The Church, as the Body of Christ, is overflowing with the divine *agape*. In the Church, the prayer of St Paul could be fulfilled, 'that Christ may dwell in your hearts by faith, that ye, being rooted and grounded in love, may be able to comprehend with all saints what is the breadth, and length, and depth, and height; and to know the love of Christ which passeth knowledge, that ye might be filled with all the fulness of God.'[1] When St Paul speaks of the Church as the Body of Christ he is speaking of its oneness with Christ in love; the oneness is a mystery rooted in the divine purpose (*πρόθεσις, προτίθεσθαι*).[2] It is not for nothing or by accident that the same figure, *corpus Christi*, is used of both Church and Eucharist; nor is it by accident, in Calvin's view, that the figure had been in both cases radically distorted in the Middle Ages.

The appositeness of the figure, *corpus Christi*, is not less striking in Calvin's treatment of the organization of the Church. As elsewhere, Calvin's final appeal is, of course, to Scripture; but the influence of the decretalists and of the conciliarist discussions on his way of thinking is apparent. Legalist by temperament and training, Calvin was always, for good or ill, a traditionalist. As will be shown later in the present chapter, it was this traditionalism combined with his overwhelming sense of the majesty of God that made him, in unfortunate circumstances, a fairly judicious liturgist. On the question of ecclesiastical order, both in the ministry of Christ's holy mysteries of Word and Sacrament and in the government and discipline of the Church, all is constantly referred to the Headship of Christ. There is no other absolute criterion for determining any matter concerning the

[1] Ephesians iii. 17–19.
[2] Rom. iii. 25; viii. 28; ix. 11; Ephesians i. 9; i. 11; iii. 11; 2 Tim. i. 9.

order of the Church. Though Calvin argues from Scripture and primitive practice in favour of every safeguard from the notorious abuses with which he was familiar in the medieval Church, he nowhere proposes any fundamental principle of Church order, government or discipline except the Headship of Christ.[1] His principal concern is to arrive at an ordering of the Church that shall preclude the usurping of Christ's place. He thinks this is usurped not only by a pope who, under pretext of viceregency, presumes to exercise *dominium*[2] over the Body of Christ, but no less by a mob that by ignorant and thoughtless procedures arbitrarily introduces confusion into the Body in which Christ alone has the right to reign. The practical absurdities connected with the hierarchical system as interpreted by papalist lawyers are easily exposed. It is not against bishops as such, or even archbishops and patriarchs and popes, that Calvin directs his criticism of medieval practice; it is, rather, against their being chosen on the false principle that they may be appointed as a landowner appoints agents and bailiffs and stewards to farm his land.[3] He notes that, worst of all, 'even boys, scarcely ten years of age, have by papal permission been made bishops.'[4] But he is no less opposed to mob rule, and his opposition to this is for the same reason as his opposition to papalism. 'I confess,' he says, 'that there was the greatest propriety in the decree of the Council of Laodicea, that the election [of bishops] should not be left to the people. For it scarcely ever happens that so many heads concur in one opinion for the settlement of any business; and almost every case verifies the observation, that the uncertain vulgar are divided by contrary inclinations.'[5] He goes on to approve the mode of episcopal election that continued to be practised in Gregory's time, according to which 'the clergy were neither at liberty to elect whom they pleased, nor under the necessity of obeying the foolish wishes of the people'.[6]

Calvin is really establishing the conciliarist interpretation of

[1] Cf. *Institutio*, IV, vi, 9. [2] *Op. cit.*, IV, iv, 4. [3] *Op. cit.*, IV, v, 11.
[4] *Op. cit.*, IV, v, 1. [5] *Op. cit.*, IV, iv, 12. [6] *Loc. cit.*

the corporation theory on the highest theological ground. Behind the whole conception of the episcopate must always be put the fact that Christ alone is the Shepherd and Bishop[1] of the Church; therefore all ministry in the Body of Christ must be related to the connexion that all members of the Body have to the Head.[2] So bishops, presbyters or others are all, without exception, only administrators of the one Bishopric of Christ. As such they act as joint trustees rather than as individual agents, and as joint trustees they cannot be formed into any kind of hierarchy.[3]

Two points must, however, be noted. The first is that this does not preclude the assignment to individuals of special offices. But for the extreme disrepute into which the papacy had fallen, and the blasphemous doctrine of viceregency, with all its consequences, that the papalist interpretation of the corporation theory had enabled some canonists to devise, it need not have excluded even a constitutional papacy. This is admittedly a theoretical point, since it was precisely the failure of the conciliarists to realize such a constitutional papacy that had forced upon the Reformers the total repudiation of a papal form of government. Nevertheless, the point is of crucial importance: no ordering of the Church can be essentially wrong that preserves the essential relationship between members of the Body and their only Head, and provides for the ministry that is essential to the health of the Body. Distinctions of rank within the ministry are not to be condemned; indeed, they may be highly desirable: 'The political distinction of ranks is not to be rejected, for natural reason itself dictates this for the purpose of eliminating confusion; but whatever shall have this object in view will be so arranged that it may neither obscure the glory of Christ, nor serve tyranny or ambition, nor prevent the cultivation among the ministers of brotherhood with equal liberties and rights.'[4]

[1] 1 Peter ii. 25.
[2] *Op. cit.*, IV, ii, 6. Calvin is here indebted to Cyprian, from whose *De simplic. Praelat.* he quotes.
[3] Cf. Calvin's *Comm. in Eph.*, iv, 11, in which he quotes Cyprian's *De unitate Ecclesiae*, ii.
[4] *Comm. in Num.*, iii, 5. But cf. *Institutio*, IV, iii, 8.

The second, certainly no less vital, point is that the ministry, which is inseparable from the presence of Christ in His Church, is indispensable. Not only is it a teaching ministry that is ordained by God; it is a ministry endued with the plenitude of Christ's authority so long as it preserves the essential relationship, not seeking to usurp the place of the one Shepherd and Bishop, the only Head of the Church. The fact that Calvin enjoined and cultivated a greater participation by the laity in the work of the Church than had been for many centuries practicable, ought not to be allowed to obscure his insistence on the unique function of the ministry in the Church. The ministry is placed by Christ within the Body as His gift to the Church. No ecclesiology has ever more exalted the ministry, under Christ, than does Calvin's. The ministry is entrusted to frail humanity; but Christ's power sustains the feeble instrument of His choosing. The ministry is a weak vessel; but the precious freight that the vessel carries caulks her cracks. In this vessel He has deposited the keys of the Kingdom.[1] 'God Himself appears, and as the author of this ordinance requires His presence to be recognized in His own institution.'[2] The ministers of the Church are the ambassadors of Christ.[3] Yet not one of them, whatever rank or function may have been assigned to him, can have this authority alone: each holds it jointly with the whole ministry. God calls men to the oversight of others only to maintain His own sovereignty.[4]

The kind of authority that Calvin appears to have envisaged is perhaps more like the *sobornost*[5] of the Graeco-Russian Church

[1] *Institutio*, IV, i, 1, 5, 20, 22; IV, iii, 1.

[2] *Op. cit.*, IV, i, 5.

[3] *Op. cit.*, IV, iii, 1: 'personam suam repraesentent.'

[4] *Corpus Reformatorum*, xlviii, 109. *Infra*, c. xi.

[5] Cf. Nicolas Berdyaev, *Truth and Revelation* (London, Geoffrey Bles, 1953), p. 39 f.: 'An objective authoritative standard of religious truth assumes a subjective belief in it, but it is a subjective belief which in the course of history has taken on a collective and socialized character. From one form of subjectivity we inevitably come back to another. Subjectivity by no means invariably indicates that which is arbitrary nor is it due to what people are fond of calling "individualism". It may be an attribute of a group, it may be the expression of the inward attitude of mind of a community. That to which Khomyakov gave the name of "*sobornost*" and which it is difficult to define in rational terms, is not an "objective", collective reality, it is an interior quality. When I am within existential subjectivity I am far from

than anything to be found in the medieval Western Church before the Reformation. Yet the case may be argued that Calvin was but providing a theological solution to the problem that conciliarism could never have solved by its canonistic methods. For the conciliarists, laudable as were their efforts, had never found the answer to a great difficulty inherent in their position. They had opposed the papalist conception of authority as power committed by Christ directly to the Bishop of Rome and delegated by the latter down and through the ranks of the hierarchy as from a general to minor officers in an army. In resisting this notion they had appealed to ancient phrases, *universitas fidelium* and the like, which they had identified with the *corpus mysticum*, and which by the conciliar era had acquired highly legalistic connotations. The conciliarists' fundamental difficulty was this: if that same *kind* of power or authority claimed by the Pope for his office really lay in the *universitas fidelium*, then the bishops, it would seem, ought to be instructed by their people, perhaps through the intermediary of the lower clergy, concerning the action they should take at a synod or council of bishops. This was plainly absurd, not only because of the illiteracy and ignorance prevalent among the people, but for the far more vital reason that such a view of the matter, however it might conform to the more extreme views of popular sovereignty excogitated by the Bologna jurists, could not be applied to the Church as it might to the State. For it did not take into account either the peculiar nature of ecclesiastical assemblies, guided by the Holy Ghost, or the sacramental, contradistinguished from the executive, judicial or administrative, functions of bishops and other prelates, and of the clergy generally. The conciliarists could see the theological difficulties; yet they could not or dared not find a solution except in canonis-

being in a state of isolation. I am by no means "an individualist". Rather I become "an individualist" when I am precipitated into objectivity and a state of objectification. . . . Individualism and isolation are among the things to which objectification gives birth.' A. G. Herbert (*The Form of the Church* (London, 1944), p. 67) connects *sobornost* with 'that spirit of the liturgy which the New Testament calls *koinonia*.' It should be noted that the *sobornost* theology has not been explicitly formulated or officially recognized by the Orthodox Church: it has been called, rather, a *theologoumenon*.

tic terms, and these in themselves could provide no solution at all. A Turrecremata could say, not without some justification, that his case was theologically more sound than that of any conciliarist, whatever difficulties it might present in face of the ancient phrases. Calvin may therefore be said to have provided a theological answer to a legalistic puzzle. He traced the hierarchical notion that had done such incalculable hurt to the conception of the Church in the Middle Ages, and hindered for centuries the growth of a sound ecclesiology, to writers such as the Pseudo-Dionysius who had provided a pattern for the hierarchical conception of the Church in his disquisitions upon the celestial hierarchy. That writer had been indubitably very influential in the Middle Ages. Calvin acknowledged that he was subtle and acute; but he noted that a critical examination of his theories would show that he had been engaged in airy speculations, so that what he said was 'mere babbling'. The duty of the theologian, Calvin insisted, was not 'to please the ear with empty sounds' but to examine the evidence from Scripture and 'confirm the conscience by teaching things which are true, certain and profitable'. In contrast to the reticence of St Paul, who would disclose nothing of what had been his mystical experience in the 'third heaven' to which he had been caught up, the Pseudo-Dionysius, Calvin complained, talked glibly about the ranks of the celestial hosts as though he had for long companied with them in heaven.

Calvin's conception of the Church is such that he envisages considerable divergencies not only of government but also of doctrine within it. He speaks of doctrines 'which are the subject of controversy within the Churches' and which nevertheless 'do not destroy the unity of the Faith'. By way of example, he cites differences of opinion concerning the future life. On the other hand, certain doctrines may be regarded as 'the proper essentials of religion; for instance, that God is one, that Christ is God and the Son of God, that our salvation is dependent on God's mercy, and the like'.[1] However, doctrine is really of paramount

[1] *Institutio*, IV, i, 12.

importance, for Calvin's conception of the Church is an historical one: while he repudiated the notion of an 'automatic' theory of succession in the ministry of the Church, he implied an apostolic succession of doctrine. His application of the Scriptural test cannot but seem uncritical to modern scholars; but it was critical in terms of sixteenth-century standards of Biblical exegesis. With Scripture as his final authority, he used patristic and other documents with good historical sense in terms of the scholarship of his age. This is important in estimating Calvin's attitude towards order, discipline and liturgy, all of which, of course, reflect his doctrine of the Church. In such matters Calvin found himself in a special, 'abnormal' situation. He could not arrange matters exactly as he would have wished. Not only had he to take into account opposition from the magistrates; he had to bear in mind the necessity for avoiding even the appearance of falling into the superstition the Reformers condemned, and he had also to consider the reproaches to be incurred from adherents to Rome if his practice should ever suggest support for the gibe, naturally current in such hostile quarters, that the Reformation was calculated to provide men with an easier religion. Since it is to be presumed that he endeavoured to concentrate on essentials, let us see from the documents what he accounted these to be.

Though the regular liturgy at Geneva was based upon medieval practice in important respects, Calvin's arrangements for the ordination of ministers appear to have been divorced from medieval practice, owing nothing to the ordinals. Much importance seems to have been attached to the procedure leading up to ordination. To the ministers belonged the prerogative of selecting and examining a candidate who, if approved, was then submitted to the City Council for approval, and finally to the people. A period of time was then allowed in case anyone should find just cause to oppose the ordination. When no such objection was made, and the people had formally elected the candidate, notice was given appointing a day for the ordination to take place.[1] This procedure was an expression of the historic principle that the ministry is Christ's gift to His Church. The ordinands were proposed by the ministers and submitted to the people for election. Practice varied slightly; for instance, in the case of the congregation of English refugees at Geneva, the elders were associated with the ministers in examining the candidates with regard to their gifts, learning and manner of life. At the ordination itself, however, in all cases, only the ministers took part in the liturgical ceremony. Though the laying on of hands (*impositio manuum*) was not customary at Geneva in Calvin's time, prayer by the ordained presbyters over the ordinand and in the Triune Name attested the intention of which the *impositio* (later general in the Reformed Church)[2] is a symbol.[3]

Calvin's attitude towards discipline reflects the peculiarity of the circumstances at Geneva; but though the practice there was extraordinarily severe—to a modern ear it often sounds absurd[4]—

[1] Calvin, *Opera* (in *C. R.*), x, i, 17–18.

[2] Cf. *The Book of Common Order of the Church of Scotland* (ed. by G. W. Sprott and T. Leishman; Edinburgh, Blackwood, 1868), p. xlviii (Sprott): 'For a few years after the Reformation imposition of hands was judged "not necessary", but most of the early clergy had been ordained priests, and the Second Book of Discipline, agreed upon in the Assembly of 1578, says, the "ceremonies of ordination are fasting, earnest prayer, and imposition of hands." These were henceforth observed by all parties.' On the subject of apostolic succession in the Scottish ministry, Sprott refers to a series of articles in the *Edinburgh Christian Instructor*, 1839. The *impositio* is prescribed in the *Liturgie des Eglises Réformées de France* (Paris, Berger-Levrault, 1897), p. 190: 'A ce moment tous les pasteurs se lèvent et placent leur main droite sur la tête du candidat.'

[3] Cf. St Augustine, *De Bap.*, iii, 16: 'Quid aliud est manuum impositio quam oratio super hominem?' Duchesne (*Christian Worship: Its Origin and Evolution*, 5th ed., London, 1923, p. 377), after reviewing evidence from the ordinals, observes: 'We see that in all these rites the ceremony of ordination consists especially of a prayer recited over the candidate in a public and solemn assembly. This prayer is accompanied by the imposition of hands.' But he goes on, in a footnote, to remark that Augustine's view is reflected in the fact that 'the imposition of hands in express terms is frequently omitted in the books of ritual.' Cf. Calvin's *Institutio*, IV, xxxi, 6; R. H. Story, *The Apostolic Ministry in the Scottish Church* (Baird Lectures, 1897), p. 242 ff. In the Greek Liturgies, χειροθεσία may often mean simply 'blessing'. Cf. Origen, *Hom. in Lev.*, ii, 4. Calvin himself recommended *impositio*. Cf. *Proj. d'ordon.*, 1541, in *Opera* x, i): 'Quant a la maniere de lintroduyre, jl seroit bon de user limposition des mains, laquelle ceremonye a este gardee des apostres et puys en lesglise ancienne, moyennant que cela se face sans superstition au temps passe et quil sen pourroit en suivre du scandalle on sen abstient pour linfirmite du temps.'

[4] E.g., (*Registres du Consistoire*, 1548, in *Opera*, xxi, p. 422), a widow was disciplined for saying 'requiescat in pace' over her husband's grave; action was also taken (1557, *loc. cit.*, p. 669) for the offence of making a noise during sermon. For documents and detailed references on this subject, see Kidd, *op. cit.*, p. 629 ff.

the principle of ecclesiastical discipline is fundamental to the ecclesiology of Calvin. He considered it to be the inalienable prerogative of the Church to administer censures upon all who cause public scandal, and in the last resort to pass sentence of excommunication. Without ecclesiastical obedience the Church degenerates into anarchy and becomes a 'seed-bed of quarrels';[1] but such obedience is to be 'without superstition' and for the sake of concord.[2] In Calvin's view, the loss of the rigorous discipline that had been so prominent in the life of the primitive Church, was one of the main causes of the Church's degeneracy before the Reform. While the manner in which discipline is exercised, and the scale and gravity of the offences, may vary considerably from place to place and from age to age according to circumstances, the principle remains vital: without a due regard for ecclesiastical discipline, the Church inevitably becomes corrupt. To attempt the reform of doctrine and worship without also reforming discipline would have seemed to Calvin to be courting disaster. Luther's experience in Germany had shown how tragic could be the results of purifying doctrine without providing an adequate discipline to match it. Above all, however, discipline must always be for the good of the whole Church, the Body of Christ. It must be executed in accordance with the vital principle of the Body; that is, in accordance with the law of love. But in the organization of the Body it is an essential factor.

There is no doubt that Calvin had as his liturgical ideal the liturgy of the early Church, so far as he knew and understood this. At any rate, his basic conception of regular Sunday morning worship was that it should consist of the celebration of the Eucharist, preceded by prayer, Scripture reading and sermon. He had no liking for the medieval Mass;[3] yet the liturgy he adopted for use in Geneva was descended from this. At Strassburg, whither Calvin had gone in 1538, having had to leave

[1] *Institutio*, IV, x, 31.
[2] *Op. cit.*, IV, x, 27.
[3] Cf. his letter, *De fugiendis impiorum illicitis sacris* (1537) in *Corpus Reformatorum*, xxxiii, 239.

Geneva partly at least because of his sacramentarian views, a German translation of the Mass, by Diebold Schwarz (Theobaldus Niger), had been in use for some time during 1524 and 1525.[1] Many unessential but beautiful ceremonies had been retained, including the *asperges* and the *lavabo*, but all reference to sacrifice and all invocation of the Virgin Mary and the saints had been eliminated; the *confiteor*, for instance, was retained in a modified form. The most striking change, no doubt, was that the whole Mass was audible. The Canon, recited standing, with upraised hands, included thanksgiving, intercessions and anamnesis. Under Bucer's influence, later on, however, considerable modifications were made. Bucer appears to have had little liturgical sense. By introducing greater variety of choice into the prayers, and leaving some of them to be devised by the celebrant, he took away much of the simplicity and vigour of the liturgy, and the prolixity of many of the alternative prayers supplied only aggravated the impoverishment. By 1537, the year before Calvin's arrival in Strassburg, the black gown and cassock, formerly used only for preaching, had superseded the eucharistic vestments. Worst of all, perhaps, the elimination of the responses divested the liturgy of its character as the corporate worship of the congregation.

Calvin, who knew no German, and who came to Strassburg to serve the congregation of French refugees there, urgently required a liturgy for their use. He therefore got a friend to make a translation for him, from which he composed a version of his own. His description of the result of his labours reveals his liturgical sense: 'We begin with confession of our sins,' he says, 'adding verses from the Law and Gospel,[2] . . . and after we are assured that, as Jesus Christ has righteousness and life in Himself, and that . . . we are justified in Him and live in the new life through the same Christ Jesus, . . . we continue with psalms, hymns of praise, the reading of the Gospel, the con-

[1] For the text, see F. Hubert, *Die Strassburger liturgischen Ordnungen im Zeitalter der Reformation* (Gottingen, 1900), p. 57 ff. Cf. J. Smend, *Der erste evangelische Gottesdienst in Strassburg* (Strassburg, 1897).

[2] The words of absolution.

fession of our faith,[1] and the holy oblations and offerings. . . . And, . . . quickened and stirred by the reading and preaching of the Gospel and the confession of our faith, . . . it follows that we must pray for the salvation of all men, for the life of Christ should be much inflamed within us. Now, the life of Christ consists in this, namely, to seek and to save that which is lost; it is fitting, then, that we pray for all men. And since we truly receive Jesus Christ in this Sacrament, . . . we do worship Him in spirit and in truth; and with great reverence receive we the Eucharist, concluding the whole mystery with praise and thanksgiving. This, then, is the whole order and reason for its administration in this manner; and it also accords with the administration in the ancient Church of the Apostles, of the martyrs, and of the holy Fathers.'[2]

This is not the place to consider the doctrine of the Eucharist in the Reformed tradition. A later chapter will be devoted to this. But it is perhaps not too early to question whether Gregory Dix, for all his customary insight into such matters, does full justice to Calvin when, after appreciating how readily Calvin acknowledged a 'Real Presence' in the Eucharist,[3] he goes on to say that 'The real eucharistic action is for Calvin individual and internal, not corporate. It is one more example of the intractability of the scriptural sacraments to the protestant theory, and the impossibility of adapting to a "religion of the spirit" and pure individualism the institutions of a "religion of incarnation" which presupposes the organic community of the renewed Israel.'[4] For if Calvin's ecclesiology was anything at all like what our examination of the facts has revealed it to be, his eucharistic theory could not possibly have been only 'individual and internal' in the sense plainly intended by Dix, who thinks that the Reformers, including Calvin, 'were unable to fit the external sacramental actions at all comfortably into their theological and devotional scheme of Christianity.'[5] It would

[1] The Apostles' Creed.
[2] *Corpus Reformatorum*, xxxiv, 194 ff.
[3] *Institutio*, IV, xvii, 19.
[4] Dix, *The Shape of the Liturgy* (1952), p. 633.
[5] *Loc. cit.*

be odd that a man who felt such *malaise* should, especially in the embarrassing situations in which Calvin's liturgical arrangements were developed, not only write of the Eucharist with such profound reverence but repeatedly urge its weekly celebration against the will of his patrons in such a manner as to endanger, at any rate in his earlier ministry, his prospects as a leader of the Reformation. It would surely be difficult to hold the view Dix suggests and yet direct the celebrant, as Valérand Pullain, Calvin's successor at Strassburg, does, to utter the prayer of consecration 'with the whole Church'.[1] The evidence points, rather, to the conclusion that Calvin's emphasis on the Eucharist springs naturally from his doctrine of the Church as the living Body of Christ which, being endued with the gift of the sacred ministry and subjected by discipline to its only Head, is united in the Eucharist to glorify the same.

[1] Pullain, *Liturgia sacra* (London, 1551), p. 7. (There is a copy in the British Museum.) The direction referring to the prayer of consecration reads: 'Finito Symbolo, cum tota Ecclesia summa veneratione se dat orationi, pastor ipse his verbis praeit.'

CHAPTER IV

ECCLESIA SCOTICANA

The claim of the Scottish Church to continuity is at first sight a curious one, and a preliminary investigation of it makes it seem no less so.[1] It is repeatedly asserted, both in public acts and by individual divines, both in Reformation times and at the present day, that the Kirk is, as the *Ecclesia Scoticana*, both before and after the Reformation, part of the One Holy Catholic Church. The significance, implications and grounds of this claim call for close inspection. No merely systematic examination of ecclesiological ideas or phrases could in itself provide an answer to the questions raised by the claim. For instance, the fact that many of the Scottish divines used the phrase *corpus Christi* of the Church does not in itself, of course, point to an ecclesiological tradition. Separatists use the Biblical figure, though plainly to convey a very different notion from what is intended by, say, St Augustine. In sixteenth-century Anglican divinity we find Hooker, Ridley, Cranmer and Field, all using the phrase; but they do not all mean exactly the same by their use of it.[2] So exceedingly complex is the history of the Scottish Church, not least since the Reformation, and so labyrinthine the paths of Presbyterian schism since 1689, that not only does it seem out of the question to hope to find any common doctrine of the Church; the discovery of even a dominant ecclesiological tradition seems peculiarly improbable. It was, however, out of the turmoil of internal strife and resistance to external forces that interest in ecclesiological questions in Scotland was most vigorously aroused. It had not been aroused by

[1] *Supra*, pp. 18 ff. Cf. G. D. Henderson, *The Claims of the Church of Scotland* (London, Hodder and Stoughton, 1951), pp. 1–19.

[2] Cf. H. F. Woodhouse, *The Doctrine of the Church in Anglican Theology, 1547–1603* (London, S. P. C. K., 1954), p. 43 ff.

Scotland's inheritance from Calvin, for Calvin's doctrine of the Church, being written as it was into the confessional statements of the Reformed Church in Scotland, seems to have been taken for granted. Before we turn, however to the Scottish divines who devoted special attention to the problem of the nature of the Church as this problem presented itself to them in a unique set of circumstances, we must survey these circumstances.

By the time that papal jurisdiction was abolished by the Scottish Parliament in 1560, Christianity had already been the religion of Scotland for a thousand years. The Christian Church had therefore a longer pre-Reformation history in this country than it had in other far-northern lands. At the time of the Reformation, Scotland was, moreover, in an extraordinary position. For some centuries it had, chiefly to secure support in its struggle to maintain its much-cherished political independence, tied itself more closely to the papacy than had perhaps any other country in Europe. With an exceedingly weak monarchy and very powerful nobles, its situation was quite unlike that of England, for example, and the corruption of the medieval Church in Scotland was without parallel even in a Europe where the Church was everywhere corrupt.

Dissatisfaction with the medieval Church was widespread in Scotland long before the sixteenth century. There appears to be no documentary evidence conclusively proving that Lollardy was imported to Scotland from Oxford; but between 1357 and 1389 safe-conducts were very frequently issued to Scottish students to enable them to proceed to Oxford, then a centre of Lollardy.[1] In 1398 the contagion had spread sufficiently to make it expedient for the King of Scotland to take a special oath at his coronation to suppress the heresy.[2] Masters of Arts at the University of St Andrews were required, almost from its beginnings in 1412, to undertake to defend the Church against Lollardy.[3] Throughout the fifteenth century there are recorded prosecutions, and in the course of the century two foreign

[1] Cf. *Scottish Historical Review*, April 1904, p. 266 f.
[2] *Act. Parl. Scot.*, i, p. 572 f.
[3] T. McCrie, *Life of Andrew Melville* (London, 1824), vol. i, p. 420.

martyrs went to the stake in Scotland, one a Lollard and the other a Hussite,[1] and acts of Parliament were passed against the heresy.[2] A translation into Scots by Murdoch Nisbet of Wyclif's New Testament, dating from early in the sixteenth century,[3] attests the persistence of Lollardy down to the time of Patrick Hamilton, the first native Scottish martyr, who was burned in 1528 for the Lutheran opinions he had imbibed at Paris, and it appears that Luther's views were so acceptable to Nisbet that the latter added to his New Testament the German Reformer's preface to his, as he later adopted also Tyndale's prologue to the Epistle to the Romans.[4] In 1525 an act was passed by Parliament forbidding the import of Lutheran books.[5]

That Lollardy should have occasionally provided a cloak for wild and irresponsible anarchists of various sorts is not surprising. Nor would it be difficult to find support in Wyclif himself for later ecclesiological theories that he could not even have understood; the use of the same anachronistic hermeneutic in the case of Biblical writers is a proceeding with which we are but too familiar. But in view of Wyclif's lack of any notable or novel ecclesiological principles, it is a reasonable presumption that Lollardy, though it prepared Scotland for the work of Knox and his associates in the sixteenth-century Reformation, provided its adherents with no ecclesiological preconceptions implying separation from the historic Church in favour of a perfectionist group distinct from it. The men who passed on Wyclif's torch to show a way to purify the Church were men who in their hearts deeply loved the Church though they could not love the evil that seemed to have choked its arteries. Lutheran influence in Scotland, though not negligible, was too limited and short-lived to have much influence. By the time of Wishart's preaching in Scotland in 1545, when Knox fell under his spell, Swiss Pro-

[1] John Resby and Paul Craw.

[2] One in 1425 (*Act. Parl. Scot.*, ii, p. 7); the other in 1443 (*op. cit.*, p. 33).

[3] Law, *The New Testament in Scots* (Scottish Text Society, 1901). Cf. *Scottish Historical Review*, April 1904, p. 260 f.

[4] *Loc. cit.*

[5] *Act. Parl. Scot.*, ii, p. 295.

testantism had been divided by Zwinglian and Calvinistic views of ecclesiastical organization and discipline, and Wishart is known to have been Zwinglian rather than Calvinistic.[1] Wishart bequeathed to the Scots a translation of the Helvetic Confession[2] for their guidance in organizing themselves according to Reformed principles, and it appears that Knox's first and brief appointment in Scotland, in 1547, as a minister of the Reformed Church was in accordance with the principles of the Helvetic Confession which, making no provision for the eldership, places the exercise of discipline in the hands of the minister, supported, where possible, by the magistracy.[3] Knox seems always to have insisted upon being called to his pastoral charge by a minister, in this case John Rough, not merely by (though nevertheless with the consent of) the people. This indicates conformity to the Confession.[4]

There is no evidence that, even in the disorderly state of affairs that prevailed in Scotland during the decades preceding the year 1560, either the reforming preachers or their flocks intended to repudiate the historic conception of the Church as the Body of Christ, in favour of a Separatist ecclesiology in which the minister or pastor would be called by a 'gathered' congregation to act as their preacher.[5] Knox had no liking for the Anabaptists: in common with most churchmen of his day he looked upon them with unbounded suspicion. 'The Church

[1] Cf. MacEwen, *History of the Church in Scotland*, vol. i (1913), p. 476 f.

[2] Rogers, *George Wishart* (Edinburgh, 1886), p. 17, p. 63 ff.

[3] Rogers, *op. cit.*, pp. 69, 72.

[4] Rogers, *op. cit.*, p. 68.

[5] MacEwen (*op. cit.*, p. 476 f) says that Wishart's adherents probably 'received the supper from him in both kinds' and that 'he was the first to see, or at least the first to show that in Scotland the Reformation must be shaped into a separate Church.' Some of the older historians (Buchanan, Spottiswoode, Pitscottie; not Row) say that Wishart celebrated the Eucharist. Knox, however, who was closely associated with Wishart's Scottish mission, makes no mention of such a celebration in the course of a detailed account (*John Knox's History of the Reformation in Scotland*, ed. W. Croft Dickinson, Edinburgh, Nelson, 1949, vol. i, p. 60 ff), and Janet G. MacGregor (*The Scottish Presbyterian Polity*, Edinburgh, Oliver and Boyd, 1926, p. 138 ff) summarizes the facts, showing that 'the most reliable direct evidence, and the greater and most convincing part of the indirect evidence' is against the reports of Wishart having celebrated. While at Wishart's trial before Cardinal Beaton it is recorded that he was charged with preaching without authority, there is no record of the charge—a graver one in the eyes of his judges—that he had celebrated the Eucharist unlawfully, after the fashion of the Reformed Church.

of God,' he wrote of them on the eve of the Scottish Reformation, 'may look for no other thing at your hand but for the confusion of all God's ordinances and for more cruel persecution than ever yet it did sustain since the days of the Apostles.'[1] When Dudley offered Knox the bishopric of Rochester in 1552, he explained to Cecil that not only would Knox be 'a whetstone to quicken and sharp the Bishop of Canterbury, whereof he hath need'; he would also be 'a great confounder of the anabaptists lately sprung up in Kent'.[2]

Knox and his associates, in devising the polity of the Reformed Church of Scotland in 1560, were indebted to many sources, including, for instance, the Church of England in which Knox had served as chaplain to Edward VI, as well as Geneva, Basel and Zurich. Certain features described in the *First Buik of Discipline*, such as the provision of superintendents and readers[3] for the Kirk were peculiar to Scotland, designed for the special circumstances and to meet the needs of an ambitious and far-reaching national programme of reform. But the fact that the Scottish Reformers organized the Kirk according to a pattern that seemed to them to fit the needs of the case without committing themselves absolutely, at any rate in the first generation after the overthrow of the papacy, to either Presbyterianism or Episcopacy, must not be taken to imply that they did not care about the ministerial office or did not regard themselves as succeeding to the ministry of the pre-Reformed Church that they believed to have been so shamefully abused. It is true that they would have probably subscribed to Melanchthon's one-sided statement that the Church is 'an assembly bound not to succession of office, but to the Word of God. The Church is

[1] Lord Eustace Percy, *John Knox* (London, Hodder and Stoughton, 1937), p. 113.

[2] *Op. cit.*, p. 154.

[3] The readers were men insufficiently trained to be admitted to the ministry but qualified to serve in parishes for which ministers could not yet be found; they were not permitted to administer the sacraments, nor even to preach, until the superintendents accounted them qualified. The superintendents had the pastoral and administrative functions of bishops and were placed over regions described as dioceses; in 1572 the Kirk adopted instead the designation 'bishops' and 'archbishops'. For the first provisions concerning readers, ministers and superintendents, see *The Books of Discipline* (Edinburgh, 1836), p. 25 ff. The plan was to appoint ten superintendents; in fact only five were appointed.

reborn wherever God restores doctrine and bestows the Holy Ghost'.[1] But this would not have meant to them what it might have meant to controversialists of a later age. Sixteenth-century Scotland was and felt itself to be, as much if not more than its southern neighbour, a definite and isolated national unit. The only Church known to the many thousands of Scotsmen who had never travelled beyond the Cheviots was the Church as they saw it in their native land. The Body of Christ was for them that Church alone or it was nothing, for to them what lay beyond seemed in its way almost as remote as the Kingdom of God itself. The Reformers knew that the Church throughout the world could not be reformed in one piece; the work must be done nation by nation, or, *faute de mieux*, city by city or even house by house. The Church in Scotland was indeed being restored by the gift of the Holy Ghost and the preaching of the Word; but it was the same Body, ruled and directed by Christ, its Head. That a unit as large and sharply defined as Scotland then seemed to be should be the locus of reform; that the old Church, the historic *Ecclesia Scoticana*, should be loosed from its bonds; that the old church buildings, many of which had stood empty and mute for generations, should be restored to use, so that in them men might begin to find that the Body of Christ was not, as some had been fearing it might only be, a phantom, but a vivid reality; these were among the blessings the Scottish Reformers saw attending their labours. The notion of separation from the old Church could not well be in the Scottish Reformers' minds, since in 1560, of the thirteen Roman Sees, four were vacant officially while five others were for practical purposes vacant, so that apart from questions of ecclesiology, which was still everywhere immature if not inchoate, it would have seemed more natural to the Scottish Reformers to view their action as casting off the Kirk's bonds than of separating from these.

These considerations ought to be taken into account as we

[1] Melanchthon, *De Ecclesia et auctoritate verbi Dei* (1539) in *Corpus Reformatorum*, xxiii, 598: 'Est coetus non alligatus ad ordinarium successionem sed ad verbum Dei. Ibi renascitur Ecclesia ubi Deus restituit doctrinam et dat Spiritum sanctum.'

now turn to examine the Scottish Reformers' definition of the True Church, and their attitude, expressed in the violent language everywhere customary in their day, towards what they called 'papistry'. As early as 1547, not long after Knox had first publicly embraced the Reformation cause,[1] he offered a definition of the Church to Dean John Annand, in the course of a public disputation with the latter in the parish church of St Andrews. 'Before we hold ourselves,' said Knox, 'or that ye can prove us sufficiently convicted, we must define the Church, by the right notes given to us in God's Scriptures of the trüe Church. We must discern the immaculate spouse of Jesus Christ, from the mother of confusion, spiritual Babylon, lest that imprudently we embrace a harlot instead of the chaste spouse; yea, to speak it in plain words, lest that we submit ourselves to Sathan, thinking that we submit ourselves to Jesus Christ. For, as for your Roman Kirk, as it is now corrupted, and the authority thereof, wherein stands the hope of your victory,[2] I no more doubt but that it is the synagogue of Sathan, and the head thereof, called the Pope, to be that man of sin, of whom the Apostle speaks, than that I doubt that Jesus Christ suffered by the procurement of the visible Kirk of Jerusalem.'[3] Knox was anything other than an original theologian; he had, least of all at that early period in his career, no systematic ecclesiology to offer. But his definition of the True Church reflects his conception of it as continuous with the old Israel whose law Christ came not to destroy but to fulfil.[4] Satan's emissaries had been as active in seeking to bind and paralyse the Old Israel as in later ages they were in seeking to devour the New; but the True Church had never been entirely paralysed or devoured.[5] That the invisible

[1] At this time he had not come under Calvin's influence. Having in all probability never travelled beyond Scotland, he was hoping then 'to have visited the schools of Germany'. (*John Knox's History of the Reformation in Scotland, ed. cit.*, vol. 1, p. 82).

[2] His antagonist had appealed to the authority of the Church, which, he said, 'damned all Lutherans and heretics' (*op. cit.*, p. 83).

[3] *Op. cit.*, p. 83 f.

[4] Matt. v. 17.

[5] Among the articles charged against Knox at this time was one affirming that it was because the Pope is 'an Antichrist' that he can be 'no member of Christ's mystical body' (*op. cit.*, p. 87).

Church is also visible is a notion that would have been conformable to Lutheran doctrine.[1]

In the *Confessio Scoticana*, the Church is plainly defined as one, for it is 'ane company and multitude of men chosen of God, who richtly worship and imbrace him be trew faith in Christ Jesus, quha is the only head of the same Kirk, quhilk alswa is the bodie and spouse of Christ Jesus, quhilk Kirk is catholike, that is, universal, because it conteinis the Elect of all ages, of all realmes, nations and tongues, be they of the Jewes, or be they of the Gentiles, quha have communioun and societie with God the Father, and with his Son Christ Jesus, throw the sanctificatioun of his haly Spirit: and therefore it is called the communioun, not of prophane persounes, bot of Saincts, quha as citizenis of the heavenly Jerusalem, have the fruitioun of the maist inestimable benefites, to wit, of ane God, ane Lord Jesus, ane faith, and ane baptisme: Out of the quhilk Kirk, there is nouther lyfe, nor eternall felicitie. And therefore we utterly abhorre the blasphemie of them that affirme, that men quhilk live according to equitie and justice, sal be saved, quhat Religioun that ever they have professed.'[2] This Church, said to be 'invisible, knawen onelie to God, quha alane knawis whome he hes chosen', is the *corpus mysticum* of the elect;[3] yet, a little later on,[4] the 'notes' or marks of the True Church (Word, Sacraments, Discipline) are clearly predicated of the visible Church, which consists of 'particular' Churches. Such Churches the Reformers claimed 'to have in our citties, townes and places reformed'; they are likened to those that were 'in Corinthus, Galatia, Ephesus, and uther places, in quhilk the ministrie wes planted by Paull, and were of himselfe named the kirks of God'.[5]

[1] That is, the visible elements of the True Church are discernible to faith, Lutheran theologians today seem to vary considerably in their emphasis on this. Very 'spiritual' interpretations are to be found, for instance, in G. Wehrung, *Kirche nach evangelischen Verstandnis* (Gutersloh, 1947) and W. Haugg and E. Wolff in *Evangelische Selbstprufung* (Stuttgart, 1947), p. 136 ff.

[2] *Scots Confession, 1560* (ed. G. D. Henderson, Edinburgh 1937), art. xvi, p. 71. Text in Scots and Latin.

[3] It includes the 'Kirk Triumphant' (*loc. cit.*).

[4] *Op. cit.*, art. xviii, p. 75.

[5] *Op. cit.*, p. 77.

The relation between the visible and the invisible Church was to become, as we shall see, a question of great interest to and much discussed by the later Scottish divines. For the present, however, it is sufficient to observe that though the men who framed the Scots Confession seem to have had unclear notions of the relation, they thought of the Church as a *coetus hominum*.[1] Nourished as they were on an Aristotelian doctrine of man, they could not but think of soul and body as inseparable in a *coetus* such as the Church. It is true that they insisted, as did the other Reformers, upon the susceptibility of the external or 'corporal' aspect of the Church to corruption, and that their conception of the soul animating the body was as much Platonic and Augustinian as it was Aristotelian. But the Scottish Reformers appear to have thought (*a*) that the Church is necessarily embodied, (*b*) that the embodiment is always a good in itself, (*c*) that the embodiment is nevertheless liable to disease, and (*d*) that the radical surgery the cure may entail is the work of Christ, the Head, by the Holy Spirit working through the ministry. The 'Kirk Malignant' is not really another Church at all, for the Church is one; it is, rather, a parasite on the True Church. It could not live by itself, for it is its life to feed upon the Church it seeks to devour. All this was consonant with Calvin's ecclesiology. Though other foreign influences affected the Scots, it was to Geneva, at this time, that they principally looked for guidance. But they did so not as importing a foreign theology for building a new Church. They saw themselves as, rather, borrowing theological ideas for the work of restoring their own Church to health.

The *Ecclesia Scoticana* they were bent on restoring was in many ways anomalous and paradoxical. In Columban times, for instance, it had had features that would be inconsistent with modern Presbyterian, Anglican and Roman prac-

[1] Cf. the *Confessio Montana*, art. viii, in W. Elert, *Morphologie des Luthertums*, vol. i (Munich, 1931), p. 233, where the Church is defined: 'coetus visibilis audientium, credentium et amplectentium puram et incorruptam doctrinam Evangelii et utentium Sacramentis; in quo coetu Deus per ministerium est efficax et multos ad vitam aeternam regenerat, cui in hac vita adjuncti sunt multi non renati, sed tamen de doctrina consentientes.'

tice alike. Its primates, presbyter-abbots, had no commission from Rome; its bishops were *nullius dioceseos* and subject to the authority of presbyters; its presbyters did not exercise episcopal functions corporately or otherwise, reserving these strictly to the bishops acting as individuals yet under presbyteral direction.[1]

The history of the Pictish and Scoto-Pictish Church is obscure; but what is known about this period, which extends from the eighth century till the coming of Queen Margaret about 1070, reveals further anomalies. It is known that early in the eighth century the King of the Picts discarded the customs of the Columban Church, and that he adopted some of the Roman usages without, however, ceding independence. In the middle of the ninth century the Scots and Picts were united under Kenneth, and it is about this time that we have at last a hint of a diocesan episcopacy. We are told that Girig, who reigned later on in that century, 'was the first to give liberty to the Scottish Church, which was in servitude up to that time after the custom and fashion of the Picts.'[2] Here, before Scotland itself fully emerges as a nation, we have for the first time the phrase *Ecclesia Scoticana.* In the tenth century we find this Church in marked hostility to the Roman Church, the Church of political enemies, and with the marriage, about 1070, of Malcolm III to the princess Margaret, who had been reared partly at the court of Stephen I of Hungary and partly in England, at the court of Edward the Confessor, the systematic romanization of the Church takes place.[3] There were remnants of the old Pictish Church to be dealt with even in the twelfth century, under David I, a munificent founder of abbeys and monasteries of the various orders within the Roman obedience; but by the end of the thirteenth century, which brought the friars to all the chief towns, the Scottish Church, now thoroughly

[1] J. A. Duke, *The Columban Church* (Edinburgh, Oliver and Boyd, 1957), p. 123.

[2] W. F. Skene, *Chronicles of the Picts, Chronicles of the Scots, and other Early Memorials of Scottish History* (1867), p. 151.

[3] In a Bull, *Cum universi*, dated 1188, Clement III, addressing the King of Scots as his 'dearest son in Christ', decreed that the *Ecclesia Scoticana* owed immediate subjection to the Apostolic See, 'whose special daughter she is, none intervening.'

organized, had identified itself with the cause of maintaining national independence and the ferocious patriotism this cause evoked. David, Bishop of Moray, taught his people that to join with Bruce against the English was in God's sight as meritorious as going forth on a crusade against the Saracens in the Holy Land. We hear of a bishop putting on armour, mounting horse, and, at the head of a little army of his own, driving invaders back with slaughter.[1] On the field of Bannockburn, before Scotland's proudest victory against the English, Maurice, Abbot of Inchaffray and later Bishop of Dunblane, shrove Robert the Bruce, celebrated Mass in the midst of the kneeling troops, and then, bearing the Crucifix along the lines, earnestly exhorted the soldiers to fight to the death for their sacred cause.[2]

To these memories of the association of the Church with the national independence that was so dear to the Scots, were added other memories, no less indelible, of what the papacy had done. Boniface VIII, for example, after severely rebuking the English Edward I, in 1299, for unlawfully invading Scotland and infringing upon the rights and liberties of the Church, wrote the Scottish bishops in 1302 turning the blame upon them for troubling his 'dearest son in Christ, Edward, illustrious King of England'. After repeated papal perfidies of this kind had been followed by a century of bounties eagerly showered upon Scotland by rival popes competing, during the Schism, for her favour, it was easy for even the most thoughtless Scotsman to see the *Ecclesia Scoticana* apart from Rome and infinitely more precious. And if such a distinction could be made by the man in the market place, it was not difficult for the more thoughtful and theologically-minded to distinguish between the Body of Christ and that which sought its destruction. The *Ecclesia Scoticana* must be revived and healed: in seeing themselves within it, loving it and grieving for it, men saw themselves within the Body of Christ, loving it and grieving because of the bonds that

[1] Bower, *Scotichronicon*, xii, 25.

[2] *Op. cit.*, xii, 21. The Crucifix was unknown in Scotland before the coming of Queen Margaret in the eleventh century.

were suffocating it. Scholars spoke of the Scottish Church;[1] to plain men it seemed no more inseparable from Rome than their country, which before the Reformation had come to have strong French ties, was inseparable from France. Of course such a conception of the Church was not theologically adequate. The theological importance of its being held by the plain man is not, however, to be underestimated. The ecclesiology of the Reformed tradition could not but be in important respects determined by the fact that to the sixteenth-century Scotsman separation was meaningless and continuity taken for granted.

The relation between Church and Bible in the minds of the Scottish Reformers is of no less importance for understanding the principle of continuity in the *Ecclesia Scoticana*. The Bible which had been in an important sense rediscovered at the time of the Reformation was a source of endless delight to those who could read it. No praise seemed too high for it. It was proclaimed the supreme standard of authority.[2] But the Scottish Reformers did not intend by this, as has often been charged against them, that the Bible was to be given the place the Koran holds in Islam. Their words have often been wrenched from their context, as have likewise been those of Chillingworth, who in criticizing the Tridentine doctrine that Scripture and tradition were co-ordinate sources of revelation, uttered the famous and widely misunderstood words: 'The BIBLE, I say, the BIBLE only, is the Religion of Protestants.'[3] The reason why the Scriptures are not to be regarded as deriving their authority from the Church is crucial: it is because the True Church *hears* the voice of its own 'Spouse and Pastor' and does not presume to exercise authority

[1] For instance, Knox, in his early days, studied for the priesthood at St Andrews under John Major, a conciliarist who was out of sympathy with Knox's later views, though Knox was naturally influenced by him. The phrase *Ecclesia Scotiae* or *Ecclesia Scotica* came as naturally from the lips of John Major as it did from those of John Knox. Cf. *Historia maioris Britanniae, tam Angliae quam Scotiae, per Ioannem Maiorem, nomine quidem Scotum, professione autem Theologum, e veterum monumentis concinnata* (Edinburgh, 1521), V, xxiii, fo. 111.

[2] *Scots Confession, 1560*, art. xix.

[3] William Chillingworth, *The Religion of Protestants. A Safe Way to Salvation* (1637), vi. The frequent and influential abuse of this phrase by controversialists provides a salutary reminder to scholars against wresting utterances from context.

over that voice.[1] While Knox and his associates, in common with the other Reformers, proclaimed the Bible to be the supreme standard, they acknowledged in practice that the Bible itself had a 'centre'. Scripture is 'sufficient' because it contains and makes known what is necessary for salvation; but the basis of the authority is the authority of God from whom the Scriptures proceed and whose incarnation in Christ they attest. There was nothing in this that was alien to the spirit of the early Fathers,[2] and it was also typical of the attitude of the Reformers in other countries. The Scriptures 'belonged' to the Church in the sense that Christ 'belonged' to it; that is, the Church received and proclaimed them but did not control them.[3]

Far from Scripture being given over to private interpretation, it was one of the principal functions of the ministry to interpret it to the people. But this work of interpretation was subject to a code of rules. The Church is a witness to God's Word, not its master. So the meaning of Scripture could never be absolutely settled even by the unanimous testimony either of the Fathers

[1] *Scots Confession, 1560*, xix: 'We affirme, therefore, that sik as allege the Scripture to have na uther authoritie bot that quhilk it hes received from the Kirk, to be blasphemous against God, and injurious to the trew Kirk, quhilk alwaies heares and obeyis the voice of her awin Spouse and Pastor; bot takis not upon her to be maistres over the samin.'

[2] Cf. Hippolytus, *Contra Noetum*, ix. But for the relation between Scripture and tradition cf. Tertullian, *Liber de praescriptionibus*, xix, xxi.

[3] It should be noted that the Reformers' position on the relation of Church to Bible was opposed to Roman practice rather than Roman theory. Cf. Francis de Vitoria (d. 1546), *Comm. in IIam IIae*, q. 1, a. 10 (ed. Salamanca, Beltran de Heredia, 1932), p. 55, where he refers to the Church after the death of the apostles: 'Ecclesia non habet potestatem determinandi nisi ex scriptura . . . habet suas regulas ex scriptura sacra et ex his quae derivata sunt ad nos ex apostolis et factis Christi.' Francis of Sales is even more explicit (*Controverses*, III, iii, 1, in *Oeuvres* (ed. Annecy), vol. i, p. 206 f): 'Ce n'est pas l'Ecriture qui a besoin de règle ni de lumière étrangère, comme Bèze pense que nous croyons; ce sont nos gloses, nos conséquences, intelligences, interprétations, conjectures, additions et autres semblables ménages du cerveau de l'homme qui, ne pouvant demeurer coi, s'embesogne toujours à nouvelles inventions. . . .' These writers express the Roman theory fairly enough. But the authority claimed by the Roman Church in interpreting Scripture (cf. Conc. Trid., s. 4; Conc. Vat., *De Fide Catholica*, c. 2) is such that, from the point of view of the Reformers, the voice of God in Scripture is muffled. The Reformers' protest is against the Church treating the Scriptures as though it controlled them. The notion that the Roman Church is the absolute mistress of Scripture was certainly widespread; it appears, for example, in Louis de Blois (d. 1556): 'Neque enim dependet auctoritas Ecclesiae ex testimonio Scripturarum, sed potius auctoritas Scripturarum dependet ex approbatione Ecclesiae (*Institutio spirit. Epistola ad Florentinum*, i, in *Opera* (ed. Monast. Campidonensis, 1672), vol. 1, p. 502).

or of contemporary churchmen. By modern standards of Biblical criticism, the hermeneutics of the Scottish Reformers leave much to be desired; but this fact ought not to mislead us into supposing that they or their continental counterparts were literalistic in the later sense of this term. They did not approve of the patristic and scholastic theory of Scripture being written at various 'levels' of allegory, and in this, from the point of view of modern scholarship, their position was less misleading than that of the Fathers and schoolmen. They laid great stress on the importance, indeed the necessity, of using all available linguistic and historical materials that might shed light upon the meaning of difficult passages.[1] But they thought that there was in Scripture a central teaching so evident to men of faith that such scholarly interpretation was for the purpose of throwing additional light only. Through the Scriptures the Spouse of Christ plainly understands her Lord's meaning; yet she would not be a true spouse if she did not always seek to use every means to understand it more fully. The Reformers certainly knew very much less than we do about the editing that had gone into the compilation of the Scriptures in the form in which they knew them. But it is difficult to believe that this knowledge would have very profoundly disturbed them, since in fact they did so much editing themselves. For Knox, like Calvin, edited the whole Scriptures in the light of what he accounted the central doctrines. These doctrines lived in his heart, and they were essentially the doctrines that Nicaea and Chalcedon had endeavoured to formulate. The Scriptures were a precious 'discovery'; but they were precious only to the True Church, which recognized in them the authentic voice of its Head. The fact that the Bible acquired the immense prestige it did among the

[1] Cf. *Second Helvetic Confession*, ii, 1: 'Illam duntaxat Scripturarum interpretationem pro orthodoxa et genuina agnoscimus, quae ex ipsis est petita Scripturis (ex ingenio utique ejus linguae, in qua sunt scriptae, secundum circumstantias item expensae, et pro ratione locorum vel similium vel dissimilium, plurium quoque et clariorum expositae). . . .' In the *Formula Concordiae* (*praef.*, ii) the Scriptures are said to have a content, which is the 'Catholic Christian faith' and it is this which stands out preeminently in them. The *Westminster Confession*, later the principal standard in the Scottish Church, refers (xx, 4) similarly to the 'known principles of Christianity'.

common people of Scotland must be understood in the light of these considerations.[1] Nor should it be forgotten that the Scots preferred to leave hundreds of parishes without an ordained minister than ordain men who were not accounted qualified to interpret the Scriptures.[2] They recognized that they had to face, for the present, a 'raritie of godlie and learned men', and make the best of the situation.

On the continent of Europe the Churches that shared the Reformation heritage eventually distinguished themselves from one another in terms of doctrine rather than of government or order. In Britain, by the end of the seventeenth century, it was government and order rather than doctrine that constituted the most obvious and sharpest division between the English and Scottish Churches. Probably the most important historic fact to be borne in mind for an understanding of this situation is that in England the attack on papal supremacy had enjoyed episcopal support while in Scotland the case was very much otherwise. Yet it had been not until 1592 that the full Presbyterian system of ecclesiastical courts, as set forth in Andrew Melville's *Second Buik of Discipline*, was accepted by the Scottish Parliament,[3] and before the Settlement of 1689 the Scots had had several kinds of episcopacy.[4] A full account of the story of seventeenth-century

[1] In the use of the phrase 'the Word' there was, of course, much scope for linguistic confusion, since sometimes it meant Christ, the Head of the Church, and sometimes Holy Writ. Cf. *Theses Bernenses*, i: 'Sancta Christiana Ecclesia, cujus unicum caput est Christus, nata est ex Verbo Dei, in eoque permanet, nec vocem audit alieni.' The transition from one idea to the other could be very unfortunate; nor is it to be denied that the Scots, no less than the Anabaptists and English Puritans, indulged in superstitious and magical practices such as turning up a place at random for an answer to a moral problem, and 'reading a chapter' as if the process had talismanic value. That the Scots were aware of the danger of bibliolatry is evident from many sources; for example, reference was made at the funeral of Henry Scougal, a seventeenth-century Scottish divine, to those guilty of 'making a lottery of the Holy Scriptures' (G. Garden, *A Sermon at the Funeral of Mr Henry Scougal* in H. Scougal, *Works* (ed. 1726), p. 418).

[2] In 1567 there were 269 ministers and 659 readers and other substitutes.

[3] *The Second Buik of Discipline, or Heids and Conclusiones of the Policie of the Kirk, agreed upon in the General Assembly 1578* was inserted in the Registers of Assembly in 1581 and sworn to in the National Covenant, 1638.

[4] That is, if the superintendents be accounted an episcopacy. Besides the episcopacy officially set up in Scotland in 1612 which Charles I was obliged to abolish in 1639, there was another episcopacy from 1662 to 1690, generally called the 'Second Episcopacy'. The use of the term 'superintendent' by the Scottish Reformers was not original, and by it they intended simply to convey that the office of a bishop is

ecclesiastical strife in Scotland would, of course, be entirely out of place here, and even a summary of it is unnecessary for our purpose. It should be noted, however, since we shall be concerned in our next chapter with the development of the doctrine of the Church in the seventeenth-century Scottish divines, that despite the considerable influence of English Independency on the Kirk after the signing of the 'Solemn League and Covenant' in 1643, it was possible for a Scottish writer at the Restoration in 1660 to declare that while sectaries were 'very few and inconsiderable in comparison to the body of the Church, scarce one to a thousand, yet is the infection such as ought not to be despised or neglected.'[1]

In 1652, however, a small group in Aberdeen formally declared that 'the Congregational way comes nearer to the pattern of the Word than our Classical form', and that the Church should consist exclusively of those of a 'blameless and gospel-like behaviour'.[2] When they had presented a document to this effect to the Synod of Aberdeen and it had been pronounced contrary to the Word and to the mind of the Church, the group 'separated themsellfes from the discipline and government of this Kirk to Independencie'. The signatories were men of distinction and, in some cases, learning, and soon there were said

pastoral; the term 'bishop' carried too many overtones of *dominium*. John Poynet, Bishop of Winchester wrote: 'Who knoweth not that the name *bishop* hath been so abused, that when it was spoken the people understood nothing else but a great lord, that went in a white rochet with a wide shaven crown. . . . Now to bring people from this abuse, what better means can be devised than to teach the people their error by another word out of Scripture of the same significance: which thing, by the term *Superintendent* would in time have been well brought to pass; . . . and the word *superintendent* being a very Latin word, made English by us, should in time have taught the people, by the very etymology and proper signification, what thing was meant when they heard that name. . . .' (Quoted by J. Strype, *Ecclesiastical Memorials* (1553), II, ii, 141.) Jewel recalls 'that a superintendent is an ancient name and signifieth none other but a bishop. St Augustine saith: Vocabulum episcopatus inde ductum est, quod ille, qui praeficitur, eis, quibus praeficitur, superintendit. . . . Ergo ἐπισκοπεῖν . . . Latine dicere possumus superintendere. Again he saith: Quod Graece dicitur Episcopus, hoc Latine superintentor interpretatur. Chrysostom saith: Episcopus, ex eo dictus quod omnes inspiciat. St Hierome saith: ἐπισκοποῦντες, id est, superintendentes. . . . Your own Thomas of Aquine saith: Episcopi dicuntur ex eo, quod superintendunt.' (Jewel, *Works*, IV, p. 906.).

[1] J. Guthrie, quoted by G. D. Henderson, *Religious Life in Seventeenth-century Scotland* (Cambridge U. P., 1937), p. 106.

[2] G. D. Henderson, *op. cit.*, p. 108.

to be many 'Apostates in the Colledge of Aberdeen'. They held a Communion Service of their own at Marischal College, but afterwards abandoned the idea of forming themselves into a separate Church.[1] The result of this movement was negligible; but the Aberdeen Independents, as they came to be called, are of considerable interest to us, for their movement illustrates how deeply rooted in Scotland was the idea of the historic Church, and how alien from the minds and hearts of the Scots was English Independency. The Scottish nobles and others who signed the National Covenant in Greyfriars Church, Edinburgh, in 1638,[2] did so because they believed, rightly or wrongly, that under James I and more especially under Charles I fresh bonds had been devised for binding the Kirk, the historic *Ecclesia Scoticana*. There were, after all, at this time men in their eighties who were born before the Reformation; some of them could even remember the burning of Walter Myln.[3] It is not surprising that they were uncommonly suspicious of anything that looked in the least like a return to those days. Laud, who did not understand the Scots, had unwittingly provoked them to call for the abolition of episcopacy, which they had now come to identify with forces destructive of the Church they loved.

The men who signed the 'Solemn League and Covenant'—a very different document—in 1643, hoping thereby to secure the Scottish Church against what they believed to be political tyranny, were acutely disappointed at the alliance they had made. For they found to their dismay that their English allies were Independents rather than Presbyterians as the Scots understood this term. Their English allies were also Republican rather than Monarchist—uncongenial, therefore, to the Scots

[1] *Loc. cit.* One of the members of this group, John Row, who, under Cromwell's government, had become Principal of King's College, Aberdeen, was the grandson of an associate of Knox, John Row, who was a doctor of Laws of Padua and, before the Reformation, an agent at Rome for the Scottish clergy. A letter of Principal Row's to his brother expresses the opinion that 'We think a member of a congregatione of Christ ought to be a visible saint'. The same letter also casts doubt upon the right of the Courts of the Church to overrule congregations (*op. cit.*, p. 109 ff.).

[2] Some symbolized their zeal for it by signing their names with their blood.

[3] Myln, an octogenarian, was burned for heresy at St Andrews in 1558.

from a political as well as from a religious point of view. The alliance in this troubled time gave the Scottish Church its *Westminster Confession* and the extreme, often vulgar hostility to even the most restrained types of ecclesiastical art and moderate liturgical ceremonial that was characteristic of English Puritanism. The catastrophic effect of this spirit on liturgical worship in Scotland for over two hundred years is well known.[1] Yet the Scots were essentially unaffected by any Separatist doctrine of the Church. As we shall see, a Scottish ecclesiological literature was in process of development at this time; but of course it was not this that stayed the spread of Independency one might have expected in the circumstances. There was a much livelier force behind the Scots' almost complete invulnerability to a Separatist ecclesiology. The turmoil of the age had but clarified the Scottish vision of the Church as the Body of Christ, wounded and bleeding, yet assured of His blessed Presence always. Throughout the lamentable strife that filled most of the remainder of the seventeenth century in Scotland, from the cruel persecution of the Covenanters during the 'killing time' to the stupid 'rabbling of the curates' that grimly marked the end of the Second Episcopacy, there was still one 'face of Kirk', one *Ecclesia Scoticana*. There were indeed parties within it, parties whose bitterness towards each other far exceeded anything in modern Christendom, where acrimony is still not unknown; yet Protester and Resolutioner were within one Church which both loved, each in his own way, taking that Church to be the Body of Christ. Nor did the grim realism of the seventeenth century in Scotland encourage the Scots to think in terms of a company of visible saints. The very few ministers who were interested in the notion found their congregations singularly unresponsive to it.

The party division of the next age was of another kind. As the Kirk slowly passed from the bitterness of the seventeenth to the settled calm of the eighteenth century, the distinction that

[1] Cf. G. W. Sprott, *The Worship of the Church of Scotland during the Covenantine Period, 1638–61* (Lee Lecture; Edinburgh, 1893). Cf. also W. McMillan, *The Worship of the Scottish Reformed Church, 1550–1638* (London, James Clarke, 1931).

gradually emerged was between the Moderates[1] and the Evangelicals. The Kirk, with William Carstares as its chosen leader, was assured of a mediating policy; but even with this good fortune and the memory of men such as the saintly Robert Leighton which lived on in the hearts of many to temper the asperities they had inherited, the old wounds had bitten deep, and the opening years of the eighteenth century were passed in an atmosphere of extraordinarily sullen gloom. There is no doubt that the Puritan attitudes of mind the Scots had imported from England at the time of the 'Solemn League' were peculiarly unfortunate. They ill suited the Scottish temperament, and the circumstances of the time aggravated their adverse effect. They were by far the worst influence that Scotland ever imported from across the Border, for though they did not affect the fundamental ecclesiology of the Scottish Church, their effect on its ethos as well as its liturgy was calamitous.[2] Their superimposition upon the fundamentally historic conception of the Church that had proved to be inalienable from the *Ecclesia Scoticana* produced, in an age in which the country was at last united under a strongly consolidated ecclesiastical institution, a peculiar atmosphere of gloom. Sunday observance was enforced with severe penalties, while the seasons of the Christian Year were, because of their association with the distrusted episcopacy, studiously ignored. Satan seemed ever round the corner; so much so that when witch-hunting waned at this time there were some who attributed the innumerable ills of the day to the leniency in this matter that seemed to them to betoken a decline

[1] The Moderates took their name from the words addressed by William of Orange to the Kirk after the Revolution Settlement: 'A calm and peaceable procedure will be no less pleasing to Us than it becometh you. We never could be of the mind that violence was suited to the advancing of true religion, nor do we intend that Our authority shall ever be a tool to the irregular passions of any party. Moderation is what religion enjoins, neighbouring Churches expect from you, and We recommend to you.' Cf. A. J. Campbell, *Two Centuries of the Church of Scotland 1707–1929* (Hastie Lectures, University of Glasgow; Paisley, Alexander Gardner, 1930), p. 19 f. This work (317 pp.) is still the best available account of the period.

[2] So great was the antipathy to set forms of prayer that it was not until 1802 that one was published, anonymously, under the title, *The Scotch Minister's Assistant*. It was printed in Inverness. Such a spirit was as alien to Knox as it was to Laud.

in morals.[1] A perverse caricature of Calvin's predestinarian theology was preached, and his lofty doctrine of the sovereignty of God turned into a picture of a very unamiable deity. Hell and the Last Judgment were among the most popular subjects in the pulpit, and some travelled thirty or forty miles to hear a sermon upon them by an outstanding preacher.

Nevertheless, the centrality of the Eucharist was maintained, and the significance of this for the purpose of our study can hardly be overestimated. The Eucharist was not at this time regarded as a parochial celebration: in rural areas, when it was announced that it was to be celebrated in a certain church, neighbouring churches were closed while ministers and their flocks went off on a sacramental pilgrimage to what was often called, in the language of ploughmen and fisherfolk, 'the Great Work.'[2] That such an apposite colloquialism should have been used by the common man attests the fact that despite the havoc wrought upon the liturgical tradition of the Reformed Church in Scotland by that time, the historic significance of λειτουργία had not been lost. The thousands who attended a celebration of the Eucharist in such a parish created great practical difficulties, for the devotions lasted from Thursday to Monday, and lodging had, of course, to be found for the visiting congregations. These gatherings were social occasions, and young people, according to Burns, sometimes used them as cover for discreet saturnalia of their own.[3] Some preachers felt impelled to discourage their flocks from too much 'running from Supper to Supper'. During the summer months in many districts it was possible to go almost every other week to one of these lengthy celebrations, and some did go as often as that, though a celebration in a particular parish might be as rare as once a year or even once in two or three years. But these gatherings were on the whole, in spite of aberrations, deeply liturgical in spirit.

The relation between Church and State defined in the Revolution Settlement had at that time been taken for granted. The idea of a national Church general in Reformation times, had

[1] A. J. Campbell, *op. cit.*, p. 29. [2] *Op. cit.*, p. 30. [3] Cf. Robert Burns, *The Holy Fair.*

lingered on. In Scotland, at the time of the Revolution Settlement, there were but two very small sections of the population, representing the extremists of both sides, who proved themselves willing to carry their old animosities to the point of standing out from the National Church. The latter inevitably included, therefore, people of very different temperaments, and there were many shades of opinion on the old controversies. That national sentiment and a sense of patriotic duty were not the only or the principal forces uniting the early eighteenth-century Scots in the Kirk, and that there was a fundamental ecclesiological unity, is exhibited, paradoxically, in the *kind* of secessions that began to take place as soon as the old principle of the co-extension of Church and State collapsed.[1] For these secessions, which unfortunately gave rise to renewed bitterness, were, though also associated with party differences between the Moderates and the Evangelicals, fundamentally concerned with questions of Church-State relations. The characteristic motivation on the part of the seceders was a righteous-minded jealousy for the *ecclesiological* purity of the Church, a fear that the Body of Christ was being strangled by corrupt influences in the State with which it was, in their opinion, too closely allied. Though the secessions and the Disruption brought fresh strife, they betokened a commendable care for principle which since the final healing in 1929 has seemed to many to mitigate the memory of the evils that attended the schisms. The chief points to be borne in mind for our present study are as follows: (*a*) all the bodies maintained Presbyterian government and discipline; (*b*) the Disruption certainly did not imply Separatist principles, for both sides considered the Church to be in schism and neither

[1] The First Secession took place in 1733, on a question of State interference; the Second Secession, similar in motivation, came in 1761. The seceding bodies splintered in various ways, but the resulting bodies were for the most part reunited in 1847 in the United Presbyterian Church. In 1843, the Disruption in the Church of Scotland, also on the question of Church-State relations, resulted in the Free Church and the Established Church competing for the allegiance of the nation. In 1900 the United Presbyterian Church and the Free Church joined, under the name of the United Free Church, which continued apart from the Established Church until 1929, when these were reunited. The causes of disunity had by this time been mainly removed, leaving no differences of principle but only of outlook and opinion. No more than remnants of these secessions remain.

looked upon the other as separated from the Body of Christ, while there existed also on both sides a sense of the sin of schism; and (*c*) even the earlier secessions did not generally imply Separatist principles,[1] though many of the seceders were indubitably affected by Independency, and while they held to Scottish Presbyterianism they did not always exhibit a very profound understanding of its ecclesiology.[2]

In the *Ecclesia Scoticana*, to which Presbyterian Churches in other parts of the world have always looked with special interest, the doctrine of the Church in the Reformed tradition has been maintained and developed in unique circumstances. The adoption of a special emblem, the Burning Bush, accompanied by the motto, *Nec tamen consumebatur*, symbolizes these special circumstances rather than the doctrine itself.[3] It was, of course, in no

[1] In 1841 the leaders of a group later known as Morisonians were expelled from the seceding synod to which they belonged, on account of their heterodoxy. They founded the Evangelical Union, the majority of whose congregations joined the Congregational Union of Scotland in 1896. But this was a special case; moreover, the Congregational Union, founded in 1798, was never strong in Scotland.

[2] It was a widespread ignorance of the ecclesiological principles of the Reformed tradition that led to the situation that alarmed certain leaders of the Established Church in the last quarter of the nineteenth century. William Milligan, in his moderatorial charge in 1882, referred to the widespread doubt among educated people in Scotland 'with regard to the claims of Christianity as an actually Divine revelation and of the Church as an actually Divine institution in the world'. It was not, he said, Establishment that was at stake; it was the Church of Christ. (Cf. H. J. Wotherspoon, *James Cooper* (London, Longmans, 1926), p. 161.) The Evangelical movement of the early seventies, having had too meagre a theology, had exhausted itself. There was, Wotherspoon complained, a modification of 'the *ethos* of the clergy' and an assimilation of 'the tone of Church life to that of Dissent'. The consciousness of such churchmen of the need for recovery of better churchmanship led to the foundation, in 1892, of the Scottish Church Society, whose purpose was declared to be 'to defend and advance Catholic doctrine as set forth in the ancient Creeds and embodied in the Standards of the Church of Scotland. . . .' First among the Society's aims was the affirmation of 'the Divine basis, supernatural life and heavenly calling of the Church'; other aims referred to the historical continuity of the Church, ordination, the sacraments, and the pastoral discipline of clergy and people. (*Op. cit.*, c. vii.). While the leaders of this movement were distinguished in historical and liturgical scholarship, and its aims most laudable, its ecclesiology has never been sufficiently developed. An account of the formation and a full statement of the Constitution of the Society may be found in C. G. McCrie, *Public Worship of Presbyterian Scotland* (Cunningham Lectures, 1892) (Edinburgh, Blackwood, 1892), Appendix P, p. 450 ff. On the subject of liturgical history there is a good brief modern sketch in W. D. Maxwell, *A History of Worship in the Church of Scotland* (Baird Lectures, 1953; Oxford U. P., 1955). The account (c. vi) of developments since 1750 is especially well done; but it exhibits a singular inattention to theological and ecclesiological principles.

[3] The Burning Bush appears in an old Huguenot seal, dated 1559. This bears the motto *flagror non consumor*, and within the emblem is inscribed the tetragramma-

way intended to supplant the Scriptural figure, the Body of Christ. The Commission appointed by the General Assembly of the Church of Scotland in 1940 'for the interpretation of God's Will in the present crisis' presented reports in which, among other recommendations, was urged new emphasis on the doctrine of the Church. 'There is therefore great need today,' said John Baillie, reporting in 1942 as convener of the Commission, 'for laying fresh emphasis upon the doctrine of the Church. . . . We must correct the widespread notion that Christianity is merely an affair of the individual soul. . . . We must therefore teach men afresh that the blessings of the Gospel cannot be enjoyed by the single individual in his singleness, but only in his incorporation into Christ's Mystical Body, the Holy Catholic Church.'[1]

ton. The use of this emblem in the Reformed Church has been exhaustively studied by G. D. Henderson in *The Burning Bush* (Edinburgh, St Andrew Press, 1958), since the publication of which the General Assembly of the Church of Scotland has resolved to register a design embodying its traditional emblem and motto, together with a St Andrew's Cross, at the Court of the Lord Lyon.

[1] *God's Will in Our Time* (London, S.C.M. Press, 1942), p. 16 f. This report is included in the series published in 1946 under the title, *God's Will for Church and Nation*.

CHAPTER V

THE SEVENTEENTH-CENTURY SCOTTISH DIVINES

It is hardly to be expected that the seventeenth century should have produced, in Scotland, theologians of great originality or vision. There were too many obstacles in the way, not least the intense and almost incessant ecclesiastical strife. On the other hand, this very circumstance did bring ecclesiological problems before the minds of the most thoughtful divines; hence the importance of these for our purpose. The Scottish divines of the period were often very learned in their way,[1] and they produced a body of solid divinity. Much of it is dull reading, for the prose of these writers is tedious and ornamented with elaborate and often absurd metaphors.

[1] The state of education in seventeenth-century Scotland should be noted, for it indicates how these divines were equipped, to what extent they were, from a modern viewpoint, handicapped, and in what measure the common people were able to follow the disputations of the learned, or become acquainted with the theological issues of the day. *The First Buik of Discipline* (c. vii) provided, *inter alia,* that there should be an elementary school in every parish: no longer were the sons of the rich to be allowed to spend their youth 'in vaine idlenesse', while the sons of the poor were to be required, if they showed any aptitude for learning, to go to the parish school. The turmoil of the seventeenth century did not mitigate the difficulties of carrying out this ambitious programme, and until 1696, or later, many parishes, especially in the Highlands, had no organized school; nor was attendance always fully enforced by the Kirk Session even where a school had been provided. Illiteracy, therefore, was still widespread. On the other hand, considering the poverty of the Kirk and the unsettled conditions, the educational achievement is impressive.

Education at all levels was very medieval in form. At the grammar schools Latin was studied for five years to prepare boys for the university, where lectures were in Latin and where Aristotle was still the basis of the four-year curriculum in Arts. Modern thinkers were not neglected entirely; but a student was likely to know more about the *Isagoge* than about the *Discours de la méthode.* Scholastic disputation habituated men to controversy in later life. Candidates for the ministry, who took the further four-year Divinity course, were taught Hebrew, and in some cases even a little Syriac; but the average attainment in Hebrew was probably low, and in some cases negligible. The standard of Greek was apparently very respectable, however, and there was at any rate an immense respect for Biblical learning. One writer, quoting Musculus, says: 'Visne esse bonus Theologus? Cura ut sis bonus Biblicus.' (William Douglas, *Academiarum Vindiciae* (1659), p. 39.) Ministers who merely engaged in the usual Latin controversies without having solid Biblical scholarship behind them did not usually impress their colleagues. Probably the

Foreign influence was considerable. Switzerland was naturally a focus of interest. Germany exercised little influence on the Scots at this time, though some students went to Heidelberg, and the Heidelberg Catechism was studied in Scotland, as were also the commentaries of Pareus and the earlier works of Zanchius and Olivianus. The Union of the Crowns did not destroy the old ties with France, and in the early part of the century there were, in the Reformed colleges in France, large numbers of Scottish students and teachers, while it was by no means uncommon for parish ministers in Scotland to have had some training in France. The French Reformed Church continued to influence Scotland in matters of ecclesiastical government. Gradually, however, French influence waned.[1] England was naturally an important influence. The work of the great English divines was well known to most of the theologians north of the Border. The Scots were suspicious of Episcopacy because they feared the political motives they thought they detected, and many of them on that account no doubt wished they could have liked the Independents. We have already seen that there was much influence from Independency, especially through the Westminster Confession. But experience of both English Episcopacy and English Independency convinced the Scots of that day that neither was to their liking, and so reinforced nationalistic sentiment. Nevertheless, we shall see that the ecclesiology of the Scots was much nearer to that of the Anglican divines than it was to that of the Independents.

Scotland's closest tie in the seventeenth century was with the Netherlands. The two countries traded, lent each other military aid, and evinced much interest in each other's affairs. There were Dutch merchants in every Scottish port, and likewise

greatest advantage the Scottish clergy enjoyed in those days was the 'presbytery exercise' which, being taken very seriously indeed, obliged even the least studious to make an attempt to keep up with his more learned colleagues, for if he badly failed to do so he was publicly rebuked. A presbytery could afford to be indulgent towards a student whose attainments in Hebrew did not fulfil the requirements, since no minister was ever allowed to neglect his studies in later life; of even the least gifted something was demanded long after ordination.

[1] Huguenot refugees, coming to Scotland after the revocation of the Edict of Nantes in 1685, no doubt revived the old alliance.

many Scots in Holland. Dutch students attended the Scottish universities, and the Scots went to Leyden and Utrecht in large numbers. The theological influence of Holland would be difficult to exaggerate. The Scots had a high regard for the decrees of the Synod of Dort, and the Scottish divines frequently referred to it. The Arminian controversy greatly interested the Scots who vigorously opposed the Remonstrants: John Forbes of Corse, for instance, called them 'the Semi-Pelagians of this century'.[1] David Dickson,[2] Robert Baillie[3] and John Strang,[4] all of Glasgow, were involved in the controversy, and the last was probably the most learned in it.[5] As an infralapsarian he was less popular, however, than the ardently supralapsarian Samuel Rutherford of St Andrews.[6]

Rutherford's special interest for our purpose lies in his vigorous opposition to Separatist ideas. In *A Peaceable and Tem-*

[1] John Forbes (1593–1648) *Instructiones Historico-Theologicae* (ed. 1645), p. 409; cf. p. 388, p. 435 f. where he quotes the *Historia Pelagiana* of Vossius. On Forbes, *infra*, p. 109, n. 1.

[2] C. 1583–1663.

[3] Robert Baillie (1599–1662), a learned Hebraist, fiercely opposed the sectaries in works such as *A Dissuasive from the Errours of the Time; wherein the Principall Sects, especially of the Independents, are drawn together in a Map* (1645–46), and *Anabaptism, the True Fountaine of Independency, Brownisme, Antinomy, Familisme, etc., or a Second Part of the Dissuasive from the Errours of the Time* (1647).

[4] 1584–1654.

[5] This may be seen from Strang's *De Voluntate Dei et Actionibus circa Peccatum* (Amsterdam, 1657), which exhibits considerable knowledge of patristic and medieval sources, of the Reformers, of the English divines, and of the Dutch, including Maccovius, Amesius, Arminius, Rivetus, Grotius, Maresius, Trelcatius and others. His *De Interpretatione et Perfectione Scripturae* (Rotterdam, 1663) was influential in its time. Strang was suspected of Amyraldism. Subjected to investigation by a committee of Scottish divines, he was exonerated on subscribing to the decrees of the Synod of Dort. For an exposition of Amyraldism, see Hodge, *Systematic Theology*, vol. ii, p. 205 f, p. 322. It was a modified Calvinism, so called after Moses Amyraldus or Amyraut (1596–1664), who taught that Christ died for all men (*supra*, p. 49).

[6] Rutherford (1600–61) was a very remarkable man, a deeply devotional and mystical writer (cf. Adam Philip, *The Devotional Literature of Scotland* (London, James Clarke, n. d.), pp. 116–25), as well as an indefatigable controversialist and learned exponent of Dutch divinity. John Row alleges that Rutherford's bishop (Sydserf) was an Arminian (*The History of the Kirk of Scotland* (ed. 1842), p. 396); Rutherford's *Exercitationes Apologeticae pro Divina Gratia* (Amsterdam, 1636) attacked Arminius, and in *De Divina Providentia* (1651) and the posthumous *Examen Arminianismi* (1668), Rutherford's own position is more fully developed. His *Spiritual Letters* was for long a devotional classic in Scotland. In his *Lex Rex* (London, 1644), he considers the source of royal power, and argues that the monarch receives his power from the people, not absolutely, as some held, but conditionally. Rutherford quotes, usually with exact references, from sources that show his wide interests, e.g., Luther, Cajetan, Bellarmine, Salmasius and Hooker.

perate Plea for Paul's Presbytery in Scotland, published in 1642, he undertakes to uphold a Presbyterian view, and two years later, in *Due Right of Presbyteries; or, a Peaceable Plea for the Government of the Church of Scotland*, he attacks the New England Independents. After another two years he wrote upholding, against Erasmus, the power of the Church to excommunicate, in *Divine Right of Church-government and Excommunication.* Rutherford, making much of the distinction between the visible and the invisible Church, endeavours to uphold the thesis that the Separatists and Romanists err together in predicating of the visible Church what may be predicated only of the invisible Church. Maintaining that only visible profession is essential to the visible Church, he goes so far as to propose that, since many persons do in fact adhere to the Church for 'favour of men' and other such unworthy motives, the Christian magistrate may compel men to attach themselves to the True Church.[1] He recognizes that a saving knowledge of Christ cannot be achieved by compulsion, 'by the dint and violence of the sword'; but he thinks that a Christian magistrate is entitled to punish irreligion. He argues that the magistrate does not command outward performances as service to God, but forbids, rather, their omission, because this is destructive of society. So neglect of church attendance is punishable, since it causes scandal, being offensive to those who lead 'a quiet and peaceable life in all godliness and honesty'.[2]

The notion, repugnant to many, that a Christian magistrate has the moral right to exercise powers such as this belongs to the 'covenant' or 'federal' scheme of theology that was elaborately developed by some of the Dutch, English and Scottish divines in the seventeenth century.[3] Rutherford's special interest for our

[1] *A Peaceable and Temperate Plea*, p. 111.

[2] *A Free Disputation against pretended Liberty of Conscience* (London, 1649), pp. 50–2. In this work Rutherford criticized the position of John Goodwin and Jeremy Taylor.

[3] Federalism or 'covenant theology' was fully elaborated only after the Westminster Assembly, and is essentially a seventeenth-century product. It has no place in the ancient creeds or in the confessional statements of the Roman, Lutheran or Continental Reformed Churches; nor is it to be found in any of the Church of England formularies from 1536 to 1571, or the Scottish confessions from 1560 to 1616. There is a mention of 'the covenant of the law' in the Irish Articles of 1615. The Westminster Confession, however, represents the dealings of God with man

purpose lies in the extreme position he adopts in opposing Separatism. He puts himself the question, 'Whether or no do some warrantably teach that Baptism should be administered only to infants born of one at least parent known to be a believer and within the covenant, and who are to be admitted to the Lord's Supper?'[1] In answering this question he first calls attention to the distinction between an 'inherent' and a 'covenant' holiness. The latter gives a right to the means of salvation only. He then distinguishes between those who are in the covenant by faith in Christ, according to election, and those who are there by profession as hearers of the Word, as members of the visible Church. The holiness of a nation is to be distinguished from the holiness of an individual; the covenant holiness *de jure* of infants born in the visible Church and not yet baptized, from the *de facto* holiness of the baptized members of the visible Church. Baptism is the right of all infants in a society that is within the covenant, for such a society enjoys God's promise to be the God of the seed of His people. Admission to Holy Communion requires the capacity to 'discern the Lord's body', so that children, mentally deficient persons, and others of whom such discernment could not be expected, must be excluded; nevertheless, no definite evidence of inward conversion is to be demanded, for the Church may not judge the inward state of a man, but only his visible profession. The Apostles received Ananias and Sapphira[2] and Simon Magus[3]. Such persons must be admitted to communion

both in nature and in grace as 'covenants': there is a 'covenant of works' and a 'covenant of grace'. Henry Bullinger had published, two years before the first edition of Calvin's *Institutio*, his *De Testamento seu Foedere Dei unico et eterno* (1534). Peter Martyr, in lectures at Oxford on the Epistle to the Romans, also made some use of the covenant idea, as did Martin Bucer at Cambridge and John Alasco at London. The English Puritans were affected by it: cf. John Preston of Cambridge, *Treatise on the New Covenant; or, the Saint's Portion* (1629), John Ball of Oxford, *Treatise of the Covenant of Grace* (1645), and the very influential book published anonymously in two parts, *The Marrow of Modern Divinity* (1645 and 1649) which gave rise to an Antinomian controversy. The Dutch divine, John Cocceius, a pupil of the English Puritan William Ames, arranged a whole theological system in a work published after the Westminster Confession had appeared: *Summa Doctrinae de Foedere et Testamenti Dei Explicata* (1654). (Cf. J. Walker, *The Theology and Theologians of Scotland* (Edinburgh, 1872), p. 73 ff.) Herman Witsius, his disciple, was popular in Scotland.

[1] *A Peaceable and Temperate Plea*, c. xii.

[2] Acts v. 1–11.

[3] Acts viii. 9 ff.

upon making formal profession; but they may be put out of communion as soon as evidence is available that their lives are plainly incompatible with it.

'Rome,' says Rutherford, 'made the separation from the Reformed Churches and not we from them, as the rotten wall maketh the schism in the house, when the house standeth still and the rotten wall falleth.'[1] A Christian cannot separate himself from the Church but only from the corruptions that spring up in the Church. Rutherford distinguishes between the Church Mystical and the Church Ministerial. The power of the keys is given to the latter *for* the former. John Robinson, whose companions had gone in considerable numbers to New England, had argued, in Separatist fashion, that any two or three persons might gather together in the name of Christ and so constitute a Church, without having any officers at all. Rutherford was comparatively gentle towards Robinson and his friends, for though they were Separatists they were much less fanatical in their Separatism than were the Anabaptists. He regarded them as erring, yet as erring in good faith. 'Why should we strive?' he says, 'for we be brethren, the Sons of one father, the born Citizens of one mother Jerusalem.'[2] But he insisted that there is no 'practice or precept' in Scripture for the use of the keys by a Church without officers.[3] 'Men may be a Church of Christians, and a mystical Church before they have a ministry, but they are not a governing Church, having the power of the keys, so long as they want officers, who only have warrant ordinary of Christ to use the keys.'[4] So he develops a high view of the ministry: it is from the ministry that a man receives ordination, and the power that is bestowed is the power of those who confer it, not being restricted by the limitations of place or time to which a particular congregation is subject. Against the English Independents, Rutherford insisted that a man is ordained to the ministry *in* the Universal Church; he exercises his ministry *to*

[1] *A Peaceable and Temperate Plea*, p. 122.
[2] *The Due Right of Presbyteries* (London, 1644), p. ii.
[3] *Op. cit.*, c. viii, p. 179.
[4] *Op. cit.*, p. 177.

congregations. He cannot be deprived of his ministerial status even if his whole congregation should forsake him.[1] Whether this means that ordination confers an indelible mark or character is not entirely clear. According to Willet, an Anglican divine, the notion that such an indelible character is conferred at ordination is without warrant in St Augustine or other ancient source, and is to be rejected.[2] Rutherford, not unmindful of the fact that the ministry exists for the Church, would certainly have agreed with Hooker that those who have been ordained to the ministry 'may not think to put it off and on like a cloak as the weather serveth', and he would probably have approved Hooker's view that since by ordination a man is 'consecrated unto God', neither deposition from the ministry nor restoration to it can 'iterate the first knot'.[3] At any rate, Hooker's summary of the essential nature of the ministry indubitably expresses Rutherford's view: 'Whether we preach, pray, baptize, communicate, condemn, give absolution, or whatsoever, as disposers of God's mysteries, our words, judgments, acts and deeds, are not ours but the Holy Ghost's.'[4] The power of the keys belongs to the ministry. Moreover, such is Rutherford's stress on the unity of the Church that he insists that any disciplinary action by a particular Church, which is done according to the order and discipline accepted by that Church, is to be recognized throughout the Universal Church. Not to recognize it would be to declare that Church outside the Universal Church.[5]

One of the most learned treatises produced by the Scottish divines was Robert Boyd's commentary on Ephesians.[6] The

[1] *A Peaceable and Temperate Plea*, c. xii.
[2] A. Willet, *Synopsis Papismi* (1594; ed. 1852), vol. vi, p. 366 f.
[3] Richard Hooker, *The Laws of Ecclesiastical Polity*, lxxvii, 3.
[4] *Op. cit.*, lxxvii, 8.
[5] *A Peaceable and Temperate Plea*, c. xvii.
[6] Robert Boyd (1578–1627), *In Epistolam Pauli Apostoli ad Ephesios Praelectiones*, published posthumously in 1652. His father, James Boyd, laird of Trochrig, Ayrshire, was the first Archbishop of Glasgow after the Reformation, and also became Moderator of the General Assembly. Robert, after taking the degree of M.A. at Edinburgh, went in 1599 to France where he became, at the age of twenty-one, professor of philosophy at Montauban. Seven years later he became professor of theology at Saumur, and it is said that his command of French in the pulpit was

doctrine of the Church which he expounds in it is set forth in reference to the work of the Jesuit theologian, Robert Bellarmine, whose statement of the Roman doctrine of the Church had appeared about twenty years previously. Bellarmine, who had spoken of 'the levity of heretics in matters pertaining to the sacraments',[1] charged Protestants generally with 'making the True Church invisible', since, he said, they require internal graces of men before these may be constituted members of the Church. With this Bellarmine contrasted the Roman view that, while all graces are to be found in the Church, it is not necessary for anyone, in order to be called a member of the Church, to have any internal grace; only an external profession of faith and the partaking of the sacraments is required.[2] Bellarmine described the Church as a living organism, consisting of soul and body: the soul is the inward graces, the body the outward profession of faith and participation in the sacraments. He distinguished three classes of members of the Church: (*a*) those who are members in the fullest sense, being 'of the soul and the body'; (*b*) those who are of the soul but not of the body, such as catechumens and others who are spiritually united with the Church, yet are not of the body; and (*c*) those who, making profession without lively faith, are of the body but not of the soul of the Church. The Church is an external institution in which men may be sanctified, but which consists of good and bad members.[3]

Boyd questions what sort of living body it could be in which some of the members were of the soul yet not of the body, while

much admired. In 1615, he accepted an invitation from James VI to return to Scotland as Principal of the University of Glasgow. It seems he was a scholar rather than a teacher; at any rate he found the students' boisterousness irksome and resigned in 1621. For a very brief period later he was Principal of the University of Edinburgh; but most of his remaining years were spent in retirement at his ancestral home. His *Ephesians*, based on lectures given at Saumur and Glasgow, contains well over a million words and is written in a style more terse than was then common. He quotes over two hundred writers, including Augustine, Chrysostom, Bernard, Bellarmine, Bede, Perkins and Whittaker, as well as the Scottish divines.

[1] Bellarmine, pref. to *Controv. de sacram.* in *Disputationes de controversiis christianae fidei*, vol. iii.

[2] Bellarmine, *De Ecclesia militante*, ii, in *Disputationes, loc. cit.*

[3] *Loc. cit.*

others are of the body yet not of the soul. Must not it be monstrous or paralysed? He refers to Aristotle, who says that an eye deprived of the power of seeing is no more an eye than if it were the eye of a statue or a painted representation of an eye.[1] He is on surer ground when he suggests that the difference between the Reformed and the Roman doctrines of the Church springs from a different conception of the nature of faith. The Roman conception of faith as essentially intellectual assent permits of the distinction between *fides informis*, a mere knowledge of and acquiescence in what the Church teaches, and *fides formata*, a knowledge of the truth affecting one's heart and life. In Reformed theology, Boyd maintains, *fides informis* has no place. Boyd's position, though it inclines to, is nevertheless distinguishable from, Separatism. It is his insistence upon the Headship of Christ that seems to him to preclude Bellarmine's conception of the Body as consisting in part of persons whose faith is *informis*. It is one thing to recognize that hypocrites attach themselves to the Body of Christ, and to acknowledge that even within the living Body there are incorporated members who have not yet fully realized the life that is being given them; it is a very different thing to suppose that a man can be incorporated into the Body of Christ by giving intellectual assent to theological propositions, or even by saying, 'O God, I believe in all Thy Church doth teach.' Christ dwells in the hearts of the faithful that they, being rooted and grounded in love, may know the love of Christ.[2] It is of our oneness with Christ in love that we speak when we speak of being in the Body of Christ. A Christian's faith may be imperfect; it cannot be loveless. In some measure it must always affect his heart and life; otherwise it is not faith at all. Boyd opposes Bellarmine's conception because it appears to him to injure the Headship of Christ and to suggest that the Church may pretend to keep

[1] Aristotle, *De Anima*, 412 b. It might be contended, however, that the 'bad' members correspond, in Aristotelian terms, not to a dead eye but to one that exists in potentiality. This seems to be Bellarmine's view; it is also implicit in Rutherford's position.

[2] Cf. Ephesians iii. 17–19.

a part of itself autonomous, independent of the sovereignty of its Lord.

John Brown of Wamphray,[1] who is among the Scottish divines who argue for the 'divine right of Presbytery',[2] likens the Church to a workshop (*officina*).[3] He contends that God desires even unregenerate persons to be received into it, so that they may become regenerate. The ministry is the instrument of this regeneration, which takes place within the Church. He maintains that the Jews admitted proselytes upon an external profession of faith and that such a profession was accounted sufficient in apostolic times.[4] The life of the Church, which is Christ Himself, must quicken all who are incorporated into it.[5]

A pamphlet[6] published shortly after the establishment of Presbyterianism under the Settlement complains of the poor state of the book trade in Scotland at that time, declaring that 'the Episcopall are not in circumstances for buying',[7] while the Presbyterians appear to be content with a very few books from which they 'take the heads of their sermons and the instructions which they tender the people', such as 'Durham on the Can-

[1] John Brown of Wamphray (c. 1610–79) was for some time minister at the Scots Church in Rotterdam. His *opus maximum, De causa Dei contra anti-sabbatarios*, which treats many subjects, is particularly concerned with questions about the sanctions of law and the law of God; other works include *The Life of Justification Opened* (1695) and *Quakerism the Pathway to Paganism* (1678).

[2] Cf. his *An Apologetical Relation* (1665), an influential work in its day, in which he questions (ed. 1846, p. 146) the lawfulness of ordaining priests, *more Anglicano*, by 'the sole warrant and mission of the prelate' and with 'no imposition of hands of the Presbytery'. But his theory of the divine right of Presbytery was associated with his strongly anti-Erastian polemic. This was indeed the case, in varying degree, with all who held to it. (On the notion of this 'divine right', cf. *French Conf.*, art xxix; *Belgic Conf.*, art. xxx. It did not imply complete uniformity: cf. Calvin, *Institutio*, IV, i, 2; IV, iv, 10; *Second Helvetic Conf.*, xvii, 13; *Belgic Conf.*, xxviii.) The 'divine right of Presbyteries' was not upheld by the Westminster Assembly in any of its official pronouncements. Moreover, Brown was, like all the divines of the tradition considered in the present chapter, far too deeply concerned for the unity of the Church to permit any radical exclusiveness here: he is defending the 'divine right' in what seems to him an 'Erastian situation', in which the 'crown rights of the Redeemer' appeared to be infringed.

[3] John Brown, *Contra Wolzogium et Velthusium* (Amsterdam, 1670), preface, s. 8. Wolzogius was a Socinian. Lambert Velthuysen, a Dutch physician, had written a work that Brown accounted Erastian.

[4] *Loc. cit.*

[5] *Infra*, c. vii.

[6] *An Historical Relation*, (1691), p. 49 f.

[7] *Supra*, p. 83.

ticles'.[1] James Durham,[2] who drew a distinction between the medieval practice of 'fastening many senses upon one Scripture' (which he disapproved) and 'drawing plain doctrine' out of passages that are clearly allegorical, treats the Song of Solomon as such a passage, on the ground that since the literal meaning does not edify, and all Scripture is for edification, this book must be intended as an allegory. Like St Bernard, he interprets it as a mystical account of the relation between Christ and His Church.[3]

But Durham's principal stress is upon the unity of the Church and the sin of schism. 'Never,' he says, 'did men run to quench fire in a city, lest all should be destroyed, with more diligence than men ought to bestir themselves to quench this in the Church.'[4] He thinks there can be no division among true Christians that cannot be healed, and that in trying to heal such a division we must not insist upon agreement on details. We may

[1] *Infra*, n. 3.

[2] James Durham (1622–58) was born in the parish of Monifieth and ordained to the ministry at Glasgow in 1647. Appointed one of the King's chaplains, he became, in 1651, minister at the Inner Kirk in Glasgow Cathedral. For a man who died at such a very early age his learning is astonishing. Wodrow (*Analecta*, iii, p. 108) records one judgment that though he was, in the pulpit, 'full of great substantiall matter', he 'had not a popular or plausible way of speaking'; his father-in-law, John Carstares, claimed, however (introduction to Durham's *Revelation*) that 'in preaching the Gospel, he liked not to soar and hide himself from the hearers in a cloud of words.' Besides his commentaries on the Song of Solomon (*Clavis Cantici*), on Revelation and on Job, he wrote *The Dying Man's Testament to the Church of Scotland; or, A Treatise concerning Scandal* (1659). According to the *Dict. Nat. Biog.*, Cromwell, who may have heard Durham preach, accounted him a 'very great man'.

[3] *Clavis Cantici* (1669). This interpretation of the Song of Solomon was very popular in seventeenth-century Scotland. Rutherford popularized the notion for the Scots in his *Letters*, and Archbishop Leighton abundantly used it. The 'Gude and Godlie Ballates' (*supra*, p. 19, n. 1) may possibly have disposed people towards this sort of interpretation: many profane love-songs had been given a 'sanctified' dress, e.g., 'Quho is at my windo?' (*ed. cit.*, p. 116 ff). This use of popular songs for religious instruction and edification was by no means peculiar to the Scots; but it had played a special role in Scotland in the sixteenth century in spreading Reformed doctrine. Bernard's interpretation of the Song of Solomon no doubt appealed to the Scots for two reasons: (*a*) for its implied emphasis on the doctrine of the Church, and (*b*) for the devotional values suggested in passages such as that in which Bernard remarks that there are many 'canals' in the Church, but too few 'reservoirs', and in which he enjoins the reader to 'show yourself rather as a reservoir than as a canal' (Bernard, *Cant.*, xviii. 2, 3). It is perhaps noteworthy, in view of the fact that the debt of the Scottish Calvinists to a one-sided Augustinianism has often been exaggerated, that Dom Cuthbert Butler (*Western Mysticism*, 2nd. ed., 1927, p. 277 ff) has demonstrated admirably that Dean Inge's opinion (*Christian Mysticism*, p. 140), that Bernard depends on Augustine for the mystical side of his teaching, is to be doubted.

[4] *The Dying Man's Testament* (ed. 1680), IV, vi, p. 288.

find that, in our view, the practice of another Church is defective, as for instance, where discipline is badly administered; but even serious defects and corruptions cannot excuse schism, except in an extraordinary case. He provides six rules for determining whether corruption is sufficient to justify schism. (1) Nothing can ever warrant maintaining a division that would not warrant a breach; so it is as sinful to neglect to heal a needless breach as it would be to make a schism needlessly. (2) Division is warrantable only when the defect or corruption makes communion with the Church sinful. There can be no warrantable division merely because many abuse the means of grace. (3) 'Men may keep communion with a Church when their calling leadeth them thereto upon the one side and they have access to the discharge of the same upon the other.' A minister has a special duty here. He must continue in his duty 'whilst there is no physical or moral impediment barring him in the same, and others being defective in their duty will not absolve him from his, which he oweth by virtue of his station'. (4) Division is not warrantable even though there be widespread failure in applying the general principle that the ordinances must edify the Church. (5) Schism can never be justified when the evils it entails are greater than the evils it is intended to avoid, no matter how great these may be, unless they entail what is unquestionably sinful. (6) 'When men may unite without personal guilt or accession to the defects or guilt of others, there may and ought to be union, even though there be failings and defects of several kinds in the Church.' Three impediments are recognized, however: (*a*) 'if a person be put to condemn anything he thinketh lawful in his own former practice, or the practice of others, or in some point of doctrine, though never so extrinsic, if it be to him a point of truth;' (*b*) if he be required to approve the deed of others that he accounts sinful or affirm as truth what he accounts error; (*c*) 'when some engagement is required for the future which doth restrain from any duty called for, or that may afterwards be called for.'[1]

[1] *Op. cit.*, IV, vii.

Durham's criterion for deciding what is radically corrupt and what is not, is, of course, Scripture: in this he is at one with other divines of the period, Presbyterian and Anglican, and he shares with the Anglicans also a deep reverence for the opinions of the Fathers and especially for early Christian custom. His whole attitude to schism is, indeed, very similar to that of the sixteenth-century Anglican divines as well as that of the continental Reformers. Jewel points out that if it were always unlawful to leave the fellowship in which one was brought up, then Christ and the apostles would have been guilty of schism.[1] Field contends that there are circumstances that warrant schism,[2] and he also maintains that even where there is schism the divided parts remain parts of the Church, the sin of schism notwithstanding.[3] Unity consists, according to Durham and the Scottish divines generally, of loyalty to one faith, one baptism, one Gospel, and this view is expressed by many of the Anglicans.[4] Even where the latter stressed the episcopate as a bond of unity, and where the Presbyterians upheld the 'divine right of Presbytery', it was not generally maintained that either Bishop or Presbytery was the only means of maintaining visible unity. Field notes three kinds of unity: (*a*) unity of faith; (*b*) unity of the people under pastors lawfully chosen; (*c*) unity of the due connection of pastors with each other and with their flocks.[5]

Durham's teaching on ecclesiastical discipline provides an important illustration of the radical difference between the doctrine of the Church in the Reformed tradition and the Separatist ecclesiology. Scottish discipline was, after the Reformation, notoriously severe. The old church records abound in references to the 'place' or 'stool' or 'pillar' of repentance, occupied by offenders during sermon. Persons were excommunicated with terrible solemnity. They were addressed by

[1] Jewel, *Works* (Parker Soc.), vol. iii, p. 91; but cf. Overall, *Convocation Book* (1606) (Anglo-Catholic Library), p. 109.
[2] Field, *Of the Church* (ed. 1847), vol. i, p. 163.
[3] Field, *op. cit.*, vol. i, p. 42.
[4] E.g., Jewel, *op, cit.*, vol. 1, p. 401 f.; Overall, *op. cit.*, p. 203.
[5] Field, *op. cit.*, vol. i, p. 330 f.

'the Minister, in public audience of the People,' as follows: 'It is clearly known unto us that N., sometimes baptized in the name of the Father, and of the Son, and of the Holy Ghost, and so reputed and accounted for a Christian, hath fearfully fallen from the society of Christ's body, by committing of cruel and wilful murder (or by committing filthy adultery, &c.), which crime, by the law of God, deserveth death. And because the civil sword is in the hand of God's Magistrate, who, notwithstanding, oft winks at such crimes, We, having place in the Ministry, with grief and dolour of our hearts, are compelled to draw the sword granted by God to His Church; that is, to excommunicate from the society of Christ Jesus, from His body the Church, from participation of sacraments and prayers with the same, the said N. And, therefore, in the name and authority of the Eternal God, and of His Son Jesus Christ, We pronounce the said N. excommunicate and accursed in that his wicked fact. . . .'[1] In some cases an excommunicated person was required to stand in the 'jogges'[2] at the church door, 'barefooted and bareheaded, clothed in base and abject apparel,'[3] for twenty or thirty Sundays, before being deemed ready to exhibit 'the signs of repentance', make his public confession, and be publicly reminded of the gravity of his sin and the mercies of God. Only after the Church was satisfied that the offender had, as far as possible, made amends to all whom he had injured, 'shall the Minister pronounce his sin to be remitted according to his repentance; and shall exhort the Church to embrace him as a brother.'[4] The form of excommunication delineated here was used only for heinous public crimes; there was a less severe procedure for lesser offences, and no offence, however grave in itself, was held to require excommunication unless it were

[1] G. W. Sprott and T. Leishman, *The Book of Common Order* (Edinburgh, 1868), p. 35. Cf. W. McMillan, *The Worship of the Scottish Reformed Church, 1550–1638* (London, James Clarke, n.d.), p. 334 ff.

[2] Iron rings for the neck, from *jugum*. They are still to be seen in a few parish churches, e.g., at Duddingston, Edinburgh. Sprott says (*op. cit.*, lii, n.) that till the middle of the nineteenth century it was still common to hear parents threaten their children that 'the minister will put you in the jogges.'

[3] Sackcloth. Sprott, *op. cit.*, p. 37.

[4] Sprott, *op. cit.*, p. 38.

scandalous.[1] There was, in theory at any rate, no prying into private sins, for the discipline of the visible Church can relate only to visible offences. Durham insists on a superabundance of charity and forbearance in such matters, urging that the Church ought to make every conceivable effort to show patience, in the hope that love may soften the offender's heart before public penance of any kind should become necessary. He recommends such a gentle course even when the offender evinces a contemptuous attitude towards those who are exercising the forbearance.[2] Nor should the Church be too exacting in judging repentance: it is not entitled to demand more than a sober, serious acknowledgement of sin, sufficient to show that, *prima facie*, there is no hypocrisy. There may indeed be hypocrisy; it is enough that it be not blatant. 'By Divines this is called moral seriousness or sincerity, as it is distinguished from that which is gracious.'[3]

Distinguishing between the 'key of doctrine' and the 'key of discipline', Durham says that the former reaches to the thoughts and heart, and judges them, while the latter is intended 'only to restrain, regulate, and judge the outward man'.[4] The distinction was a customary one in the discussions of some of the older divines on the subject of the 'power of the keys',[5] and it was, in its context, an important one, because of its bearing on the nature of excommunication in the Reformed Church. By the 'key of doctrine' was meant the preaching of the Word (including private admonition,[6] counselling and instruction, as well as sermon in church) and the administration of the Sacraments. The 'key of discipline' comprised, strictly speaking, all the rest of the administration of the Church as a visible, institutional society, though in practice the phrase was more com-

[1] Cf. Edward Stillingfleet, *A Discourse concerning the Power of Excommunication in a Christian Church* (London, 1662), published as an appendix to the second edition (1662) of *Irenicum* (1659).
[2] Durham, *op. cit.*, II, v.
[3] Durham, *op. cit.*, II, viii.
[4] *Loc. cit.*
[5] Matt. xvi. 19.
[6] Private admonition is not a censure of the Church.

monly restricted to the infliction of the various censures[1] of the Church and their removal. Durham points out that censure is absolute in its way: by the use of the key of discipline, the Church absolutely does what it intends to do, for example, in shutting out a person from an ordinance, or in admitting him to it. But in the use of the key of discipline the Church condemns or approves only a man's outward practice; that is why its condemnation or approval can be absolute. It does not pretend to open or close the gates of heaven to any individual, on the ground of any conduct, however reprehensible or exemplary it may seem. It is not given to the Body of Christ to do what pertains only to the Head. On the other hand, the key of doctrine absolutely debars from the saving promises, and, on condition of faith and true, inward repentance, absolutely opens the gates of heaven. Saving grace is the condition of absolution in the exercise of the key of doctrine; serious profession, outward decency, is the condition of absolution in the exercise of the key of discipline.[2] The distinction was not, in practice, by any means as clear as Durham's formulation implies;[3] nevertheless the principle he enunciates is fundamental. The Body of Christ is living: it does not consist of a collection of individuals arranged in such a fashion that an individual may be added or taken away absolutely, as a man is admitted to or expelled from membership of a club.

[1] These are, in ascending order of severity: public admonition, rebuke (admonition with reproof), suspension (from office or from communion), deposition (from office), excommunication.

[2] *Loc. cit.*

[3] Cf. the *Form of Excommunication* (Sprott, *op. cit.*, p. 52 ff.), which provides that the minister shall say: 'It cannot be but dolorous to the body that any one member thereof should be cut off and perish: and yet, it ought to be more fearful to the member than to the body, for the member cut off can do nothing but putrefy and perish, and yet the body may retain life and strength. . . . Lawful excommunication . . . is the cutting off from the body of Jesus Christ, from participation of His holy Sacraments, and from public prayers with His Church, by public and solemned [solemn] sentence, all obstinate and impenitent persons, after due admonitions, which sentence, lawfully pronounced on earth, is ratified in heaven, by binding of the same sins that they bind on earth. The danger hereof is greater than man can suddenly espy: for seeing that without the body of Jesus Christ there abideth nothing but death and damnation to mankind, in what estate shall we judge them to stand that justly are cut off from the same?' (p. 57 f.). It may be argued, however, that in pronouncing sentence of excommunication the Church uses *both* keys.

The Scottish divines of this period are all, in principle, opposed to even the slightest interference by the civil power in the ordering of the affairs of the Church. But not only do they resist the notion that the civil rulers and magistrates may actively interfere in any way in ecclesiastical government or discipline; they demand that they actively support the Church as a visible institution, apparently on the ground that neglect of this is a sort of passive interference. Though bound up, as we have seen, with the 'covenant' theology, this view also sprang from their insistence upon the Headship of Christ. Since Christ is the Head, any ruler who meddles in the affairs of the Church is meddling with the Body of which Christ is the Head, and is therefore, according to the measure of the meddling, a rebel against Christ. But it is no less intolerable that rulers and magistrates should, under pretence of aloofness from 'spiritual' matters, injure the Body of Christ by neglecting to give it the external support that it is their duty to give it as the visible Body. It is not the duty of a Christian magistrate to preach or even to lend his aid to the ministry in the exercise of the 'key of doctrine'. In this no more is required of him than is required of the humblest private citizen. But it is his most solemn duty to support the ministry in its exercise of the 'key of discipline', by every lawful means in his power. His duty in this is of the same kind as the duty of a father as head of his household. The father of a family is not only bound to abstain from putting difficulties in the way of his children's attendance upon sermon and the other regular ordinances of the Church; he is required to see that they attend, for this is his responsibility as a father. He is not responsible for their inward state of heart, but only for their outward performance. His responsibility for this is not towards them, but towards the whole Church, for their neglect of the outward performance would be an injury to others: it would be directly injurious to the local congregation, and indirectly injurious to the whole Church. The duty of rulers and magistrates is that of the head of a household: it differs only in the extent of their jurisdiction.

Durham holds that the civil ruler ought to require his subjects to 'keep the Ordinances', for this, he affirms, 'is but a constraining of them to the means whereby Religion worketh, and a making them, as it were, to give God a hearing, leaving their yielding and consenting to Him, when they have heard Him, to their own wills, which cannot be forced; yet it is reason that, when God cometh by His Ordinances to treat with a people, that a magistrate should so far respect His glory and their good as to interpose his authority to make them hear.'[1] Durham goes much further than some when he opines that magistrates may and ought to remind ministers of their ministerial duties, and to make known their negligence.[2] Since it is 'no just liberty to have liberty to hurt others,' the magistrate ought also to use his power to prevent the dissemination of heretical or impious literature,[3] and he 'may and ought to restrain and censure all blasphemous and irreverent expressions and speeches against the Majesty of God and His Ordinances ... and to make such persons incapable of public places of trust, and remove them from such.'[4] Not all would have agreed with Durham's exposition; but the acceptance of the principle was general. Another writer[5] considers the magistrate to be the keeper and defender of the Church in the sense that, while he does not judge or interpret Scripture, he is to use his magisterial rod in guarding and defending the Body of Christ. He acts neither for nor against the ministry; but he may and ought to act *with* it.[6] What, precisely, it meant for the State to act *with* the Church was unclear, and this fact was at the root of almost all the ecclesiastical controversies in Scotland after the Settlement of 1690.

The ecclesiological principle underlying the polemic of the

[1] Durham, *op. cit.*, III, xiv, p. 231.

[2] It is difficult to see on what ground Durham maintains this. It would appear to be an arrogation by the magistrate of the function of the Presbytery. Cf. *op. cit.*, p. 232.

[3] *Op. cit.*, p. 232.

[4] *Op. cit.*, p. 233.

[5] George Gillespie (1613–48). He was, at the age of thirty, one of the Scottish Commissioners to the Westminster Assembly.

[6] George Gillespie, *Aaron's Rod Blossoming* (1646), p. 116.

seventeenth-century divines is independent of the special historical circumstances they faced, and in which they formulated the principle. It is hardly to be expected that the distinction should always have been clear to them. The ideal of all the Reformers had, of course, been universal Reformation. While this did not seem to be immediately realizable, experience soon proved that it was reasonable to hope that the vision might be fulfilled piece by piece. In Germany the maxim *cujus regio, ejus religio* provided a solution to certain practical problems: the principality should follow the prince. Though Calvin's conception of the Church-and-State relation was, as is well known, more 'Hildebrandian' than the Lutheran one, the exigencies he faced were similar: the Reformation must proceed city by city, and, God willing, nation by nation. The rise of the nation as a political unit naturally pointed to it as the unit with which God would deal. When God, through His Church, dealt with a nation, it seemed plain that there was a very close tie between nation and Church. God singularly blessed the nation; it was plainly the duty of the nation *as such* to be thankful for it. It was taken for granted that even the least spiritual man ought to perceive much that demanded common gratitude according to the natural law. In a land in which the Word is purely preached and Christian people are daily bringing forth the fruits of the Holy Spirit, there are, besides the priceless blessings discernible only to faith, innumerable advantages that must delight the heart of even the most worldly prince whose good fortune it is to have such favours showered upon his land, such as widespread honesty and industry, providence and thrift. The least to be expected of the ruler and magistrates of such a land is that they should lend whatever authority and power they possess to the support of the Church through which the land has been so bountifully blessed.

To the seventeenth-century Scottish divines it appeared to be a fundamental presupposition that God dealt with Scotland as a nation. It was not, perhaps, theologically axiomatic that He should do so, though there was indeed a unique example of such a covenant in Scripture; but it was, in the existential situation, an inevitable presupposition that God dealt with the nation. That He should deal with Scotland rather than with, say, only Edinburgh and Aberdeen, was both a blessing and a responsibility. The Settlement that followed the turmoil of a century was based on the doctrine that Church and nation were co-extensive.[1] But the Church-and-State relation had never been formulated with sufficient precision, and great difficulties soon presented themselves.[2]

The divines whom we have so far considered were among those who opposed Episcopacy. There was, however, another side to the Reformed tradition in seventeenth-century Scotland, represented by an important and interesting school of divines, commonly called 'the Aberdeen Doctors', who favoured Episcopacy. These owed their inspiration chiefly to Patrick Forbes of Corse, Bishop of Aberdeen.[3]

The Aberdeen doctors were Calvinist in their theology. But their Calvinism was moderate, infralapsarian, and in an age when party feeling ran high Rutherford and other supra-

[1] By the Union with Scotland Act, 1707 (6 Anne, c. 11), art. xxv, ss. 4, 8, every British Sovereign, on accession to the throne, subscribes to an oath for the security of the Church of Scotland; the oath for the security of the Church of England is taken separately, at the coronation. Both oaths are to be distinguished from the declaration of Protestant faith and intention that the Sovereign also makes.

[2] For example, as a defence against ecclesiastical intrigue, the Church sought the embodiment of a doctrinal formula (to be subscribed by ministers) in an Act of Parliament, which was duly passed in 1693. But then the Church could not alter the formula without Parliament. This was just the kind of situation that the Reformed Church does not approve in principle, yet it insists in principle on the duty of the civil magistrate to support it. It is not surprising that the controversies that later rent the Scottish Church were almost all on questions concerning the extent, if any, to which the freedom of the Church might be limited without injuring the principle of independence. The Church-State question, though involving ecclesiological principles, is notoriously inclined to obscure these. In Presbyterian Scotland, some, remaining loyal to the Establishment, believed that the principle of support by the civil power was so important that the Church ought not to forego such support even when there were some minor infringements of the principle of independence. Others, notably those who led the Disruption in 1843, were willing to sacrifice the support that Establishment provided, rather than countenance the slightest infringement of the other principle. But these were not ecclesiological differences; they were, rather, differences of judgment upon the Church's duty in practical situations.

[3] 1564–1635; consecrated bishop in 1618. His principal work was a commentary on the Apocalypse (1613). On his influence on the Aberdeen Doctors and indirectly on later theological thought, see G. D. Henderson, *Religious Life in Seventeenth-century Scotland* (Cambridge U. P. 1937), c. ii.

lapsarians suspected them of an Arminianism which they themselves disowned.[1] By far their greatest concern was the unity of the Church that had been, they liked to emphasize, reformed, under God's gracious Providence, from Roman corruptions. Learned in the Fathers, they saw in these abundant testimony to the fundamental principles of the Reformation, which they stressed. It should be remembered that the north-east of Scotland had been less responsive to the Reformation than had been the more accessible parts of the country, and there were remote regions that it had not even touched. The Doctors were more concerned to refute Rome than to develop a special ecclesiology of their own. Their chief interest for our study lies in the fact that they provide abundant testimony to the breadth of the Reformed tradition. Their conception of Episcopacy was not that of Laud: they looked upon apostolic succession, for instance, as a succession of faith or doctrine rather than as being guaranteed by sacramental rite. They seem to have had no doubt about the validity of Presbyterian orders,[2] yet they regarded bishops as of the *melius esse*[3] of the Church, seeing in them not only a bond of unity with the Universal Church but a convenient instrument for the spread of the Reformed faith and the good government of the Church. They did not sign the National Covenant. Nevertheless, in their doctrine of the Church they were fundamentally indistinguishable from those who did.

[1] *Supra*, p. 91, n. 1. John Forbes (1593–1648), the second son of Patrick Forbes, was one of the Aberdeen Doctors. He is not to be confused with Patrick's brother, John, who took the Presbyterian side. It should also be noted that William Forbes (1585–1634), Bishop of Edinburgh, was not one of the Doctors: his views were, rather, those of Laud.

[2] Patrick Forbes' son John received Presbyterian ordination abroad from his uncle John and other presbyters, while his father was Bishop of Aberdeen. (Cf. G. W. Sprott, *Scottish Liturgies of the Reign of James VI* (Edinburgh, Blackwood, 1901), p. xi, n.). It is likewise noteworthy that Laud himself made Vossius a prebendary of Canterbury Cathedral and installed him there in 1629. Moreover, the Aberdeen Doctors generally would have been in sympathy with the view expressed by John Menzeis in *Roma Mendax* (1675), p. 380, that Presbyterian orders are valid *in spite of* their having been derived from Rome. The presuppositions of such a view of succession will be considered later (*infra*, pp. 210 ff. 220 ff).

[3] Cf. John Forbes (Patrick's son), *Irenicum Amatoribus Veritatis et Pacis in Ecclesia Scoticana* (Aberdeen, 1629), II, xi, 13. For 'The Form and Maner of Consecrating ane Archbishope, or Bishope', used in the Scottish Church at this time, see Sprott, *op. cit.*, p. 124 ff.

PART TWO

CHAPTER VI

"ΕΚΚΛΗΣΙΑ"

As we proceed to a more theological analysis of the subject before us, there is at the outset one affirmation to be made with confidence. Every formulation of a doctrine of the nature of the Church depends upon and implies a christological foundation.[1] This is not to say that to know a man's christology is to know his ecclesiology equally well. A Nestorian's doctrine of the Church may take one of several forms, and it is possible to detect Docetic or Monophysite tendencies in what an individual 'Protestant' says about the Church as well as in what is said about it by an individual 'Catholic'. But to know a man's christology is nevertheless to know a great deal, at least negatively, about his ecclesiology. To this point, the importance of which cannot easily be exaggerated, we must return. The reason for beginning with it is to call attention to the fact that it is useless to look for a doctrine of the nature of the Church before there is a doctrine of the Person of Christ. We are bound to inquire carefully into the meaning of the word ἐκκλησία. We ought not, however, to expect too much of the endeavour. No more is to be expected of it than the provision of some signposts.

A very useful study of the word ἐκκλησία has been made by Karl Ludwig Schmidt in his now well-known article in Kittel's Theological Dictionary of the New Testament.[2] Schmidt follows, however, a view that Deissmann expresses in a misleading fashion when he asserts an analogy between the primitive Chris-

[1] This is well recognized by both Yves Congar and T. W. Manson. The latter roundly says that 'the doctrine of the Church is a branch of Christology' (T. W. Manson, *The Church's Ministry* (London, 1948), p. 20).

[2] *Theologisches Worterbuch zum neuen Testament*, edited by Gerhard Kittel and, after his death in 1948, Gerhard Friedrich. Schmidt's article on ἐκκλησία, first published at Stuttgart, 1938, is translated by J. R. Coates under the title, *The Church* (London, A. and C. Black, 1950). Cf. also Schmidt's 'Die Kirche des Urchristentums' in *Festgabe fur A. Deissmann*, 1927.

tian use of ἐκκλησία and the use of the word *Versammlung* for 'congregation' by the 'Pietistic' folk in the valley of the Dill, to the south of Giessen.[1] As George Johnston points out in an important study of the New Testament doctrine, the notion that 'as ἐκκλησία the Church is a community called *out of the world* by God' is one that 'may legitimately be deduced from passages in the New Testament, according as the "world" is defined, but it is not present in the word itself'.[2]

The word ἐκκλησία, from ἐκκαλέω ('to call out'), is used by secular writers such as Thucydides to denote an assembly of citizens summoned by a herald to gather for specific business at an appointed place. There is nothing particularly significant about the fact that they are so summoned; no more than there is in the fact that nowadays they would probably be circularized. As Johnston remarks, it is the 'purposiveness' of the assembled community that is emphasized. The word is used in this ordinary sense even in a chapter of the New Testament.[3] It is doubtful whether the word ever had a religious sense in ordinary Greek usage. On the other hand, the word occurs frequently in the Septuagint, where it is always a translation of the Hebrew *qāhāl* or, in a few cases, of a word closely associated with this and having the same root. The word *qāhāl* means 'assembly'; but it is much used, especially in post-exilic literature, in the sense of 'the assembly of the Congregation of Israel'.[4] The word *'edhah* has also a general meaning ('company' or 'band') and in this sense it is applicable to animals[5] and angels[6] as well as men. When applied to Israel, *'edhah* denotes the people, considered as an organic whole, not as assembled.[7] Sometimes, in Exodus,

[1] Adolf Deissmann, *Light from the Ancient East* (trans. by L. R. M. Strachan, London, Hodder and Stoughton, 1927), p. 112.

[2] George Johnston, *The Doctrine of the Church in the New Testament* (Cambridge U. P., 1943), p. 35. Cf. Schmidt, *The Church* (*ed. cit.*), p. 24.

[3] Acts xix. 32, 39 f.

[4] But cf. J. Y. Campbell, 'The Origin and Meaning of the Christian Use of the Word *EKKLESIA*' in the *Journal of Theological Studies*, XLIX (1948), p. 133 ff.

[5] Ps. lxviii. 30.

[6] Ps. lxxxii. 1.

[7] When assembly is to be indicated, *'edhah* becomes *qāhāl*: the Hiphil is used; so Exod. xxxv. 1. But *'edhah* can mean 'court of justice' (cf. Num. xxxv. 24). It has also been translated *sanhedrin* (Num. xxv. 7) in *Targum Jonathan* and *Jer. Sanhedrin* X, 2, 28d: see H. A. Wolfson, *Philo* (Harvard U. P., 1947) vol. ii, p. 351, n. 203.

Numbers and Leviticus, the word *συναγωγή* is used to translate both *'edhah* and *qāhāl*; elsewhere *qāhāl* is translated *ἐκκλησία*.

The evidence from Philo is interesting. Professor Wolfson of Harvard, a leading authority on Philo, points out that Philo's undertaking is to treat that 'assembly (*ἐκκλησία*) of the Lord' or 'congregation (*συναγωγή*) of the Lord' as a polity (*πολιτεία*), as a political state governed by a constitution embodied in the laws of Moses, and to show how the constitution of that state defines with clearness and precision as well as with fairness the status of the various classes of inhabitants.[1] Without any direct reference to other constitutions, he describes the status of the various classes of inhabitants under the Mosaic constitution in such a way as to be indirectly a criticism of their status under other constitutions. Under the man-made constitutions discussed by Aristotle, he would seem to argue, a citizen must have the ability not only to be ruled but also to rule. . . . No one born under the Law can be excluded from citizenship; no alien who is willing to accept the Law can be refused citizenship.'[2] Philo calls this second class of citizens sometimes by the Septuagintal name, proselytes (*προσήλυτοι*),[3] sometimes by the term epelytes (*ἐπηλύται*),[4] that is, 'the incomers'. They are to be received and treated as if they were born Jews.[5] According to Philo, this indicates that the basis of the polity is not race but the common heritage of the Law, a spiritual rather than a genetic kinship.[6]

[1] Neither *ἐκκλησία* nor *συναγωγή* is applied by Philo to the Jewish people of his own day. By the time of Philo, the Septuagintal term *συναγωγή* had come to mean a place of prayer and study. Professor Wolfson has drawn my attention to the fact that when Philo did happen to allude to its Septuagintal use as synonymous with *ἐκκλησία*, he substituted for it the term *σύλλογος* (Somn. ii, 184). But both *ἐκκλησία* and *συναγωγή* are transformed in his mind into what the Greek thinkers called *πολιτεία*. When in *Legatio ad Gaium*, 194, he describes the whole Jewish people as *ἡ καθολικωτέρα πολιτεία* which bears the name of Israel (cf. Wolfson, *Philo*, ii, p. 397, n. 8), he had in mind the Pentateuchal expression which is more often translated in the Septuagint by *πᾶσα συναγωγὴ υἱῶν 'Ισραήλ* than by *πᾶσα ἐκκλησία υἱῶν 'Ισραήλ*.

[2] H. A. Wolfson, *op. cit.*, vol. ii, p. 354.

[3] E.g., *Spec.*, I, ix, 51.

[4] E.g., *Virt.*, xx, 102.

[5] *Virt.*, xx, 103; cf. Lev. xix. 34; Deut. x. 19.

[6] Cf. Aristotle's observation (*Eth. Nicom.* VIII, 1156b) that 'perfect friendship is the friendship of those who are good, and alike in virtue', though there are other kinds of friendship, such as that which is based on blood ties.

By way of illustration, Wolfson quotes rabbinic authority for excluding an apostate Jew from eating of the paschal lamb which a proselyte is allowed to eat.[1]

Johnston does not think that the evidence from Philo, or even the fact that Josephus sometimes appears to show a marked preference for ἐκκλησία, deliberately substituting it, on nine occasions, for an original συναγωγή, is sufficient to warrant Goodenough's conclusion 'that early Christianity could take ἐκκλησία for its community directly from Greek Judaism'.[2] While the preference for ἐκκλησία, in the Septuagint, in Philo, in Josephus, and elsewhere, is certainly interesting and noteworthy, it does not prove that this term had come to possess, by New Testament times, any highly stylized connotation beyond various meanings such as have been already indicated. There is no evidence for its having been used in a specific sense that would at all justify, for instance, a translation such as 'Church of Israel' or 'Jewish Church'. By contrast, the word συναγωγή had acquired a distinctive character, 'a place of meeting.' It could still denote a local community of Jews; but, like προσευχή it was regularly used for the place in which they met rather than for the collection of persons. Johnston notes that Paul not only never uses συναγωγή but is reported in Acts as using ἐκκλησία even where he would appear to be echoing an Old Testament phrase in which the Septuagint has συναγωγή.[3]

In Aramaic, one word, *k'nishta*, does service for both *'edhah*= συναγωγή and *qāhāl*=ἐκκλησιά. It has been suggested,[4] that Jesus actually used the word *k'nishta*,[5] thereby indicating the true Israel of His followers. According to this view, the disciples would use *k'nishta* of their community, expressing thereby both the idea of divine calling (ἐκκλησία) and also that of assembly

[1] *Op. cit*, p. 357, n. 239.
[2] Johnston, *op. cit.*, p. 39.
[3] *Op. cit.*, p. 40 f. Cf. Acts xx. 28 and Psalm lxxiv. 2.
[4] E.g., by Schmidt, *op. cit.*, p. 48 ff.; cf. F. Kattenbusch in *Festgabe fur Harnack*, p. 166 f. For a contrary view, cf. W. G. Kummel, *Kirchenbegriff und Geschichtsbewusstsein in der Urgemeinde und bei Jesus*, (Uppsala and Zurich, 1943), p. 23; A. V. Strom, *Vetekornet* (Stockholm, 1944), p. 434.
[5] Matt. xvi. 18.

for worship (συναγωγή). But for the spread of the Gospel to the Gentile world, the Christian community might then have become generally known as the *k'nishta.* At any rate, the Gospel soon had to be proclaimed in Greek, and the word used to designate the Christian community was ἐκκλησία. This was singularly apposite, whether or not the choice was determined by any conscious piece of reasoning. It would express the idea of the congregation of God, and all that was conveyed by the term *k'nishta.* It had a special advantage: it was suitable both for converts of Jewish and for converts of Gentile background. For while it was a word that conveyed to a Gentile ear no specifically Jewish sound, it could recall to a Jewish Christian that sense of universality that we have seen Philo give it when using it of the people bound by the Law, whether born Jews or proselytes. So the Christian of Jewish background could discover a very deep and rich meaning in the word as applied to the Christian community.

The appositeness of ἐκκλησία lay in what it could comprehend rather than in what it defined. From the point of view of Loisy, its very comprehensiveness opened the way to Christian arrogance, for in his account, the Christians originally claimed to be the realization of the long-promised Kingdom of God, and it was when the majority of the Jews declined to see in Jesus the awaited Messiah that the Christians, exasperated by such obstinacy, asserted that they were 'the True Church' and 'denied the claim of the Jews to the very attribute it (Christianity) had borrowed from them'.[1] While Loisy's interpretation cannot well be supported by the linguistic evidence, it does draw attention to a peculiarity in the term, its susceptibility to development. On the assumption that Jesus was not what Christians account Him to be, the choice of the term is to be regretted for the very reason that commends the choice of the term when it is assumed that the claim concerning Jesus is true. On the latter assumption, the process of Christian realization of the

[1] Alfred Loisy, *The Birth of the Christian Religion* (Eng. trans. of *La naissance du Christianisme*, 1933) (London, 1948), p. 285 f.

meaning of ἐκκλησία would be inevitably gradual. Jalland rightly reminds us that 'the cleavage between Judaism and Christianity was essentially gradual, almost imperceptible'.[1] It is, indeed, difficult to suppose that any member of the original *ecclesia* at Jerusalem, the Twelve not excepted, could have understood the problem underlying the question that springs so readily to modern lips, 'Did Jesus found a Church or did He find one?' For the members of that *ecclesia* 'were continually in the Temple praising God';[2] 'day after day they continued to frequent the Temple in a body.'[3] Adhering to the Torah, observing the fasts, reading the prophets, they were externally indistinguishable from other Jews; no doubt one could hardly have guessed, in a casual encounter with a group of them, that they were in any way different, unless, of course, one could have gone with them to watch them break bread and hear them lovingly rehearse the events of their Master's life. Had not these Nazarenes been arrested and persecuted by the Jewish leaders, they might have continued, presumably, in this way, endeavouring to win their compatriots to their view and so to bring all Israel to what they believed to be the truth about Jesus, namely, that the Messiah had come and had suffered and died to effect the atonement.

The Qumran literature reveals some interesting aspects of the terminological background. The word *qāhāl* appears several times, signifying, for instance, now a judicial assembly,[4] now an army.[5] We find the phrase 'the *qāhāl* of God' used to designate the convocation of God's people;[6] it is also a sign on a banner.[7] But in this literature it would seem to be much less important than the words *'edhah*, *yachad*, *'etsah*, and *sod*. *'Edhah* is characteristic of 1 QM, common in 1 QSa, rare in 1 QS. It is often used of an army, whether of angels or men,[8] and it is also used of a congregation of people, local or national.[9] The Zadokite

[1] T. G. Jalland, *The Origin and Evolution of the Christian Church* (London, Hutchinson's University Library, n.d.), p. 73; cf. p. 69.
[2] Luke xxiv. 53.
[3] Acts ii. 46.
[4] 1 QSa 1.25.
[5] 1QM 1.10.
[6] 1 QSa.
[7] 1 QM 4.10.
[8] E.g., 1 QM 1.10.
[9] E.g., 1 QSa 1.1.

Covenanters themselves were an *'edhah.*[1] Israel is the *'edhah* over which the anointed High Priest and King are to rule.[2] *Yachad*, though it has several shades of meaning, is used in the *Manual of Discipline* in a technical sense to denote the Qumran brotherhood, and as such it seems to be used not in any contradistinction to Israel, but rather as embodying the 'True Israel': it is, indeed, the '*yachad* of truth'.[3] That is to say, it is a sort of union of those Jews who, believing that the Law is the truth of God, pledged themselves, probably annually, to the covenant of Sinai.[4] These Covenanters pledged themselves to observe the Mosaic Law and to live together in fraternal love.[5] The Zadokites were an esoteric brotherhood founded by a priest, the 'Teacher of Righteousness', and led by priests. They stressed ritual purity through frequent ablutions and were hierarchically arranged: priests, levites and 'the Israel'; there were also proselytes. Whatever their relation to other parties in Judaism such as the Pharisees, Sadducees and Essenes, they were an ascetic and priestly community, and as such they would seem to be quite unlike the disciples of Jesus. Were the disciples in any way organized by Jesus as a *yachad* within Israel? There is little evidence for His having organized anything in the least resembling the Zadokite community. His public ministry was, after all, extremely brief—probably between two and three years, perhaps even less. He may have thought of his *k'nishta* as a *yachad*, in a general way; but that He organized it with formal rules and the like is extremely unlikely. If He had done so, His disciples would probably have dispersed less easily than they did on Good Friday. The reason that they dispersed would seem to be, rather, that there was nothing to hold them together, since they were without a constitution or formal bond of any kind. It was only after Easter that the question of organization could arise for the Nazarenes.

[1] 4 Q p Ps. 37.24. [2] E.g., 1 QSa 2.12, 22. [3] 1 QS 1.24.

[4] Barthélemy-Milik, *Discoveries in the Judaean Desert I: Qumran Cave I* (1955), p. 154.

[5] Professor George Johnston of Toronto has suggested to me that the *κοινωνία* of Acts ii. 42 and elsewhere in the New Testament may perhaps represent this technical usage of *yachad*. There is a Greek version of 1 Chron. xii. 17 in which *yachad* is rendered *κοινωνία*.

These Nazarenes were in an unique position. They could by no means easily assert a claim to be the true Israel, the *ecclesia* of God. They were Jews both by ritual circumcision and by due observance of religious duties. They belonged to Israel, and they could cease to belong to it only by contracting out of it. But how could they contract out of it, maintaining, as they did, that their Lord was the fulfilment of the prophecies and 'a greater than Moses'? They kept the covenant of their fathers, for to have broken the covenant would have seemed as incompatible with their position as would have been the withdrawal of their claim that their Master was the Messiah. They asserted, rather, that into the elect race had been born He who was foretold in prophecy, and that since this Messiah was above Moses and the prophets, a true Israelite would hearken unto Him. Their claim was, then, that while Israel had indeed been called to be the *ecclesia* of God, it now rejected the call to the extent that it rejected Jesus.[1]

So they were naturally treated as a sect;[2] but they did not regard themselves as a sect. They not only regarded themselves as belonging to the true *ecclesia*; they claimed that only they belonged to it, for now they only were the true *ecclesia*.[3] Their claim was no more and no less arrogant than the claim that their Master was the Messiah; that is to say, their ecclesiology already matched their christology. The first Christians could have regarded themselves as a sect within Israel only if they had regarded their Master as but a prophet within Israel. Because they regarded Him as above the prophets, and indeed above Israel itself, they could not possibly regard themselves as a sect. True, they had not yet a fully developed ecclesiology. Their thoughts on this subject had yet to be geared to the new situation of faith in which they found themselves.[4] No doubt they did

[1] Cf. Romans ix. 7: 'They are not all Israel, which are of Israel.'

[2] Acts xxiv. 5; xxviii. 22.

[3] The contention of J. Y. Campbell that the Christians first used ἐκκλησία in a neutral sense (a gathering) and then later invested it with the meaning of 'Universal Church' is singularly difficult to uphold. Cf. his article in the *Journal of Theological Studies*, XLIX (1948), p. 133.

[4] Cf. O. Michel, *Das Zeugnis des Neuen Testaments von der Gemeinde* (Göttingen, 1941) p. 1

not put into the word ἐκκλησία all that was going to be put into it. But neither did they put into the word κύριος, as applied to Jesus, all that was to be put into it at, say, Chalcedon. Still, the uniqueness of what they claimed for their Lord was already reflected in the uniqueness of what they claimed for the community that they were. The uniqueness of the community lay in the fact that it was both continuous with the old Israel and discontinuous with it. The continuity and the discontinuity were alike derived from their Lord; for the former depended on His being the fulfilment of Hebrew prophecy, while the latter depended on His being the Saviour of mankind. Only He had risen from the dead, and whatever this meant to the first Christians after Easter Day would determine the content of their ecclesiology. Pentecost confirmed their ecclesiological beliefs as it confirmed their christological ones.

The Old Testament notion of the faithful Remnant could not fail to suggest itself immediately to these Christians in the situation in which they found themselves. It is hardly possible that St Paul's idea on this subject could have been original with him.[1] On the other hand, Jesus is not recorded as having ever explicitly referred to the Remnant, though the notion is suggested by His reference to His 'little flock'. To what extent, if any, this implied the definite notion that St Paul presents is conjectural. Some scholars have looked on Jesus as embodying in Himself the Remnant of Israel; that is to say, the Remnant had been reduced to the point at which, but for Him, it would have disappeared.[2] It has been said that after the disciples forsook Jesus, 'at the end of the first Good Friday there remained perhaps one completely loyal Christian in the world, and he apparently dead.'[3] But according to Visser 't Hooft, 'While Jesus climbs towards Golgotha, He *alone* is the people of God. He bears the whole weight of God's work for this world. At that moment there

[1] Romans xi. 1–5; ix. 27; cf. 1 Kings xix. 18.

[2] Cf. A. G. Hebert, *The Throne of David* (London, 1941), p. 238; A. M. Ramsey, *The Gospel and the Catholic Church* (London, 1936), p. 21; D. M. Baillie, *God was in Christ* (London, 1948), p. 207.

[3] A. C. Bouquet, *Comparative Religion* (London, Penguin Books, 4th ed., 1953), p. 242. In the present writer's opinion, 'apparently' is misleading here.

was not even a Remnant, but only a Man who obeyed even unto death on the Cross.'[1] There is no evidence that the disciples received any explicit doctrine from their Master concerning their status as a 'little flock'. As Dahl puts it, 'The group of disciples is not for Jesus the object of a special theological reflection.'[2] They had to discover their own ecclesiology, and they discovered it *pari passu* with their growing understanding of the Person and mission of their Lord.

Inseparable from this growing understanding in the minds of the believers was a conviction that they were living in extraordinary times. Pentecost attested their conviction that God's reign had begun. What is preached is that men must repent and believe in the Risen Christ, for the time is fulfilled. It was 'urgent' preaching. To ask how the preachers may have formulated their conception of the *ecclesia*, its function and destiny, is to underestimate the urgency of their message and perhaps even to misunderstand the character of the urgency. But that there was a close connexion between the notion of the *ecclesia* and the notion of the Kingdom (βασιλεία) is plain. On the other hand, what precisely was the connexion is by no means so easily determined. According to Cullmann, the first Christians believed and taught that there was a new dimension of time: the Lord had ended history and introduced a new order of time. The Christians were living, not in history, but under the reign of Christ which is beyond history. The new dimension of time was *die Endzeit*, 'end-time' or '*eschaton*-time'. Pentecost was the *endzeitliche* birthday of the Church, fulfilling the *ecclesia* in the *eschaton*.[3] This is, however, a speculative view. There is no evidence for such a belief in a new order of time. That the Kingdom of God, a well established conception among the Jews of the

[1] W. A. Visser 't Hooft, *The Wretchedness and Greatness of the Church* (London, 1944), p. 15.

[2] N. A. Dahl, *Das Volk Gottes. Eine Untersuchung zum Kirchenbewusstsein des Urchristentums* (Oslo, 1941), p. 161 f. On the significance of the names (apostles, disciples, etc.) used of the adherents of Jesus, cf. F. J. A. Hort, *The Christian Ecclesia* (1897), pp. 22–9.

[3] Oscar Cullmann, *Königsherrschaft Christi und Kirche im Neuen Testament* (Zurich, 1946), p. 20. (Eng. tr. in *The Early Church*, S.C.M., 1956.)

day,[1] denoting in its widest application the reign of God, had *begun* or *was now 'there'*, is plainly the belief that is proclaimed.[2] The proclamation (κήρυγμα) is that the Kingdom is at hand (ἤγγικεν) and every man must make a decision about it, an 'either-or' decision, such as Moses had called upon the people to make when he had 'stood in the gate of the camp, and said, Who is on the Lord's side?'[3] Every man must make a decision for or against the reign of Christ. Far from being in contrast with the doctrine of the Church that is developing as a result of the Easter experience and is corroborated by that of Pentecost, the proclamation of the Kingdom is an essential basis for the development of the doctrine of the Church.

The *ecclesia* before the Kingdom had been *expectant*; whatever it is now, it is not that. In discussions of the attitude of the first-century Christians towards the *parousia*, the impression is often given that they were waiting for Christ to come to reign, and that they were therefore puzzled and disappointed when He did not come as they expected. There is, of course, some truth in this; but it is a very misleading notion. Their faith was that their Lord was reigning *now*. This faith did not depend on His return at any particular time, otherwise, they must have been not merely disappointed, but increasingly disillusioned. The *parousia* was a hope rather than a faith; the *basileia* was a faith rather than a hope. To say that the reign had begun is not, however, to say that it had been consummated. The subjects of the Kingdom are in time; while they may hope that some may not taste death, they are no longer afraid of death. Nothing distinguished the Christians from the old Israel more vividly than the fact that, as Ramsey has well said, they had the faith that enabled them to look upon death as no longer a problem.[4] Christ had overcome death, and by His conquest of it He was reigning.

[1] Doctrine about it was derived from Dan. ii. 44; vi. 26; vii. 13, 14, 27. Cf. Ps. ciii. 19; cxlv. 11–13; Isaiah xxxvii. 16; Dan. iv. 34; Wisd. of Solomon, x. 10; Tobit, xiii. 1.

[2] Cf. Johannes Weiss, *Die Predigt Jesu vom Reiche Gottes* (2nd ed., 1900), p. 69: 'Die Zeit des Wartens ist vorbei, die Wendung ist da.'

[3] Exod. xxxii. 26.

[4] A. M. Ramsey, *The Gospel and the Catholic Church* (London, 1936), p. 18.

Ontologically, every man was a subject of the Kingdom; but one might be a willing subject or an unwilling one. The willing subjects, those who acknowledged the Kingship of Christ and welcomed His reign, were the *ecclesia*. But the eschatological attitude of the members of this *ecclesia* might change without their losing faith that they were the New Israel. As Dodd says, the first Christians did not look upon the various events, resurrection, exaltation, and second coming, as an eschatological series, but rather as one event, so that 'it was not an *early* advent that they proclaimed, but an *immediate* advent.'[1] No doubt they had a very definite picture of this in their minds for a few years after Pentecost; gradually thereafter they had to revise their eschatology. Dodd thinks the necessity for this was a 'principal cause for the development of early Christian thought'.[2] That revision was possible demonstrates that the apocalyptic notions of the *basileia*, *parousia*, and the like, and even the messianic notion itself, could be subordinated and had to be subordinated to the growing doctrine of the Church. More and more they were seen to be only guideposts to the Church's realization of itself and of its true nature. This did not imply a change of belief about the nature of the Church, however, but a development of the implications of the doctrine that had been born of the Easter experience. The Christians' growing discovery of themselves as participating in the life of the Risen Christ did not merely mitigate a disappointment about the *parousia*, so as to enable them to accept with serenity what happened; it unfolded to them what had at first been partially obscured, or imperfectly grasped: to be in the *ecclesia* was to be in the life of the Risen Christ, to enjoy that peculiar quality of life (ζωή) of which He is the source. History goes on; one's life-span (βίος) proceeds and is to be terminated either by death or, it may be, by the completion of the *eschaton*. But in the *ecclesia*, come what may, is known and experienced the life (ζωή) that is eternal and so qualitatively superior to all temporal blessings and more im-

[1] C. H. Dodd, *The Apostolic Preaching and Its Developments* (London, 1936), p. 33.
[2] *Op. cit.*, p. 34 f.

portant than all temporal events. Thus does the slowly developing sense of what it means to belong to the *ecclesia* take precedence over all messianic expectation and eschatological modes of thought, without, of course, ever casting these off.

The mysteries of the Kingdom had been expounded in the parables. In the parable of the Tares, the Kingdom is depicted as a community of good and evil men living in the world and hardly distinguishable from each other; but the evil are to be plucked out, so that in the end the good will shine forth as the sun.[1] In the parables of the Draw-net, the Mustard Seed and the Leaven, similar ideas are presented.[2] These ideas appear to be recast as Christ's teaching is presented to the Gentiles. They were, of course, thoroughly Jewish ideas. 'Seek ye first the kingdom of God, and his righteousness,' says Jesus.[3] St Paul, on the other hand, says that the Kingdom is 'righteousness and peace, and joy in the Holy Ghost'.[4] The Church is not the reign of Christ; nevertheless, it is the instrument of that reign, and this gives the Church the unique status that it possesses.

The notion that the Christian Church was explicitly founded by Christ before His death rests, of course, on the famous passage in Matthew[5] that is the *locus classicus* for the supremacy of St Peter and has been made to support, however precariously, the ecclesiology delineated in the decrees of the fourth session of the Vatican Council.[6] The passage is under suspicion. Much is to be said both for and against its authenticity.[7] This question is an extremely complicated one, and since it is of limited relevance to a study of the nature of the Church in the Reformed tradition, it is unnecessary to consider it in detail. It is to be noted, however, that here we have one of the only two occurrences of the

[1] Matt. xiii. 24–30; 36–43.
[2] Matt. xiii. 31–3; 47–50.
[3] Matt. vi. 33.
[4] Rom. xiv. 17. Cf. W. Sanday, 'St Paul's Equivalent for the "Kingdom of Heaven" ' in the *Journal of Theological Studies* (1900) I, p. 481.
[5] Matt. xvi. 18.
[6] *Acta et decreta sacrosancti œcumenici Concilii Vaticani* (Rome, 1872), 'Constitutio dogmatica prima de ecclesia Christi.'
[7] Cf. Schmidt, *op. cit.*, pp. 35–50; O. Linton, *Das Problem der Urkirche in der neueren Forschung* (Uppsala, 1932), pp. 157–83.

word ἐκκλησία in the Gospels. The other one is in the passage[1] in which an erring brother who neglects to hear the church is to be treated as a Gentile. This passage is also suspect; but, as Schmidt recognizes,[2] if both passages are accepted as authentic there remains a serious difficulty in view of the indisputable fact that the word ἐκκλησία cannot easily be interpreted as meaning the same thing in both cases. Schmidt speaks of Jesus' concern with the *k'nishta*, and so deprecates Bultmann's assertion that it is of no consequence, so far as the first passage is concerned, whether ἐκκλησία represents *qāhāl* or *'edhah* or *k'nishta*. But wherein lay Jesus' concern for the *k'nishta*? It is one thing to say He loved His 'little flock', another to say that He had a concern for His *k'nishta* in the sense of the ἐκκλησία that He was to build. The use of the future tense[3] indicates that, though the foundation of the Church is being laid, the 'building' of the Church is yet to take place.

This, together with the fact that the exegesis of the other passage is so difficult that some scholars[4] have resorted to the theory that here ἐκκλησία means the local synagogue as ordinarily understood among the Jews, does not mitigate the complexity of the question; nor does it diminish the suspicion of the authenticity of these passages. It is not very easy to suppose that their authenticity would ever have been defended had not the authenticity of one of them seemed so vital for upholding a certain ecclesiological theory. This passage is so a-typical that if it were authentic it could hardly have been overlooked: one would expect to find it looming large in the New Testament writers. But, on the contrary, since no other New Testament writer ever refers to it at all, there is no evidence for its having been in their minds. That the other evangelists should have been ignorant of it is as incredible as that they should have neglected or suppressed it. Moreover, even if one overlooks all such difficulties, the passage still strikes an odd note. For if the events of Easter and Pentecost are to be taken seriously, and in

[1] Matt. xviii. 15–17.
[2] *Op. cit.*, p. 35 f.
[3] οἰκοδομήσω.
[4] E.g., Schmidt, *loc. cit.*

the Reformed tradition they have certainly been taken very seriously indeed, such a prediction about the Church is a little curious. The disciples were to forsake Christ on the Cross and were later to acknowledge their faith in Him and 'know' Him, in 'breaking of bread'.[1] It would appear that either the prediction of the 'building' of the *ecclesia* would have been an important element in the *kerygma*, which it was not, or else it would have seemed redundant or insignificant in face of the reality of the life in the *ecclesia* that was lived in the presence of the Risen Christ and that had as its principle the Spirit whom He had sent.

With certain exceptions,[2] the term ἐκκλησία, as used elsewhere in the New Testament, always means the Christian Church. But as local communities of Christians were formed in various places, a name had to be found by which to designate them. Though there was apparently no special rule or principle adopted in this matter,[3] the plural ἐκκλησίαι is used, notably by St Paul, to designate not only local communities but house-meetings of Christians. St Paul writes to the Corinthians: 'The ἐκκλησίαι of Asia salute you. Aquila and Prisca salute you much in the Lord, with the ἐκκλησία that is in their house.'[4] So the singular, ἐκκλησία, can refer to one of these ἐκκλησίαι, and either in the sense of a community or else in the sense of a gathering or group in a certain place. But there is no sound reason to support any view implying a deliberate choice of term rather than an unreflecting adoption of a word that seemed natural. On the other hand, while it is foolish to concoct subtleties that could hardly have been in the minds of the first-century Christians, it is legitimate to consider why it seemed natural to them to call the local community by the same name as that which was being used to designate the New Israel. It might mean that they were

[1] Luke xxiv. 35.

[2] These are: Acts vii. 38, where it is used to denote the assembly of Israel; Acts xix. 32, 39, 41, where it has the 'neutral' or commonplace meaning as in secular Greek usage; Hebrews xii. 23, where it refers to an assembly of the celestial hosts.

[3] The Jewish Christians in Trans-Jordan seem to have called both their communities and their buildings synagogues. Cf. Epiphanius, *Haer.* xxx, 18, 2; also, cf. James ii. 2 and v. 14. But this is an intricate question and, though interesting, not of fundamental importance for our purpose.

[4] 1 Cor. xvi. 19.

thinking of the ἐκκλησία that 'was in' Aquila's house as a part of the ἐκκλησία that is the New Israel. Or it might mean, rather, that the ἐκκλησία in Aquila's house was the New Israel in microcosm. 'The part is equal to the whole,' argues Sir Edwyn Hoskyns, 'because each part possesses, not a fragment of the Christ, but the whole Christ, and consequently, in accordance with the mathematical definition, the *ekklesia* is of the order of infinity.'[1] A similar view is taken by Headlam,[2] and others. The 'fellowship' (κοινωνία) is to be found in the microcosmic and in the macrocosmic ἐκκλησία, in the 'little church' where the members care for each other's needs and in which the teachers of the Word share in the blessings of life that the hearers enjoy,[3] and in the 'Great Church' within which is to be found one community of Christians taking up a collection on behalf of another without regard to race, distance, or any other such consideration. This does not show in what relation, precisely, the microcosm stood to the macrocosm; but it provides a clue. Not only is it impossible that one 'little church', however renowned, can have authority or precedence over another; each 'little Church' is universalized in and by and through its relation to Christ. As the various local communities grew up physically separated from each other in parts of the world that seemed then distant, they could have no meeting together and could communicate with each other only occasionally by letter or visit. Yet if Christ is with His Church, He must be with His Church at Corinth, at Antioch, at Rome. Physical 'togetherness' is not necessary. What, then, is the principle of the 'togetherness' that one church has with another in the conditions that gradually emerged?

Johnston contends that there is little warrant in St Paul for Ramsey's view that 'the organization of the Church is an utterance of the Gospel,' that the historic episcopate, 'as the guided result of the primitive order,' is indispensable, and that 'the minister at the Eucharist must represent the one universal and

[1] E. H. Hoskyns and F. N. Davey, *The Riddle of the New Testament* (London, 3rd ed., 1947), p. 25.

[2] A. C. Headlam, *op. cit.*, p. 77 ff.

[3] Gal. vi. 6.

historic society'.[1] 'Church unity,' Johnston maintains, 'is inward and spiritual. Each congregation represented the whole Church of God in its own area; its officers had sufficient commission when they had its appointment. The bishops or elders are local ministers.'[2] But surely an important distinction is neglected here Unity does not require uniformity; but this is not to say that it is unrelated to external order, or that it is expressed only, as Johnston affirms, 'in the practical help of one part of the Body for another.'[3] It is true that one might be baptized according to one form in this church and according to another form in that one; nevertheless, Baptism must mean the same in both. There may be, and it appears that there were, various organizations of the ministry; but this is not to say that the ministry was not essentially the same. The variety of organization does not preclude the possibility that the ministry itself is of such a nature that it provides an external bond of unity. The visible ordering of the churches is not a regimentation: all must serve the form of the Church in love. But Christians are incorporated not into the Church at Antioch or the Church at Corinth, but into one Body. The unity that this gives finds expression in the Eucharist,[4] where the form of the life of the Church is seen to be derived from a source beyond the Church itself. As the gift of the ascended Christ to the Church, the ministry, if it be a true ministry, cannot but manifest a unity in the Church.

These are, of course, extremely complex questions which cannot well be discussed till we have had an opportunity to consider the peculiarly important Pauline figure of the Body of Christ. They are mentioned now only to help us to draw the very modest conclusion that is all that we can claim to be able to draw from the present chapter. We find that in the history of the word ἐκκλησία as it was adopted and developed in primitive Christian usage, there is little to justify the precise formulation of any positive ecclesiology. It would be no less difficult to

[1] George Johnston, *op. cit.*, p. 96, referring to A. M. Ramsey, *The Gospel and the Catholic Church*, p. 46 ff., p. 59.
[2] *Loc. cit.* [3] *Loc. cit.* [4] Cf. 1 Cor. x. 16 f.; xii. 12 f.

formulate a christology on the basis of a study of the terms used by the first Christians to designate their Lord. Nevertheless, certain ecclesiological conceptions seem to be excluded. Out of its own life, whose source it believed to be beyond itself, the Church gradually discovered what it took to be its own nature. Only as a result of such discovery could a doctrine of the Church begin to be evolved. The articulation of the doctrine was retarded by the circumstances that forced the Christians of the first centuries to turn their attention to other problems, notably the christological one, and by the time a christology had been articulated other circumstances forced themselves upon the Church in such a way as to obscure ecclesiological questions and further retard serious thought about them. From a later, Reformation, standpoint it became plain that while the Church's awareness of itself as a living Body whose Head is Christ had never been entirely lost, it had been numbed under the weight of an institutionalism that had distorted the form of the Church and enfeebled its life. The imperfectly articulated self-awareness of the Church in its earliest days is therefore of paramount interest to the Reformed tradition; yet an understanding of what is revealed by such a study of that self-awareness precludes any slavish copying of primitive practices, and should encourage, rather, the recapture of the living form and of an order which, though not fixed with mechanical rigidity, exhibits the principle of the Church's life.

CHAPTER VII

INCORPORATION BY THE HOLY SPIRIT

To say, as does Alan Richardson, that the primitive Christians knew nothing of a baptism that was not of the Spirit[1] is misleading. For it would appear that some persons had already received the Holy Spirit before they were baptized,[2] while on the other hand we learn of others who, having been baptized by John Baptist, had not even heard 'whether there be any Holy Ghost' and were thereupon baptized by Paul, after which 'Paul laid his hands upon them, the Holy Ghost came upon them; and they spake with tongues, and prophesied'.[3] Doubt has been cast, moreover, by some scholars,[4] on the passage in Acts in which Peter urges his hearers to repent, be baptized, and so receive the gift of the Holy Spirit.[5] Nevertheless, it was indubitably held that the Holy Spirit worked in the post-pentecostal rite of Baptism. One of the most prolific sources of error, however, about the nature of the Church is the notion that the Holy Spirit is given to individuals in Baptism as a prerequisite of their being admitted into the *koinonia*. It is in the incorporation of the individual into the life of the Church that the Holy Spirit is given to the individual in Baptism.[6]

The Holy Spirit and the Church are ecclesiologically inseparable. Without Him the figure of the Body of Christ would be quite meaningless. This is not to say that the first-century Christians had a fully developed trinitarian doctrine, which of course they had not; nor did they always use 'Spirit' in its now

[1] Alan Richardson, 'Une Interprétation anglicane de l'Eglise,' in *La Sainte Eglise universelle* (Neuchâtel, 1948), p. 139.
[2] Acts x. 47.
[3] Acts xix. 2–6.
[4] E.g., F. J. Foakes-Jackson, *The Acts of the Apostles* (London, 1931), p. 18 f.
[5] Acts ii. 37 f.
[6] Cf. Oscar Cullmann, *Die Tauflehre des Neuen Testaments* (Zurich, 1948), p. 35.

theological meaning and never in a general, providential sense. But they could not have talked of the work of Christ in the Church as they did without thinking of God's presence and activity in it through the Creator Spirit who bestows the divine life upon it. The Creator Spirit operates by creating the Body of Christ out of the world. His work is unique.[1] We might perhaps say, borrowing Aristotle's language, that He is the efficient cause of the life of the Church while Christ is the formal cause, since St Paul speaks of the Spirit as the agent who transforms us into the likeness of Christ.[2] Through the descent of the Holy Spirit the baptized are 'added' to the Body; but in the 'addition' there is nothing mechanical or arithmetical: it is a dynamic increase in the sense that through the Holy Spirit they are incorporated (*σύμφυτοι*) into the Body of Christ. It is also through the Holy Spirit that the Body reaches out to fulfilment (*πλήρωμα*). This *πλήρωμα* begins in the Church and reaches out to all creation.[3] Through the operation of the Holy Spirit in Word and Sacrament, the Church, which is the Body of Christ, reaches out to its fulness and may so be said to be 'enlarged', as the Word is said, in Acts, to have been 'multiplied' and 'increased'.[4]

The Holy Spirit thus operates in history through one Body,

[1] There is a different emphasis in Latin theology and in the Greek Fathers on the subject of the work of the Spirit, and this reappears in modern discussions. The Latins generally accept the principle: *opera Trinitatis ad extra sunt indivisa.* The Greeks have preferred to say that the Holy Spirit is more especially the principle of sanctification because, in the revelation that is given to us of the mystery of God, the Holy Spirit is represented as being turned towards men and consequently the immediate principle of all *ad extra* operations, so that, while Father and Son act, they act through the Holy Spirit. (Cf. Didymus of Alexandria, *De Trin.* II, vi, 2; St Thomas, *S. Theol.*, I, q. 45, a. 6 ad 2.) Calvin, in the Genevan Catechism, describes the Holy Spirit as God's 'virtus per omnia quidem diffusa, quae tamen perpetuo in ipso resideat'. We recall the words of the *Quicumque*: 'Spiritus sanctus a Patre et Filio, non factus nec creatus nec genitus, sed procedens.' The Greek Fathers put it, rather, that the Holy Spirit is the *τέλος*, the 'limit' of the divine life, which, however, stretches out in time and space to touch our souls and animate them with the life of the Trinity. So, since the Holy Spirit is the 'limit' of the divine life, it is He that is the principle of the new life; hence he is called *δάκτυλος τοῦ θεοῦ*. (Cf. Leonard Hodgson, *The Doctrine of the Trinity* (London, 1943), p. 80 ff. and appendix, p. 226 ff.). It is a question of emphasis: as we are reminded by St Augustine (*Hom. in Joh.*, lxxvii), it is the Trinity that speaks and teaches, but the Persons must be intimated so that we should 'both hear Them in Their distinctness and understand Them in Their inseparableness'.

[2] 2 Cor. iii. 18.

[3] Romans viii. 19–29; Eph. i. 9 f.

[4] Acts vi. 7; xii. 24; xix. 20.

the Church. The content of the doctrine of the Spirit that is to be found in the New Testament is simply the New Testament christology; for the Holy Spirit is sent to reveal Christ and unite us to Him in such a manner that Christ, through Him, may dwell in us and with us.[1] The meaning of the Body of Christ cannot be understood apart from the relation between the outpouring of the Spirit and the great christological mysteries, the Incarnation, Passion, Death, Resurrection and Ascension of Christ. In the Incarnation, the fulness (πλήρωμα) of the Godhead dwelt bodily (σωματικός) in Christ;[2] at Pentecost the fulness (πλήρωμα) of the life of Christ overflows into the Church which is His Body (σῶμα Χριστοῦ), so that the Church is complete in Him.[3]

The place of Baptism in the life of the Church is of peculiar importance in the Reformed tradition, not least because it is a link between the Old Covenant and the New. Baptism, according to Calvin, and according to all the historic confessions and catechisms of the Reformed Church, is the sacrament of 'the Covenant of Grace', in which God, in his paternal goodness to us, takes us for His children, allying Himself with us as our Saviour. Christ is the Head of a new humanity which, being taken up into the Covenant, constitutes His Body. So to be baptized into Christ is to be taken into Christ's Body in personal union with Christ, not merely in a legal relationship, for the relationship we have with Him is a living and growing one, nourished and sustained by the Holy Spirit. Baptism is 'from the hand of God': the rite that is performed is essentially 'passive'.[4] In circumcision God had 'inscribed His covenant in the flesh of Abraham. For circumcision was a solemn memorial of that adoption by which the family of Abraham had been elected as the peculiar people of God'.[5] To the Jews, however, Christ had been given only by way of promise: they partook of Christ, but

[1] John xiv. 16–26; xvi. 7–11.
[2] Col. ii. 9. Cf. the excellent brief discussion of this text in C. F. D. Moule, *The Epistles of Paul the Apostle to the Colossians and to Philemon* (Cambridge, 1957), p. 92 ff.
[3] Col. ii. 10.
[4] Calvin, *Institutio*, IV, xiv, 26; xv, 1–2; *Comm. in Gal*, v, 3.
[5] Calvin, *Comm. in Gen.*, xvii, 9.

they could be said to possess Him only 'as one hidden and, so to speak, absent—absent, I say, not in the power of grace, but because He was not yet manifest in the flesh'.[1] Circumcision was abrogated to make way for another sign that would figure the reality now completely fulfilled in the Body of Christ.[2] All that had been promised by circumcision to the Old Israel was given to the New Israel. Baptism, which is given to children as well as to adults, to Gentiles as well as to Jews, is given because the Covenant has now been fulfilled on our behalf in Christ. 'He gives me, so to say, His own robe; He speaks for me, and I present myself in His name, even as though I were Himself, because it has pleased Him to be so gracious as to unite me to Himself.'[3]

It is of much importance for the study of the meaning of the phrase 'Body of Christ' upon which we shall later embark, to note that the rite of Christian Baptism, because of its Semitic origin, implies no mind-matter dualism. Man is envisaged as a unity. If his soul is tainted by sin, so also is his body: the uncleanness of a man's body and soul are not separable. That is why it had seemed natural and fitting to employ physical means to purify the soul. By the time of Christ there was of course a strong Greek influence in Judaism, not least among the Pharisees, who were therefore able to distinguish between ritual or ceremonial uncleanness and moral uncleanness. The New Testament writers, however, in interpreting Baptism, return to the earlier conception of the unity of body and soul.[4] So close, moreover, is the connection between the old rite and the new that Baptism is actually called 'the circumcision of Christ',[5] with whom we are 'buried in baptism'.[6] It should not be forgotten that the circumcision rite had undergone an interesting development in Judaism. To the original rite, which was administered

[1] Calvin, *Comm. in 1 Pet.*, i, 12.
[2] Calvin, *Comm. in Col.*, ii, 11 f.
[3] Calvin, *Sermon on Galatians*, iii, 29.
[4] E.g., 1 Peter iii. 21.
[5] Col. ii. 11.
[6] Col. ii. 12. It should be noted that according to the Manual of Discipline of the Zadokite community, contemporary with Jesus, baptism, administered to women and children also, was apparently regarded as a covenanting rite (cf. D. Barthélemy in *Revue Biblique* (1952), p. 204).

the eighth day after the child's birth, had come to be added a baptismal ablution, administered on the eleventh day.[1] The New Testament writers could therefore see a symbolism in Christian Baptism that is generally overlooked by us: the bloody part of the ancient rite was abrogated because Christ by His sacrifice on the Cross had ended the shedding of blood; but the ablutionary part of the old rite was perpetuated and transformed. The attitude of the Jews towards the circumcision of proselytes is also relevant to our study. The Gentile convert was looked upon as 'coming from the grave'; his uncleanness was, therefore, considered to be the uncleanness of a corpse.[2] Since the Exodus, circumcision and the Passover had been closely connected: it was generally at the Passover season that the proselyte was incorporated into Israel,[3] so that he could begin his life as an Israelite fully and immediately by participating in the Passover.[4] At the Passover, the convert could symbolically consider himself to have 'crossed the Red Sea',[5] being 'redeemed out of Egypt', so that he was truly participating in the great redemptive acts of God. All this symbolism in proselyte circumcision and baptism lies behind the Pauline conception of Christian Baptism and the Eucharist. To the latter, St Paul gives the same name, *τὸ σῶμα τοῦ Χριστοῦ*, as he gives to the Church itself.

Calvin insists on connecting every Christian baptismal ceremony with the Baptism of Christ in the Jordan, seeing in this an important symbolism that is also connected with the Body of Christ, the Church. It was, he says, to assure believers that they are ingrafted into Christ's Body, and that they are buried with Him in Baptism so that they may rise to newness of life,[6] that 'Christ received the same Baptism with us'.[7] 'The general reason why Christ received Baptism was that He might render unto the Father full obedience; the special reason was that He might consecrate Baptism in His own Body, so that we might have it in common with Him.'[8] Again, Calvin says that Christ

[1] *Mishnah, Shabbath*, ix, 3.
[2] *Mishnah, Pesaḥim*, viii, 8.
[3] *Loc. cit.*
[4] *Bab. Jebamoth*, 47 b.
[5] *Jer. Pesaḥim*, x, 5; cf. ix, 8.
[6] Romans vi. 4; cf. Col. xi. 12.
[7] Calvin, *Comm. in Matt.*, iii, 13,
[8] *Loc. cit.*

'consecrated and sanctified Baptism in His own Body that He might have it in common with us as the firmest bond of union and fellowship which He deigned to form with us; and so Paul proves us to be the sons of God from the fact that in Baptism we put on Christ'.[1] Baptism is therefore, according to Calvin, essentially an incorporation. 'The whole Church' is baptized in Christ.[2] 'Confiteor unum baptisma' does not merely mean that Baptism, in contradistinction to the Eucharist, is received once; it means that there is one Baptism common to all, and each individual Baptism is grounded in this one common Baptism.[3] 'We all have the same Baptism whereby we are ingrafted into the common Body of Christ; yet His Baptism is conferred on every individual so that all may acknowledge that they share in the adoption and are members of the Church.'[4] Baptism does not necessarily imply conversion any more than it guarantees salvation. Those who receive it may later be cut off; yet so long as they remain in the Body of Christ there is hope for them. Indeed, being in the Body of Christ, they have been given every hope of salvation, whether they have received Baptism as believers or as the children of believers. Only if they 'do not abide' in Christ are they cast off.[5]

'If we give proper consideration to the end for which Baptism was instituted,' says Calvin, 'we perceive clearly that it is not less applicable to children than to those of more advanced years.'[6] It is this end that we ought to bear in mind rather than the various other, less theological, arguments that Calvin provides for infant Baptism, such as are implied in his reminder that though Christ did not baptize infants, He embraced them and commended them to His Father with prayer and benediction.[7] That John Baptist was 'sanctified from his mother's womb' as 'an example of what he was able to do for others' is

[1] Calvin, *Institutio*, IV, xv, 6; cf. Gal. iii. 27.

[2] *Op. cit.*, IV, xv, 2; xvi, 22; *Comm. in Eph.*, v, 26.

[3] Calvin appears to mean that Baptism, though different from the Eucharist in function, is in its own way no less a 'corporate' sacrament.

[4] Calvin, *Comm. in Exod.*, xii, 11.

[5] Cf. Calvin, *Comm. in Rom.*, xi, 22 f.

[6] *Institutio*, IV, xvi, 8.

[7] *Institutio*, IV, xvi, 7; cf. M. Goguel, *L'Eglise primitive* (Paris, 1947), p. 325.

not, Calvin maintains, merely an argument from 'a single case': its strength lies in its drawing attention to the limitless power of God, which we should not 'unjustly confine'.[1] But surely no arguments of this kind need be adduced if it is established that Christian Baptism, having the Jewish rite of circumcision of infants as its prototype, is the sign of God's Covenant. True, it differs from circumcision as we have seen; but it has also 'a very complete likeness' in 'the internal office, the promise, the use and the effect'.[2]

The Biblical emphasis of the Reformed tradition excludes all notions of Baptism as a transaction between God and individuals only. For, as Barth points out, 'the Bible takes no independent interest in the individuality of man, determined, so to speak, from below or from within. What constitutes the members of the body of Christ the members of the Church as such (and therefore as individuals) is not the peculiar quality that this or that individual brings under his personal name and as his personal contribution to the discipleship of Jesus and to the Church. The Old and New Testaments do not know anything of those "Bible character sketches" that people, particularly in modern times, have endeavoured to find in them.'[3] The initiative in Baptism comes from God, and God does not enter into a covenant with individuals: he incorporates individuals into the Body of Christ under His Covenant of Grace. It is for this reason that the Reformed Church has generally discouraged the private administration of Baptism. According to Calvin, this sacrament should be administered in the midst of the people; this symbolizes the nature of Baptism, which is entry into the Body of Christ.[4] In the Form prescribed in the Book of Common Order

[1] *Institutio*, IV, xvi, 17. [2] *Institutio*, IV, xvi, 16.

[3] K. Barth, *Kirchliche Dogmatik*, 1/2 (Zurich, 1945), p. 789. To that radically false approach to Scripture Barth (*ad loc.*) attributes the misunderstanding behind a certain type of Biblical criticism: 'Die Leben-Jesu-Forschung ist mit daran gescheitert, dass man das so lange nicht wahr haben wollte.'

[4] *Institutio*, IV, xv, 13, 15, 19. The Scottish Church was so strict in this matter that a minister is reported to have been suspended and required to do public penance for having baptized children in private houses (G. W. Sprott, *The Worship and Offices of the Church of Scotland* (Edinburgh, 1882), p. 57). The First Prayer Book of Edward VI, though it provided for house baptism in case of necessity, recommended public baptism in principle.

commonly known as 'Knox's Liturgy', which was regulative in the Scottish Church between 1564 and 1645, the rubric declares that 'it is evident that the Sacraments are not ordained of God to be used in private corners, as charms, or sorceries, but left to the Congregation, and necessarily annexed to God's Word as seals of the same. Therefore, the infant that is to be baptized shall be brought to the Church on the day appointed to Common Prayer and Preaching, accompanied with the Father and Godfather, so that, after the Sermon, the child being presented to the Minister, he demandeth this question: Do ye here present this child to be baptized, earnestly desiring that he may be ingrafted in the mystical body of Jesus Christ?'[1] After a lengthy exposition of the Twelve Articles of the Creed, the Minister, before uttering the words of Baptism, prays God to 'sanctify with Thy Spirit, and to receive into the number of Thy children, this Infant whom we shall baptize according to Thy Word, to the end that he, coming to perfect age, may confess Thee only, the true God, and whom Thou hast sent, Jesus Christ, and so serve Him, and be profitable unto His Church in the whole course of his life, that after his life be ended, he may be brought, as a lively member of His body, unto the full fruition of Thy joys. . . .'[2]

While Calvin repudiates all tendencies to divide Baptism into three separate operations, he recognizes that 'the fruit and efficacy of Baptism proceed from God the Father adopting us through His Son, after having, through the Spirit, cleansed us from the pollutions of the flesh so as to create us anew unto righteousness'.[3] What Calvin calls the 'matter' or 'substance' of Baptism is found exclusively in Christ: it consists of our restoration to favour with God by the death of Christ who has fulfilled God's Covenant. To be baptized in[4] the name of Christ means

[1] *The Book of Common Order* (ed. Sprott and Leishman; Edinburgh, 1868), p. 135.

[2] *Op. cit.*, p. 147 f.

[3] Calvin, *Comm. in Matt.*, xxviii, 19.

[4] Baptism in the Reformed Church has always been *in* the Triune Name, following the medieval Latin formula. A more literal rendering of the Greek (εἰς τὸ ὄνομα) has, however, sometimes been used in Scotland: Alexander Henderson, writing in 1641, prescribes the formula '*into* the Name. . . . ' (William McMillan, (*The Worship of the Scottish Reformed Church, 1560–1638* (London, 1931), p. 262).

that believers are to 'live out of themselves; that is, live in Christ'.[1] It is through Christ alone that we obtain the mercy of God, and so 'when we wish to sum up in short compass the efficacy of Baptism we make mention of Christ alone; but when we wish to speak with greater minuteness, it is necessary to introduce expressly the name of the Father and that of the Spirit'.[2] It is not by reason of our faith that we are baptized; on the contrary, both Baptism and faith depend upon God's promise.[3] However, Baptism is not effective apart from faith, and so we require the Holy Spirit in order that we may be made into new creatures. Barth, in his exposition of the Scots Confession, indicates that the Christian would be incapable of repentance and thankfulness, but for Christ's daily coming to him in the Holy Spirit.[4] The calling by the Holy Spirit is a calling into the Church, which, says Barth, possesses its 'true nature, unity and holiness' in the 'electing, calling, directing and comforting' of the Holy Spirit.[5]

The practice of infant Baptism in the Christian Church today however, is such that it is commonly dissociated in the popular mind from the doctrine of the Holy Spirit, and has given rise to such widespread misunderstanding, not to say vulgar superstition, that several distinguished theologians have called for drastic remedies to help to remove this. Barth has called into question the Scriptural authority for infant Baptism.[6] Brunner has deplored the contemporary practice as little less than scandalous.[7] Phythian-Adams, pointing to the serious departure from the New Testament conception in which Baptism was so essentially 'with the Holy Ghost and with fire',[8] reminds us of the manner in which the connection between Baptism and the Holy Spirit was lost sight of in later practice, through the sepa-

[1] Calvin, *Comm. in Gal.*, ii, 20.
[2] Calvin, *Comm. in 1 Cor.*, i, 13; cf. *Comm. in Matt.*, xxviii, 19.
[3] Cf. Mark xvi. 16.
[4] Karl Barth, *The Knowledge of God and the Service of God* (London, 1938) p. 122 f.
[5] *Op. cit.*, p. 157; cf. E. Lohmeyer, *Grundlagen paulinischer Theologie* (Tubingen, 1929), p. 185.
[6] Karl Barth, *The Teaching of the Church regarding Baptism* (London, 1948), p. 49.
[7] Emil Brunner, *The Divine-Human Encounter* (London, 1944), p. 132.
[8] Matt. iii. 11; Luke iii. 16; cf. Mark i. 8; Acts i. 5; ii. 4; x. 45; 1 C r. xii. 13.

ration of the 'washing' part and the laying on of hands with invocation of the Holy Spirit. The latter part, after having then become, as Confirmation, a separate sacrament, lost its sacramental status in the Reformed Church. The result was that, with Baptism retained as one of the two sacraments believed to be Scripturally authenticated, and with Confirmation relegated to the status of an additional, non-sacramental rite[1] for those who, being of riper years,[2] could be accounted eligible for it, Baptism came to be more than ever deprived of its proper connection with the doctrine of the Holy Spirit, and so associated more than ever with 'washing'. The same writer recognizes that

[1] No provision for a form for the confirmation of baptismal vows was made either in the Book of Common Order (1564) or the Westminster Directory (1645). But the *First Buik of Discipline* set forth, in an appendix 'for the Instruction of Ministers and Reidaris in thair Office' (xiii: The Tabill) the following injunction: 'The ministratioun of the tabill suld never be without scharp examinatioun ganging befoir; cheiflie of thame quhais life, ignorance, or religioun is suspectit. Quha can nocht say the Lordis Prayer, the Articles of the Faith [i.e., the Creed] and declare the soume of the law [i.e., the Ten Commandments], suld not be admittit.' These provisions are similar to the requirements set forth at the beginning of the Order of Confirmation in the English Book of Common Prayer. Cf. also Herman's note: 'This custome hath beene obserued in the olde, and newe testament, of the institution of God, that those, whiche in theyr fyrst infancie were receiued into the grace of the Lorde, . . . assone as they had understande thys benifyte of God, whiche they had receyued, and assone as they hadde afore conceyued fayeth in God, they themselues shoulde professe theyr fayeth in the congregation, and they them selues shoulde bynde them selues to the obedience of God, and of the congregation' (*Hermanni Einfaltigs Bedencken von der Reformation* (1543); English translation, *A simple and religious Consultation of us, Herman by the grace of God Archbishop of Colone, and Prince Electoure* . . . (London, 1548), fol. 171). It is well known to liturgists that Bucer and Melanchthon drew up liturgical offices for Herman, and that the latter, a personal friend of Cranmer, exercised, through his *Consultation*, a great influence on the First Prayer Book of Edward VI. In Scotland a form of service almost certainly accompanied the examination (cf. Bonar, *Catechisms of the Scottish Reformation*, pp. 324–57); but it seems plain that there was no laying on of hands even during the First Episcopacy, for the Aberdeen Doctors admitted that even the bishops themselves refrained from it (cf. Grub, *An Ecclesiastical History of Scotland* (4 vols., Edinburgh, 1861), ii, p. 361). A form for the confirmation of baptismal vows was provided in the Scottish Church Service Society's Book of Common Order (1867), and the present Book of Common Order authorized by the General Assembly provides one that includes the prayer for the sevenfold gifts of the Holy Ghost. In some churches the laying on of hands at Confirmation is now customary. In France the laying on of hands is likewise practised in some churches only (*Liturgie des Eglises réformées de France* (Paris, 1897), p. 158.

[2] In the sixteenth and seventeenth centuries children were admitted to Holy Communion at a much earlier age than is now generally encouraged in the Reformed Church. The 21st General Assembly (1570) ordained that children should be examined three times, at nine, at twelve, and at fourteen years of age (*The Booke of the Universall Kirk of Scotland* (ed. Peterkin; Edinburgh, 1839), p. 121), which indicates admission at fourteen. Earlier admissions are, however, recorded.

the Baptists are, to say the least, in no better a case than the Reformed Church, so far as this danger is concerned, since their dramatic emphasis on the 'washing' can aggravate the misleading association.[1]

The popular misunderstanding of the significance of Baptism lies in a deeper misunderstanding of the nature of the Church, however, rather than in any other prevailing condition. That such is the case is indicated by the fact that no satisfactory solution of the practical problem has been offered from any doctrinal point of view. Baptists as well as Anglicans and others recognize that Baptism is an entry into the Church;[2] but the meaning of 'entry into the Church' depends, of course, on what is meant by 'the Church', and a Baptist does not mean by this what an Anglican does. A Baptist theologian's concern about popular misunderstanding of the significance of Baptism is by no means the same as that of a theologian in the Reformed Church, because his Separatist doctrine of the Church is radically different from any that is warranted in the Reformed tradition. The significance of Baptism by immersion may be, from a Baptist viewpoint, popularly misconstrued; but its powerful psychological effect is obvious, and it is not difficult in principle to explain to people that the significance lies beyond the 'washing'.[3] Moreover, because of the presumably vivid memory of such a rite in the mind of a participant, a fuller realization of what was intended may be developed later by meditation upon the experience in retrospect, in the light of preaching. For it is universally admitted that faith is demanded after as well as during Baptism, and it cannot be denied on any theory that a fuller appreciation of the significance of it may be attained long after the rite is over. It is said that Luther, to encourage his own faith, was in the habit of saying to himself, 'Baptizatus sum.'

[1] W. J. Phythian-Adams, *The Way of At-one-ment* (London, 1944), p. 100 ff.

[2] Wheeler Robinson, for instance, says (*Baptist Principles*, p. 25) that Baptism is 'the door of entrance to the church'.

[3] The 'washing' was much emphasized in early Christian literature. Pseudo-Clement, for instance, suggests that the soul that is washed in Baptism is not easily enkindled by 'the fire of the demons' (*Recognitions*, xii, 10 f.).

After all, there is no sacrament that is not susceptible to misunderstanding;[1] nor could there be. That is one of the reasons why the Reformers generally insisted so vigorously on the indivisibility of Word and Sacrament. Even if, as a substitute for or addition to the 'washing' symbol of Baptism, a 'fire' or 'burning' symbol were to be used to indicate the action of the Holy Spirit (for instance, a token scorching with a lighted taper), it would indubitably be liable to misconstruction. In any case, He is 'fons vivus' and 'spiritalis unctio' as much as He is 'ignis'. Despite the evidence that immersion was widely used in early times, and the fact that the verb *βαπτίζω* seems to imply it, it is arguable that there is reasonable doubt whether the immersion was generally total, and even some doubt whether there was always immersion at all: the immersion of three thousand persons on one day in Jerusalem,[2] for instance, would seem to present practical difficulties. But it seems trivial to argue for or against immersion on those grounds. It might be argued, on the other hand, that sprinkling is a more fitting symbol of the bestowal of the Holy Spirit than immersion, and therefore is to be preferred. Culmann has, indeed, suggested that the later introduction of the laying on of hands as a symbol of the bestowal of the Holy Spirit was due to the notion that dipping seemed less appropriate, when Baptism was considered apart from the Baptism of Jesus. But whether this be so or not, it is not an argument that provides any solution to the practical problem raised in the minds of those who note the common misunderstandings about Baptism.

It is questioned by many scholars whether Baptism was enjoined by Jesus. The Marcan passage[3] indicating a dominical authority for Baptism is generally repudiated, and there are

[1] The Roman Pontifical directs the bishop to give the newly confirmed a slight blow on the cheek. ('*Deinde leviter eum in maxilla caedit, dicens:* Pax tecum.') One Roman Catholic, interpreting the significance of Confirmation to the present writer, said: 'Confirmation is the sacrament where you get a slap in the face from the bishop to show you what you have to "take" from the world.' Even from a Tridentine standpoint this is indeed an inadequate account of the significance of Confirmation.

[2] Acts ii. 41.

[3] Mark xvi. 16.

grounds for doubt about the authenticity of the Matthaean one,[1] which enjoins Baptism into the Triune Name, while it seems plain from Acts that Baptism was customarily 'into the Name of Christ', in the early days of the Church. Moreover, it is well known to Biblical scholars that when Eusebius cites the Matthaean passage, which he does often, he nearly always omits the injunction to baptize, so indicating that he may have been familiar with an earlier text that did not include the injunction. On the other hand, the fact that while there is evidence in the New Testament of controversies on many subjects, there appears to be unanimity about Baptism, and it is plainly regarded as the one door into the Christian Church. A good case for dominical authority for Baptism is made by Flemington[2] who, besides drawing attention to this unanimity, reminds us of the work of John Baptist, and of how closely the mission of John was connected with that of Jesus. John was apparently well known in Jewish circles: Josephus refers to him as the Baptizer. Among contemporary scholars there is, however, much disparity on the question of the institution of Baptism. While Schweitzer maintains that Christian Baptism was never, down to the time of Eusebius, connected with Christ's Baptism by John,[3] Barth would have it that it was at His Baptism at the hands of John that Christ instituted the sacrament.[4]

It is plain that from Pentecost onwards Baptism was thought about in diverse ways. We are no doubt far too much inclined to be distracted by the variety of symbolism that the early writers were capable of seeing in Baptism, and to ignore what was its essential significance. It was inevitable, for example, that it should be associated with the death and resurrection of Christ: the baptized person dies to sin and rises to new life. Cleansing was also indubitably much in the minds of all who participated

[1] Matthew xxviii. 19.

[2] W. F. Flemington, *The New Testament Doctrine of Baptism* (London, S.P.C.K., 1948).

[3] Albert Schweitzer, *The Mysticism of Paul the Apostle* (London, 1931), p. 234.

[4] Karl Barth, *The Teaching of the Church regarding Baptism* (London, 1948), p. 18 ff. Ambrose (*In Luc.*, ii, 83) and Chrysostom (*Hom. in Matt.*, xii, 3) are among the Fathers who take this view. Cf. St Thomas, *Summa Theol.*, III, q. 66, a. 2.

in the baptismal ceremony. Both water and fire are symbols of cleansing, and both are symbols of life. It is a Talmudic notion that when a child is in the womb, a light burns on its head, in which the child's spirit is manifest as fire.[1] It will be remembered that Moses, when he came down from Mount Sinai, manifested a peculiar glow: 'the skin of his face shone, and they were afraid to come nigh him.'[2] He was no doubt believed to be showing forth the Spirit of Yahweh, who had, so to speak, imparted His own glow to Moses. The glory (δόξα) that is such a predominant notion in the New Testament has its roots in the Hebrew conception, *kabhodh*, a fiery or shining radiance from a visible fire.[3] The Jews put an oil-lamp on their tombs to represent the spirit, and there is evidence that this notion goes back to antiquity, even that the lamp was used in the places where children had formerly been sacrificed: the lamp was a substitute for the child-sacrifice.[4] A man's spirit (*n'shama*) is Yahweh's lamp, which searches the innermost parts of the belly.[5] The Spirit descended upon Christ in the form of a dove, a well-known symbol of spirit, continued in the Christian catacombs, where the dove drinking water from a basin apparently represents the human spirit drinking the water of life. Echoes of primitive water-symbolism are even more obvious. Among the Greeks and Romans water was the sap of life: the dead were ἀλίβαντες; that is, lacking moisture (α—λιβας). Indeed the word 'skeleton' (σκελετός) surely means 'dried up' (σκέλλω, to dry up). In Hebrew lore, death is symbolized by dry bones, and is contrasted with the water of life which is with God.[6] So the baptismal water expresses not merely cleansing; it is the infusion of new life.[7] Resurrection was widely associated with the falling of

[1] *Niddah*, 30 b. John Baptist was 'filled with the Holy Ghost, even from his mother's womb' (Luke i. 15).

[2] Exod. xxxiv. 30.

[3] Cf. Gen. xlix. 6; Exod. xxiv. 16 f.; Psalm vii. 5; xvi. 9 (note LXX translation: γλῶσσα); Isaiah, x. 16; Ezek. i. 27 f.; x. 4; Luke ix. 29–32; Acts xxii. 11; 1 Cor. xv. 41; 2 Cor. iii. 7, 18; iv. 6.

[4] Cf. *Palestine Exploration Fund Quarterly Statement*, 1903, pp. 10, 11, 228, 299, 306 ff.

[5] Proverbs xx. 27.

[6] Psalm xxxvi. 9; cf. Rev. xxii. 1, 17.

[7] Cf. F. C. Conybeare's *Rituale Armenorum*, p. 106, where it is said that Baptism 'in the language of the world is called Life'.

dew or rain. Water, oil, fire, the dove, were all symbols naturally connected with baptismal ritual for they were all connected with life and immortality. But of course we look in vain among them for elucidation of the characteristically Christian doctrine.

Nor should practice be determined simply by what seems to tend to or away from superstition. Modern writers are often much less clear-sighted than were the Reformers in this matter. Notions that are notoriously productive of superstition may be retained when they can be rendered innocuous, and they can be rendered innocuous when they are put into a framework or context which, by subordinating them, takes away their danger. Tertullian defends Christian Baptism by means of an image that sounds highly fanciful to modern ears. He says that it is not surprising that a heresy had arisen that would destroy Baptism, because it is characteristic of vipers and basilisks to frequent arid deserts, while, in contrast, 'we, little fishes, after the example of our Fish,[1] Jesus Christ, are born of water, nor have we safety otherwise than by permanently resting in water.'[2] He connects water with the Spirit of God who hovered over the water in the beginning,[3] as well as with other Old Testament parallels. He is ready to interpret the 'one Baptism'[4] as signifying that, because we enter the *lavacrum* once, 'once are sins washed away' and ought never to be repeated.[5]

But Tertullian is not to be charged with superstition on the grounds of the imagery used in his treatise on this subject. His teaching is not different from that of Calvin, even in his interpretation of Christian Baptism in terms of 'onceness' rather than 'oneness'. He is less theological in his exposition than is Calvin in the passages we cited.[6] What makes Christian Baptism different from any other baptismal rite is not water or fire or oil. Baptism might be *fluminis*, *flaminis* or *sanguinis*, yet be other than

[1] *ΙΧΘΥΣ*, well known in iconography.

[2] Tertullian, *De Bapt.*, i: 'Nos pisciculi secundum ἰχθῦν nostrum Jesum Christum in aqua nascimur: nec aliter quam in aqua permanendo salvi sumus.'

[3] *Op. cit.*, iii, iv; cf. Gen. i. 1–2.

[4] *Op. cit.*, xv.

[5] *Loc. cit.*

[6] *Institutio*, IV, xv, 2; xvi. 22. *Supra*, p. 133, n. 3.

Christian Baptism. Only incorporation into Christ makes Christian Baptism different from any other kind. Tertullian may use his fanciful language with impunity, when he urges us to 'stay in the water', because he is urging us to see the water as that in which we, the little fish, are joined to the great Fish. Fancy may have free rein so long as the essential theological idea is preserved. The genius of Calvin lay in his ability to see which are the essential theological safeguards against the pleasant, but generally vain and sometimes dangerous imaginings of men. The Reformed tradition has shown wisdom where it has followed him here, emphasizing, as Knox did, that Baptism is above all ingrafting or incorporation by the Holy Spirit into the Body of Christ, the Church.

Were not Christian Baptism in danger of being detached from the central idea upon which it depends, incorporation into Christ, there need be no fear that concentration upon the 'washing' or any other aspect might lead to undesirable results. For the cleansing of the candidate for Baptism is indeed a work of the Holy Spirit, and the Church must rejoice in it. Likewise, Baptism is rightly associated with the death and resurrection of Christ: the baptized person dies to sin and rises to new life. This is also the work of the Holy Spirit: *emitte Spiritum tuum et creabuntur, et renovabis faciem terrae*. The peculiarity of the Christian doctrine is that the baptized person does not rise to *a* new life, but to *the* new life, for it is ἡ ζωή, life in Him who *is* ζωή. Only by pseudo-pentecostalism and pseudo-individualism does Christian Baptism stand in any kind of danger. So long as the Reformed tradition is faithful to its ecclesiology and insists upon Baptism being understood only as incorporation, as Calvin understood it, it need not be unduly concerned about the practical problems to which perhaps too much attention has been given in recent discussions. Even to delineate the process of regeneration is of less consequence than to establish and affirm the fundamental doctrine that Christian Baptism is nothing if not incorporation by the Holy Spirit into Christ.

CHAPTER VIII

THE UNIQUE INSTRUMENT

Various figures are used in the New Testament to describe the Church and the relationship in which it stands to Christ. St Paul tells the Corinthians that 'the temple of God is holy, which temple ye are'.[1] The author of Ephesians[2] addresses his readers as 'built upon the foundation of the apostles and prophets, Jesus Christ himself being the chief corner stone; in whom all the building fitly framed together groweth into an holy temple in the Lord; in whom ye are also builded[3] together for an habitation of God through the Spirit'.[4] It is reported that Christ enjoins His disciples to abide in Him, for He is the 'true Vine' and they the branches.[5] Those branches that break off from the Vine wither and are burned in Gehenna; the 'abiding' branches are fructiferous. The Church is also called the 'Bride' of Christ.[6] This figure likewise typifies the vital relation that exists between Christ and the Church. Husband and wife were accounted 'one flesh',[7] and the husband was the 'Head' of the wife, who according to the prevailing custom was virtually purchased by the bridegroom. We have noted[8] the predilection of the Scottish divines as well as St Bernard of Clairvaux for this figure. The Church is also considered as a family or household. Many allegories and symbols have been developed: in iconography the Church becomes sometimes Noah's ark, sometimes

[1] 1 Cor. iii. 17.

[2] Ephesians, though written after the manner of St Paul, is believed by many scholars to be non-Pauline.

[3] Calvin erroneously interprets *συνοικοδομεῖσθε* as imperative; that it is indicative is plain from what precedes. It should be noted that the verb is in the present tense: the building is in process. Cf. 1 Peter ii. 5.

[4] Eph. ii. 19 ff.

[5] John xv. 1 ff.

[6] Eph. v. 22–33; cf. John iii. 29; Rev. xxi. 2; xxii. 17.

[7] Gen. ii. 24.

[8] *Supra*, p. 99, n. 3.

the bark[1] of Peter, in which the apostles knew themselves safe in the presence of Christ and in hearing His Word in the midst of the stormy lake of Gennesaret.

The phrase 'the Body of Christ' might well be taken as one more metaphor of a similar kind, and some modern writers apparently so regard it. Scholarly opinion on the subject is so diverse, however, and there is so much confusion in the interpretation of the phrase that one must for this as well as for other reasons take very seriously the suggestion that we are here confronted with a very special kind of metaphor indeed. Chavasse, for instance, apparently treats the phrase as but another of the many poetic figures and less felicitous than some of these. He prefers the 'Bride' and even the 'Vine', saying that 'the Body of Christ' cannot express 'the fundamental and original apartness of Man and the Word of God, nor the astounding love which impelled the Bridegroom, to come down from heaven, to humble himself to the level of his Creation, that, in uniting himself to humanity, he might raise humanity to the heaven from which he came'.[2] On the other hand, Thornton says: 'All that happened to the physical organism of His body (suffering, death, burial and resurrection) now happens to us also. It happened to Him in the literal facts of history. It happens to us in a mystical order. . . . Our incorporation into Christ identifies us with the history of the new organism to which we now belong.'[3] This is to take the figure far more seriously than many scholars do. We are warned by one writer that 'we must constantly remember that it *is* a metaphor. . . . The "members" of the body are not so much raw material, out of which a new material object is fashioned'.[4] Yet another writer, who seems to agree that the phrase is to be regarded as a metaphor of the same kind as the Vine or the Temple,[5] says elsewhere, apparently without dis-

[1] The 'nave' of a church, though the word may be a corrupt form of *ναός* (temple) is generally thought to be derived from *navis*, a ship.

[2] Claude Chavasse, *The Bride of Christ* (London, 1940), p. 17.

[3] L. S. Thornton, 'The Body of Christ' in *The Apostolic Ministry*, edited by Kenneth Kirk (London, 1946), p. 77.

[4] H. W. Robinson, *The Christian Experience of the Holy Spirit* (London, 1928), p. 149 f.

[5] E. F. Scott, *The Epistles of Paul to the Colossians, to Philemon and to the Ephesians* (London, 1930), p. 24.

approval: 'From an early time the idea grew up that the Church was the new incarnation of Christ.'[1]

But acceptance of the notion that the Church is an incarnation of Christ, or an extension of the Incarnation, or even 'the incarnation of Christ *par excellence*'[2] does not seem to be correlative to the 'level' at which the Pauline language is placed. Thornton and Chavasse, for instance, whose interpretations of the phrase have been contrasted, both regard the Church as in some sense an extension of the Incarnation.[3] Nor does the outlook upon this question appear to be determinable according to the churchmanship of the writer. Lacey[4] and some other Anglicans indicate only moderate sympathy with the notion that the Church is an extension of the Incarnation; Torrance, a Church of Scotland theologian, says 'there can be no talk of an extension of the Incarnation';[5] Reinhold Niebuhr, who belongs to the Evangelical and Reformed Church, warns us that this idea 'represents a significant shift of emphasis from the Pauline-Biblical doctrine that the Church is the "body of Christ" '.[6] Whale, an English Congregationalist, on the other hand, insists that the Church is 'rightly known by all Christians as "an extension of the Incarnation" '.[7] Barth, who in an early volume of his *opus maximum* said that the Incarnation of the Word of God in Jesus Christ is given, through the Spirit, a repetition (*Wiederholung*), in the historical existence of the Church,[8] seems to abandon this concept in a later volume.[9] It would appear that, alarmed by the resemblance he has seen between Bultmann's conception of the existential repetition of Christ's work in the subjectivity of faith and the Roman doctrine that the Mass is a repetition of Calvary, Barth has preferred to fall

[1] E. F. Scott, *The Nature of the Early Church* (New York, 1941), p. 115.
[2] Robert Will, 'La conception protestante de l'Eglise considérée comme le corpus Christi' in *Revue d'histoire et de philosophie religieuses*, XII (1932), p. 482.
[3] L. S. Thornton, *The Common Life in the Body of Christ* (London, 1942), p. 315; C. Chavasse, *op. cit.*, p. 70.
[4] T. A. Lacey, *The One Body and the One Spirit* (London, James Clarke, n.d.), c. ii.
[5] T. F. Torrance, reviewing *Catholicity* in *Scottish Journal of Theology* (1949), p. 88.
[6] R. Niebuhr, *The Nature and Destiny of Man*, vol. ii (New York, 1943), p. 144 f.
[7] J. S. Whale, *Christian Doctrine* (Cambridge, 1941), p. 140.
[8] Karl Barth, *Kirchliche Dogmatik*, 1/2 (Zurich 1945), p. 135 ff.
[9] *Op. cit.*, 4/1, p. 857 ff.

back on what he takes to be less misleading or less dangerous analogies.

More than merely verbal circumspection is required in formulating any theory about the incarnation of God in the Church. The notion is, however, an interesting one and ought to be thoroughly explored. It is suggested, of course, by the Pauline phrase 'the Body of Christ'. That divinity and humanity somehow meet in the Church would be generally admitted by all who take the idea of the Church seriously at all. But when we are called upon to explain how they meet, a great many other questions must first be asked before we can attempt an answer. The notion that the Church reproduces the conditions of Christ's earthly life has been widely entertained.[1] In the latter part of the nineteenth century and the first decade of the present one, when kenotic theories were intellectually fashionable in christological discussions,[2] there were some attempts to apply them to the Church.[3]

The kenotic theory is, of course, much older than these discussions: it is rooted in the New Testament,[4] and there are some faint suggestions of it in Irenaeus.[5] The Lutheran divines drew a sharp distinction between the incarnation and the humiliation or kenosis. The Logos, they held, surrendered nothing of the divine majesty: it was the God-man, respecting his human nature, who was the subject of the kenosis, which consisted only in his making no habitual use of the divine qualities conveyed to his humanity by its union with the Logos. So they could speak

[1] E.g., L. S. Thornton, 'The Body of Christ' in *The Apostolic Ministry* (ed. K. Kirk; London, 1946); Robert Hugh Benson, *Christ in the Church* (London, 1911); E. Mersch, *La théologie du Corps mystique* (Paris-Brussels, 1944).

[2] Notable expositions were: Thomassius, *Beiträge zur kirchlichen christologie* (1845); *Christi Person und Werke* (1853); W. F. Gess, *Die Lehre von der Person Christi* (1854); Bruce, *Humiliation of Christ* (1881); Bensow, *Die Lehre von der Kenose* (1903); Gore, 'The Consciousness of Our Lord in His Mortal Life' in *Dissertations on Subjects connected with the Incarnation* (1895), pp. 69–226; Mason, *Conditions of our Lord's Life on Earth* (1896); Powell, *Principle of the Incarnation* (1896); Forrest, *The Authority of Christ* (1906); Garvie, *The Christian Doctrine of the Godhead* (1925).

[3] E.g., W. R. Carson, 'The Kenosis of the Church' in *Reunion Essays* (London, 1903), pp. 157–72.

[4] Philip. ii. 5–11.

[5] Irenaeus, *adv. Haer.*, iv, 4, 2: 'Well spake he who said that the unmeasurable Father was Himself subjected to measure in the Son; for the Son is the measure of the Father, since He also comprehends Him.' Cf. also iv, 20, 5.

of the divine Infant ruling the universe, though He did so 'secretly'. These notions were connected with the peculiarly Lutheran doctrine of the transference of qualities (*communicatio idiomatum*) in the hypostatic union.[1] From this doctrine they went on to take the view that the divine attributes might be predicated of the human nature, because there was a real transference of properties in Christ, whose two natures exchanged something of their substance by a process of endosmosis (*genus majestaticum*). So even in His human nature Christ is omnipotent and omniscient; the sacramental ubiquity or multipresence of Christ's Body might therefore be explained christologically. Such ideas were a sort of continuation of Alexandrian speculation, and they accorded with the Lutheran maxim: *finitum est capax infiniti*.

Reformed christology, on the other hand, took a Chalcedonian starting-point, categorically opposing the Lutheran maxim and saying instead: *finitum non est capax infiniti*. The subject of the humiliation, it was maintained, is not the God-man; it is the pre-incarnate Son. All the Calvinist divines insisted very strongly on the humanity of Christ, whose human nature, though conjoined to the awful Majesty of God in personal union (the mystery *par excellence* according to the Reformed tradition), is as fully human as our own. So they had no difficulty in thinking of Jesus as growing, as gaining in human experience, knowledge, holiness and power. In superficial estimates of Calvin, his emphasis upon the awful, transcendent Majesty of God is commonly divorced from his christology in such a way as to divest it of all Christian meaning. When the Reformed theology is so divorced from the Reformed christology it is scarcely distinguishable from the theology of Islam. The Logos was indeed present in Jesus Christ, yet existent outside Him: *totus extra carnem*, yet *totus in carne*. 'Though the boundless essence of the Word,' says Calvin, 'was united with human nature into one person, we have no idea of its imprisonment or confinement. The Son of God descended miraculously from heaven, yet with-

[1] The Lutherans appealed to Col. ii. 9.

out abandoning heaven; He chose to be conceived by a miracle in the womb of the Virgin, to live on earth, to hang upon the Cross, yet He always filled the world as from the beginning.'[1] The Lutherans mistook this for a sort of neo-Nestorianism; they spoke disparagingly of 'illud "extra" Calvinisticum'. But the only 'extra' is the mystery of the Incarnation itself, which no theological speculation can eliminate or even mitigate. The Reformed christology is thoroughly Chalcedonian and is a vigorous protest against the very strong tendencies away from Chalcedon that had for long been apparent in medieval piety.[2] For there is no doubt that the well-known tendencies in medieval devotion, from about the twelfth century onwards especially, to replace the Mediator by the Mediatrix, were possible only by an unofficial but nevertheless immensely influential revival of Monophysitism. As the Monothelite controversy, two and a half centuries after Chalcedon, plainly shows, Monophysite tendencies did not readily die out, not least because there must have been many besides Pope Honorius who could not see anything important at stake.[3]

[1] *Institutio*, II, xiii *ad fin.*

[2] The Reformers, while protesting against the typical medieval tendency to replace the Mediator by the Mediatrix, did not deny Mary the designation *Theotokos*. Even Zwingli speaks of Mary with the utmost reverence, saying, in the idiom of Chalcedon, that 'deiparam θεοτόκος apellari iusto vocabulo iudicamus et probamus' (*Fidei Christianae Expositio* in *Opera*, iv, 74). At Zurich, Zwingli encouraged the use of the *Ave Maria* and upheld the ancient Marian feasts (cf. *Kirchenblatt fur die reformierte Schweiz*, Feb. 1, 1951, p. 34 ff.). Calvin, in explicitly repudiating the errors, as he calls them, of both Eutyches and Nestorius, affirms (*Institutio*, II, xiv, 4) that 'the Virgin herself is called "the Mother of our Lord" '. Though Calvin does not use the designation *Deipara*, he does not reject it or indicate that it is to be rejected. What the Reformers did all emphatically reject was the notion of co-operation by Mary in the work of redemption, a notion that has no support whatsoever either in the Council of Ephesus or in that of Chalcedon, but is prominent in Roman mariology where it is frequently and explicitly affirmed. As early as the twelfth century Mary was being hailed as Mediatrix: St Bernard of Clairvaux, in a well-known sermon, said (Migne, *P. L.*, clxxxiii, 429 f.) that 'we need a mediator in order to reach Christ our mediator, and we find none better than our Lady'. But for the development of such tendencies, which the Reformers could not but regard as heretical, the Reformed Church might have encouraged devotional expressions of the special love that every Christian must surely feel towards her who bore the divine Redeemer. Only the dangers that are all too obvious can justify the restraint that the Reformed Church has felt compelled to exercise, but which is not in itself an essential element in the Reformed tradition.

[3] Honorius wrote (Migne, *P. L.*; lxxx, 473) that 'whether it is necessary to think or say that on account of His divinity or His humanity there is one operation in Him or there are two does not interest us at all. We leave such questions to gram-

It is easy to see that the slightest tendency towards Monophysitism in christology makes it exceedingly dangerous to develop an ecclesiological theory that would make the Church in any way a 'new Incarnation' or an 'extension of the Incarnation'. Such a christology suggests to anyone engaged on such ecclesiological speculation that God and humanity are somehow mysteriously fused together in the Church; even, indeed, that the mystery of the Church consists in their fusion. It may be that the triumph of Chalcedon was not an unmixed blessing, and that, as Prestige says, 'the clumsy Occident intervened as teacher in a matter which it had not properly learned and did not really understand.'[1] But at the least Chalcedon drew attention to ways of thinking about Christ which, if pursued, emasculate the Christian religion. If these ways of thinking are pursued ecclesiologically, the results are disastrous. For if, on the one hand, with Eutyches, we deny that Christ is consubstantial with us, and then go on to think of the Church as an extension of the Incarnation, or even virtually to identify it with Him, as some have been bold enough to do,[2] we are either launching upon an

marians who sell the results of their word-games to little children'. As Père Galtier remarks (*L'Unité du Christ* (Paris, 1939), p. 278), 'the grammarians have taken their revenge: when theology falls asleep it prepares a sad awakening for the Church.' Cf. Eugene Masure (*The Christian Sacrifice* (London, 1944), p. 109): 'Monophysitism is the regular temptation of pious but ignorant people. The Christ whom they adore is, as they say, the *good God.* And they understand by that—God making more or less a semblance of being man to put himself within our reach. They do not refuse him a body, like the Docetists: this too crude form of heresy has definitely disappeared. But this body is only the historic vesture of God, who is thus visible and lives among us with all his love and intelligence; and this love and this intelligence are the eternal love, the infinite intelligence of him who bends towards his creatures in their borrowed garments. God became Incarnate. But the idea of the Incarnation does not mean a Substantive to these heedless spirits; it only brings before their eyes an adjective. . . . All the realism of Christianity has then evaporated. It is a religion without force or originality. Unfortunately it is widely spread in a diffuse form in pious writers, and it is hard to diagnose and to expel, like a subtle microbe.' Cf. also Galtier, *op. cit.*, pp. 273–87, and 'La religion du Fils' in *Revue d'Ascétique et de Mystique*, xix (1938), pp. 337–75, esp. p. 344, and J. Jungmann, *Die Stellung Christi in liturgischen Gebet* (Munster, 1925). For a penetrating criticism, in terms of official Roman doctrine, of the extremely strong Monophysite tendencies in popular eucharistic devotions in the Roman Church, cf. Moeller, 'En marge du quinzième centenaire du Concile de Chalcédoine' in *Collectanea Mechlinensia*, xxxvi (1951), p. 216 f.

[1] G. L. Prestige, *God in Patristic Thought* (London, S.P.C.K., 1952), p. 279.

[2] E.g., G. Aulén says in 'The Church in the Light of the New Testament' in *The Universal Church in God's Design* (W.C.C.) (London and New York, 1948), p. 20: 'The Church is not the Body isolated from the Head, but the Body of Christ.

ecclesiology perilously near a blasphemy from which no kenotic theory, however ingenious, can deliver us, or else we are making the Church so 'spiritual' that it does not even touch us who are accounted, in Pauline language, its members. And if, on the other hand, with Nestorius, we separate the divinity and humanity of Christ, giving to each an individuality of its own, like the individuality of two boards lightly glued together, then, far from being able to take *corpus Christi* seriously, we degrade the Church, as Lecerf puts it, 'to the level of a debating club',[1] making it, in Kierkegaard's phrase, 'finiteness from end to end.'[2]

The Church is nothing if not man's trysting-place with God, who is present in it uniquely. It is therefore also nothing if not thoroughly human. By the Holy Spirit it is given to the Church to participate in the embodiment of the divine *agape* in the Incarnate Son, and this participation is indeed its essential nature and being. The Church participates in the humanity of Christ, who is the divine *agape* outpoured for us and for our salvation. But the Church in its human nature does not and cannot hope to exhibit the perfect sinlessness of the human nature of Christ; far from it. Like Christ it has the 'form of a servant'; but its form, unlike His, is not that of a sinless servant.[3] It is proper to the Church, whose inestimable privilege it is to share in the humanity of Christ without having His sinlessness, to be not only humble, as He was, but penitent. It is not for nothing that, even as it approaches the sacred Feast of His *agape*, it says the *confiteor*. Christ who, in His humanity, joins with the Church in thanksgiving, does not utter that prayer without which the Church dare not approach the mysteries. Roman as well as other theologians recognize that there is an essential frailty in the

The Body of Christ is Christ Himself, the Risen Christ, alive and active on earth.' Similarly, A. Nygren, as quoted by E. Wahlstrom, 'A Book about the Church' in *Christendom*, xiii (1948), p. 232: 'The Body of Christ is Christ Himself. The Church is Christ as He after the resurrection is present among us and meets us here on earth.'

[1] *Supra*, p. 51.

[2] Quoted from Kierkegaard's *Efterladte Papirer* by Walter Lowrie, *Kierkegaard* (Oxford, 1938), p. 523.

[3] This distinction appears to be frequently overlooked. Cf. A. G. Hebert, *The Form of the Church* (London, 1945), p. 36 ff.

Church,[1] on its human side, that is more than, and in part other than, Christ's frailty as Man. But the implications of the distinction are not always fully drawn out. When grievous crimes are committed under the aegis of the Church, it is not enough to say that they cannot be condoned but that, since they are due to the 'human element' in the Church, and the Church is divinely instituted, it is improper for the Church to be penitent for them. That such penitence is proper to the Church is precisely what is recognized in the maxim of the Reformed tradition, *Ecclesia Reformata, semper reformanda*. Yet it is also essential to the Reformed tradition to recognize that the Church is not only the *congregatio* or *societas* gathered to wait upon its Lord. For such is the mysterious love of God that the Church is to be accounted the Body of its Lord. To say, however, that this means it is an extension of the Incarnation is to fall into an intolerable error about the Incarnation itself. It is not only that, as Niebuhr reminds us, 'the deification of the Church is spiritually dangerous, however conceived,'[2] and that we must remember that the Church 'when conceived as the body . . . remains subject to the laws of historical reality'.[3] The Church is not only not to be identified with the divine nature of Christ; it is not even to be wholly identified with His human nature. Christ, in His human frailty, stumbled under the weight of the Cross he carried to Calvary; yet His stumbling was sinless. The Church, in its human frailty, stumbles sinfully, the redemptive process notwithstanding. It is indeed the unique instrument of Christ who by means of it continues the fulfilment of the loving purpose of God. But while Christ proclaims Himself one with the Father,[4] the Church, in proclaiming Him, cries *Christe eleison*. Were the Church properly described as an incarnation of God, there

[1] Cf. P. Simon, *Das Menschliche in der Kirche Christi* (Friburg, 1936), P. Sladek, 'Gottliches und Menschliches in der Kirche. Ein Betrag zur Frage aus der Sicht des Grenzlandes' in *Theolog. Quartalsch.*, 1941, pp. 175–90; K. Adam, 'Das Problem des Geschichtlichen im Leben der Kirche' in *Theolog. Quartalsch.*, 1948, pp. 257–300; I. Fr. Gorres, 'Briefe uber die Kirche' in *Frankfurter Hefte*, 1946, pp. 715–33.

[2] R. Niebuhr, *loc. cit.*

[3] *Loc. cit.*

[4] John x. 30.

would be 'no need for it to point beyond itself to Christ—as true preaching must do'.[1] It would be *alter Christus*, which it cannot be, for He is *Filius unicus*. Besides, the Incarnation is completed; it is the redemptive process that continues.

Yet when all that is said it remains true that the Church is united to Christ in His risen Body. The members of the Church have been, in Baptism, buried with Christ, and by the Holy Spirit they have been ingrafted into His Body. We are to consider, in the next chapter, the very difficult problem of interpreting the Pauline phrase τὸ σῶμα τοῦ Χριστοῦ; but we may say now that whatever else it may mean, it means that the Church is a divine mystery. It is a mystery in itself; it is not merely the locus of our corporate encounter with the mystery of Christ. It is a mystery in that, being sinful, it is organically united to the sinless Christ. It is precisely the uniqueness of this relationship that makes it improper to speak of the Church as an extension of the Incarnation. The mystery lies in the fact that it is given to the Church to participate in the sinless humanity of the Risen Christ. The dignity of the Christian ministry is the dignity bestowed upon it in its participation in the ministry of Christ. The voice of the Reformed tradition is unanimous in repudiating both the notion that at some point or other the Church's ministry is simply to be identified with Christ's ministry and the notion that it is a human, though hallowed, activity entirely separate from the ministry of Christ. The doctrine here stressed in the Reformed tradition cannot be understood apart from the context of the Biblical idea of 'headship', of which we must constantly remind ourselves when we refer to the *corpus Christi* figure. It is proper to call the Church the Body only because the relation between Head and Body is such that the Head is to be

[1] J. E. Lesslie Newbigin, *The Reunion of the Church* (London, 1948), p. 61. The same writer elsewhere complains (*The Household of God: Lectures on the Nature of the Church* (London, 1953), p. 83) that one verse of Neale's hymn, 'Christ is gone up' (*English Hymnal*, 166), sung on Ember Days, makes the Church seem 'to have become a purely historical institution, the trustee of an absent landlord':

'So age by age, and year by year,
His grace was handed on;
And still the holy Church is here,
Although her Lord is gone.'

conceived, in characteristically oriental fashion, as Master and Lord, not merely as one part of the organic whole of which the Body is another part. The figure of the Body is proper for the Church because the Body comprises the movement, which is the Church's ministry, received from the Head and then returned to the Head. The Body is the 'slave' (δοῦλος) of the Head, yet it is enslaved by love. Every member of the Body is called upon to surrender himself in love *within* the Body, yet *to* the Head. Christ's authority is not delegated to anyone; it is submitted to by all corporately. The corporate ministry of the Church speaks indeed by His authority, but in speaking it says, not 'I say' or 'We say', but 'Thus saith the Lord'. Nevertheless, in uttering such words according to the old prophetic formula, the ministry of the Church makes proclamation for and to the Church, which, in virtue of the gift of the Holy Spirit, shares in the ministry of Christ himself. The Church's ministry is indefinable by analogy with any human service because it is unique, being the ministry within the unique instrument that is the Church.

This uniqueness of the Church had been recognized in some measure by the later medieval canonists who endeavoured to apply the proctorial principle. Wyclif had likewise perceived, in his own way, when he repudiated the concept of *dominium*, the uniqueness of the Christian ministry. The dignity of the individual minister is not taken away with the loss of *dominium*; on the contrary, the loss of *dominium* restores the minister's unique dignity. For this is neither the dignity that springs from popular acclamation nor that which is conferred upon the officer of a great institution when he receives his commission. The Christian minister receives more than such a commission and much more than popular acclamation. The authority with which he is invested is likewise unparalleled, proceeding neither from rank nor from election. Yet it does not come from God directly to the individual minister, after the manner in which, we are to suppose, an angel receives a divine commission. That which gives the Christian minister his unique dignity and unparalleled authority is that he *shares* or *participates* in the corporate ministry within the living Body that is united to the living Christ Himself.

The uniqueness can never be said to lie in anything that the Church may be said to 'have', but must be said to reside only in what it *is*. That is to say, it is always misleading to speak of the Church as 'having' a ministry and sacraments, of 'having' the apostolic succession, of 'having' the Word. For no possession can give it the uniqueness that distinguishes it from all other societies. The uniqueness of the Church is seen, not when it is presented as having sacraments, but when it confronts us as the eucharistic *koinōnia*; not when it is said to possess a ministry, but when it is proclaimed to be a ministry; not when it seems to uphold its claim to have this or that kind of succession, but when its continuity is such as to exhibit its apostolicity. The marks of the Church are exhibited in its function rather than in its possession. There is indeed a visible continuity in the Church, for it is entirely repugnant to the Reformed tradition to suppose that Churches may spring up in separation from the historic Church. But the visible, earthly continuity that the Church manifests is a continuity of function. So the *esse* and the *bene esse* of the Church must be determined by function, not by possession, for the Church has no possessions, as its ministers have no *dominium*. The marks of the Church, according to the Reformed tradition, are commonly said to be: Word, Sacrament and Discipline; but more strictly, they are: the proclamation of the Word, the administration of the Sacraments, the exercise of Discipline. The Reformed Church should not think of itself as having or not having this or that kind of officer; it should think of itself as exercising a corporate episcopate through the ministry that is gifted to it. To the extent that the individual minister is but the mouthpiece of a people, or but the delegate of another minister, or only a member of a sort of committee of presbyters, each only *representing* the presbytery as a partner represents a partnership, his ministry has been defiled; it has become describable in terms of analogies with other human institutions such as an army or a committee of the House of Commons. According to the Reformed tradition, there are, strictly speaking, no individual ministers, but, rather, individuals within the Church whose unique privilege it is to *participate* in the corporate ministry of Christ, the only Head of the Church.

CHAPTER IX

THE BODY OF CHRIST

The Pauline use of the phrase 'the Body of Christ' (τὸ σῶμα τοῦ Χριστοῦ) is crucial. The phrase is used both of the Eucharist and of the Church, and in several of the epistles.[1] The exegesis is difficult: while the phrase is plainly figurative, it is not at all clear precisely what kind of figure it is. Nor is it by any means clear whether the use of the phrase in regard to the Eucharist has little or much or nothing or everything to do with its use in reference to the Church. Modern scholars have rightly considered the phrase to require the most careful analysis, for the theological and ecclesiological consequences of its interpretation are far-reaching.

The English word 'body' has several commonplace meanings, including, for example, 'corpse' and 'living person' (as in the pronoun 'everybody') as well as 'body' in the even more ordinary, physiological sense. All these meanings were present in the Greek word σῶμα. This word could also mean 'slave', and it was used figuratively to illustrate the organic principle. For instance, Plato, in the *Republic*, makes Glaucon admit to Socrates that the best ordered State is like a σῶμα: 'when but a finger of one of us is hurt, the whole frame' feels the pain of it.[2] Lacey thinks that Paul may have had in mind, in his use of the phrase, something 'drawn from Stoicism but transfigured. For the Stoics, the whole universe was a living thing, a Body, the life or spirit of which was God—God exclusively immanent, without any transcendence. But into the Church are poured spiritual *charismata* from Beyond, the gift of the transcendent God'.[3] The notion that the

[1] E.g., Rom. xii. 5; 1 Cor. x. 16; xii. 27; Eph. iv. 12; Col. ii. 17.
[2] *Republic*, V, 462.
[3] T. A. Lacey, *The One Body and the One Spirit*, p. 56 f.

whole universe was living and breathing like a vast body is very ancient, being found in the Vedas, and it passed into Gnostic mythology, for example, in the Anthropos myth, in which the deity descends to earth and accomplishes human salvation by assimilating the human race into his body, so bearing it heavenwards. Loisy, Bultmann, and other scholars have argued for the influence of Gnostic ideas on the mind of St Paul.[1]

It has for long been well known that Gnostic ideas were very pervasive in the time of St Paul, and that occultism from the east spread to the Hellenic world, influencing not only the adherents of the mystery religions but the general climate of thought about religion and philosophy. Some decades ago[2] there was a general tendency among scholars to look, therefore, to such ideas for the explanation of the manner in which Christian practices took shape. That these methods were carried too far and their results often much exaggerated is now widely admitted. There is also a fuller appreciation by many of the importance of a more profound study of the Hebrew background of Christianity, not least as this was developed in the mind of the Cilician Jew who became the great Apostle of Christ to the Gentiles. For however estranged a Jew in the Hellenistic world might seem to be from the old currents of Hebrew thought, these were still exceedingly powerful influences on his mind. The Hellenistic Jew maintained a close association with Jerusalem, paying his annual subscription of two drachmae, and visiting, if possible, the temple within which he could feel himself invested with exclusive privilege. Paul was indubitably very Jewish in his thinking, reckoning his journeys as a Christian missionary according to the Jewish calendar,[3] frequently boasting of his Jewish ancestry,[4] of his descent from the tribe of Benjamin,[5] and ex-

[1] A. Loisy, *The Birth of the Christian Religion*, p. 289; Rudolf Bultmann, *Theologie des Neuen Testaments*, i (Tubingen, 1948), p. 178; cf. Heinrich Schlier, *Christus und die Kirche im Epheserbrief* (Tubingen, 1930), p. 39; Otto Michel, *Das Zeugnis des Neuen Testaments von der Gemeinde* (Gottingen, 1941), p. 46 ff.

[2] *Infra*, p. 163, n. 4.

[3] 1 Cor. xvi. 8; cf. Acts xxvii. 9.

[4] Rom. iv. 1, 16; ix. 10; xi. 1; 1 Cor. x. 1; 2 Cor. xi. 22; Gal. vi. 16; Philipp. iii. 5.

[5] Philipp. iii. 5.

pressing his love for his brother-Jews whom he calls his kinsmen *κατὰ σάρκα*.[1]

On the other hand, it is well known that Hellenic ideas had profoundly affected Hellenistic Judaism. St Paul's predilection for allegorical interpretation of the Septuagint, for instance, was not a traditionally Jewish attitude; it was an attitude borrowed by Jews from the Hellenistic world in which allegorical interpretation had become fashionable among those who felt, preciously perhaps, in some cases, that their old literature was disfigured by primitive religious ideas repugnant to the cultivated taste of the day. There were many besides the learned Philo to whom the allegorical method had opened up seemingly unbounded possibilities.[2] The extent of Paul's debt to Philo is not easy to determine; what is certain is that both men, different though they were in background, temperament and inclination, were Hellenistic Jews faced with similar cultural problems. While they shared a common heritage, their interests were different; yet their methods were circumscribed by the limitations of their age. By modern standards, even Philo's use of the allegorical method is often undiscriminating. There was, in his day, no brake upon the use of such a method, no rigorous distinction drawn between one sort of metaphor and another. There was no Russell or Tarski to restrain speculative philosophers from extravagances; no theory of 'types' or of 'levels' of language to caution or dispirit the imaginative. The modern reader of St Paul, a less learned man than Philo, must be vigilant, therefore, lest he read into his use of figurative language a kind of precision that could not possibly be there.

It should be emphasized, moreover, that although, in Stoic, Gnostic and rabbinic literature, examples may be found to show the use of the word *σῶμα* in the sense of 'a body of people' or 'a society of people', the word did not readily conjure up any such notion.[3] It appears to have been very much less common than is

[1] Rom. ix. 3.
[2] Cf. G. Klein, *Der alteste christliche Katechismus und die judische Propaganda-Literatur* (Berlin, 1909), p. 42 f.
[3] Cf. J. A. T. Robinson, *The Body* (London, 1952), p. 50.

the case with the modern English word 'body', so that the use of *σῶμα* in this sense probably seemed far-fetched to those who encountered it in these writings. In any case, what is striking in the phrase under consideration here does not lie so much in the metaphorical use of the word *σῶμα*; it lies, rather, in the conjunction of this with the genitive *τοῦ Χριστοῦ*. It is not as though St Paul had used a phrase such as *τὸ σῶμα τῶν Ἑλληνικῶν* where, say, Herodotus would have used *τὸ Ἑλληνικόν*, to designate the body of the Greek people.

There is, indeed, another and perhaps far more dangerous pitfall for the modern interpreter of St Paul. We may appreciate the complex influences at work in his mind, the rabbinic lore, the echoes of occult speculation, what might even be a Philonic allegorizing of the Septuagint, and so forth, estimating also with judicious care the various aspects of his complex personality, his volcanic power as a preacher, his wide range of human experience, the reflective turn of his mind. Yet we shall certainly fail to understand his figurative language unless we keep before us that which had transformed his life and thought, his awareness of encounter with the Risen Christ: 'He was seen of me also.'[1] Every student of Gnosticism knows that the vast range of eclectic tendencies in the ancient world that are gathered up under this convenient term are baffling in their diversity and at least as insusceptible to rigorous classification as are modern forms of theosophy. Nevertheless, the Gnostics did have one common notion: whatever a Gnostic teacher taught his pupil, he purported to teach him *gnosis*, and the man who sought to acquire such *gnosis* went about his task as one who seeks to *lay hold* of esoteric knowledge. St Paul indicates that he shared in the fashionable longing to unravel the hidden mysteries of the universe; but it is not out of this quest that his transforming experience sprang. It sprang, rather, from an experience quite alien to the presuppositions of the fashionable quest. Paul did not lay hold of what he sought; Christ laid hold of him.[2] He has

[1] 1 Cor. xv. 8: *ὤφθη κἀμοί*.

[2] Philipp. iii. 12: *κατελήφθην ὑπὸ Χριστοῦ Ἰησοῦ*. (*καταλαμβάνω* means to catch, capture, seize, lay hold of, surprise, arrest; cf. Mark ix. 18; Rom. ix. 30; 1 Cor. ix.

no interest, thereafter, in figurative language to delineate the religious quests of the Hellenic world; his interest in allegorical language now lies in its possibilities in helping him to communicate experiences of this kind. However we are to interpret *σῶμα Χριστοῦ*, let us bear in mind that Paul is describing what he takes to be a unique, living reality, and that this consideration is more important for an understanding of his meaning than anything, however interesting, that we may discover by way of echoes from a complex background.

It is impossible to prove that Paul was not influenced by Gnostic notions such as the Anthropos myth; but even if it were possible to show conclusively that he was, it is likely that the result would be less important than some scholars have seemed to suppose it would be.[1] In any case, it is highly improbable that any such notion was dominant in Paul's mind. For Paul did not have to go further than the Hebrew ways of thought that were dear and familiar to him to find inspiration in describing, in terms of a body, the reality he wanted to describe. The Hebrews found it quite natural to express the notion of a whole people in terms of one man. We need not refer to anything so difficult or controversial as the figure of the Suffering Servant. Adam was the human race; Abraham was the people of God. The notion preserved in modern times as a legal fiction in the English courts, in which criminals are sued by the Queen, was a commonplace in Hebrew thought: Moses was not merely the revered, ancient lawgiver; he was the manifestation of Yahweh's demands upon the chosen people. He personified the race, as the Crown, in English legal theory, still personifies the State. So there was, in principle, no difficulty for either Paul or his Jewish hearers in concluding that Christ embodies the people of Christ, who are consequently His Body.[2] One of the central contrasts in

24. It also means to overtake; cf. John i. 5; xii. 35; 1 Thess. v. 4. In mid. aorist it may be used in the sense of grasping with the intellect, as in German *begriffen*.)

[1] The interpretation of *σῶμα Χριστοῦ* in terms of the Anthropos myth has been rejected by many scholars, e.g., H. Kohnlein, 'La notion de l'Eglise chez l'Apôtre Paul' in *Revue d'histoire et de philosophie religieuses*, xvii (1937), p. 364 f.

[2] Cf. Stig Hanson, *The Unity of the Church in the New Testament* (Uppsala, 1949), p. 68 ff.; J. Knox, *Christ the Lord* (New York, 1945), p. 120 ff.

Paul's mind was that of Adam and Christ: mankind is typified by Adam; redeemed mankind is typified by Christ, the second Adam.[1]

It is usual to stress the fact that while it seemed to come naturally to the Greek mind to follow Pythagoras in placing the body, as 'matter', on the bad side of the dualistic inventory, the Hebrews, seeing the human body as the handiwork of the Creator, regarded it as good, and that this constitutes a sharp cleavage between Hellenic and Hebraic ways of thought. It is to be noted, however, that there were differences of rabbinic opinion about the relation of body and soul. In general, the body was not regarded as impure; yet it was sometimes called impure in contrast to the soul.[2] It is true that the Hebrews commonly regarded the soul and the body as inseparable.[3] Body and soul are alike responsible for deeds committed. Aaron ben Elijah bases his argument in favour of resurrection on this joint responsibility.[4] It was also held that the body, having been once the temple or tabernacle of the soul, is to be respected after death, and that the bodies of the risen are reproductions of those that they tenanted while living, so that cripples, for instance, rise with their deformity. The importance of the notion of the human body in Hebrew thought is also illustrated in the curious legend that an almost shapeless body (*golem*) came from the Creator's hand, and that of this body, which was bisexual and two-faced, man now retains, in his nails, a vestige of an original coat of light.[5] The number of his bones and nerves were even computed to correspond with the number of the commandments and prohibitions of the law respectively.[6] Not least striking is the notion that the dust of which Adam's body was formed came from all parts of the world: his trunk, for instance, according to R. Oshiah, came from Babylon, his limbs from various other lands,

[1] Cf. Rom. v. 12 ff.; 1 Cor. xv. 22, 45.

[2] Mek. Beshallah, *Shirah*, 2; cf. *Sanhedrin*, xi, 91 a–b.

[3] Cf. R. Bultmann, *Theologie des Neuen Testaments*, p. 189; also W. Gutbrod, *Die paulinische Anthropologie* (Stuttgart, 1934).

[4] *Ez Hayyim*, cxii.

[5] *Rashi*, *Gen.*, ii, 21.

[6] *Targum Yer.*, *Gen.*, i, 27.

and his head, being the most exalted part, came from the most exalted land, *Eretz Yisrael*, before these various contributions were kneaded into a rough shape.[1]

All this seems to support the view of Hanson and others who think the *σῶμα Χριστοῦ* figure is an expression of Jewish thought rather than Hellenic or Oriental notions.[2] The human body was, for the Jew, an 'earthy' conception; yet into it was infused a soul, and both body and soul were alike the work of the Creator. Gathered from the ends of the earth, it had within itself the principle of universality. From such ideas it was not a far cry to the notion that the Church, the new creation, is the Body of Christ. Besides, such a way of looking at the question, while thoroughly Hebrew, need not have been entirely repugnant to Gnostic ideas that might have been, more vaguely and remotely, in the mind of St Paul.

The phrase *τὸ σῶμα τοῦ Χριστοῦ* is used also of the Eucharist by St Paul,[3] and in interpreting the relation—a controversial question for some modern scholars—between the use of the phrase to denote the Eucharist and the use of the phrase to denote the Church, the background we have just delineated is peculiarly relevant. We have stressed the fact that, however Paul's thinking may have been moulded, his purpose is clear: the description of what he took to be living reality. It is not perhaps inconceivable, though detailed exegesis would make it a difficult thesis to maintain, that there was no more than a vague connection in Paul's mind between the two uses of the phrase. An appreciation of the Hebraic mould of Paul's thought would seem, however, to undermine if not entirely destroy the plausibility of such an opinion. The Judaism that Paul knew was profoundly sacramentarian.[4] There was no need for him to import

[1] *Sanhedrin*, IV, 38 a–b: we are even told that R. Joḥanan b. Hanina computes the exact time of each operation—the first hour of the day of Adam's creation, for instance, was occupied by the gathering of the dust; the second by the kneading into the shapeless mass; the third by the process of extending the limbs; and so forth.

[2] Cf. also F. Gavin, *The Jewish Antecedents of the Christian Sacraments* (London 1928), esp. the first lecture.

[3] E.g., 1 Cor. x. 16.

[4] Cf. F. Gavin, *op. cit.* Charles Gore (*The Holy Spirit and the Church* (London, 1924), p. 92) had denied this, perhaps through an insufficiently critical reading of Bousset

into Christian doctrine or practice any novel interpretation of the Last Supper or of its relation to the Death of Christ. At the Last Supper, Christ had invested the familiar Jewish *chabūrah* with new meaning. This *chabūrah* was the ancestor of both Eucharist and Agape,[1] and whatever else these meant for Paul, they had Christ as their centre. He asks: 'The bread which we break, is it not the κοινωνία of the body of Christ?'[2] It is generally agreed that κοινωνία, though it has several shades of meaning, fundamentally implies participation: to have κοινωνία is to have a share with others *in* something.[3] Etymologically, the English word 'fellowship' is in a similar case; but the senses in which it is now most generally used in modern English are so different from that which is primarily conveyed by the word κοινωνία in the New Testament that it seems to the present writer to be a peculiarly unfortunate rendering of the Greek term. It suggests 'convention' rather than 'participation'.[4]

This is not to say that there are no intrinsic difficulties in interpreting the word κοινωνία in the New Testament. It may be, however, that the difficulties are exaggerated when scholars neglect to keep in view the New Testament preoccupation with an object that stands outside and is independent of the κοινωνία.

and Reitzenstein, who had played leading roles in the growth of the *Religionsgeschichtliche Schule* which, under Hegelian influence, had adpted the historical methods of von Ranke and Mommsen to a study of Christian origins and had concluded with theories that displayed imagination rather than insight into the nature of religions in general and Christianity in particular.

[1] The Greek term εὐχαριστία, in the sacramental sense, translates the Hebrew *berakah*, while ἀγάπη, in the sense of the love-feast which originally accompanied the Eucharist, translates the Hebrew *chabūrah.* At what point the separation of Eucharist from Agape took place has not been determined with certainty or precision. Ignatius (*ad. Smyrn.*, viii) writes as though he were distinguishing them in such a way as to indicate that they had in fact become separate, and it is probable that before that date (*circa* A.D. 115) they had already been separated for a considerable time.

[2] 1 Cor. x. 16.

[3] Cf. J. Y. Campbell, 'Koinōnia and Its Cognates in the New Testament' in *Journal of Biblical Literature*, li (1932), p. 353 ff.

[4] The German *Gemeinschaft* is, of course, in much the same case; nor does *gemeinsames Anteilhaben*, suggested by H. Seesemann (*Der Begriff Koinōnia* im Neuen Testament (Giessen, 1933), p. 87 ff.), convey the meaning. How remote is the modern English word 'fellowship' from the New Testament may be illustrated by the fact that the best one can do with it in French is to render it 'communion', suggesting a vague similarity of feeling, or 'communauté', suggesting joint possession, while the primary French equivalent is 'camaraderie'! The lovelessness of modern individualism is one of the principal difficulties in translating the Bible into modern speech.

For instance, the writer of Acts relates how the Christians persevered in the doctrine of the apostles and in the *κοινωνία*, and in the breaking of the bread, and in the prayers.[1] It has been held by some[2] that the *κοινωνία* is participation in the Eucharist. The Vulgate, indeed, renders the phrase so as to attach the participation to the breaking of the bread.[3] It is difficult to see how this interpretation may be sustained: the Greek text does not warrant it. The passage is obscure in the sense that the object of the participation is not specified; but is the obscurity as great as it appears? The fact that the object is omitted draws attention, once again, to the fact that the New Testament writers were describing what they took to be a living reality. It is left open to us to speculate, with the help of such exegetical techniques as may be at our disposal, whether we are to say, for instance, that it is a participation in the Spirit that is intended,[4] or that the writer was thinking, rather, of some other aspect of the living reality. To ask whether such a writer was thinking of the Spirit or of the Eucharist or of the Risen Christ or in some other terms, seems important only in detachment from the reality that the writer knew. We do not inquire, surely, to whom the prayers of which he speaks were addressed: why should not we be content with the notion of participation, though he does not specify the object, accepting the view that he left the object unspecified because of its vivacity in his mind?

We now return to the question of the relationship between Eucharist and Church in the Pauline passages on the Eucharist. George Johnston, writing on the phrase 'discerning the Lord's Body',[5] observes that some commentators see a connection with the Church, others repudiate this, while others again do not seem even to take into account the possibility that *σῶμα* may

[1] Acts ii. 42: *τῇ διδαχῇ τῶν ἀποστόλων καὶ τῇ κοινωνίᾳ, τῇ κλάσει τοῦ ἄρτου καὶ ταῖς προσευχαῖς*

[2] Notably by C. H. Dodd, a weighty authority in such matters, in *The Johannine Epistles* (London, 1946), p. 7. But he does not there produce evidence for the view; nor is the writer acquainted with any defence of it that he makes elsewhere.

[3] 'Erant autem perseverantes in doctrina apostolorum, et communicatione fractionis panis, et orationibus.'

[4] Cf. Philipp. ii. 1.

[5] 1 Cor. xi. 29.

refer to the Church.[1] One might argue similarly about the phrase τοῦ σώματος τοῦ Χριστοῦ.[2] But surely St Paul is looking at a total reality without binding himself exclusively to the one aspect of it that is foremost in his mind in this or that use of the phrase. Throughout the whole passage under consideration,[3] Paul's mind seems to flit from one aspect of the reality to the other in his use of the crucial phrase. The human body has many parts; each is separate, yet all are one—'so also is Christ.'[4] In conclusion, Paul reminds his readers that they are 'the Body of Christ and individually members of it'.[5] As they participate in the Eucharist, so they participate in the Church: the patristic Church rightly understood St Paul when in it, as Gregory Dix puts it, 'the twin realities of the church and the sacrament as Body of Christ were inseparably connected, and were regarded in a sense as cause and effect.'[6] Dix remarks on what he calls the 'curious "reversibility" ' of these realities in the thought of the Fathers. 'Sometimes (and perhaps this is on the whole commoner in pre-Nicene writers),' he says, 'the sacrament becomes the Body of Christ *because* it is offered by the church which is the Body of Christ. Sometimes, as in S. Augustine, the church is the Body of Christ *because* it receives the sacrament which is His Body. Both ideas are true, and both go back to S. Paul in 1 Cor. for their starting-point.'[7]

The notion of participation in an object is further brought out in Paul's charge to the Corinthians to abstain from fornication with harlots.[8] It is plain that in enjoining them to 'flee

[1] *The Doctrine of the Church in the New Testament* (Cambridge, 1943), p. 90: 'Johannes Weiss rejects the interpretation given of μὴ διακρίνων τὸ σῶμα in 1 Cor. xi. 29 as referring to the Church; but it seems justified by the use of ἓν σῶμα in 1 Cor. x. 17 and especially by the whole' context. Johnston cites Moffat, Anderson Scott, Stanley, as favouring this view, and Goudge, Robertson, Plummer, as well as Weiss, as rejecting it.

[2] 1 Cor. x. 16.

[3] 1 Cor. x, xi, xii.

[4] 1 Cor. xii. 12. Cf. the rabbinic notion of the number of the bones corresponding to the number of the commandments of the law, *supra*, p. 162. Christ is the fulfilment, completion of the law. Cf. Rom. vii. 4.

[5] 1 Cor. xii. 27.

[6] Gregory Dix, *The Shape of the Liturgy* (*ed. cit.*), p. 251.

[7] *Loc. cit.*, n. 1.

[8] 1 Cor. vi. 15.

fornication' he is reminding them that they who participate in the Body of Christ must not 'participate in' a harlot. For *κοινωνία* had also a base sense: it meant coition.[1] There can be little doubt that this would be in St Paul's view as he reminded the Corinthians that 'he which is joined to an harlot is one body' with her.[2] The notion is peculiarly abhorrent, since in Hebrew thought body and soul are inseparable, so that the question may be put thus: shall he who fully participates in Christ allow himself so to participate in a prostitute?

The technical problem of the authorship of Ephesians and Colossians is one that need not be discussed here. Their genuineness is doubtful; but they are thoroughly Pauline in tone, and in both of these letters the figure of the Body of Christ is elaborated in such a way as to provide a basis for an ecclesiology.[3] Christ is declared to be the head of the Church that is His Body.[4] Here also is a basis for the principle that has been repeatedly urged in the present study, that christology and ecclesiology are interdependent. The interpretation of the figure, as this is elaborated in these letters, is, however, by no means simple.

In recent and contemporary discussions the question is often raised in the form: is the phrase *τὸ σῶμα τοῦ Χριστοῦ* to be taken literally or metaphorically?[5] This is surely in principle a very misleading antithesis, and it would in any case be absurd to suggest that the 'Head and Body' figure is to be taken 'literally'. Certainly not even the most intrepid exponent of the Church as the incarnation of Christ would be able so to take it. And if the 'Head and Body' figure is not to be taken 'literally', what would it mean to say that the phrase 'the Body of Christ' is to be so taken? We are not faced with an alternative, as often seems to

[1] E.g., Euripides, *Bacchæ*, 1277: *ἐμῇ τε καὶ πατρὸς κοινωνίᾳ*

[2] I Cor. vi. 16.

[3] Eph. i. 23; ii. 16; iii. 6; iv. 4, 12; Coloss. i. 18, 24; ii. 9, 19; iii. 15.

[4] Eph. i. 22; iv. 15; v. 23; Coloss. i. 18; ii. 19.

[5] E.g., B. S. Easton ('The Church in the New Testament' in *Anglican Theological Review*, xxii (1940), p. 166) writes: 'The "Body", therefore, is nothing less than the veritable Body of Christ, in which He lives and through which He acts on this earth.' Brunner, on the other hand, says (*The Divine Imperative* (London, 1937), p. 300) that the Body of Christ is 'only a simile, it is not an organic principle'. Johnston (*op. cit.*, p. 93) says: 'There is no need to look for literal realities in the presentation of the doctrine. If only dimly, we perceive the adoring wonder of the thought.'

be suggested in modern discussions, of taking this language 'literally' or treating it as but one of the several metaphors used of the Church, such as 'bride' and 'building' and 'household'. The question that should confront us is, rather: is the figurative language here used, especially in Ephesians and Colossians, of the same kind as the figurative language used elsewhere? Is the figure perhaps even of the same kind as that of the 'ship' of later symbolism?

When the Church is likened to a building or a ship, attention is drawn to an aspect of the Church's function. Such language is not radically different from the language used, for instance, of Mary in the Litany of the Virgin: she is a house of gold, a tower of ivory. Metaphors of this sort abound in ordinary literature and there is nothing very remarkable about them. They are designed to call attention to a poetic aspect of the situation that the reader might overlook. It is otherwise when the figure is intended to describe an ontological reality, as when theologians speak, for instance, of the processions in the Trinity or of the begetting of the Son by the Father. To say that God 'reigns on high' is to speak figuratively; for reigning is a human activity, and height is but another figure to express a value-judgment. Yet language of this kind is very different from the language employed by Cowper when he says of God that 'He plants His footsteps in the sea and rides upon the storm'. Metaphysical and theological concepts, if they are to be expressed at all, must be expressed in metaphorical language; but the metaphors become what have been called 'root' metaphors;[1] they are to be distinguished from the more ephemeral figures of speech that every poetic imagination is continually creating. The phrase *τὸ σῶμα τοῦ Χριστοῦ*, however it is to be interpreted, must be understood in its relation to other fundamental metaphors. It depends, for instance, on a connection with the ancient Hebrew figure according to which the spirit of a man is his breath (*ruaḥ*). The Breath of God comes as a rushing mighty wind.[2] It fills the Body

[1] Cf. S. C. Pepper, 'The Root Metaphor Theory of Metaphysics' in *Journal of Philosophy*, XXXII, July 4, 1935.

[2] Acts II. 2.

of Christ. It is poured out upon the Gentiles,[1] for since it is associated in ancient Hebrew thought with the seed,[2] the notion of 'outpouring' is in character with the figure. The figure σῶμα Χριστοῦ fits into the language already in use for the description of ontological realities. The nature of the Church is ἀγάπη: it is so united with Christ that it is filled to overflowing with the divine love. This ἀγάπη is not a quality, merely, such as 'redness' or 'courage': it is itself an ontological reality. God is love, and only by being 'rooted and grounded in love' can we be 'filled with all the fulness of God'.[3] The being of the Church is grounded upon the ontological reality of the divine love that 'flows into' it and 'fills' it.

The significance of the σῶμα Χριστοῦ figure may be more fully appreciated by a reference to what it is not. Neither is it a casual poetic figure, an element in a myth in the dyslogistic sense, nor yet can it be a religious symbol the historical or temporal element in which is in exactly the same case as, say, the Cross. One cannot point to the Body of Christ in the same way in which one might conceivably have pointed to the chief instrument of the Passion, saying, 'Behold the very Cross on which Christ died for us men and for our salvation.' But this is not to say, in the manner of the Symbolo-Fideists, that 'the Body of Christ' has a moral significance only. It has a sacramental significance, for it draws attention to the fact that the Church is, indeed, the 'total' Sacrament. Hence the inseparability of the phrase σῶμα Χριστοῦ as applied to the Eucharist and as applied to the Church. Neither can the visible Church nor the visible elements of the Eucharist be identified with the Body of Christ *simpliciter*; yet both are static, visible aspects of the dynamic, ontological reality that is the Christian Church. If the predicate of fatherhood may be applied to God *per analogiam*, it follows that we may be accounted, however unworthily, His children.

[1] Acts x. 45.

[2] Isaiah lxiv. 3.

[3] Eph. iii. 17, 19. Cf. Goodspeed's translation: 'the indisputable head of the church, which is his body, filled by him who fills everything everywhere.' Cf. also Hanson, *op. cit.*, p. 129; Thornton, *The Common Life in the Body of Christ* (London, 1942), p. 306.

The Lordship of Christ is expressed in acclaiming Him the Head; whence it follows that they who have been united to Him in His Church form His Body. The Incarnation does indeed point to a special ground for the metaphor, since it makes it possible for us to ally the figure of the Body as an ontological reality to the ontological reality of the Risen Body of Christ, so that, by reason of the divine action, the figure acquires a peculiar appositeness for us. On the other hand, metaphors such as 'Father' and 'Logos' remain metaphysical and abstract in the sense that they are predicated of a divine reality to which we finite beings cannot be united as we are to Christ as Head of the Church.

Again, it is plain that the *σῶμα Χριστοῦ* figure is of a different character from figures such as the quaint metaphor used by Bradford of the Holy Ghost who, wrote that English divine, 'shadoweth and sitteth' upon the Church 'to hatch and cherish it, as a hen her chickens'.[1] This fanciful, poetic extension of the figure of the brooding Dove may be picturesque and didactic. It has, however, no direct connection with the *σῶμα Χριστοῦ* figure, which is grounded in a metaphysics, essentially Hebrew, that appears to have been what Urban called an 'organicist' theory of reality.[2] In contradistinction to, say, an idealist metaphysics, which uses the category of mind metaphorically, the metaphysics of St Paul expresses itself in the metaphorical use of the category of life: it uses organic metaphors in expressing its fundamental[3] concepts. The *σῶμα Χριστοῦ* figure belongs to the 'categorial scheme' of Hebrew thought. When Bradford refers, on the other hand, to the Church 'partaking' of Christ,[4] he is, of course, returning to that 'categorial scheme'.

The same 'categorial scheme' appears to be the context of the thought in a difficult passage in Colossians.[5] The writer of the epistle, exhorting the Colossians to constancy in Christ, charges them not to allow themselves to be judged in terms of

[1] J. Bradford, *Sermons* (Parker Society), p. 146.

[2] W. M. Urban, *Language and Reality* (New York, Macmillan, 1939), p. 658.

[3] Urban uses the term 'fundamental metaphor' in preference to Pepper's use of 'root metaphor'; but the notion is very similar.

[4] *Loc. cit.*

[5] Coloss. ii. 16 f.

the observance of dietary rules or the keeping of holy days and the like, for such matters, he says, are but 'a shadow of things to come; but the body is of Christ' (*ἅ ἐστι σκιὰ τῶν μελλόντων, τὸ δὲ σῶμα τοῦ Χριστοῦ*).[1] Calvin and others took *σκιά* to mean 'a sketch' as distinguished from 'a picture'. But *σκιά* is not contrasted with a picture; it is contrasted with a body. The *σκιά* is surely to be related directly to the *σῶμα*. It is the unsubstantial image, the shadow, of the living Body of Christ. Observances such as those mentioned are in themselves lifeless; yet they typify, in their way, the 'shape' of the living Body. Dependent for their meaning upon the life that is their source, they are as the shadow that is cast by the Body. The shadow precedes the Body in the sense that the eye first rests upon it, and it does indeed present the beholder with some notion of the 'shape'; but as the eye is then raised to the living Body itself, the shadow is seen for what it is worth and is to be forgotten in the encounter with the living Body whose life-principle is the Spirit of God and whose Head is Christ. False teachers talk of angels: in encouraging the worship of these they may impress those who are easily taken in by talk of this kind, which they suppose betokens religious humility and what people nowadays might call a 'spiritual outlook'.[2] But no one need be deceived who is truly ingrafted into the Body of Christ, whose ligaments (*σύνδεσμα*) are connected together and are together directly dependent upon the Head.[3] To those who know only the shadow, the talk of such false teachers sounds lofty and uplifting; but that is because they do not enjoy *κοινωνία* in the Body of Christ. To those who are in fact within the Body of Christ, all talk of that kind, with its pretensions to esoteric *γνῶσις* and its affectation of humility, can sound only empty chatter.

The figure of the Body of Christ is used of the Church by several early Christian writers. Methodius says that 'it will be most certainly agreed that the Church is formed out of His bones and flesh'.[4] Origen reports that 'the holy Scriptures declare the Body of Christ, animated by the Son of God, to be the whole

[1] Coloss. ii. 17. [2] Coloss. ii. 18. [3] Coloss. ii. 19. [4] Methodius, *Symposium*, iii. 8.

Church of God and the members of this Body—considered as a whole—to consist of those who are believers; for, as a soul vivifies and moves the body, which of itself has not the natural power of motion as has a living body, so the Word, arousing and moving the whole Body, the Church, to befitting action, awakens, moreover, each individual member belonging to the Church, so that they do nothing apart from the Word'.[1] The most remarkable use and development of the notion among the early writers, however, is to be found in Ignatius of Antioch who, alone among the Apostolic Fathers, uses the term ἕνωσις[2] (union), applying it to various relations, including the relation between Christ and His Church.

Ignatius takes ἕνωσις to be a fundamental principle in the whole redemptive process. Reflecting in some way the union between Christ and the Father,[3] it is at the heart of the Church's life. When Ignatius says that wherever Christ is, there is the Catholic Church,[4] it is plain that he is not merely defining the Catholic Church as the company of those who truly follow Him: Christ and His Church are quite inseparable. Christ is said to be the Head of the Church in the sense that 'the head cannot be born without members, since God promises union, that is, Himself'.[5] It is by the Cross that Christ 'calls you through His Passion, as being His members'.[6] Apparently Ignatius thinks of the union between Christ and the Church as having its beginning when the eternal Logos united itself to flesh,[7] and that this union was consummated through the Death and Resurrection of Christ. By Christ's Death and Resurrection the baptized are united to Christ through the Church, which participates in the divine πλήρωμα and may therefore be said to be 'filled with God'.[8] God is, indeed, called ἕνωσις.[9]

[1] Origen, *Cels.*, vi, 48.
[2] Ignatius, *Magn.*, 12, 13; *Phild.*, 4, 7, 8; *Polc.*, 1, *Trall.*, 11.
[3] *Magn.*, 7, 13; *Smyrn*, 3. Cf. John x. 30.
[4] *Smyrn.*, 8. Ignatius is the first Christian writer to use the phrase ἡ καθολικὴ ἐκκλησία.
[5] *Trall.*, 11. Cf. Clem. Alex., *Stromata*, iv, 23. [6] *Loc. cit.*
[7] Cf. 2 *Clem.* xiv. 1 f. For discussion of Gnostic influence on Ignatius, such as is apparent here, cf. A. Hilgenfeld, *Die Apostolischen Vater*, p. 226 ff., p. 251 f.
[8] *Magn.*, 14. [9] *Trall.*, 11.

This is a considerable departure from the Pauline conception of the Body of Christ. Ignatius, it is well known, was a zealous opponent of all that seemed to lead to heresy or schism, and he saw in the episcopate the Church's safeguard against such ills. It seems that he took up the Pauline conception without any attempt to work it out in context, and that his development of it in terms of his own thought led him to an exaggerated statement of the Christ-Church relation that may be the ancestor of the 'incarnational' ecclesiologies we have already mentioned.[1] In some measure, it would appear, union with Christ is made dependent upon the unity of the Church, a solicitude for which is characteristic of this writer. He has a constant care for unity, seeing it as the essential principle of God Himself. This notion he connects with the Church, the unique instrument. It seems to be Christ and the Church together, as Head and Body, that constitute the 'new Man' (καινὸς ἄνθρωπος), on which subject Ignatius tells the Ephesians that he intended to write them a separate treatise.[2] So it is the faith of the Church that predominates in all his thought on the subject, rather than the faith of the individual. He does not, however, ignore this. Individual faith is a preliminary to 'fleeing to the flesh of Jesus'.[3] Believing, one is then united to Christ in His Church,[4] where one may eventually 'ascend' to God: Ignatius even speaks of the Holy Spirit as a 'rope', of faith as the means of ascent, and of love as the way that leads up to God.[5]

In no writer is the ontological reality of the Church as the Body of Christ more vividly expounded. But his thought is difficult, and it is difficult because his christology, and consequently his ecclesiology, is very imperfectly worked out. He shows, however, how impressive the Pauline figure could be to a man of a background very different from that of St Paul. The difficulties of his ecclesiology must not be allowed to deflect our attention from the evidence he provides that whether a convert to the Christian Way thought Hebrew or thought Greek, he was confronted with the actuality of the Church as united with Christ.

[1] *Supra*, c. viii. [2] *Eph.*, 20. [3] *Phild.*, 5. [4] *Loc. cit.* [5] *Eph.*, 9.

Upon this fundamental experience had to be based all theological reflection. It is not too much to say that the actuality that the Pauline figure was intended to express was and remained the spring of Christian theology.

Only in the context of the doctrine of the Church that is expressed under this figure do the classic emphases of Calvin's doctrine *de Deo* have any Christian significance. The Reformed Church cannot pay too much attention to the implications of the ecclesiology that is expressed in this Pauline 'root metaphor' apart from which all bowing before the awful Majesty of God can but strike terror in the hearts of men, and even when seemingly mitigated by assurances of forgiveness to the penitent can but give rise to revivals of the old, unrealistic christological heresies that open the way to what the Reformers, in their forthright fashion, did not hesitate to dub idolatry. Taken out of the ecclesiological context, the 'Prayer commonly used in the Church of Edinburgh on the day of Common Prayer',[1] which begins, 'O dreadful and most mighty God, Thou that from the beginning has declared Thyself a consuming fire against the contemners of Thy most holy precepts,' and goes on to confess that 'We have been polluted with idolatry; we have given Thy glory to creatures', can lead only to collapse of the liturgy, as indeed it did, and to a readiness to embrace doctrines which, having their origin in human quests and fancies rather than in experience as a participant in the living reality of the Risen Christ, are as hollow and unprofitable as a course in *Religionsgeschichte* by an ineloquent teacher. Unless the significance of the only direct question the Scottish Reformers required the minister to ask of those who brought a child for Baptism[2] be fully appreciated, the rigorous refusal of the Reformed Church to countenance the practice of according *doulia* to the saints and *hyperdoulia* to Mary, or of bestowing on the latter the affectionate and charming but christologically misleading title, *Domina nostra*, cannot but seem pointlessly cold and harsh. For the Reformers'

[1] *The Book of Common Order of the Church of Scotland*, 1564 (*ed. cit.*), p. 80.

[2] *Op. cit.*, p. 135: 'Do ye here present this child to be baptized, earnestly desiring that he may be ingrafted in the mystical body of Jesus Christ?'

fundamental objection to such practices was not grounded in an abstract theology only; it was, rather, that such practices lose the meaning with which they were invested by the medieval, unreformed Church, when they come to be seen from within the living Body. It was an understanding of the essential nature of the Church that the Reformation indubitably recaptured when it made men recognize the ontological reality of their status as members of the living Body of Christ, the Holy Catholic Church.

CHAPTER X

THE EUCHARIST IN THE REFORMED CHURCH

Speaking for Eastern Orthodoxy, Father Florovsky has said that 'the sacraments constitute the Church'.[1] However startling this utterance may seem to certain contemporary Presbyterians whose ecclesiology has been affected by Separatist notions that are quite alien from the Reformed tradition, it would be far more accurate as a description of the relation between Church and Sacrament in the ecclesiology of the Reformed Church than the view expressed in the statement that the Sacraments 'do nothing that this message [the Gospel] may not conceivably do without their intervention'.[2] As we have abundantly seen, there is nothing upon which more stress has been laid in the classic documents of the Reformed Church and in its lively practice than the notion that the essential marks of the Church are Word, Sacrament and Discipline. But in what does Discipline fundamentally consist if not the exercise of the power to cast off from the Body of Christ? All other acts of Discipline are but admonitions of varying gravity, warnings that the Church has the power, and is bound by the most solemn duty to its Head to exercise this power in certain extreme cases, to cast off members whose presence within the Body is a public mockery of its Head. In regard to the relation between Word and Sacrament in the Reformed tradition, it is entirely misleading to suggest that one has any pre-eminence over the other, for the two are inseparable. To ask whether the Church is more in need of the one or of the other, is somewhat like asking

[1] Georges Florovsky, 'The Church: Her Nature and Task' in *The Universal Church in God's Design* (World Council of Churches) (London, 1948), p. 47.
[2] C. M. Jacobs, 'The Ministry and the Sacraments' in *The Ministry and the Sacraments* (London, 1937), p. 138.

whether a man's life or his body is the more important for his well-being as a physiological organism. 'Wherever we see the Word of God sincerely preached and heard,' writes Calvin, 'wherever we see the Sacraments administered according to the institution of Christ, there we cannot have any doubt that the Church of God has come into existence,'[1] The relation is well expressed by an old Scottish divine as follows: 'I take the worde sacrament, as it is tane and used in the Kirk of God, for a haly signe and seal that is annexed to the preached word of God, to seal up and confirme the truth contained in the same word, in sick sort, that I call not the seal separated fra the word a sacrament. . . . Therefore the word only cannot be a sacrament; nor the element only cannot be a sacrament: and sa Augustine said weill, Let the word come to the element and ye sal have a sacrament: then I call a sacrament the word and seal conjunctlie, the ane hung to the uther.'[2]

The nature of the Reformation protest against sacramentalism must be clarified here. The protest was against a pseudo-sacramentalism that multiplied, not to say fabricated, sacraments, while shamefully neglecting the ministry of the Word. In the view of the Reformers, the multiplication of the sacraments was by no means merely an accidental concomitant of the neglect of the Word. The two corruptions were really joint manifestations of the same disease. The true reform of the Church must always, therefore, bring about the removal of both; there is no genuine cure of the one that does not entail the cure of the other. When the Church is purified, it exhibits its healthy condition by eliminating the dichotomy between Sacrament and Word. There is, of course, but one Word, and it is arguable (and perhaps helpful) that there is really only one Sacrament. Certainly it is thoroughly misleading to say, as it is often said, that the Reformers simply reduced the number of the Sacraments from seven to two, on the ground that only these two are explicitly

[1] *Institutio*, IV, i, 9; cf. IV, i, 12; also the XXXIX Articles, article xix, the Scots Confession, article xviii, and the Westminster Confession, xxv, 4.

[2] Robert Bruce, quoted by Alexander Whyte in *A Commentary on the Shorter Catechism* (Edinburgh, T. and T. Clark, n.d.), p. 176.

warranted in Scripture. This may, indeed, be a fair description of the formal argument in which the Reformers presented their conclusions on the subject; but it is a superficial account of the role of Sacrament in the Reformed Church. The term 'sacrament' is itself, after all, entirely unscriptural. One of Tertullian's contributions to the language of Western Christendom,[1] the word *sacramentum* was used by Jerome to translate the New Testament word μυστήριον. There can really be only one mystery in the life of the Christian Church, and that mystery is indivisible, being the *corpus mysticum* itself.[2] Baptism means ingrafting into this Body which is the Eucharistic Church.

According to Calvin's doctrine on the Eucharist, which became known as Virtualism, there is no transubstantiation of the elements; nevertheless the faithful receive the power (*virtus*) of the Body and Blood of Christ. He thinks the schoolmen themselves were horrified by the kind of language that had been used in controversy against Berengarius in the eleventh-century endeavour to formulate a doctrine 'for which they [the Papists] now contend with greater earnestness than for all other articles of faith';[3] yet the schoolmen, he maintains, 'do but trifle with as much fallacy and with superior subtlety.'[4] In some ways, Berengarius's reply to Lanfranc[5] lends support to the view that he may be regarded as a precursor of Calvin in his doctrine on the Eucharist; but it would be worse than anachronistic to call Berengarius a Virtualist, not least because he appeals to Erigena and seems to be thinking in the 'Platonic' terms of those to whom the chronicler Heriman, Berengarius's contemporary, gave the name *antiqui doctores*.[6] At any rate, Calvin plainly teaches a doctrine of the real presence of Christ in the Sacra-

[1] E.g., *ad Martyres*, iii, where he uses the word in the old Roman sense.

[2] Both 'mystical' and 'mystery' come from the same onomatopoeic, Greek root μυ, whence μύω, to close (lips, eyes, ears, etc.).

[3] *Institutio*, IV, xvii, 14.

[4] *Institutio*, IV, xvii, 13.

[5] *De Sacra Coena* (ed. Deekenkamp in *Kerkistorische Studien*, ii, The Hague, 1941); cf. Darwell Stone, *A History of the Doctrine of the Eucharist* (1909), p. 244 ff.; A. J. MacDonald, *Berengar and the Reform of Sacramental Doctrine* (Longmans, 1930).

[6] *Liber de restauratione monasterii S. Martini Tornacensis* (ed. Waitz, Monumenta Germ. hist., vol. xiv, p. 275).

ment, though not in the 'species' or 'elements', for he says: 'I see not how any man can attain a solid confidence that he has redemption and righteousness in the cross of Christ, and life in his death, unless he first have a real communion with Christ himself; for those blessings would never be imparted to us, did not Christ first make Himself ours. I say, therefore, that in the mystery of the Supper, under the symbols of bread and wine, Christ is truly exhibited to[1] us, even His Body and Blood, in which He has fulfilled all obedience to procure our justification. And the design of this exhibition is, first, that we may be united into one Body with Him, and, secondly, that being made partakers of His substance, we may experience His power in the communication of His blessings.'[2]

According to Calvin, Church and Eucharist are allied together in such an intimate way that it is hardly to exaggerate if we say that the one is an aspect of the other.[3] The infant who is baptized is ingrafted into the Body, within which he is to grow till he can fully participate in the Body; thereupon he is admitted to the Eucharist, in which the Head is 'exhibited to' him. Calvin can say that 'our souls are fed by the flesh and blood of Christ, just as our corporeal life is preserved and sustained by bread and wine'.[4] He recognizes that 'the power of giving life to us is not an essential attribute of the Body of Christ, which, in its original condition, was subject to mortality and now lives by an immortality not its own',[5] and he accuses of reviving Marcion's error those who say that the Body given by Christ at the Last Supper to his disciples was a 'glorious and immortal Body' not subject to space or time. 'What a door doth this open to Marcion's error,' he says, 'if the Body of Christ appeared in one place

[1] That is, 'administered to,' 'delivered over to.' George Gillespie, expounding the meaning of 'exhibitive sign' in the theology of the Reformed Church, says: 'I answer, that *exhibition* is a real, effectual, lively application of Christ, and of all His benefits, to every one that believeth, for the staying, strengthening, confirming, and comforting of the soul' (*Aaron's Rod Blossoming* (1646), III, xii). Cf. also *Herman's Consultation*, fol. 211: 'At the exhibition of the body, let the pastoure saye. . . .'

[2] *Institutio*, IV, xvii, 11.

[3] Cf. St Augustine, quoted at the outset of this study: *supra*, p. 7.

[4] *Institutio*, IV, xvii, 10.

[5] *Institutio*, IV, xvii, 9.

mortal and mean, and in another was received as immortal and glorious.'[1] Nevertheless, though Christ's earthly body was subject to death, 'it is rightly represented as the source of life, for it is endued with a fulness of life to communicate to us.'[2] Calvin has no sympathy with the 'too narrow description'[3] given by those who 'represent us merely as partakers of His Spirit, but make no mention of His flesh and blood, as though there were no meaning in these and other such expressions: that His flesh is meat indeed; that His blood is drink indeed; that except we eat His flesh and drink His blood, we have no life in us'.[4] Calvin's close association of Church and Eucharist permeates all that he says of the Supper. For instance, 'Who does not see,' he asks, 'that a participation of the Body and Blood of Christ is necessary to all who aspire to heavenly life? This is implied in those passages of the Apostle, that the Church is the Body of Christ and His fulness;[5] that He is the Head, from whom the whole Body, joined together and compacted by that which every joint supplieth, maketh increase of the Body;[6] that our bodies are the members of Christ;[7] that there are things which we know cannot be effected otherwise than by His entire union both of Body and Spirit with us. But that most intimate communion, by which we are united with His flesh, the Apostle has illustrated in a still more striking representation, saying, "We are members of His Body, of His flesh, and of His bones."[8] At length, to declare the subject to be above all description, he concludes his discourse by exclaiming, "This is a great mystery."[9] It would be extreme stupidity, therefore, to acknowledge no communion of believers with the Body and Blood of the Lord, which the Apostle declares to be so great that he would rather wonder at it than express it.'[10] Calvin's rejection of transubstantiation, a doctrine that implies the adoration of the consecrated species as such does not lead him to the slightest doubt that in the Eucharist it

[1] *Institutio*, IV, xvii, 17.
[2] *Institutio*, IV, xvii, 9.
[3] *Institutio*, IV, xvii, 7.
[4] *Loc. cit.*
[5] Cf. Eph. i. 23.
[6] Cf. Eph. iv. 15 f.
[7] Cf. 1 Cor. vi. 15.
[8] Cf. Eph. v. 30. Cf. Hooker, *supra*, p. 13, n. 3.
[9] Cf. Eph. v. 32.
[10] *Institutio*, IV, xvii, 9.

is the Body of Christ that 'feeds' the faithful. On the contrary, he insists upon this. 'If it be true,' he says, 'that the visible sign is given to us to seal the gift of the invisible substance, we ought to entertain a confident assurance that in receiving the symbol of His Body, we at the same time truly receive the Body itself.'[1]

We have already seen,[2] that Calvin earnestly desired a weekly celebration of the Eucharist, and that it was only unfortunate circumstances that prevented him from realizing this aim. But it was not Calvin only who stressed the Eucharist in the Reformed Church. This emphasis so permeates the Reformed tradition that it is not till late in the nineteenth century that alien influences penetrated it sufficiently to permit of anything to the contrary being taken seriously within it. Robert Bruce picturesquely expresses the characteristic sentiment of the Reformed Church of Scotland on the peculiar importance of the Eucharist: 'Speers thou[3] quhat new thing we get in the sacrament?' he inquires. 'I say, we get Christ better nor we did before: we get a better grip of Christ now. That same thing quhilk thou possessed be the hearing of the word, thou possesses now more largely. For be the sacrament my faith is nurished, the bounds of my soull are enlarged, and sa, quhen I had but a little grip of Christ before, as it were betwixt my finger and my thumb, now I get Him in my haill hand: for aye the mair my faith growes, the better grip I get of Christ Jesus.'[4] This may be taken as typical of the older style of preaching at the 'action sermon' as the sermon before Holy Communion was called.[5] The Reformers' natural suspicion of all pseudo-sacramentalism that is separated from the proclamation of the Word ought not to mislead us into the erroneous and quite unrealistic view that the Sacrament itself is considered to have an attenuated importance. For the contrary is the case: the insistence upon the association of Word and Sacrament is calculated to exalt the latter no less than the former.

[1] *Institutio*, IV, xvii, 10. [2] E.g., *supra*, p. 53, n. 1. [3] I.e., 'Do you ask?'

[4] Quoted by Alexander Whyte, *op. cit.*, p. 185 f.

[5] The 'action sermon' was the sermon before the 'action'; that is, the 'actio gratiarum' which is the Eucharist.

It is surely a misinterpretation of Calvin to impute to him, as Dix has done, the doctrine that 'in the eucharist Jesus bestows His Spirit on the spirit of the individual who believes in Him as Redeemer and partakes of the bread and wine as He had commanded',[1] and to say that 'The real eucharistic action is for Calvin individual and internal, not corporate'.[2] Such a view is out of keeping with Calvin's whole ecclesiology as well as being repugnant, as we have seen, to the ethos of the Reformed Church. Nor is any conclusion on this subject to be deduced from either the omission or the use of the epiclesis[3] in the liturgies of the Reformed Church. Calvin himself prescribed nothing that can. be called an epiclesis. He shared, of course, the distaste of all the Reformers for the cleavage between priest and people that was associated with the Mass,[4] both in the 'grande messe' and those 'où le Prestre seul murmure et barbotte'.[5] The epiclesis was commonly omitted by the Reformers: it seems they had reason to fear its being mistaken for a focal point substituted for the 'moment of consecration' in the Mass.[6] The need for a blessing of the elements appears to have been felt in Scotland soon after

[1] Gregory Dix, *The Shape of the Liturgy* (*ed. cit.*), p. 633.

[2] *Loc. cit.*

[3] The epiclesis, a prayer in the anaphora of the eucharistic liturgy, in which God the Father is invoked to send down the Holy Spirit upon the elements, is to be found in various forms in the liturgies of the Eastern Church, but is omitted from the Roman Mass. The question is complicated but important, and is much disputed among theologians and liturgists.

[4] Cf. Guillaume Farel, *Summaire déclaration*, c. xix: 'La messe est pour donner à entendre la grosse différence entre le prebstre et le peuple.'

[5] Calvin, *Institution de la religion chrestienne* (*ed. cit.*), vol. iv, p. 57.

[6] It was omitted, for example, from the Consecration in the English Book of Common Prayer, from 1552 onwards. The epiclesis had become such a 'moment' in the Greek Church, as the words of institution had become such a 'moment' in the West. The emergence in the fourth century of the quest for such a 'moment' was due, as Dix has described with admirable vigour (cf. *The Shape of the Liturgy* (*ed. cit.*), p. 240 ff., 299 f., 301 f.), to a forgetfulness in the Church, by that time thoroughly Hellenized, of the Hebrew background of the liturgy, and to a correspondingly growing misunderstanding of the inner structure of the eucharistic service. It is important to note here that the notion of such a 'moment' is alien to the Reformed tradition, and that the use of the epiclesis, far from being calculated to change the place of the 'moment', was stressed partly to diminish the danger of a refocussing of attention on what was still remembered as the 'hoarse whisper' (so Calvin had called it) of the Mass. The Reformation distaste for the notion of the 'moment' was instinctive—it was widely felt to be magical—but the instinct may be shown to have been sound, not least in the light of what is now known of Christian liturgical origins.

the Reformation, however, for we find Row, a strong partisan of the 'anti-prelatic' side, complaining that in Aberdeen, on 'Pasch-day', 1622, there was, in the prayer of consecration at Holy Communion, 'not one word of Lord blesse the elements or action'.[1] The reason for protests of this kind is of some importance in determining the doctrine of the Eucharist in the Reformed Church of Scotland. There was no question of denying or modifying Calvin's doctrine that in the Eucharist 'Christ is truly exhibited to us, even His Body and Blood'.[2] The prayer for the illapse of the Holy Spirit upon the elements soon came to be insisted upon, however. It seems that the chief reason for this was a suspicion that the 'prelatic' party were plotting, in a political interest, the restoration of the Mass, and were therefore reviving an emphasis upon the words of institution so as to make them, as in the Mass, the 'moment of consecration'. In support of this popular sentiment, the learned were able to invoke, as did Gillespie, for example, the testimony of ancient authorities in the Greek Church that the elements are 'sanctified by the Word of God and prayer.'[3] In 1629 the use of the following petition in the consecration prayer was suggested to the Assembly: 'Send doune o Lord thy blissing upon this Sacrament that it may be unto us the effectual exhibitive[4] instrument of the Lord Jesus.'[5] One of the features of Laud's book that would have met with favour throughout Scotland, had not the circumstances of the book's appearance disposed the Scots against everything connected with it, was the provision of an epiclesis.[6] The use of

[1] John Row, *The History of the Kirk of Scotland* (Edinburgh, 1842), p. 331.

[2] *Institutio*, IV, xvii, 11.

[3] Cf. G. W. Sprott, *Scottish Liturgies of the Reign of James VI* (*ed. cit.*), p. 152. Sprott also (*ad loc.*) quotes Boston, a later divine, as saying that 'The Popish Consecration hits not the mark, for these words, "This is My Body," were uttered by our Lord after the Consecration'.

[4] *Supra*, p. 179, n. 1. Sprott (*op. cit.*, p. 151) quotes Cowper, who probably had much to do with the proposed form, as saying that the elements 'are not only signs representing Christ crucified, nor seals confirming our faith in Him, but also effectual instruments of exhibition, whereby the Holy Spirit makes an inward application of Christ crucified to all that are His'.

[5] G. W. Sprott, *op. cit.*, p. 93.

[6] This is placed, in Laud's book, immediately before the words of institution. It is now found, though in a different arrangement, in the liturgies of the Scottish Episcopal Church, which has always approved of it, and of the American Episcopal Church, whose liturgy closely follows the Scottish Episcopal use.

the epiclesis, expressly enjoined by the Westminster *Directory*,[1] became common practice in Scotland and seems now to be general in Presbyterian churches throughout the English-speaking world.[2]

A Latin account of the liturgical practice in Scotland in or about the year 1620, in the celebration of the Eucharist, reveals the importance of its place in the Church life of the Scots and their care for its solemnity. 'Among us,' says the writer of the account, 'the Minister, having concluded his discourse, recites (*recitat*) the words of institution and gives a short exhortation (*exhortatiunculum*) and admonition. Then he blesses (*deinde benedicit*).[3] The blessing or thanksgiving being finished, he says, "Our Lord in that night in which He was betrayed took bread, and gave thanks as we have now done, and break as I now also break bread, and gave to His disciples, saying (here he hands to those nearest on right and left), 'This is my Body,' " etc. He adds nothing to the words of Christ; he changes nothing; he omits nothing. Those next then break off a particle from the larger fragment or portion, and what is left they hand to those sitting nearest, so long as any part of the fragment remains. Then, when one fragment is finished, those who serve the tables offer the paten from which another, in like manner, takes a similar larger piece or fragment, which, breaking, he hands to the nearest person, and so on. The Minister delivers the cup to those nearest, in like manner, repeating the words of Christ, without addition, mixture, change or omission, and these per-

[1] Sprott and Leishman, *The Book of Common Order* (*ed. cit.*), p. 310.

[2] In the 'liturgie de la sainte Cène' of the French Reformed Church there is no trace of an epiclesis. (Cf. *Liturgie des Eglises Réformées de France* (*ed. cit.*), pp. 131–8.) But the eucharistic liturgy of that Church is defective in many points, being generally impoverished to such a degree as to express almost nothing of Calvin's emphasis upon the Sacrament and to be curiously divorced from the historic eucharistic liturgies of Christendom. The reasons for this are complicated. The Savoy Liturgy (1660) provided an epiclesis (cf. P. Hall, *Reliquiae Liturgicae* (Bath, 1847), vol. iv, p. 68). An epiclesis is provided immediately after the anamnesis and before the 'Great Intercession' in the elaborate, scholarly and beautiful form proposed by H. J. Wotherspoon in a now rare pamphlet, *The Divine Service* (*'Η θεία λειτουργία*)*: a Eucharistic Office according to Forms of the Primitive Church* (Glasgow, James MacLehose, 1893), p. 22 f.

[3] Liturgists consider this to refer to a form of epiclesis, associated with anamnesis.

sons hand it to those seated next to them, and when the wine is finished those serving replenish the cup. As soon as he has delivered both elements to those sitting nearest him, using only the words of Christ while they are distributing the bread and the cup among themselves, the Minister addresses[1] those at the table, as long as the action continues. . . . While they [the communicants] are rising from the table and others are taking their place, the Minister observes silence; those leaving and those coming to the table, together with the entire congregation, sing, or else the Reader reads aloud the story of the Passion.'[2] The narrator adds that the Scottish Church had been so celebrating the Eucharist for sixty years. Nothing had been said in the Scottish *Book of Common Order* on the order of receiving; but in the form proposed in 1629 an express injunction appears in the rubric: 'Then shall the Minister first receive the communion in both kyndes himself, and next delyver it unto other ministers (if anie be there present) that they may help the chiefe minister, and after to the people in there hands they kneeling. . . .'[3]

That the Eucharist retained the high place it indubitably did in Scotland, even under the most unfavourable conditions, being for long, as we have seen,[4] celebrated infrequently and with

[1] This practice of giving a brief exhortation to each set of communicants, as they assembled at the table, was still usual at the beginning of the nineteenth century, and perhaps persists in some rural parishes in Scotland down to the present time.

[2] David Calderwood, *Altare Damascenum* (Woodrow Soc.), p. 777 f.

[3] G. W. Sprott, *Scottish Liturgies of the Reign of James VI* (*ed. cit.*), p. 94. The phrase 'that they may help the chiefe minister', which does not appear in the corresponding rubric in the English *B. C. P.*, refers, of course, to the distribution of the elements. But it also recalls the practice of concelebration, which appears to have been normal in the Columban Church, and is still common in the Eastern Church. It is found in the Latin West only in curious survivals, e.g., on Holy Thursday at Lyons (a Gallican survival) and at the Mass in the ordination service. Its virtual disappearance in the West is explained by A. K. Fortescue (*The Mass: a Study in the Roman Liturgy* (London, ed. 1922), p. 187) as follows: 'the older system of assistance and communion or concelebration was replaced in the early Middle Ages by a separate mass said apart by each priest. . . . Each mass as a propitiatory sacrifice has a definite value before God; therefore two masses are worth twice as much as one.' This was indubitably the chief reason why concelebration fell into desuetude in the West. (It may be pointed out in passing that the reasoning is nevertheless bad Roman theology: since each mass is of *infinite* worth, how can two be better than one?) The spirit of the Gallican liturgy which, though less terse, was far more dramatically symbolic than the Roman rite, has always tended to survive and to be revived in post-Reformation Scotland.

[4] *Supra*, c. iv.

much sombre prolixity, justifies the conclusion that it is central to the worship of the Reformed Church.[1] Calvin's desire for its weekly celebration was no merely personal inclination or taste. No man of Calvin's perspicacity could have failed to see that the most fundamental principles behind the Reformation, notably the insistence on continuity and the claim to be the One Church, demanded that the Eucharist should remain the heart of the liturgy. Above all, the Reformation doctrine of the Church itself, the teaching that the Church is the Body of Christ into which we are ingrafted at Baptism, was sufficient to ensure, so long as it was remembered, that the Eucharist would have central place in the Church's worship. It is through the Eucharist (inseparable from the Word) that the Church, which is the Body of Christ, is continually renewed. The eccentric infrequency of its celebration, arbitrarily out of accord with the known practice of the Church of the first centuries which it was the declared purpose of the Reformers to restore, cannot be justified as the liturgical norm in the Reformed tradition, howevery it may be held to have been excusable in particular historical circumstances.

The tradition of the Reformed Church, being grounded in Scripture, recognizes that everything the Church does must be directed towards that *agape* that is its *esse*, given to it through union with Christ, and manifested in the Church in suffering and service.[2] The celebration of the Eucharist, with the proclamation of the Word, does not in itself guarantee that all is well with the Church: only by its being ordered in love, only in

[1] It seems to have partially survived even the introduction in some parish churches in Scotland and many elsewhere of what has come to be known, by a euphemism, as the 'individual cup', which James Cooper, whose charitableness was proverbial among his contemporaries, called a 'horrible proposal' (cf. H. J. Wotherspoon, *James Cooper* (*ed. cit.*), pp. 224 f, 242). It should be noted, however, that this monstrous device, though superficially appearing to be anti-eucharistic in character, and whose accompanying paraphernalia cannot with decency be described, has no doctrinal significance. It was first introduced into those seceding churches in Scotland that in 1847 had united as the United Presbyterian Church (*supra*, c. iv), in which unruly sections of the congregation had power to exercise pressure on a timid pastor. It has nothing to do, positively or negatively, with the Reformed tradition, being due to general vulgarity rather than to anything to be dignified by the name of liturgical error. But cf. *supra*, p. 87, n. 2.

[2] 1 Cor. xiii. 3 ff.

subordinating all to love, can the Church be built up as the Body of Christ. But when the *χαρίσματα* are used in the eucharistic *κοινωνία*, in subordination to love, the *κοινωνία* becomes the sphere of the activity of the Risen Christ, whose real presence in the Body, through the Spirit, is thus assured. Order is indispensable, however, in the life of the worshipping Church. That 'all things are to be done decently and in order',[1] is a special and traditional maxim of the Reformed Church. The Reformers had a peculiar distaste for anarchy. One reason for this is well known: they feared its spread within the movement they had fostered and the consequent destruction of their work. But another reason, more often forgotten, is that they saw ecclesiastical anarchy as the cause of most of the evils against which they were protesting.

All the Reformation formularies repudiated the medieval conception of the sacrifice in the Mass. On the subject of the Eucharist, the *Westminster Confession* says: 'In this sacrament Christ is not offered up to His Father, nor any real sacrifice made at all for the remission of sins of the quick or dead, but only a commemoration of that one offering up of Himself, by Himself, upon the Cross, once for all, and a spiritual oblation of all possible praise unto God for the same: so that the Popish Sacrifice of the Mass (as they call it) is most abominably injurious to Christ's one only sacrifice, the alone propitiation for all the sins of the elect.'[2] The word 'oblation' is noteworthy, and we shall return to it.[3]

The Reformers commonly took the Mass to be a parody of the Eucharist. Its theological basis was, of course, the doctrine of transubstantiation, in attacking which they knew they were attacking the foundation of the structure they accounted idolatry masquerading as Christian worship. The Mass had seemed to justify the extremely sharp cleavage between the clerical and the lay state, for by the unique power in the hands of the priest, he was held to be able not only to transform the elements into the

[1] 1 Cor. xiv. 40. [2] *Westminster Confession*, xxix.
[3] *Infra*, p. 190 and, more especially, p. 245 ff.

Body and Blood of Christ, but to offer Christ Himself to God Himself in the sacrifice of the altar. Because of his exclusive power to offer this all-powerful sacrifice, which alone could be a worthy sacrifice to God, the priest was placed in an extraordinarily privileged position, since it could not but seem that, in vivid contrast to the helplessness of the layman, the priest had the Son of God at his disposal. It was this notion of sacrifice that was so repugnant to the Reformers, causing them to use language that, even allowing for the robustness of speech that was customary in their day, sounds extravagant to modern ears, as when we hear, for instance, that John Knox, whose views were quite typical, declared that the saying of one Mass in Scotland was more detestable to him than would be the presence of a whole foreign army of occupation.

It is necessary to bear in mind how much this detestation of the Mass affected the attitude of the Reformers towards the notion of sacrifice itself. It is by no means improbable that their rejection of the medieval doctrine that Christ's sacrifice was 'repeated' or 'renewed' in the Mass coloured their thought on the subject of eucharistic sacrifice so as to cause them to overlook certain theological questions of considerable importance for the Reformed tradition. That the Eucharist was from the earliest times accounted in some sense a sacrifice is abundantly plain. The *Didache*, for example, contains the following injunction: 'And on the Lord's own day gather yourselves together and break bread and give thanks, first confessing your transgressions, that your sacrifice may be pure (ὅπως καθαρὰ ἡ θυσία ὑμῶν ᾖ). And let no man, having his dispute with his fellow, join your assembly till they have been reconciled, that your sacrifice may not be defiled; for this sacrifice it is that was spoken of by the Lord: In every place and at every time offer Me a pure sacrifice; for I am a great king, saith the Lord, and My name is wonderful among the nations.'[1] Moreover, in the ancient liturgies and in the early Fathers there are abundant references to sacrifice, showing a universal association of this

[1] *Didache*, xiv.

with the Eucharist in an age that was innocent of the abuses towards which the Reformers' attention was directed and which had their centre in the doctrine of transubstantiation as this was developed in the later Middle Ages.[1] Some scholars would even argue that in the words of institution themselves the notion of sacrifice is present, since in the Septuagint the verb *ποιέω* translates a Hebrew word that has not only the meaning of 'I do' ('This do in remembrance of me') but also 'I offer' and 'I sacrifice',[2] so that the words might be rendered, 'Make this sacrifice in remembrance of me.' It has even been maintained that the word *ἀνάμνησις* itself is fraught with a sacrificial meaning that is not included in the English word 'remembrance'. While such interpretations have been received with reserve by some scholars and too readily accepted by others, it cannot be denied that there is a certain force in them. It may be incautious to see in the words of institution an explicit injunction to offer sacrifice; but it is difficult to resist the conclusion that the notion of sacrifice is, to say the least, hinted at. Nor is this surprising. Once again, the essentially Hebraic background of the Christian liturgy must be recalled. So deeply rooted was the idea of sacrifice that it would have required an explicit repudiation of it to eliminate it from the content of the dominical command.

It is characteristic of the ethos of the Reformed Church to emphasize by all possible means that man has nothing in himself worthy of being offered to God. Christ alone could and did make a worthy sacrifice, and He made it once-for-all on Calvary. It seems plausible, therefore, to say, as has very often been said within the Reformed tradition, that for us to presume to offer any sacrifice to God is for us to attempt to derogate from the sacrifice offered by Christ. The Hebrews, it is pointed out,

[1] Innumerable examples might be cited, including the opening of the Great Intercession in the Greek Liturgy of St James, and the following striking passage from St Augustine (*De Civ. Dei*, x, 6): 'Efficitur, ut tota ipsa redempta Civitas, hoc est, congregatio societasque sanctorum, universale sacrificium offeratur Deo per Sacerdotem magnum. . . . Hoc (sc. Rom. xii. 3) est sacrificium Christianorum: multi unum corpus in Christo. Quod etiam sacramento altaris fidelibus noto frequentat Ecclesia, ubi ea demonstratur, quod in ea re quam offert, ipsa offeratur.' Cf. *Liturg. Basil. Text. Const.*, 162; St Chrysostom, *Hom xxxiii in Joan.*

[2] Cf. Exod. xxix. 38 ff; 1 Kings xi. 33.

made sacrifices, but these could only foreshadow the sacrifice of Christ. In themselves they had no value; they were but relics of a primitive religion, and this was seen by the great prophets of Israel themselves. But the Hebrews, while they came to recognize that 'thou desirest not sacrifice; else would I give it,'[1] perceived also that 'The sacrifices of God are a broken spirit: a broken and a contrite heart, O God, thou wilt not despise'.[2] It might be said that the sacrifice of Christ, being complete, makes even this 'interior' sacrifice unnecessary, and that it now behoves the Christian simply to accept Christ's offering on his behalf. But not only does such a view injure the whole conception of the Church as *corpus Christi*; it is surely a striking contradiction of the teaching of the New Testament itself, for we read, in a passage that warns against 'strange doctrines' and proclaims Jesus Christ to be 'the same yesterday, and today, and for ever', that 'We have an altar, whereof they have no right to eat which serve the tabernacle', and 'By him [Christ] therefore let us offer the sacrifice (θυσία) of praise to God continually, that is, the fruit of our lips giving thanks (ὁμολογούντων)[3] to his name'.[4] The whole passage is plainly written with both the Eucharist and the Church in mind. It concludes with an injunction not to forget to do good and not to forget 'the sharing' (κοινωνία), 'for with such sacrifices God is well pleased.'[5]

We have already drawn attention to the word 'oblation' in the *Westminster Confession*. No 'real sacrifice', it is said, is offered up in the Eucharist, but only a commemoration of the one sacrifice of God *and* 'a spiritual oblation' to God 'for the same'. An oblation to God is nothing if not the bringing[6] of something to God, and what is this but a sacrifice?[7] So while the Reformed

[1] Psalms li. 16. [2] Psalms li. 17.

[3] ὁμολογέω as used here appears to be a Hebraism. The Vulgate renders the phrase 'fructum labiorum confitentium nomini ejus'; but modern scholars prefer to render the verb in this case as, 'I give thanks' or 'I praise' or 'I celebrate'.

[4] Hebrews xiii. 8–15. [5] Hebrews xiii. 16.

[6] From *latus*, the past participle of *ferre*. But see *infra*, p. 245 ff., for discussion of a traditional distinction between *oblatio* and *sacrificio*.

[7] The term 'oblation' is used by the Reformers of the sacrifice of Christ on the Cross. Cf. the 'Prayer upon the Fortieth Psalme' in the 1595 edition of the Scottish Psalter, of which the 'prayers upon the psalmes' is a peculiar feature: 'O Lord, that

Church indubitably repudiates one doctrine of sacrifice in the Eucharist, it cannot be said that the Reformed tradition excludes the notion of sacrifice entirely. Prayer is defined in the *Shorter Catechism, agreed upon by the Assembly of Divines at Westminster*, as 'an offering up of our desires unto God for things agreeable to His will, in the name of Christ, with confession of our sins, and thankful acknowledgement of his mercies'.[1] The Eucharist is most properly called liturgy, the Church's work, since it is expressly commanded by Christ, for 'works' are not condemned, if they be done 'in faith' and at God's command. In the words of the Scots Confession, 'gude warkes we affirme to be thir onlie, that are done in faith, and at Gods commandment, quha in his Lawe hes expressed what the thingis be that pleis him.'[2] What is rejected is only dependence on those works which have 'na uther assurance bot the inventioun and opinioun of man'.[3] So while it is a truism, according to the Reformed tradition, to say that we have nothing to offer to God that is worthy of Him, it is not to be denied that God, notwithstanding, desires us to bring our offerings of prayer, such as they are, and what greater offering and oblation can we bring than the Eucharist which He has commanded us to 'do'?

The Reformed Church is therefore expressing its fundamental tradition upon this question when it prays at the Eucharist in terms such as these: 'And here we offer and present unto Thee ourselves, our souls and bodies, to be a reasonable, holy, and living sacrifice; and we beseech Thee mercifully to accept this our sacrifice of praise and thanksgiving. . . .'[4] 'This kind of sacrifice,' Calvin reminds us, 'has no tendency to appease the wrath of God, to procure remission of sins, or to obtain righteousness: its sole object is to magnify and exalt the glory of God. For it

be thy Prouidence gydis and gouvernis all things, and that hes send to vs thy weilbelouit Sonne, for to delyuer vs from sinne and deith, be the oblatioun of his bodie on the Croce. Graunt that wee continuallie may acknawledge this thy great and inestimabill benefite. . . .'

[1] Q. xcviii.

[2] *Confessio Scoticana*, xiv.

[3] *Loc. cit.*

[4] *Book of Common Order of the Church of Scotland* (1940) (Oxford University Press, 1940), p. 120.

cannot be acceptable and pleasing to God, except from the hands of those whom He has already favoured with the remission of their sins, reconciled to Himself and absolved from guilt; and it is so necessary to the Church as to be altogether indispensable. Therefore will it continue to be offered for ever, as long as the people of God shall exist. . . . For so far are we from wishing to abolish it, that in that sense we are glad to understand the following prediction: 'From the rising of the sun, even unto the going down of the same, my name shall be great among the Gentiles; and in every place incense shall be offered unto my name, and a pure offering; for my name shall be great among the heathen, saith the Lord of hosts. . . .'[1] So all the good works of believers are spiritual sacrifices.'[2] Calvin goes on to declare that 'This kind of sacrifice is indispensable in the Lord's Supper, in which, while we commemorate and declare His death, and give thanks, we do no other than offer the sacrifice of praise. From this sacrificial employment, all Christians are called "a royal priesthood";[3] because, as the Apostle says, "By Christ we offer the sacrifice of praise to God, that is, the fruit of our lips, giving thanks to His name." For we do not appear in the presence of God with our oblations without an intercessor; Christ is the Mediator, by whom we offer ourselves and all that we have to the Father. He is our High Priest, who, having entered into the celestial sanctuary, opens up the way of access for us. He is our altar, upon which we place our oblations, that whatsoever we undertake to do, we may attempt in Him. In short, it is He that "hath made us kings and priests to God".'[4]

It has been too often forgotten that the Reformers did not conceive their task as the abolition of the priesthood, but, rather, as the fuller appreciation of its nature as the priesthood of the whole Church. The negative attitudes of mind that have characterized the thought of some exponents of the doctrines of the Reformed Church have ill disposed these exponents to express what Calvin so clearly expresses in the passages just quoted. The misunder-

[1] Malachi i. 11.
[2] *Institutio,* IV, xviii, 16
[3] 1 Peter ii.9.
[4] *Institutio,* IV, xviii, 17.

standing and neglect of the Reformed tradition that distressed the nineteenth-century divines who were associated with the formation of the Scottish Church Society[1]—men such as James Cooper, William Milligan, George Sprott, Matthew Leishman and Duncan MacGregor—has been nowhere more disastrous than in the loss in many places of the doctrine of oblation in the Eucharist to which the *Westminster Confession* refers, and consequently of the sense of jubilant praise and thanksgiving in eucharistic worship without which the celebration of the Lord's Supper cannot but become an empty 'commemorative sign'. Against such an interpretation of the Eucharist the *Scots Confession* inveighed with no less robust vigour than that which it displayed in its denunciation of the Mass. For it is declared in that document that 'we utterlie damne the vanitie of thay that affirme Sacraments to be nathing ellis bot naked and baire signes. No, wee assuredlie beleeve . . . that in the Supper richtlie used, Christ Jesus is so joined with us, that hee becummis very nurishment and fude of our saules . . . we affirme that the faithfull, in the richt use of the Lords Table, hes conjunctioun with Christ Jesus, as the natural man can not apprehend. . . . For the haly Spirite, quhilk can never be divided fra the richt institution of the Lord Jesus, will not frustrat the faithfull of the fruit of that mysticall action. . . . And therefore, whosoever sclanders us, as that we affirme or beleeve Sacraments to be naked and bair Signes, do injurie unto us, and speaks against the manifest trueth.'[2]

The 'mysticall action' is, of course, the action of the whole Church:[3] if the Reformers affirmed anything, they affirmed this.

[1] *Supra*, p. 87, n. 2. [2] *Confessio Scoticana*, xxi.

[3] St Augustine, *De civ. Dei*, x, 7: 'Hoc est sacrificium Christianorum, multi unum corpus in Christo. Quod etiam sacramento altaris fidelibus noto frequentat Ecclesia ubi ei demonstratur quod in ea re quam offert, ipsa offeratur.' The importance of the people's part in the Eucharistic celebration is evident in the Eastern liturgies, where not only are the salutations between priest and people frequent, but the people interpolate repeated 'amens' even in the most solemn parts of the celebration. Cf. also St Chrysostom (*Hom. xviii in 2 Ep. ad Cor.*) who reminds his hearers that 'in the most tremendous mysteries the priest prays for the people and the people pray for the priest. For these words "and with Thy Spirit" are nothing other than this. Again, the giving of thanks is common to both. For the priest gives, not thanks alone, but the whole people also. . . . Now I have said all this so that . . .

There could be no question for them of thinking of the Supper as a sacramental device through which individuals could have their 'private', individualistic mystical experiences. Such piety in regard to the Eucharist was possible to the medieval mind only as a means of escape from the petrifying effects of the pre-Reformation development of the doctrine of the Mass. It did not come naturally to the medieval mind to think *theologically* after such a fashion, and thinking of this kind must never be read into the minds of the Reformers. They could hardly have understood the force of Dodd's remark, for instance, that 'Sacramental communion is not a purely mystical experience, to which history, as embodied in the form and matter of the sacrament, would be in the last resort irrelevant; it is bound up with a corporate memory of real events'.[1] It is only because Reformed Church doctrine, as expressed by Calvin and the great confessional documents of the Reformed Church, has been adulterated by influences alien from Christianity itself—influences very similar to those which Newman found so stultifying in the English Church of his day—that Dodd's well-known reminder is meaningful and timely. So long as there is a lively apprehension of the nature of the Church as the Body of Christ there can be no question of 'mystical experience' detached from the corporate experience of the Eucharist that nourishes the members of the Body in their *κοινωνία* with the Head, which Eucharist He continually enables them to offer without the question of their personal unworthiness being permitted to deter them from their eucharistic praise.

The eschatological element in the words of institution, which

we may learn that we are all one single body, differing from one another only as members differ from other members; and that we may not throw all upon the priests, but may also ourselves have care for the whole Church, as for our common body'. Even as late as the twelfth century we have a remarkable expression of this essentially liturgical notion by the abbot Guerricus, a friend and disciple of St Bernard, in these words (Guerrici Abbatis, *De purific. beatae Mariae*, serm. v, in *Opera S. Bernardi*): 'Neque enim credere debemus quod soli sacerdoti supradictae virtutes sint necessariae, quasi solus consecret, et sacrificet corpus Christi. Non solus sacrificat, non solus consecrat, sed totus conventus fidelium qui adstat, cum illo consecrat, cum illo sacrificat. Nec solus ligni faber facit domum; sed alius virgas, alius ligna, alius trabes, etc., comportat.'

[1] C. H. Dodd, *The Apostolic Preaching and Its Developments* (London, 1936), p. 235.

Dix[1] and others have stressed, is important; yet it is just that eschatological element that ought most vividly to bring to our notice the theological doctrine of the Real Presence that is fundamental to the Reformed tradition. For it is because the *anamnesis* is not merely a looking-back but also a looking-forward that the Eucharist can be an *event* in the present.[2] That it is such an event is what is meant when we speak, in the Reformed tradition, of the Real Presence.[3] The doctrine of the Real Presence of Christ in the Eucharist is so vital to the Reformed tradition that even the slightest neglect of it leads rapidly to catastrophic decline in the life of the Church. So closely is it related to the Reformed ecclesiology that its repudiation would imply the repudiation of the doctrine of the Church itself, and the substitution for this of a Separatist ecclesiology in which both Eucharist and Church would have even less justification than the use of holy water may be said to have had in pre-Reformation times. That is to say, they become 'aids to devotion' with more extensive possibilities of idolatry than sacramentals could ever have. For the Eucharist cannot become, in the Reformed Church, a mere 'naked and bare sign' without the Church itself becoming likewise a 'naked and bare sign', and therefore to talk of a general duty of church attendance would be not only indefensible but immoral, since it could never be enjoined as a general moral duty to do what is not generally profitable, being only an 'aid to devotion' for those patient enough to bear the irksomeness of a prop they are too weak to do without. The doctrines of the Eucharist and of the Church are so central in the Reformed tradition that they must serve their true purpose or none at all. *Corruptio optimi pessima*: the loftiest idol is the most dangerous, and whenever Church and Eucharist can be regarded as less than indispensable, they have

[1] Gregory Dix, *The Shape of the Liturgy* (*ed. cit.*), p. 263 ff.: 'It is not merely,' he says (p. 263) 'that the language of the earliest prayers is full of eschatological reminiscences. . . . The whole conception of *anamnesis* is in itself eschatological.

[2] The whole action of the Eucharist is both *anamnesis* and *prolepsis*.

[3] The 'how' of the Real Presence is, of course, a mystery. The acknowledgement of this is not peculiar to the Reformed tradition. Even the *Roman Catechism* (II, art. 226) forbids inquiry into it: 'quo modo fiat, curiosius non inquirendum.'

already become, for those who so regard them, potential enemies of the spiritual life. Only by the conjunction of Eucharist and Word at the heart of the Church's life is this danger to be averted.

How faithfully the patristic notion of the Church as 'one bread' in Christ has been preserved in the Reformed tradition may be strikingly demonstrated from the Liturgy of the Dutch Reformed Church as used at the present day in Holland and elsewhere, for example at the Marble Collegiate Church in Fifth Avenue, New York. Cyprian, in a well known passage, says that 'the Body of the Lord cannot be flour alone or water alone, unless both should be united and joined together and compacted in the mass of one bread; in which very sacrament our people are shown to be made one, so that as many grains, collected and ground and mixed together into one mass, make one bread, so in Christ, who is the bread of heaven, we may know that there is one Body, with which our number is joined and united'.[1] This figure, which recurs in Augustine[2] and was a favourite among the Reformers, is conserved in the order for the celebration of the Eucharist in the Dutch Reformed Liturgy, appearing in a picturesque form in the derivative Liturgy of the Reformed Church in America, as follows: '. . . that we, by the same Spirit, may also be united as members of one body, in true brotherly love; as the holy Apostle saith, "For we, being many, are one bread and one body; for we are all partakers of that one bread." For as out of many grains one meal is ground and one bread baked, and out of many berries being pressed together one wine floweth and mixeth itself together; so shall we all, who by a true faith are ingrafted into Christ, through brotherly love be all together one body, for the sake of Christ, our beloved Saviour, who hath so exceedingly loved us; and shall show this, not only in word, but also in very deed toward one another.'[3]

[1] Cyprian, *Ep.* *lxi*, 13.
[2] See Appendix I, 12. Cf. St Thomas, *Summa Theol.*, III, q. 73, a. 2; also q. 74, a. 4 ad resp.
[3] *The Liturgy of the Reformed Church in America* (New York, 1956), p. 34.

CHAPTER XI

THE EPISCOPATE IN THE REFORMED TRADITION

'Episcopacy has unquestionable Bible warrant,' writes an eminent Scottish Presbyterian divine,[1] 'and no Presbyterian ever denied this.' The term 'Presbyterian' itself, the same writer reminds us, is a label that acquires meaning only in the context of the 'peculiarly British controversy' of the seventeenth century. It has been bequeathed to American and other Churches in the English-speaking world; yet in continental Europe it is as foreign-sounding as is the term 'Episcopalian' in England. Much of the 'peculiarly British controversy' was rooted in the radical difference between England and Scotland in Reformation times. Reformation was needed and widely desired in both countries; but in England it received episcopal support while in Scotland the bishops opposed it. It is not surprising, therefore, that, as Sykes points out, 'next to their advocacy of the "godly prince", the Anglican reformers were at pains to restore the godly bishop, in contradistinction to the corrupt prelacy of the later middle ages, against which they had revolted.'[2] Because the Anglican Reformers had episcopal support, they naturally saw it as a part of their task to ensure that the bishops should be good pastors, not merely the holders of an honorific title. The circumstances of the Scottish Reformers, on the other hand, were similar to those that prevailed at Geneva and elsewhere: there could be no question of reforming the existing episcopacy, for the existing episcopacy collapsed in

[1] The late G. D. Henderson, Master of Christ's College, Aberdeen, and ex-Moderator of the General Assembly of the Church of Scotland, in *The Claims of the Church of Scotland* (London, 1951), p. 81.

[2] Norman Sykes, *Old Priest and New Presbyter* (Cambridge, 1956), p. 12 f. For the influence of this concept in the Roman Revival, Sykes refers to Paul Broutin, S.J., *L'Evêque dans la tradition pastorale du XVIème Siècle* (1953).

resisting reform. Melanchthon was not alone among the Reformers in desiring most earnestly to preserve the 'canonical government'; but how could one preserve a government that had fled? In Scotland, on the eve of the Reformation, there were thirteen Roman dioceses, of which four were officially vacant. Of the remaining nine, one had a layman, Lord Robert Stuart, as bishop, while Beaton of Glasgow had fled. Several of the other episcopal incumbents were notorious scoundrels even by the ecclesiastical standards of the day. When Pius IV summoned the Scottish bishops to attend a session of the Council of Trent in 1561, there were but five to whom the summons could be addressed. The reformatory aims of the Scots were not fundamentally different from those of the English; but the absence of episcopal support for their aims put them in a fundamentally different circumstance.

The Reformed Church certainly did not repudiate episcopacy. Nevertheless, it is to be noticed that, being without bishops, they did not greatly concern themselves over their absence. An understanding of the reason for this is vital to an understanding of the doctrine of the ministry in the Reformed tradition. In the first place, it is essential to draw a distinction between episcopal government and episcopal function. In the Middle Ages the bishop had come to play a role of enormous importance in the system of ecclesiastical government that the papacy fostered. Apart from his canonical functions as a bishop, the Ordinary of a diocese was, with some technical limitations, in supreme command. He was *dominus*: the restrictions upon his *dominium* that we have already considered[1] were not negligible; but they had probably little practical effect on the common estimate of the bishop as the ruler of his diocese. From this point of view he was far exalted above the clergy he ruled; yet this was due not to his having special powers which they lacked but to his having been appointed to his See.

Against all this there was opposition, and we have seen that by the time of the Reformation this opposition had had a long

[1] *Supra*, c. ii.

history. The Reformers took for granted the view that the whole concept of episcopal *dominium* was mistaken, and in this they could quote centuries of legal opinion on the subject as well as the whole conciliarist movement which, though it might seem to exalt bishops in their relation to the papacy, rested on a democratic interpretation of the principles of government in the Christian Church. That the concept of the bishop as an ecclesiastical official having *dominium* over a delineated territory should be swept away was, of course, as the Reformers wished. They had no inclination, however, to tamper with existing institutions except to the extent that seemed essential to the conduct of the Reform, and it can hardly be doubted that they would have welcomed the opportunity to do what England proposed to do in making the bishops, in Jewel's words, 'pastors, labourers, watchmen.'[1] It was not only that they recognized that bishops enlisted in their cause could be of immense value in promoting it; they saw that good bishops were good for the Church, and that the most truly reformed ministry would both need and welcome oversight. In Scotland such overseers appeared to be essential for the Reformation itself. It was by no means enough to abolish the jurisdiction of the Pope and establish the Reformed Church by law: the hearts of men must be reformed, and this task called for more than pastors in settled parishes administering the Word and Sacraments. If ever bishops were needed for the oversight of the Church, they were needed then. 'We consider,' declared the authors of the *First Buik of Discipline*, 'that if the ministers whom God hath endowed with his singular graces amongst us, should be appointed to severall places there to make their continuall residence, that then the greatest part of the realme should be destitute of all doctrine; which should not onely be the occasion of great murmur, but also be dangerous to the salvation of many. And therefore we have thought it a thing most expedient at this time, that from the whole number of godly and learned men, now presently in this realme, be selected ten or twelve (for in so many provinces we have divided the

[1] J. Jewel, *Works* (Parker Soc.), iii, p. 308.

whole), to whom charge and commandement should be given to plant and erect kirkes, to set, order, and appoint ministers.... And therefore nothing we desire more earnestly, than that Christ Jesus be universally once preached throughout this realme, which shall not suddenly be, unlesse that by you men be appointed and compelled, faithfully to travell in such provinces as to them shall be assigned.'[1]

All this was conformable to John à Lasco's system and to what was being done within the Reformed Church at Geneva and in France. But in these proceedings the Reformed Church had in mind only the advantages of episcopal government; the more profoundly ecclesiological question of episcopal function and the nature of the episcopate itself was another matter. Before Knox's death the Scottish Church was involved in the appointment of an Archbishop of St Andrews. Knox's attitude to this appointment is not quite clear: while declining to take part in it, he seems to have aquiesced. From his apparent reluctance little is to be learned, however, concerning his doctrine of the episcopate in the Reformed Church. It is well known that Knox had himself declined an English bishopric, and of course one may disapprove of a particular kind of episcopal government while earnestly desiring another. The titular bishops appointed in Scotland in the sixteenth century under the Regent Morton were by no means generally popular, for it was plain that political and financial motives had chiefly dictated their appointment.[2] After Knox's death, Andrew Melville, whose experience in continental Europe had driven him to the conclusion that under existing conditions an episcopal form of government tended to the subordination of the Church to the State, influenced the Scottish Church and the Scottish Parliament to declare in 1580

[1] *First Buik of Discipline* (*ed. cit.*), VI, i, 2, p. 36 f.

[2] Their appointment was believed by some to be politically advantageous to the Church. They had to surrender most of their emoluments to lay nobles, for which reason they were mockingly called 'tulchans': a 'tulchan' was a calf-skin stuffed with straw (or the like) and placed beside a cow to encourage her to give milk. On the other hand, there was no strong hostility to them, or even to the episcopal system officially introduced under pressure from James VI, for the life of the Church seemed to be little affected by such arrangements, far removed though they might be from the spirit of earlier provisions.

that 'the office of a bishop, as it is now used and commonly taken within this realm, hath no sure warrant, authority, or good ground out of the Book and Scriptures of God'. Even this, however, is a condemnation of a particular system rather than of the principle of episcopal government itself. In place of episcopal government, a system of government by a hierarchy of ecclesiastical courts such as is now characteristic of 'Presbyterianism' was eventually established in 1592, only to be set aside twenty years later. The later fortunes of episcopal government in Scotland in the seventeenth century have already been sufficiently indicated;[1] they could hardly have been more ill fated. The later bishops were not, on the whole, the best that might have been chosen, and most of them compared very badly with a man such as the saintly and learned Patrick Forbes.

We now turn to the more strictly ecclesiological and theological question of the episcopal function and the nature of the episcopate itself. The view of the Reformers on this question has been obscured in some measure by post-Reformation developments in Roman doctrine on the subject. It is now generally maintained by Roman theologians that the episcopate is not merely the plenitude of the priesthood but is a separate Order. This view, though it had its defenders before the Reformation, was not generally held in the Western Church. The Reformers were all, of course, nurtured on St Thomas, who had taken a very different position on this question, and the influence on Calvin and others of St Thomas's teaching on the subject of the episcopate was very considerable; so much so that it cannot easily be exaggerated.

St Thomas accepted the common medieval view that Order is a sacrament;[2] but he perceived that, as a sacrament, it imprints a character, and this character is 'specially directed to the Eucharist'.[3] (This is what had to be borne in mind when it was

[1] *Supra, c.* iv.

[2] *Summa Theol.*, III Suppl., q. 34, a. 3.

[3] *Op. cit.*, III Suppl., q. 40, a. 5 ad 2; cf. q. 37, a. 2; cf. also q. 39, a. 4, where it is argued that it is this relation of all 'orders' to the Eucharist that makes it unlawful to admit homicides to any of them.

pointed out, in scholastic fashion, that certain functions reserved to bishops, such as blessing virgins and consecrating churches, appeared to be less exalted that the proper work of a priest, the consecration of the Sacred Species.) The sacrament of Order, says St Thomas, differs from other sacraments in an important respect: other sacraments are administered in order that certain effects may be received, while Order is administered so that certain acts may be performed.[1] But while it is therefore true that 'orders' may be distinguished, 'the division of Order is not that of an integral whole into its parts, nor of a universal whole, but of a potential whole (*totius potestativi*), the nature of which is that the notion of the whole is found to be complete in one part, but in the others by some participation thereof. Thus it is in this case: for the whole fulness (*plenitudo*) of the sacrament is in one Order, to wit, the priesthood, while in the others there is a participation of Order. . . . Therefore all the orders are one sacrament.'[2] So St Thomas argues that, *sacramentally*, the episcopate is not to be regarded as an order above or separate from the priesthood.[3] In 'hierarchical actions', however, a bishop has a higher power in relation to the *corpus mysticum* (here distinguished from the *corpus verum*, the eucharistic species) than has the priest, and so in this sense the episcopate may be called an order.[4] The notion of the ecclesiastical hierarchy was connected, in the thought of the medieval theologians, with the celestial hierarchy as arranged by the Pseudo-Dionysius; indeed St Thomas finds it necessary to answer the objection that since there are nine orders of angels, ought not there to be the same number of 'orders' in the Church?[5] This association of ideas is not quite as fanciful as it tends to appear to a modern reader. It belongs to the strongly Platonic heritage in medieval thought, according to which the features of the present world reflect the forms of the eternal world, and time itself is but a passing image

[1] *Op. cit.*, III Suppl., q. 37, a. 1 ad 1.
[2] *Op. cit.*, III Suppl., q. 37, a. 1 ad 2.
[3] *Op. cit.*, III Suppl., q. 40, a. 5.
[4] *Loc. cit.*
[5] *Op. cit.*, III Suppl., q. 37, a. 2 ad 4, cf. 4 *Sent.*, d. 13, q. 1, s. 2 ad 2.

of eternity. This had much to do, of course, with the persistence of docetic notions in the Middle Ages. So a heavenly archetype had to be found for the 'orders' in the Church, even if it meant enlarging their number from seven to nine by including the tonsure[1] and the episcopate.

St Thomas is much too rigorous a thinker to allow himself to be enmeshed in speculations of this sort. So he insists upon the unity of the sacrament of Order, saying that 'although at his promotion a bishop receives a spiritual power in regard to certain sacraments, this power nevertheless does not have the nature of a character, Wherefore the episcopate is not an order in the sense in which an order is a sacrament'.[2] From what he says it is plain, not only that the episcopate is to be regarded as the plenitude of the priesthood, but that whatever 'dignity' the inferior orders have, they derive from their relation to the Eucharist, the proper work of the priest.

Calvin, in common with the Reformers generally, had no doubt that the ministry, God's gift to the Church, is a ministry of Word and Sacrament. He took over St Thomas's fundamental principle concerning the unity of Order and its special relation to the Sacrament of the Body and Blood of Christ. He could not, of course, accept the notion of 'powers' conferred upon or withheld from members of this or that 'order' in the hierarchical sense, for this conception belonged to and in one way or another depended upon the whole papal system against which the Reformers protested as being radically injurious to the life of the Body of Christ. But here we must be especially careful to run no risk of misrepresenting Calvin's position. In no sense was he seeking to oppose the ancient doctrine of the ministry, as he understood this in the light of the historical knowledge then available. What he did oppose was the notion of interference (in the last resort papal interference) with the fundamental doctrine of the unity of the ministry, which, rooted in the New Testament and expressed in early Christian literature, continued

[1] Cf. *Summa Theol.*, III Suppl., q. 40, a. 2.
[2] *Op. cit.*, III Suppl., q. 40, a. 5 ad 2.

to be expounded in St Thomas, notwithstanding later (and, from the Reformers' point of view, objectionable) innovations. Calvin wished entirely to repudiate the notion, now characteristic in Roman practice, that a bishop or priest may have a 'faculty' or 'power' withheld from him by his ecclesiastical superior.[1] He did not at all repudiate differences of ecclesiastical rank or the principle of episcopal oversight; least of all did he seek to abandon the doctrine of the episcopate as he understood this.

Calvin gives us a clear account of his understanding of the historical circumstances in which the distinction between bishops and presbyters arose.[2] 'The presbyters in each city,' he says, 'chose one of their own number (lest there should be dissension, as usually happens where there is equality), whom they distinguished by the title of *bishop*. The bishop was not, however, so superior in honour and dignity as to have any lordship (*dominium*) over his colleagues; but the functions performed by a consul in the senate, such as bringing forward questions for their consideration, collecting their opinions, presiding over the others by giving advice, admonition and exhortation, regulating the whole procedure by his authority, and executing whatever had been decreed by common consent—such were the functions of a bishop in the assembly of the presbyters. And that this arrangement was introduced by human agreement, on account of the exigencies of the times, is acknowledged by the ancient writers themselves. So Jerome, on the Epistle to Titus, says, "A presbyter is the same as a bishop. . . . Therefore, as the presbyters know that according to the custom of the Church they are subject to the bishop who presides over them, so let the bishops know that their superiority to the presbyters is from custom rather than

[1] A priest cannot, of course, be deprived of his 'power' to say Mass, nor a bishop of his 'power' to ordain; but a priest's faculty of hearing confessions may be withheld for a time on account of his youth, or for other cause, and a bishop may likewise be deprived of certain faculties that Roman bishops ordinarily enjoy. Cf. *Codex Juris Canonici*, canons 871–2.

[2] This is a highly controversial question. We are not here concerned with the adequacy or even the accuracy of Calvin's treatment of it, but only with the principle that his exposition is calculated to defend.

from the appointment of the Lord, and they ought to join together in the government of the Church. . . ."[1] To every city was assigned a certain region, which received from it presbyters and was accounted a part of that Church. Every assembly was, as I have said, solely for the preservation of order and peace, under the direction of one bishop who, while he preceded all others in dignity, was himself subject to the assembly of the brethren.'[2] Calvin goes on to note that the appointment of archbishops and patriarchs was likewise in the interest of good order and discipline.[3] His contention is that bishops were in the same case as patriarchs: appointed for the sake of good discipline, they were not intended to affect the fundamental principle of the unity of the ministry. Calvin, who in principle is disposed to favour aristocratic forms of government, welcomes even in the Church what he calls 'the political distinction of ranks'. Such a distinction, he maintains, is 'not to be repudiated, since natural reason itself dictates this for the removal of disorder; but whatever has this object in view shall be so arranged as neither to obscure the glory of Christ, nor to serve ambition or tyranny, nor to impede the cultivation by all ministers of mutual brotherhood with equal rights and liberties'.[4]

It had been affirmed by Cyprian in a famous treatise written on the occasion of the Novatian schism, that the Church, like the seamless robe of Christ, is not to be divided,[5] for it is a unity.[6] The essence of this whole treatise is contained in Cyprian's statement: 'The episcopate is one, each part of which is held by each one for the whole.'[7] Calvin, referring to the passage in which this occurs, notes that Cyprian 'after the example of Paul', deduces the origin of all ecclesiastical concord from the supreme Bishopric of Christ.[8] The faithful are united in the Body with Christ the Head: whatever the ministry be, it must flow from the ministry of Christ Himself; that is to say, the episcopate that flows from the ministry of the one Bishop, Christ, must be also

[1] Jerome, *ad Tit.*, i.
[2] *Institutio*, IV, iv, 2.
[3] *Institutio*, IV, iv, 4.
[4] Calvin, *Comm. in Num.*, iii, 5.
[5] John xix. 23 f.
[6] Cyprian, *De Unitate Eccl.*, 7.
[7] *Op. cit.*, 5.
[8] *Institutio*, IV, ii, 6.

one and indivisible.[1] Calvin points out that since, as Cyprian acknowledges, there is but one Bishop, even Christ, the administration of the one episcopate in the Church is given to individuals only as these form part of the one undivided ministry.[2] As God's gift to the Body, the episcopate, which is the ministry, participates in the inner unity of the Body, in which all coheres together by *agape*. The ranks that may be introduced into the ministry in the visible ordering of the Church, and which may properly be signified by special dress, ecclesiastical title, and the like, have nothing to do with the essential principle, which must be maintained, that when a minister in the Christian Church performs any ministerial act, he performs it on behalf of the whole ministry: to no man is it given to act by himself as the representative of Christ. No Christian minister, whatever be his rank, can ever say, 'I have this ministry from Christ.' He must say, rather, as does St Paul, 'we have this ministry.'[3]

This means that there is no essential difference in the function of the ministry, whether the minister is celebrating the Eucharist or ordaining others to the ministry. The celebration of the Eucharist with the proclamation of the word is the heart of the ministry. It would seem that concelebration well expresses the fact that each minister holds his ministry *in solidum* with the whole ministry that is given to the Church; but it is not the only possible way of expressing this fundamental fact. In the nature of the case, the Eucharist must be celebrated frequently, regularly, and in many separate places, so that concelebration, though it might be convenient in particular circumstances, could not possibly be the regular practice throughout the Christian Church. Nevertheless, every minister ought to concelebrate in spirit with all his brethren in the ministry which he shares

[1] Cf. Calvin, *Comm. in Eph.*, iv, 16.
[2] *Comm. in Eph.*, iv, 11.
[3] 2 Cor. iv. 1. It is true that in Hellenistic Greek 'we' is often used where 'I' is intended. The wisdom of rendering Paul's utterances throughout this passage in the first person singular, as Moffat does, is, however, in the present writer's opinion, questionable. Paul is speaking not only for himself but as sharing in the apostolic ministry. But cf. R. H. Strachan, *The Second Epistle of Paul to the Corinthians* (London, 1935), p. xxxv, p. 90 ff.

with them, exercises with them, and holds with them, corporately, from Christ. As he joins in the praise of God, at the Preface, 'with angels and archangels and with all the company of heaven,' so also it is in accordance with the fundamental principles of the Reformed tradition that he should unite himself in his eucharistic act with all others who have been ordained with him to the ministry. The ordination of others to the ministry is also a ministerial act, referring, as do all such acts, to the Eucharist that is at the heart of the ministry. Ordination is no more and no less an act on behalf of the whole undivided ministry, the one episcopate of the Church. But though, as has been said already, there is no fundamental difference in the function of the ministry, whether the minister is celebrating the Eucharist or performing an act of ordination, there is a practical difference whose importance must not be overlooked or minimized. Ordination, as a ministerial act, is less frequent, yet peculiarly important. Though it is performed, as are all other ministerial acts, with a view to the central act that is the heart of the ministry, it has a special solemnity of its own. The point might be illustrated with reference to the secular administration of justice: the judicial acts of the Bench from day to day are more central than the installation of a judge; yet this is properly regarded as an event to be attended by solemn ceremonial. While it may therefore be considered to be unnecessary and impracticable that the corporateness of the ministry should be regularly expressed in 'visible' concelebration of the Eucharist, there is no reason, as a rule, why it should not express itself in the act of ordination. It is therefore the universal custom in the Reformed Church for the solemn ceremony of the laying on of hands to be performed by all the ordained members of a presbytery, or as many of them as may conveniently be assembled for the purpose. Where there existed ministers of the rank of bishop or superintendent, such a minister would of course take the leading part in the ordination: it is he who would address the ordinands, give them the charges and pray over them. Nor is there any fatal objection to his being solely entrusted by his brethren with the duty of laying on of hands, without others having part in this: were this to be assigned to any one individual, it would be assigned to the bishop or superintendent; but such a practice, though not entirely to be excluded, would not seem to be as consonant with the Reformed tradition as is the practice of laying on of hands by all the ordained members of the Presbytery. It is to the Presbytery, as a court of the Church, that the individual minister is responsible, because it represents, as a conventional unit, an ecclesiastical assembly, the corporateness of the ministry. In Scotland each presbytery corporately is designated 'reverend', while the General Assembly, the supreme ecclesiastical court, is corporately designated 'venerable'.[1]

By far the most important role of the bishop, from the point of view of the Reformed tradition, is his role of signifying the unity of the Church. The practical importance of this is incalculably great. It is surely to be much regretted that the Reformed Church has made much less use than it might have made of the bishop for signifying this unity of the Church. But the bishop can never, within the Reformed tradition, be the guarantor of unity or the ground of continuity. No doctrine of apostolic succession through the episcopal *office* can ever be made to accord with the doctrine of the Church in the Reformed tradition, which entirely excludes such a notion because the ground of unity and continuity can only be the Body of Christ itself, while Christ alone, as Head of the Body, can guarantee its life.

The one episcopate in which all ministers in the Church share is a great mystery. It is not its function to offer up anything, prayer or sacrifice, to God on behalf of the people; it is its function, rather, to bring God's Word and Sacrament to the people.[2] Yet this is not to say that the ministry is a one-way movement

[1] The Moderator of the General Assembly of the Church of Scotland has for some time, by custom, been personally designated 'Right Reverend' during his tenure of office, and thereafter 'Very Reverend'. But these titles, like the title 'Reverend' itself, derive from the whole ministry: they are accorded to the individual minister by courtesy, because of his participation in the ministry of the Church, apart from which he has no right to them.

[2] Cf. A. Nygren, 'Vom geistlichen Amt' in *Zeitschrift fur systematische Theologie* (1935), p. 40 ff.

only, for the bringing of the mysteries of God to the people entails the uprising of their praise and thankfulness to God. So as the minister brings the mysteries to the people he enjoins them, in interpolated imperatives, to do their part: 'Hear the Word of God!' he bids them, and when he exclaims 'Sursum corda!' they ought to shout back, in signal, their cry of jubilant attentiveness: 'Habemus ad Dominum!'[1] To think of the ministry in the Reformed Church as the work of leading people to God is to fall into an error similar to the 'aids to devotion' error that has already been mentioned. For it represents the ministry as engaged in a technique, more or less subtle, more or less successful, for coaxing men and women into 'states of mind', developing in each individual his own individual potentialities and leading men individually to God.[2] The New Testament knows nothing of such a ministry, which is also and consequently alien from the Reformed tradition. Such a concept of the ministry, besides lacking all Scriptural warrant, is peculiarly detrimental to the moral conditions necessary for the development of the aims it purports to stress. For the Reformers profoundly understood, as have also in their own way generations of the faithful in the Reformed Church, that a genuine individualism is better attained by being forgotten than by being cultivated. This is not to say that the Christian life does not demand individual striving; on the contrary—and this is the truth that Kierkegaard so vividly perceived and so dramatically expressed[3]—it entails

[1] To the bidding, 'Hear the Word of God!' the shouted response ought to be: 'Our ears are open!'

[2] D. M. Baillie refers (*God was in Christ* (London, 1948), p. 114 ff.) to what he calls the 'paradox peculiar to Christianity' that man has a sense of genuine ability to participate creatively in the work of God and yet must acknowledge that everything he does is to be ascribed only to God. This paradox is, however, what the *corpus Christi* figure explains, when the individual is considered as a cell in the Body. The action of a cell is its own action; yet it is no less the action of the Body. It is noteworthy that the theological puzzles concerning divine grace and human freedom, which are intellectually insoluble apart from the doctrine of the Church, are within the life of the Church seen as arising from the mystery that is there encountered. They refer, indeed, to the mystery of life itself and can be profitably discussed only in terms of an organicist metaphysics.

[3] Cf. Walter Lowrie, *Kierkegaard* (Oxford, 1938), p. 525. It is true that Kierkegaard lacks all sense of the actuality of the Church as *corpus Christi*. In his day the profoundly Catholic spirit of the Reformers had been so corrupted in the Established Church of Denmark that Kierkegaard could not think in terms of recapturing

it. But it is not the work of the ministry to attempt to improve upon what God, in His watchful and merciful Providence, does with the individual lives of men and women. Because the minister acts with the whole episcopate in the Church, and because it is Christ that ministers through that episcopate, it is not the minister's function to cajole or even to persuade; it is his duty, rather, to proclaim the Gospel and to 'do' the Eucharist with the people. This is his service, his ministry, in which is reflected 'the greatness and the wretchedness' of the Body of Christ, to which this Pascalian phrase may be appositely applied since the Body, being not sinless, is united with the sinless Head.

Although it is beyond doubt that no theory of apostolic succession through the episcopal office is consistent with the ecclesiological principles of the Reformed Church, the notion of apostolic succession itself is, of course, implied in the notion of continuity that we have seen to be so fundamental in the ecclesiological thought of the Reformers. The bishop, we have said, can never be the guarantor of unity or the ground of continuity. This is so, not merely because of the view that the Reformed tradition, here essentially following St Thomas, takes of the nature of Order. For the ministry itself, the episcopate itself, is not to be accorded these functions, since to accord them to it

it. 'He was so deeply involved in the Danish situation,' writes one of his best modern interpreters (James Collins, *The Mind of Kierkegaard* (Chicago, 1953), p. 216), 'with its danger of religious *Schwärmerei* in connection with the religious community, that he found no opportunity to follow up his own remark that only in the case of the Church, as the *genus electum, gens sancta,* does the "race" or social whole again assume a primacy over the human individual. He saw only the taint of Hegelianism in his youthful statement that Christ died for each individual, but "for me" as belonging to the "many", the company of redeemed men, joined together in organic union.' Kierkegaard, for all his insight, had no real understanding of the Reformation, which in his Denmark had come to be taken with as little seriousness as the medieval Church against which it had protested. 'Catholicism was not treated by him as one of the serious alternatives in our time, but only as having taught us some valuable historical lessons, which will be useful in determining the future course of Christianity. The claims of the Catholic Church to be, in every age, the *una sancta,* the sanctifying union of men in Christ's mystical body, is not examined.' (Collins, *ad loc.*). But for all that, it is difficult to think of Kierkegaard, with his dislike of the 'odour of heartiness' that he found in the 'Grundtvigian' group (cf. Lowrie, *op. cit.*, p. 581) as a Separatist. It was, rather, that he could not discern the ecclesiological principle that had meant so much to the Reformers and apart from which the notion of the Reformed Church has no conceivable meaning.

would be to derogate from the Headship of Christ. Yet when all this is said, it must be emphasized that there remains a most important doctrine of apostolic succession to be stated and affirmed. So much did this doctrine mean to Calvin and so much has it meant within the later tradition of the Reformed Church, that its very centrality has tended to obscure it. So much rested upon it in the Reformed ecclesiology that it was taken for a truism, and the need to expound it is a modern need that our forefathers could hardly have felt in the same way as do we. In order to show what is implied in the Reformed ecclesiology concerning the apostolic succession, we must first, however, make clear certain points relevant to modern discussions of the question.

Those who defend the doctrine of apostolic succession through the episcopal office in what for convenience may be called 'the historic episcopate' are concerned with what they take to be the fact that Christ intended His authority to be transmitted to and continued in the succession of bishops. Whatever is given in this way is given, of course, to the holder of the episcopal office rather than to the person, who is merely the bearer of the office. 'Capacity to exercise authority, and *a fortiori* capacity to transmit it, must reside,' wrote Quick, 'in the office rather than in the person of him who holds it.'[1] But the office is 'attached' to a person, and it becomes therefore a question of paramount importance, in this view of apostolic succession, to determine whether or not the person has received a valid commission. The notion that there may be charismatic ministries apart from this apostolic succession is irrelevant here. No important ecclesiological theory in Christendom would assert that the Spirit is entirely fettered by the Church. Our concern is, rather; with the fact that the view of apostolic succession that is under consideration makes the Body of Christ depend for its life upon an 'organ' other than the Head.[2] So long as this 'organ' is present—and its presence can be determined, in principle, by historical

[1] O. C. Quick, *The Christian Sacraments* (London, 1932), p. 143.
[2] T. O. Wedel, *The Coming Great Church* (New York, 1945), p. 144.

inquiry not entirely unlike other 'genealogical' investigations—the essential life of the Body of Christ is assured, while on the other hand the 'death' of this 'organ' (for instance by the extermination of all bishops at a particular time, or by their universal neglect to consecrate successors) would be entirely fatal, since it would announce the death of the Church itself. In other words, what is really guaranteed by the dominical promise, according to this view, is that the episcopal succession shall not fail. *Therefore*, even though there should be a time in which Christendom should crumble to the point at which there was not a single lay congregation on earth, the continuity of the Body of Christ would be assured by the existence of, say, three bishops and their successors.

It has often been pointed out by opponents of this theory that it makes the Word dependent upon the office. 'Our protest,' says Nathaniel Micklem, 'is not against that which episcopacy represents, but only against that view which would make Word and Sacrament contingent upon the office, not the office on the Word.'[1] This is not quite strictly true, since it may be argued that the valid consecration of a bishop does require and is dependent upon the Word in the sense that St Augustine evidently had in mind when he insisted that it is the Word that 'makes' the sacrament.[2] Were it otherwise, the doctrine of succession we are considering would be a 'magical' one, and it is not this at all. Nevertheless, the protest is well grounded. For what is being neglected in this doctrine is surely the fact that it is the Spirit which, acting through the Word, vivifies the Church, constituting it *corpus Christi*. The doctrine of the Reformed tradition implies a protest against the notion that the Spirit might ever be 'conserved' in an 'organ' within the Body, and against the view that it can be given to any man, or even to the ministry as a whole, to be the curator of the Spirit, or even of the Body which receives its life from Him. 'It is the Spirit that quickeneth; the flesh profiteth nothing: the words that I speak unto you,

[1] N. Micklem, *What is the Faith?* (London, 1936), p. 215.

[2] *Hom. in Joann.*, lxxx, 3: 'Accedat verbum ad elementum et fiet sacramentum.'

they are Spirit, and they are life.'[1] Can there be a custodianship of the Spirit?

The doctrine of the episcopate in the Reformed tradition is not merely that no such custodianship has been promised or given to any man. It is, rather, that Christ's promise to be with His Church 'alway, even unto the end of the world'[2] gives no custodianship of anything even to the Church itself. The divine promise, which makes the Church truly a divine institution in the world, announces that no human custodianship of the Church is needed, for it is in the custodianship of God Himself, who cares for it by pouring out his Spirit upon it, the Body that is united with the Risen Christ. It is essential to the mystery of the union between Christ and His Church that no earthly custodianship is required. But this is not to say that the ministry, the episcopate, is not divinely bestowed. It is the gift of God. Those who share in it have no credentials, however, apart from their being called, within the Body of Christ, and ordained to participate in the ministry. A minister who has been regularly ordained is assured thereby that he truly shares in the holy ministry, even though he be personally the least worthy among his brethren, in piety and learning. With his brethren he may be said to 'carry' or 'bear' the mysteries of the Lord; but he does not 'hold' or 'guard' them, nor do they. God, whom 'the heaven and heaven of heavens cannot contain',[3] is alone the guardian of His own mysteries, including the holy episcopate that is His precious gift to His Church. The Church's safeguard of Christ's teaching and mysteries can be none other than Christ Himself, whose ministers neither can nor need provide any other guarantee.

This means that the ministry is not a special organ in the Body upon which the members must absolutely depend. In the Body of Christ there is no such dependence, except upon the Head. The ministry is therefore not so indispensable that the Church could not conceivably survive without it for a time, or that a complete break in the ministry would be fatal to the continuity

[1] John vi. 63. [2] Matt. xxviii. 20. [3] 1 Kings viii. 27.

of the Church and therefore to its life. It is, rather, that because Christ *is* the Head of the Body, the members of the Body will ever seek to profit from the ministrations of those who are corporately His gift to the Body, and will so order themselves with the ministry that the latter will be enabled to perform its function. It is such a conception of the nature of the Church as dependent upon the Head alone that justifies the important place assigned, in the Reformed Church, to lay people. It can never be held that these must in all circumstances have a voice in the ordering of the Church, for conditions vary throughout the ages. But it may be regarded as ordinarily desirable that lay people should be represented in the Church's councils, for this is beneficial, as a rule, for the life of the Church. It has, moreover, much historical precedent. The language of Tertullian, for instance, suggests that he would have regarded the voice of the laity as desirable.[1] Cyprian certainly recognizes the share that the *plebs christiana* ought to have in the essential powers of the Church.[2] The sharp cleavage between clerks and people that took place fairly early is to be associated with the erroneous doctrine of the Church that was gradually developed and that inevitably fostered false notions about the function of the ministry itself. Even so, it is well known that learned laymen occasionally exercised great influence in the medieval Church, especially in the conciliar era. Beside bishops, doctors of Sacred Theology

[1] Tertullian, *De Exhort. Castitatis*, vii: 'Nonne et laici sacerdotes sumus? Scriptum est, Regnum quoque nos et sacerdotes Deo et Patri suo fecit. Differentiam inter Ordinem et Plebem constituit Ecclesiae auctoritas, et honor per ordinis consessum sanctificatur adeo ubi Ecclesiastici ordinis non est concessus, et offers, et tinguis, et sacerdos es tibi solus. Sed ubi tres, ecclesia est, licet laici.'

[2] Cyprian, *Ep. xxxiv* (*Presbyteris et Diaconibus*): 'Cui re non potui me solum judicem dare, cum multi adhuc de clero absentes sint, nec locum suum vel sero repetendum putaverunt, et haec singulorum tractanda sit et limanda plenius ratio, non tantum cum Collegis meis, sed et cum plebe ipsa universa: expensa enim moderatione libranda et pronuncianda res est, quae in posterum circa ministros Ecclesiae constituat exemplum.' Cf. *Ep. lix* (*Cornelio*). Cyprian also writes (*Ep. xix, Presbyteris et Diaconibus*): 'Hoc enim et verecundiae et disciplinae et vitae ipsi omnium nostrum convenit: ut Praepositi cum Clero convenientes, praesente et stantium plebe, quibus et ipsis pro fide et timore suo honor habendus est, disponere omnia consilii communis religione possimus.' To this the Roman clergy replied (*Ep. xxx, Cypriano Papae Presbyteri et Diaconi Romae consistentes*) as follows: 'Quanquam nobis in tam ingenti negotio placeat, quod et tu ipse tractasti prius: Ecclesiae pacem sustinendam: deinde, sic collatione consiliorum cum episcopis, presbyteris, diaconis, confessoribus, pariter, ac stantibus laicis facta, lapsorum tractare rationem.'

were admitted to vote at the Council of Pisa. At Constance, largely through Gerson's influence, many learned men not in Orders had a full share in the consultations. But these participations by the laity in the ordering and government of the Church were exceptional. They were exceptional because the primitive conception of the nature of the Church itself had been obscured early and had survived only with difficulty and sometimes in curious ways. We find, in the fourth century, the people being expressly deprived, by ecclesiastical canons,[1] of all voice in the election of bishops and priests, which indicates, of course, that they had formerly enjoyed the exercise of that voice.

It is true, as we have noted, that the functions of the episcopate must be distinguished from its governmental role. Yet it is peculiarly important not to suppose that the two may be arbitrarily divorced. The Holy Spirit vivifies the whole Body to which the divine gift of the ministry is bestowed. The ministry receives special gifts, and so it is for the good of the Body that the proclamation of the Word and the 'doing' of the Eucharist be the special functions of the ministry. But it is because this is so that the ministry ought to have a special voice in the government of the Church. It is a symptom of corruption when the people become both mere spectators of ministerial acts and mere obedient followers of a clergy who rule the Church without consulting them at all. But it is also thoroughly unhealthy for the people to have a large say in the government of the Church and yet feel that they are in the last resort absolutely dependent upon the ministry for their very life as members of the Church, the Body of Christ. There can be no such dependence within the Body of Christ. For the Church to be entirely without a ministry, even for a very brief time, would be an immense deprivation, and the Church could not be the Body of Christ were it not, in such unfortunate circumstances, to seek by every possible means to restore to itself the ministry of which it had

[1] The canons of the Council of Laodicea, of which little is known, though it is generally believed to have been held about the year 365. From a reference to the Photinians in one of the canons, the Council could not have been held earlier than 345.

been deprived. But this deprivation would consist not only in the attenuation of worship—the substitution, for example, of a 'reader's service' for the full liturgical splendour of Word and Sacrament; it would consist also in the lack of ministerial gifts to guide the Church in the all-important matter of good order and government. For in the Reformed tradition it can never be said that Word and Sacrament alone suffice for the determination of the True Church. Discipline is no less vital, and under this head must be included the good ordering of the ministry and the government of the whole Church.

According to the general practice of the Reformed Church, representative elders have a share in the administration of Discipline—an arrangement that has proved, despite some abuses, to be a source of great strength to the Church; but it is not to be denied that in the last resort the responsibility for the right administration of Discipline lies with the ministry. This may be shown from the nature of the distinction commonly drawn in Presbyterianism between minister and elder: the fundamental nature of the minister's function is described as *teaching*, that of the elder as *ruling*. By saying that the ministerial function is that of teaching means, of course, that the ministry is the *ecclesia docens*. The elder's 'ruling' is more susceptible to misunderstanding. The verb 'rule' is used of the work of the eldership in the Reformed Church in the sense in which it is used, *mutatis mutandis*, of the work of the tailor and printer; that is to say, the elder 'measures out' the work of the ministry in the Body of Christ. The eldership is a most useful institution; but it is not a divine gift to the Church and it is by no means indispensable.[1] The elders rule not only Discipline. They rule the

[1] The nature of the eldership in the Reformed Church has been the subject of considerable controversy. Most of this has been of little theological or ecclesiological importance, and is singularly arid and dull. For it is plain that since the elders have no part in the *impositio manuum* and do not themselves receive this, they are in no sense within the corporate ministry in the Reformed Church. 'The nature of the eldership,' writes J. H. S. Burleigh (in *Relations between Anglican and Presbyterian Churches* (Edinburgh, 1957), p. 45) 'was long and hotly debated at the Westminster Assembly, where the Scots, and especially Gillespie, [*supra, c.* v] contended for it as a Scriptural office and therefore divinely authorized. They did not gain their point, and the *Form of Presbyterial Church Government*, which is still among the official standards of the Church of Scotland, accepts the eldership (office-bearers "such as in

Sacrament (that is, they 'dispense' the elements to the people) and they rule the Word, for it is part of their duty to go amongst the flock 'distributing' the Word that the minister proclaims. As a practical measure for the welfare of the Church their importance is incalculable. Ecclesiologically, however, there is nothing to be said of them that may not be said of the Body of Christ generally. It is incorrect to attribute to them ministerial functions relating to Discipline. For not only can no exercise of Discipline take place without the ministry; the ministry is distinguished from the eldership as having the teaching function, and Discipline (from *discere*, *discipulus*) is nothing if not teaching. To separate Discipline from Word and Sacrament is, as Calvin well knew, as disastrous to the Church in its way as is the separation of Sacrament from Word, which, it was contended by the Reformers, was a principal cause of the need for the Reform.

Where the ministry is properly fulfilling its function, however, it will seek to use every agency at its disposal for making itself effective in the Body of Christ, and in the eldership is to be found an agency that has proved very valuable. Its place in the life of the Church is nevertheless determined by social and political circumstances rather than ecclesiological principles. In Hungary, for instance, where the Reformed Church has for long been strong, 'feudal conditions made Kirk Sessions generally impracticable till the eighteenth century';[1] yet since then has been developed a consistorial system with a bishop and a 'lay-curator' for each ecclesiastical district. It is in the nature of the case that where the eldership is organized it will be much more closely associated with the administration of Discipline than with the administration of Word and Sacrament, for it is in the

the Reformed Churches are commonly called elders") as "warranted" by Scripture, but does not include 1. Tim. 5: 17 among the proof-texts.' There is no doubt whatsoever, as Burleigh (*ad loc.*) says, that discussions on this question within Presbyterianism 'are often coloured by emotional reactions to the terms "cleric" and "lay", and much of the debate has been a dispute about words'. The elders, though associated with the ministry, do not participate in it. On the *impositio manuum*, cf. Alexander Martin, *Presbyterian Orders and Admission of Ministers from other Churches* (pamphlet) (Edinburgh, 1941), p. 18 ff.

[1] G. D. Henderson, *The Claims of the Church of Scotland* (London, 1951), p. 209.

administration of Discipline that the ministry needs most help from the Body for the right exercise of its ministerial duties. Elders who, for lack of theological learning, could give little help to the minister in the proclamation of the Word, can give immense assistance in the administration of Discipline.

The nature of the eldership in the Reformed Church can better be understood with reference to a class of elders that is now obsolete: the 'doctors' provided for in the *First Buik of Discipline*. The doctor was an elder whose learning was sufficient to enable him to assist even in the teaching of the flock: he was, according to an old definition, 'teacher of the Catechisme, and rudiments of religione.'[1] The same source, after describing the doctor's various functions, sharply distinguishes even *his* office, closely associated though it is with the ministry, from the office of the pastor or minister: 'Bot to preache unto the peple, to minister the sacraments, and to celebrat mariagis, perteins not unto the Doctour, unles he be utherwayis ordourlie callit; howbeit the pasture [Pastor] may teache in the scoles, as he qwha hes also the gift of knawledge oftentymis meit thairfoir, as the examples of Policarpus and utheris testifie.'[2] Elders who are not doctors have the duty 'to watche diligentlie upone the flok committit unto thair charge, bayth publicklie and privatlie, that no corruptioun of religioun or maneris enter thairin. As the pastouris and doctouris sould be diligent in teacheing and sowing the seid of the word, so the eldaris sould be cairfull in seiking the fruitt of the same in the peple. It apperteins to thame to assist the pastour in examinatioun of thame that cumis to the Lordis table, and in visiting the seik. They sould be cairfull to caus the actis of the Assembleis, als weill particular as prouinciall or generall, to be put in executioun. They sould be diligent in admonisching of all mene of thair dewteis, according to the reull of the Evangell. Thingis that thay cane not correct be privie admonitioun, thay

[1] *The Booke of the Universall Kirk of Scotland* (Edinburgh, 1839, ed. Peterkin), p. 544 ('Headis and Conclusionis', cap. v, 1). This book is a reprint of the earliest records of the Reformed Church in Scotland. The original MSS. perished in the fire at the Houses of Parliament on October 16, 1834.

[2] *Loc. cit.* (cap. v, 6).

sould bring to the assembly of the elderschip.[1] Thair principall office is, to hauld assembleis with the pastouris and doctouris . . . for establisching of guid ordour, and executioun of discipline: Unto the quhilks assembleis all personis ar subject, that remane within thair boundis.'[2]

The definition of the functions of the ministers themselves shows also that it is to the corporate ministry, not to the eldership, that it *essentially* belongs to minister Discipline as well as Word and Sacrament. For it is affirmed that the pastors or bishops or ministers 'ar callit sumetymis pasturis, becaus thay feid thair congregationis, sumetymis *episcopi*, or bischoppis, becaus thay watche aboue thair flokis; sumetymes ministers, be reasone of thair service and office; and sumtyme presbyteris and seinouris, frome the grauitie in maneris, quhilk thay aucht to haue, in taking cair of the spirituall gouerament, quhilk aucht to be most deir unto thame'.[3] Finally, 'all publick denunciations that ar to be maid in the kirk befoir the congregationis, concerning ecclesiasticall effairis, belang to the office of the ministrie, for he is as messenger and herauld betwene God and the people in all thais effairis.'[4]

Certain conclusions may now be stated. The *magisterium* of the Church is recognized to be proper to the corporate ministry or episcopate in its exercise of the *ministerium* that is the divine gift to the Body. But this is to be understood always with reference to the fundamental ecclesiological doctrine that Christ alone is both Master and Minister. Therefore not only is the *ministerium*, as is often pointed out, really a subministration under Christ; the *magisterium*, which is not a divine gift but only a concomitant of the *ministerium* in the visible Body, is indubitably

[1] No such assembly may be made, however, without the presence of at least one minister. In the Kirk Session, the lowest court, the minister acts as Moderator. (Cf. W. G. Black and J. R. Christie, *The Parochial Ecclesiastical Law of Scotland* (4th ed., Edinburgh, 1928), p. 466; also J. T. Cox, *op. cit.*, p. 106.)

[2] *The Booke of the Universall Kirk of Scotland* (*ed. cit.*), p. 545 f. The minister is not, however, subject to the Kirk Session over which he presides; he is subject only to the higher courts of the Church. (Cf. Cox, *ad loc.*) The principle is that in respect of his participation in the corporate ministry or episcopate of the whole Church, he is to be judged by others who share it with him.

[3] *Op. cit.*, p. 542 f.

[4] *Op. cit.*, p. 544.

submagisterial only. The responsibility for both the *ministerium* and the *magisterium* lies essentially with the corporate ministry, the episcopate, which, however, while being responsible for the exercise of the *ministerium*, ought to have the support of the whole Body in the exercise of the *magisterium*. For this purpose the eldership has so far proved the most valuable agency, and the office of the elder is such that elders should be set apart for their office and hold it, as they do, for life.[1] In this they are distinguished from other office-bearers in the Church, who are appointed for various special purposes such as the care of ecclesiastical property and for a specified period of time. Because Discipline involves *magisterium* in a special degree, the function of the eldership is in a special manner connected with it; nevertheless, Word, Sacrament and Discipline, being inseparable, belong together and essentially to the corporate ministry.

We come at length to the question of the nature of the apostolic succession according to the Reformed ecclesiology. We have seen that the real principle of continuity must be Christ Himself. It is He who, by His promise to be with His Church always, ensures for it the only continuity it can need. The principle of continuity must not be sought elsewhere, even in the corporate ministry, the episcopate, which is the divine gift to the Church: it must be sought only in the divine Giver. In the ministry, the episcopate, may be found, however, a visible, historic expression of the continuity He provides. The continuity is not destroyed or even attenuated by any failure in the continuity of the ministry. Even were this to be for a time entirely extinguished, it would not mean that God had forsaken His Church, or that the Church was no longer *corpus Christi*. To say otherwise would be like saying that the water in a mountain stream has ceased to be the same because at some point in its course it has for a while trickled to a stop. In such a case, neither does the ground immediately become a desert, nor is the purity of the water to

[1] There seems to be no strictly ecclesiological reason for this; but there are excellent practical reasons, apart from venerable custom: the work of the elder, closely associated with that of the ministry, makes the office too sacred to be temporary.

be suspected as it spurts forth again, nor does one doubt that it comes from the same spring. The water is no more and no less likely to be contaminated in its course when the stream is flowing continuously than when it has been momentarily impeded. There is no guarantee against such contamination: *ecclesia Reformata, semper reformanda.* The water stands ever in need of purification; but because of the Source whence it comes it is purifiable. It is this, according to the Reformed tradition, that is all-important.

Even the Scriptures themselves, the norm or 'rule of faith' according to the Reformed tradition, are the norm only in the sense that they point infallibly to the Source. 'It is beyond dispute,' wrote a distinguished Scottish theologian, 'that the fundamental conviction of the Reformers was that the Gospel is true which was preached by Christ, and more fully unfolded by His apostle Paul. It was not so much that they accepted the Gospel because they knew the Bible to be the Word of God, as that they claimed all perfection for the Bible because through it they had come into possession of the vivifying gospel of the grace of God.'[1] The historical continuity of the *ministerium* may be said also to attest the promises of Christ and to direct us to him who is behind and before and within the Church. It is only that the promises cannot be made to depend on it. As well might my son suppose that my love for him and presence with him depended upon the gifts I am pleased to bestow upon him. It is a truism to say, pointing to what was once the danger of bibliolatry, that the New Testament sprang from the life of the Church. The observation must be supplemented by another: the life of the Church sprang from Christ who alone sustains it.

How, then, it may be asked, are we to distinguish between orthodoxy and heterodoxy? For, as Alan of Lille observed eight centuries ago, the textual 'authorities' have wax noses: you can turn them whichever way you please.[2] Were the Scriptures such

[1] W. P. Paterson, *The Rule of Faith* (4th ed., London, 1932), p. 76. He quotes (*ad loc.*) the *Theses Bernenses*: 'Sancta Christiana Ecclesia, cujus unicum caput est Christus, nata est ex Verbo Dei, in eoque permanet, nec vocem audit alieni.'

[2] Alan of Lille, *De Fide catholica*, I, xxx.

an 'authority' the case would indeed be hopeless; nor would it be radically improved if authority in the Church could be said to consist of Scripture and tradition as interpreted by the living voice of the episcopate. But though it be idolatrous to set up any such authority or combination or hierarchy of authorities within the Church other than Christ Himself, the value of all these as witnesses to Christ is not to be overlooked. It is as absurd to suppose that heresies are to be permitted without protest by the episcopate as it is to affirm that they may be eliminated by its decree. The real danger, however, does not lie in the spread of false doctrine, for false doctrine, though it may trouble, cannot hurt him who is truly in the *koinonia* of the Body. The real danger lies, rather, in the alienation of members of the Body from the Head in such a way that, depriving themselves of the Source of their life, they search for and find a life apart from the Body, a life that turns parasite upon the same. The importance of the apostolic ministry does not lie in its capacity to safeguard doctrine; it lies in the ministration of it. The episcopate has, indeed, a weighty responsibility to refuse ordination to candidates whose theological competence is insufficient. But it is a finite, human responsibility, for although the theological competence of such a candidate is important, the episcopate is only accrediting the man's intellectual attainments as does a college or university in laureating him. No such laureation can ensure that the man will not turn out to be far more dangerous to the Church than ever was Theophrastus von Hohenheim, who, it appears, claimed to have been laureated *Sacrae Theologiae Doctor* by God.[1] Ordination itself cannot guarantee that the ordinand, received though he is into the episcopate, shall not err in doctrine; it can no more guarantee this than it can ensure that he will not otherwise betray his Master. But the Body of Christ cannot be so dependent upon the gift of the ministry that such a betrayal might work fatal havoc within it. Ordination does, on the other hand,

[1] This Swiss physician (1493–1541) also arbitrarily assumed the name 'Paracelsus'. Cf. K. Goldammer, 'Neues zur Lebensgeschichte und Persönlichkeit des Theophrastus Paracelsus' (I: 'War Paracelsus Doktor der Theologie?') in *Theologische Zeitschrift*, III (1947), pp. 191–207.

guarantee that if the ordinand be faithful in the ministry to which he has been ordained, he shall indeed participate in it. He could receive no more. He has the unique gift of the ministry. Anyone may be instrumental in leading men to the Church; but none can minister Christ who does not share in the corporate ministry. Any competent theologian may talk about Christ, not only in learned expositions of Christian doctrine but also, it may be, with great spiritual profit to the souls of men; but the humblest minister ministers Christ Himself.

The ecclesiology expounded by a Bampton Lecturer nearly a century ago expresses in strong terms a fundamental standpoint of the Reformed tradition. 'If the holders of ministerial office and power,' he says, 'come to be regarded merely as representatives of their brethren, deriving all authority to exercise their functions from the express or implied delegation of the multitude in each successive generation—which is, I presume, more or less the extreme Protestant view—one of two consequences can hardly fail to follow: either there will be a mere congregationalism, in which every community, either great or small (and communities will gradually, by the continued operation of the same cause, become smaller and smaller), will feel itself at liberty to elect and depose its ministers, to determine without appeal upon the truth for itself, and to institute laws and rites of worship according to its own judgment—a consequence which would involve innumerable varieties of teaching and practice, and divisions or subdivisions without end—or, if it were attempted to set up any central and general authority, it would be impossible to establish, or, if it were impugned, to prove, the universal consent on which alone it could be intelligibly based, and extremely difficult to displace it if, in consequence of its becoming corrupt or tyrannical, or for any other adequate reason, that universal consent, once given, should be withheld or changed. . . . On the other hand, if the holders of such offices were to be regarded merely as descendants and inheritors of powers originally confined to twelve men, and subsequently handed down from them by direct and exclusive succession to themselves, I do not see how they could be regarded otherwise than as a body, than a separate, irresponsible, supreme company, as compared with the mass of lay Christians. . . . In short, on this theory the clergy would be the real Church, and the lay-people simply dumb recipients of whatever the clerisy—that is the Church—chose to lay upon them.'[1] But it is inevitable that corruptions such as Moberly here describes should ensue when the significance of the Church as *corpus Christi* is lost—indeed, as soon as the force of the Pauline figure is attenuated. Dix never comes nearer the heart of all ecclesiological heresies than in his vivid allusion to the eloquent exchange that took place in the Middle Ages between the phrase *corpus mysticum* and the phrase *corpus verum*. The former, he finds, seems to be applied in the first five centuries exclusively to the Sacrament. Origen can speak, on the other hand, of the Church as 'the real and more perfect Body of Christ' in comparing it with the physical body that was crucified. By the thirteenth century, however, the terms *corpus verum* and *corpus mysticum* 'had exactly changed their meanings.'[2] So by then there could be no ambiguity in the words of the hymn to the Sacred Host, *Ave verum Corpus natum*, while even in discussing the Eucharist, St Thomas could use the phrase *corpus mysticum* of the Church without any danger of ambiguity. It is hardly surprising that such a widespread loss of the sense of the actuality of the Church as the Body should have resulted in radically mistaken notions about the nature of the ministry. Though the Reformation did much to recapture the essential ecclesiological idea upon which so much else depends, the vivacity of the idea has not yet been fully recovered. In many quarters it has been entirely lost, resulting in interpretations of Christianity that would have been more abhorrent to the Reformers than the worst of that which they attributed to the Papacy. 'And it is to be feared,' Dix goes on, 'that all over the West since then the refinements of theological language have

[1] George Moberly, *The Administration of the Holy Spirit in the Body of Christ* (Oxford, 1868), p. 57 ff. Moberly, later Bishop of Salisbury, was the father of R. C. Moberly, a contributor to *Lux Mundi*.

[2] Gregory Dix, *The Shape of the Liturgy* (*ed. cit.*), p. 246 f.

greatly weakened the primitive force of the word "Body" as applied both to the church and to the sacrament by contrast with the physical Body that was born of Mary.'[1]

For the same reason, however, it appears to the present writer to be hardly less mistaken to say that 'It is the transmission of the Canon . . . from faith to faith throughout the generations that constitutes the true apostolic succession'.[2] For once again the hypothetical case must be considered: are we to say that the Church would die if every copy of the sacred text were to be destroyed? The life of the Church can no more be made to depend upon the preservation of the text of Scripture than it may be said to depend upon the 'genealogical' succession of bishops. It depends only upon Christ who, if He has not guaranteed such a 'genealogical' succession of bishops, most certainly has not given any assurance concerning the safe keeping of the Scriptures. It would indeed be grievous beyond description for the Church to lose the text of the Scriptures; but it must not be said that it would be cataclysmic, that is, that it would truly sweep away the Church. And if this be so, how can it be affirmed that the apostolic succession is in any sense constituted by the transmission of the Canon? It is constituted, rather, by the mysterious transmission of life in the individual 'cells' that together form the Body, united by the Head. Bible and episcopate are but witnesses to this. But the episcopate or corporate ministry is in a peculiar case, since it is peculiarly the divine gift to the Body.

It cannot be too emphatically stated that the ministry, though 'corporate', is not a Body organized by the Head as is the Church. To suppose it to have such a divine organization of its own is the medieval, 'hierarchical' error to which we alluded earlier. The ministry 'flows' from the Head, and the ministers participate in the current that has that divine Source. In participating in the current of Christ's gift to the Church, the individual ministers have a 'togetherness', a 'corporateness'; but

[1] *Op. cit.*, p. 247.

[2] G. S. Hendry, 'The Exposition of Holy Scripture' in *Scottish Journal of Theology*, I, 1 (1948), p. 41. P. T. Forsyth (*The Church and the Sacraments* (London, 1917), p. 59) expresses a similar idea.

ordination admits them to participation in the flow of the gift, and cannot be said to 'incorporate' them into anything, as Baptism incorporates the neophyte into the Body of Christ. This means that while the ministry is the divinely bestowed episcopate, its organization is a matter of human ordering in the sense that it has only the duty to organize itself as efficiently as possible for its ministration. In the fulfilment of this moral duty it will arrange itself, now in one way, now in another. There is no reason, on this view, why even in the visibly integrated Church that is the ecumenical hope, there should not be a variety of forms of ecclesiastical government. The episcopate itself is indispensable, for it *is* the ministry and it is one. But the arrangement into ranks is a matter of mere practical duty and the exigencies of circumstance. These circumstances vary enormously in the contemporary scene. The episcopate may in some places be failing in its duty if it does not provide for patriarchs and archbishops; elsewhere the work of the episcopate may be performed better without bishops. It should be observed, however, although no ecclesiological principle acknowledged in the Reformed tradition can be invoked here, that it is not easy in the conditions the Church faces today to justify the widespread use of a system that makes no provision for the oversight of the clergy by individual ministers set apart (that is, consecrated) for the purpose by the ministry and responsible to the same for the performance of certain singularly unenviable duties. It is true that in the past it has been possible in some circumstances to have, as in Scotland, especially in the conditions prevailing before the Industrial Revolution, a ministry which, under a 'Presbyterian' system and without bishops, was able efficiently to perform the functions of the episcopate. But neither is such an arrangement suitable to the conditions commonly prevailing today throughout the world, nor was it one that Knox deemed expedient even for sixteenth-century Scotland.

CHAPTER XII

CONCLUSION

The Reformed tradition, besides insisting on Word, Sacrament and Discipline as marks of the True Church, presupposes both the continuity and the essential unity of the Church of Christ. The Pauline figure well expresses, therefore, what is fundamentally important in the Reformed ecclesiology. Moreover, the Head-Body relation, inseparable from the idea of the Church as *corpus Christi*, not only seemed peculiarly apposite to the Reformers in their historical situation; it is central in any doctrine of the Church in the Reformed tradition. The continuity of the Church, being a continuity of life, is essentially a spiritual actuality; yet for the same reason it must express itself visibly in history. To this point we shall presently return. The continuity of the Church is especially attested in the historic continuity of the work of the corporate ministry, which, however, though it witnesses to apostolic succession cannot guarantee this. Scripture, whose divine authority is recognized by the whole Church and assured to each individual believer *testimonio Spiritus Sancti*, provides a norm standing over and apart from the Church which, though it has the duty of expounding and interpreting it, is bound by it in such a way that it can in no circumstances claim any authority over it. The doctrines of the Holy Trinity, the Incarnation, and the Person of Christ, as expressed in the formulas of Nicaea and Chalcedon are generally accepted as normative in the interpretation of Scripture; not, indeed, because of any authority conferred upon them by the Church, which could confer none, but because these doctrines are held to shine forth from Scripture itself. The reverence towards Scripture characteristic of the Reformation must not, however, be taken as indicating any abrogation of the doctrine of the Church or a diminished sense of its importance. On the contrary, the reverence for Scripture draws attention to the centrality of the doctrine of the Church: Scripture derives its authority from God whence also springs directly the life of the Church, organically united to Christ, its only Head. As God is one, so also is His Church. The Cyprianic formula, *extra ecclesiam nulla salus*, is vital to the Reformed tradition. Barth reminds us—and in this he is supported by many in the Reformed Church whose theological views on other subjects differ considerably from his—that this principle is one 'which not even the most profound humility will allow us to deny or qualify'.[1]

But the importance of the Church in the Reformed tradition far exceeds the negative conception expressed in Cyprian's phrase. The Church, as the one Body of Christ on earth and the unique instrument of Christ's redemptive process, is more than the locus of individual salvation. Only in the Church can we be ingrafted into Christ and fed by Him so that we become organically united to Him and to one another. As there is but one Christ, so there is but one Church. There is no other place whither we may go to find the life that He alone can and does impart directly from the Source of all life. The essential principle of the unity of the Church is Christ Himself; but as the continuity of the life of the Church is visibly expressed in history, so the unity of the life of the Church must likewise find visible expression. But since unity does not imply uniformity, what does it mean to say that the unity of the Church is visibly expressed? It has often been said that the unity is 'visible to faith'. In the opinion of the present writer, such a phrase obscures rather than clarifies the position. Christ, the essential principle, is truly known in the Church, and the Church is of such a nature that it cannot but give visible expression to the essential unity it enjoys. But the expression of the unity may be, for various reasons, obscured. It is a corollary of faith, and an implicate of what is known in experience in the life of the Body of Christ, that there must be visible expression of the essential

[1] K. Barth, in *Revelation* (ed. Baillie and Martin, London, 1937), p. 74.

unity of the Church; but this does not mean that I cannot help finding it, or even that I am assured of finding it if I try hard enough. In other words, to say that it is capable of being seen does not imply that it can, in all ages and in every circumstance, be clearly and easily seen. Even less does it mean that there could ever be an empirical verification of the unity of the Church, or that the unity is ever guaranteed by any visible expression of it. The external expression of unity, like the external expression of continuity, can but witness to the actuality that is, for the believer, more convincingly expressed in and by participation itself.

No attempt to discover the visible expression of the unity of the Church in the contemporary situation would be possible without some consideration of what we have called the Separatist principle. Though it cannot be pretended that there is any complete agreement on what precisely constitutes a sect, the well-known Troeltschian distinction between 'church-type' organizations and 'sect-type' organizations is now widely recognized to depend on a special theory which, whether it be good or bad sociology, throws no light on the ecclesiological problem. In actual practice, the word 'sect' usually bears a pejorative sense; yet it is not infrequently employed, perhaps especially but by no means exclusively in the United States, in a way that purports to express no value-judgment.This latter usage, however, itself generally presupposes the Separatist principle. Various attempts have been made to define the sectarian spirit or, at any rate, point to the distinctive features of the idea of the sect, contradistinguished from the idea of the Church. Gerhard Gloege has suggested that the sect, as a *haeresis*, purports to spring from the autonomous action of men, while the Church, as an *ecclesia*, purports to have been called forth by God.[1] But surely many sects not only think of themselves as having been called forth by God, but care very much for the authenticity of this calling; what they do not care about, and what in some

[1] Gerhard Gloege, *Reich Gottes und Kirche im Neuen Testament* (Gutersloh, 1929), p. 346 n.

cases they eagerly repudiate, is anything that could be construed as historic continuity with the apostolic Church, the Body of Christ. Brunner is nearer the mark when he represents the idea of the sect as really a dogmatic conception consciously or otherwise opposed to all ecclesiological principles. It is, he writes, 'not primarily a sociological principle, or an idea of Church order, but it is a dogmatic conception.'[1] That is to say, those who are more concerned to uphold a dogmatic position or system than they are for the unity of the Body of Christ are exhibiting the sectarian spirit. But this suggestion, though attractive and stimulating, presents considerable difficulties. For it is sometimes necessary for the well-being of the Church to make dogmatic protest: this was, indeed, the case at the Reformation, for example, where the health of the Church could not have been restored, so as to express more clearly its true unity and continuity, without a vigorously dogmatic protest against the papal theory that derogated from the fundamental ecclesiological principle of the Headship of Christ.

The definition of a sect that C. C. Morrison has proposed merits inspection. 'A sect,' he says, 'is a part of the body of Christ which exercises by itself and for itself those functions which belong to the unity of the whole body.'[2] This is to pursue the figurative language in such a way as to suggest that a sect is a sort of malignant growth upon the Body. The notion is reminiscent of what appears to have been in the mind of the Reformers when they spoke of Rome. But it would seem to describe a corrupt or deformed Church rather than define what is more commonly intended by the term 'sect' in traditional or contemporary usage. Many of the American sects listed, for example, by Elmer T. Clark in his useful little reference work[3] would not think in terms of the Body of Christ at all, and, while claiming the name of Christian, would repudiate all ecclesiological conceptions. Some, professing to care nothing for either unity or

[1] E. Brunner, *The Divine Imperative* (London, 1937), p. 542.
[2] C. C. Morrison, *What is Christianity?* (Chicago, 1940), p. 280.
[3] *The Small Sects in America* (Nashville, 1949).

continuity, would not, on the other hand, make any claim to exclusiveness, but would regard themselves, rather, as but groups of individuals who find it convenient or useful or edifying to be gathered together.[1] It has been suggested by an Anglican writer that while no sects as such can be accounted in any sense the Church, members of sects who have been baptized may be said to belong to the Church.[2] But even this very attractive idea presents difficulties, because it seems to presuppose that the baptismal rite as practised in sectarian groups is always intended to be Baptism in the sense of ingrafting into the one Body. In some cases, this is what is intended; in others, where there is no interest in or concern for the unity or continuity of the Church, it can hardly be said that by the baptismal rite a person is nevertheless always in fact ingrafted into the Body of Christ. It would be a magical notion indeed that a person could be ingrafted into the Body of Christ though the baptismal rite was performed within and according to the practice of a sect whose tenets implied hostility to the ecclesiological notion of the Church as the one Body of Christ. A particular minister in the Reformed Church may indeed, by reason of his being personally tinged with Separatist or 'individualist' or 'liberal' ideas, lack the intention to do what, according to the Reformed tradition, he must purport to do; yet it may well be argued that such a Baptism is not vitiated thereby, since there can be no doubt that according to the Reformed tradition the ingrafting is intended by the Church.

It is a melancholy commonplace that there is, in fact, a great deal of sectarian thinking within the Church. This fact has prompted some writers to develop the idea that both individuals and the various Christian communions belong to the Body of Christ in varying degrees. Another Anglican has written: 'What are we to say of the position at the present day? Here we are a divided Christianity; many different bodies each claiming to be the true Church or at any rate to be a true representative of

[1] *Supra*, p. 13 ff.

[2] H. Burn-Murdoch, *Church, Continuity and Unity* (Cambridge, 1945), p. 46.

Christianity. What is the position of an ordinary Christian? The Roman Church, with a self-sufficiency for which there is no justification, will call all schismatics who do not belong to its communion. Some Anglicans with equal self-sufficiency and equal want of justification will call all schismatics who do not belong to an episcopal Church. Some members of Protestant bodies are equally satisfied with their own position and condemn all who deviate even a hair's breadth from their orthodoxy. I do not think that we can feel that such attitudes have any justification. The Church which should be one is divided and of none of the separated bodies can it be said that it represents the full Apostolic tradition. We know that this is the case of every other body but our own: it is obvious that it must be true also of ourselves. . . . It is the bounden duty of all Christians to do all in their power to unite the separated members of Christ's flock, and to build up anew the Body of Christ.'[1] The same writer goes on to suggest that in modern usage the term 'Church' is so constantly used to denote a 'separated body of Christians organized together on the basis of a more or less imperfect representation of the Christian tradition and in distinction from other Christians', that it would be more correct to talk of the Anglican Schism, the Congregationalist Schism, the Presbyterian Schism, the Roman Schism, the Methodist Schism, and so forth.[2] A similar conclusion has been reached by another writer: 'the "visible" Church being manifestly divided, all bodies professing Christianity belong to it imperfectly and in varying degrees.'[3] While such language is in some ways eminently expressive of the Reformed tradition, the conception is attended by a serious difficulty. For unless there be a criterion or norm for judging the degree to which a particular 'schism' does express itself as the Body of Christ and reveal the principle of unity upon which the actuality of the Body depends, the notion of the Body of Christ itself becomes too 'mystical' to correspond to the notion of the Body of Christ as this is understood in the Reformed tradition.

[1] A. C. Headlam, *The Doctrine of the Church and Christian Reunion* (*ed. cit.*), p. 223 f.
[2] *Op. cit.*, p. 225.
[3] O. C. Quick, *The Christian Sacraments* (*ed. cit.*), p. 147.

Moreover, it is easy to lose sight of the distinction between 'schisms' which each claim to be the Church, or a branch of the Church, and 'sects' which in some cases, as we have already noted, repudiate the notion of the Church in any sense at all like that in which the term is employed in the Reformed tradition.

In accordance with the central ecclesiological tradition of the Reformation, we have maintained in the present work that the essential and only ground of the unity of the Christian Church must be Christ Himself. Man may discover, yet he cannot create that unity. The discovery of the unity in its visible expression may be difficult; nevertheless, even when schism abounds the expression of the Church's unity must be discoverable. But what, precisely, is it that we are to look for? What, indeed, is it that we should expect to see clearly, for instance, in the 'undivided Church' whose realization would answer the prayers of the ecumenical movement? It is plain that there would be, for example, diversity of organization: what we have said of the diverse expressions of the episcopate implied in the doctrine of the corporate ministry in the Reformed Church is sufficient to preclude that expectation. Certainly no liturgical uniformity would be expected, and surely we are not praying to see on earth a Christendom in which there will be no place for theological controversy, even on apparently fundamental doctrinal propositions. We are praying, indeed, for the clearer expression of the unity that we affirm must be already expressed despite the obstacles that impede our clear vision of it. But what, precisely, is the nature of the expression that we would more clearly behold? It is in the spirit of the ecumenical hope to feel, with Lacordaire, that 'the present is of little account, the future is everything';[1] but the words mean nothing in our context unless we can in some fashion delineate that future for whose sake we pronounce ourselves to be willing to forego the present.

The outward, historical, corporeal form of the Church can never be really separated from the inner form. Yet it is the out-

[1] Th. Foisset, *Vie du R. P. Lacordaire* (Paris, 1870), vol. ii, p. 48: 'J'attendrai d'autres temps et je ferai le bien quelconque qui me restera possible. Le présent est peu de chose, l'avenir est tout.'

ward form that is 'divided'. The outward form of the Church is 'divided', however, because of rather than in spite of the inward unity. It is 'divided' because in entering history the outward form is limited by history. But such is the uniqueness of the Church that the 'divisions' imposed by its entry into history are constantly being healed by the action of the Church which, through the sacred ministry, proclaims the Word, celebrates the Eucharist, and ministers Discipline. In every such action the Church actualizes itself as the Body of Christ; therefore the patterns of history do not succeed in what, in the nature of the case, they are constantly doing to break up the Body of Christ, the Church, as they do break up human institutions—empires, political clubs and religious sects. This continual, mysterious penetration of the 'divided' outward form of the Church by Christ, its essential principle of unity, is also expressed in the fraction in the Eucharist, for only in being broken does the bread become *corpus Christi*. The Word likewise, in being proclaimed, is at once enmeshed in the various historical environments of its proclamation; yet though these open up around it, as it were, to trap and stifle and so kill the living Word, the power of the same Word breaks the bonds of every such imprisonment which would otherwise be in all cases lethal. Discipline also, whose life depends upon the divine *agape* in the Church, is in every act of its ministration turned into a juridical action and would thereby die but for the power of the divine *agape* that prevents this. This is what it means to have the Real Presence of the risen and ascended Lord as Head of the Body.

It does not mean, however, that human sin is entirely powerless to *injure* the Body of Christ, as though this were miraculously immune from the effect of its being in history. The promise is that the gates of hell shall not prevail against the Church, not that they shall be incapable of disturbing it. So if we are to pursue the organistic metaphor that provides the best means of understanding the nature of the Church's unity, we may say that the pride, the self-will, that is at the root of the sin of schism can and does inflict great injury upon the Body, causing grievous lesions and terrible carcinomata. Christ may be said to be thereby, in this sense, crucified afresh in His Body, the Church.[1] It is the function of the members of the Body, not least of the ministry, to be the instruments of the Body's healing; yet only the divine life that is in the Body may be said to cicatrize the lesions and wither the carcinomata. This divine act of continual healing and renewal of the Body is a visible expression of the unity of the same. But what would be a case of it?

In the course of the past century, more than one cleavage has seemed to split Christians more strikingly, from the point of view of an observer attending to the empirical facts, than do even the 'denominational differences'. The 'face of the Church' seemed, for example, to be about to crack wide open last century as a result of sharply different attitudes taken on the subject of Biblical criticism, when this was still a highly controversial enterprise. It seemed that not only among Christians generally but also among the learned of various communions, a radical difference of outlook would lead to two fundamentally incompatible interpretations of the nature of the Christian religion itself, on the part of those who professed to adhere to this. Despite a notable reactionary outburst of emotionalism, not least in some parts of America, in the twenties, in favour of an unhistorical and untheological doctrine of the literal inerrancy of Scripture, the situation is now so altered that the whole controversy has scarcely any meaning in the life of Christendom today. It would be difficult to convince anyone intimately familiar with the temper of the controversy that raged three quarters of a century ago that either the process of dialectic or any external circumstance was in itself the cause of the healing of the breach. The more carefully one examines the historical facts, the less acceptable any such explanation becomes. While there can be, of course, no assent-compelling 'proof' in any matter of this kind, those who believe in the essential unity of the Church can see here a visible expression of the invisible principle of unity. The 'wholeness' of the faith of the Church, which is, as Hebert has

[1] Heb. vi. 6.

pointed out, more than and other than 'the sum-total of beliefs held by all Christians everywhere and always',[1] appears to have visibly triumphed over the limitations of human understanding.

Examples of such healing of doctrinal cleavages in the Church could, of course, be indefinitely multiplied, from apostolic times down to the present. The evidence, being evidence for faith, may be said to be similar, indeed, to the kind of evidence with which we are familiar in the traditional demonstrations (so-called proofs), cosmological and teleological, of the existence of God. The facts adduced could be interpreted dysteleologically, and in the nature of the case there could never be any empirical or historical method by means of which an historian who did so interpret them might be intellectually forced to change his opinions. The evidence is, however, none the less of a visible kind. That is to say, the *corpus Christi* that is visible to faith is not a *corpus mysticum* discernible only to the 'eye of the mind', but the 'visible Catholic Church' unto which 'Christ hath given the ministry, oracles, and ordinances of God'.[2] A distinction must be made between the visibility of the marks of the 'True Church' and the visibility of the principle of unity. The marks, being outward expressions of the authority of the True Church, enable me both to distinguish this from false sects of human origin and to detect corruptions in the Church itself. But the principle of unity, being the living Christ Himself, cannot be directly expressed in a static manner, as in a particular ecclesiastical order or confessional formula. It might be said, it is true, that such static expressions do in a limited fashion sometimes reflect the principle of unity in the Church. But this would be somewhat like saying that the tidiness of a man's clothes or desk reflect the tidiness of his mind: in certain favourable circumstances they may; but it would be unwarrantable to accept them as being in any sense evidence of this, since any good tailor may dress a madman in excellent taste, and any loyal secretary may make an incompetent executive's desk look orderly. The direct ex-

[1] A. G. Hebert, *The Form of the Church* (*ed. cit.*), p. 92.
[2] *Westminster Confession*, xxv, 3; cf. the *Savoy Declaration*, xxvi.

pression of a living principle must itself be living and dynamic. What is visibly presented is the divine activity operating in and through the Church, human sin and folly notwithstanding.

The manifestation of human sin and folly that most conspicuously obscures the visibility of the Church's wholeness is our failure as members of the Body of Christ to yield ourselves up entire, body and soul, to the *κοινωνία* of the Body. The concern of the Head is not only for the 'numerical' wholeness of the Church but for the complete incorporation of every member into it. The dichotomy between the 'sacred' and the 'secular' life of the individual, which is fundamentally alien to the doctrine of the Church itself according to the Reformed tradition, is bound to result in obscuring the visible expression of the essential principle of unity. 'That unity of all human living,' as one writer puts it, 'a balanced wholeness of work, craftsmanship, family life, scholarship, games, art, bound together in a living and joyful sacrifice laid before God in worship, by union with the Word made Flesh and in the power of the Holy Spirit,'[1] is what must be brought into the Body of Christ if we are to see the full visible expression of the unity of the Church. So what appears as the fragmentariness of the visible Church is but the shadow of the fragmentariness of the participation of ourselves in the life of the Body. It is not to be expected that, being ourselves imperfectly willing to realize our ingrafting into the Body, we shall be able to see more than an imperfect visible expression of the principle of unity of that Body in whose life we inadequately participate.

Because a Christian philosophy of history has never yet been sufficiently worked out in terms of Scriptural eschatology and the ecclesiology of the Reformed tradition, there have been in recent years sharp differences of opinion among theologians in this tradition on the relation between Church and Kingdom. This controversy raises theological questions that are beyond the scope of the present work; yet certain points must be noted. That there is a tension between the Church as it is now and as it

[1] O. S. Tomkins, *The Wholeness of the Church* (London, 1949), p. 71.

will be is surely implied in the basic conception of the Church as *corpus Christi*, for no living body could be without such a tension. So Vincent Taylor thinks that much of the discussion about the relation between Kingdom and Church is misguided, being a discussion whether the Kingdom be present or future when in fact it must be both present and future.[1] Brunner regards the Kingdom as beginning in the Church so that the Church is 'the earthly, historical veil' that conceals it.[2] On this question as on many others, Barth has considerably modified earlier views; but his interpretation of eschatology in terms of absolute transcendence is in some ways still difficult to relate to the Christian hope that is expressed both in the New Testament and in the life of the Church. The qualitative difference he sees between 'our time', the 'time of the Church', on the one hand, and the time of revelation in Christ, on the other,[3] does seem to injure the doctrine of the Incarnation itself. K. L. Schmidt's identification of the Kingdom of God and the Kingdom of Christ, in the New Testament, has done nothing to clarify the issues of this controversy, and is not to be uncritically accepted as sound exegesis. If a distinction be made between the Kingdom of Christ and the Kingdom of God, then we may see the Church, as Culmann does, in close relation to the former. For they belong then, to the same temporal order, and so are distinguished from the Kingdom of God which does not belong to this order. If the Kingdom of Christ is begun in the Church, as Brunner suggests, the Church must surely be the Kingdom in process of actualization; that is, the coming of the Kingdom which is to come. On this view, the coming of the Kingdom of Christ is visible in the Church which, as the Body of Christ, is the unique instrument by which 'all things shall be subdued unto him'.[4] Only when death, the 'last enemy'[5] is destroyed shall the Kingdom of Christ become the Kingdom of God, concerning the

[1] V. Taylor, *Jesus and His Sacrifice* (London, 1937), p. 9.
[2] E. Brunner, *The Divine Imperative* (London, 1937), p. 526.
[3] K. Barth, *Die kirchliche Dogmatik* (Zurich, 1945), 1/2, p. 604.
[4] 1 Cor. xv. 28.
[5] 1 Cor. xv. 26.

nature of which the less we pretend to know the more fitting it will be for our present condition.

On questions such as these there is room and need for much more theological controversy; yet within the Reformed tradition the fundamental conceptions, as in all other matters relating to the nature of the Church, are in some measure already determined by the Scriptural figure of the Body of Christ whose meaning is understood in the life of the Church itself, no matter how it be expressed in ecclesiological formulas.

However such questions may be answered, one thing is plain: there is no place in the Reformed tradition for any ecclesiological view that does not do justice to the continuity of the Church. When, in the words of the Nicene Creed, we call the Church Catholic and Apostolic, we are not really giving it two separate attributes. We are saying, rather, that both the catholicity and the apostolicity are aspects of the process in which the unity of the Church is visibly expressed. The Reformed tradition must, of course, claim to be the apostolic tradition, and implied in this claim is the doctrine that all tradition stands ever in need of reform. There is, indeed, nothing in or about the Church that is not both reformable and in process of reformation except the principle of its unity, Christ Himself, and the Holy Spirit who vivifies the Church. Within the Body, idolatry assumes a new and more terrible aspect, for it is no longer merely the worship of idols of 'silver and gold, the work of men's hands' which 'have mouths, but they speak not: eyes have they, but they see not';[1] it is, rather, the worship of that which has been, within the Body, petrified by human sin and folly, and what, within the Body of Christ, can be so petrified but the human authors of the petrifaction themselves? 'They that make them are like unto them.'[2] Within the Body, idolatry becomes self-worship—resistance to the life of the Body. It is a truism to say that there can never be any reform of the Church, if by 'reform' is meant reform of the essential principle of its life, for it has none but Christ. When we speak of the Reformation we must refer to an historical expres-

[1] Psalms cxv. 4 f.

[2] Psalms cxv. 8.

sion of the movement that is continually at work in the Church, the incessant movement that springs from the unfailing life of Christ, the Head of the Body.

This movement is continuous, incessant; but that which we, adhering to the Pauline metaphor, may call the connective tissue of the Body—the historic patterns of order and liturgy that have grown with the growth of the Body and are in some sense part of its life—cannot be lightly regarded by those who truly participate in the divine life that makes the Body what it is. As mere 'connective tissue', they are not irreformable in themselves, nor is even doctrinal formulation, however hallowed in the life of the Church; nevertheless, nothing that has ever expressed that divine life in the Church can be other than dear to all who share in this. Historic patterns of liturgy, for instance, ought never to be thoughtlessly, much less wantonly, altered, for while we dare not and would not presume to limit the forms in which the divine *agape* may express itself in the Church's living worship, we ought not in any circumstance to seek to forego what has ever enriched that worship. Where it has been partially lost or neglected, or set aside in the turmoil of an historical expression of the reforming principle at the heart of the Church, we must seek to accomplish the task, than which none is more delicate, of restoring, within the life of the Body and under the direction only of its Head, that which man, for whatever reason, has discarded of the divine splendour of the Body. The maxim, *Ecclesia Reformata, semper reformanda*, means, besides much else, that the Church is not only ever in process of building; it is ever in process of rebuilding.

What continuity means in the Reformed tradition in relation to both the Eucharist and the *eschaton* is expounded as follows by Professor Torrance: 'To participate in the Eucharist and its proclamation of the death of Christ until He come is to involve the Church in the final judgment upon the forms of history in order that its new life may appear. The repeated celebrations of the Eucharist do not mean that the Church is growing old with tradition and ancient glory, for its glory is yet to be revealed in the manifestation of the Son of Man, but it means that the Church is ever growing younger and younger, until at last it arrives at the great day when as a Bride it shall be presented to the Bridegroom for the consummation of its joy in the Marriage-Supper of the Lamb. In as much as the Eucharist is an anticipation of that day, it stands above history, and can never be subordinated to it or made relative to the fixity of its passing forms.'[1] Yet it is in the celebration of the Eucharist, the core of Christian worship and the heart of the Church, that the melancholy impoverishment of the contemporary visible expression of the Church's life is most seriously evident. For while, both within the Reformed Church and in the ecumenical movement in which it participates today, theological discussion often provides remarkable testimony to growth in the expression of the unity of the Church, the Church's worship furnishes only too often evidence of human resistance at the deepest level to the divine activity upon which alone the Church must entirely depend. Speaking at Lund on this subject, Oliver Tomkins said: 'We are liable to suspicions and misunderstandings which, at the heart of our movement, we have largely overcome in the field of theological discussion. The lack of a common language in our devotional traditions, and the way in which theological differences are more keenly felt when they are prayed, are formidable difficulties.'

A more optimistic view of this matter may, however, be taken. It may be urged that theological discussion has led whither it ought to lead, that is, to the heart of the Church's life. Here is to be seen in the most intolerable form the contrast between the essential unity of Christ and the ubiquitous sin of schism, between the riches of the divine mysteries and the dismal poverty of our enfeebled and truncated liturgies. In the Reformed Church the Sacrament must always be, as it is called by Calvin, a *vera communicatio*. 'Here, O my Lord, I see Thee face to face,' is the opening line of a Scottish hymn commonly sung by the people in eucharistic celebrations in Scotland. Yet it is here that

[1] T. F. Torrance in *Intercommunion* (London, 1952), p. 348.

the visible expression of Christian unity is mocked not only by failure to achieve what has come to be called, in ecumenical circles, 'intercommunion'—surely an untheological and perhaps also even in practice an unhappy term—but by the impoverishment of the liturgy itself. For a better understanding of its own ecclesiology, the Reformed Church must reconsider its liturgical problems at a far deeper theological level than that at which such studies have commonly been conducted. 'The theological study of liturgy', we were reminded by the Theological Commission on Ways of Worship, reporting in 1950, 'is not a matter of purely practical, still less of purely historical interest. It is a penetrating into the heart of theology.'[1] While there is no doubt, as we have seen, that the Reformers attached central importance to the Eucharist, both in theology and in practice, the task of the Reformation in the sixteenth century was, humanly speaking, exceedingly difficult, and it met with but limited success. Among the misfortunes attending this limitation was a defensive attitude on the part of the Reformed Church that resulted in its preferring an impoverished liturgy to the risk of reverting to one that was accounted corrupt to the point of idolatry. Ecclesiological study ought to draw attention to the fact that reformation, unless it be sufficiently successful to avoid schism, cannot, for psychological reasons if for no others, avoid adversely affecting the liturgical worship of both the reformed and the unreformed Church. Much reconstructive work has been done here. For instance, the old distinction between a symbolic and an instrumental view of sacramental action, which once seemed to give rise to an important controversy, has lost much of its significance with a growing appreciation of the complementary character of the two views.[2] If we think of the Eucharist only as the sign of God's continuing grace towards us, we tend to move quickly and far away from the Headship of Christ in the Church, while if we insist exclusively upon the instrumental efficacy of the Eucharist, as God's own means of

[1] *Ways of Worship* (London, 1951), p. 24.
[2] This was well exhibited in Quick's *The Gospel of Divine Action*.

imparting Himself to us, we soon lose sight of the theological truth that His activity is not bound by the Sacrament. We must find the liturgical means of ensuring that we acknowledge the symbol to be entirely instrumental to God and the instrument intrinsically symbolic of Him. Moreover, notwithstanding all that has been said in the last few decades, it remains necessary to note Brilioth's reminder that 'By making the localized presence in the elements the centre of the theology of the eucharist,' the Church 'tied down future thought and controversy to a wrong statement of the problem.'[1] The Reformed Church would do an injustice to the seriousness of the Reformers' purpose if it did not acknowledge that this theological tradition fettered Luther and Calvin in such a way as to cause them to present the eucharistic question in ways that crippled the worship of the Church they did so much to reform.

The Reformed Church may claim, perhaps, to have overcome better than is elsewhere common, this danger of localizing the Real Presence. 'The Lord Himself holds the true service within His Church. . . . It is the Lord's will to come to His Church. . . . There He stands before her as her Lord . . . thereby she becomes what she otherwise would not be, the congregation of servants called by God and so serving Him. It is this fact alone which gives reality to the divine service of the Church.'[2] But the Reformed Church nevertheless cannot pretend to have lost nothing of importance or liturgical splendour from the ancient liturgies, and what it has lost is not to be recaptured by mere tasteful historical revision of recommended liturgical service books. One has only to glance at documents such as the liturgical fragment that has come down from the Columban Church in the *Book of Deer*,[3] for example, to see something of the cost, in liturgical spontaneity and rhythm, of the consecutive processes of romanization and reform in the Scottish Church.

The question of the nature of the divine Presence in the Eucharist is really inseparable from what is, in the Reformed

[1] Y. Brilioth, *Eucharistic Faith and Practice* (London, 1930), p. 87.

[2] Julius Schweitzer in *Ways of Worship*, p. 125 f.

[3] An evangelarium of the Columban monastery at Deer, Aberdeenshire.

tradition, a very thorny question, the idea of eucharistic sacrifice. The Reformers could hardly but have been suspicious of any language that would lead anyone back into the errors they had striven to correct. But from what we have seen of their whole ecclesiological emphasis, it would not be difficult to uphold the thesis that some of the liturgical impoverishment of the Eucharist since the Reformation is hardly less repugnant to their basic conception of the nature of the Church than were the medieval corruptions against which they protested. The Eucharist must be sacrificial in some sense, if Christ is, as the Reformers continually remind us, the High Priest. If the Church is the Body of Christ, it must in some sense offer itself in the very act of being what it is, and this must be particularly true of the Church as it engages in eucharistic worship. The Reformers were bound to emphasize the uniqueness of Christ's sacrifice on Calvary, and reiterate, as they did, that it was offered once-for-all. To avoid the danger of return to the bad theology upon which the Mass had come to be founded, they stressed, rather, the receiving by the Church of the sacrifice of Christ. But one cannot really receive the sacrifice of Christ without participating in it. This does not mean that the Church is sinless, or worthy so to participate. But because it *is* the Body of Christ it must in some sense join with Him in His sacrifice. The Church rejoices that it is united, however unworthily, to Christ, and it would be not humility but rebellion for the Bride to dissociate herself from the sacrificial work of the Bridegroom, for though she has no claim whatsoever upon her Lord, yet she must share in what He does, for such is His wish. What is opposed in Reformed Church theology is the notion that the Bride may presume to take her Lord's sacrifice as His gift and then offer it on her behalf. It was this intolerable arrogance that the Reformers did not hesitate to denounce as 'the blasphemy of the Mass'. It was not a question of abuses that had crept into practice. Calvin says that he disdains even to touch upon these, and that they are too notorious to require exposition.[1] What he attacks is the fundamental con-

[1] *Institutio,* IV, xviii, 18.

ception behind the Mass, the offering by the Church of the sacrifice of Christ *as though* the Church had acquired Christ as a divine legacy, a divine gift that gave it the right to offer Christ upon the altar as in the old dispensation the Israelites had had the right to offer up a bullock. In Calvin's view, it was such a false theology that vitiated everything said and done in the Mass from the *Introibo* to the *Ite, missa est.* So 'the Mass, considered in its choicest and most estimable purity, without any of its paraphernalia, is from beginning to end full of every kind of impiety, blasphemy, idolatry and sacrilege'.[1] But Calvin does not repudiate eucharistic sacrifice; as we saw,[2] he refers to a kind of sacrifice which is *indispensable* to the Sacrament of the Lord's Supper.[3] What Calvin says in condemnation of the Mass could be said by him in condemnation of hymn-singing or prayer; that is, any worship of God can become detestable idolatry from beginning to end if it carry with it a false, an idolatrous attitude. Though I recite the dominical prayer itself, slowly and beautifully and in a most reverent tone, it immediately becomes an insult to God as soon as I say it with an idolatrous claim, such as that I have the right to *demand* of God what I am asking. The Reformation protest is that not even the whole Body of Christ has the right to do with the Head of the Body what the Roman priesthood claimed to do; nor would the whole Church have the right to say the Lord's Prayer as though it could by saying it make a *claim* upon God. But the indubitable fact that the Bride has no claim upon the Bridegroom does not mean that she ought to refrain from rejoicing that it is given to her to participate in His infinitely glorious sacrificial work. How, indeed, could she help singing when she finds herself united with the Bridegroom in His work? If she could do so, she would not be His true Bride. She is the Body of Christ: jubilantly she makes oblation of herself as obediently she unites with Him in His sacrifice.

In the Columban Church, the Eucharist was called, sometimes sacrifice (*sacorfaicc*), sometimes sacred oblation (*sacra*

[1] *Loc. cit.*
[2] *Supra*, p. 191 f.
[3] *Institutio*, IV, xviii, 17.

oblatio). The terms seem to have been used interchangeably.[1] But they appear to have been also so used of every religious act. 'Alms given to the poor, a present made to a clergyman, what corresponded to our collection taken in a church, a piece of land conveyed or bequeathed for endowment purposes, the very body and soul and even the whole life of a Christian, are all in our ancient literature regularly denominated Sacrifice, Oblations, and Immolations.'[2] St Thomas, however, makes a distinction between sacrifice and oblation: the former implies the latter, but the latter is not in itself the former. Oblation is an offering, for example an offering of money at the altar—the money is not destroyed but simply offered to God and then used for a good work such as the relief of the poor or the upkeep of the sanctuary. Oblation is, on this view, distinguished from sacrifice.[3] It is well known that in primitive religion, the sacrificial victim is killed or destroyed so that, passing from its present mode of existence, it may go up to and be received by the god. St Thomas has been interpreted by some commentators as meaning that sacrifice necessarily entails such death or destruction of the victim. Dix prefers the view that 'it is not the "destruction" of the victim, but the completeness of the offerer's surrender of it and the completeness of God's acceptance of it which together make up the reality of sacrifice'.[4] The Thomist distinction does at any

[1] 'Sacorfaicc' appears in the *Book of Deer* (ed. J. Stuart, Spalding Club, 1869) p. 90. The following is a list of the names given to the Eucharist in Adamnan's *Vita S. Columbae* (*c.* 692–7) with references to the edition made by W. F. Skene (1874) from the edition by W. Reeves printed for the Irish Archaeological Society in 1857: sacra eucharistiae mysteria (i, 32; iii, 13, 18), sacra oblationis mysteria (i, 32), sacrificale mysterium (ii, 1), mysteria (ii, 1), sacra eucharistiae ministeria (iii, 12), sacrae eucharistiae ministeria (ii, 7), sacrae oblationis obsequia (iii, 13), sacrosancta ministeria (iii, 18), sacra oblatio (iii, 18), missarum solemnia (i, 32; iii, 12, 18), missarum solemnia Dominica (iii, 24), Christi corpus (i, 35), eucharistiae (ii, 40).

[2] Duncan MacGregor, *Early Scottish Worship* (Lee Lecture, 1895) (Edinburgh, 1896), p. 6 f.

[3] *Summa Theol.*, II–IIae, q. 85, a. 3 ad 3: 'Sacrificia proprie dicuntur quando circa res Deo oblatas aliquid fit, sicut quod animalia occidebantur, quod panis frangitur, et comeditur, et benedicitur.'

[4] Gregory Dix, *The Shape of the Liturgy* (*ed. cit.*), p. 746. It is noteworthy that Dix translates the medieval Latin '*circa*', in the passage just quoted, by the English preposition 'about': 'Sacrifices are properly so called when *anything is done about things offered to God.*' (Dix italicizes.) The English Dominican translation, however, renders it 'to'.

rate correspond to an ancient ritual distinction made by the Hebrews between an offering, which was a gift brought near to the altar, and a sacrifice, which was an offering consumed in whole or in part upon the altar. St Paul says that 'Christ our Passover is sacrificed for us';[1] but he also enjoins the Romans to present their bodies 'a living sacrifice' (*θυσία*) unto God.[2] It seems plausible, of course, to argue that, in the latter instance, Paul is using characteristic poetic hyperbole, calling a sacrifice what in the nature of the case can only be an offering or oblation. But the point is, rather, that because Christ, in surrendering Himself completely, has offered up the only worthy sacrifice, there is no sacrifice or oblation or gift that a Christian may dare to offer to God *except* by participation in the Church, the Body of Christ, which, being united to Christ its Head, participates in His sacrifice since He has graciously willed to unite it to Himself as His Body. It is not as individuals that we 'offer and present unto Thee ourselves, our souls and bodies';[3] only the Church, *corpus Christi*, dare do this, must do it, and does it with jubilant thanksgiving. Only as it surrenders itself is it truly *corpus Christi*; only as I surrender myself with it am I truly a member *corporis Christi*. The Church, in receiving Christ in the Sacrament, offers itself with Christ. What is unfortunate in the wording of the *Westminster Confession* is that it makes it appear as though nothing really happens in the Eucharist because everything has happened already, so that we are not to be allowed to do anything but pay homage to the memory of this. The Westminster divines, in guarding against the danger of reversion to the attitude that had engendered the Mass ('abominably injurious to Christ's one only sacrifice'),[4] used language that fails to draw attention to

[1] I Cor. v. 7.

[2] Romans xii. 1.

[3] *Book of Common Order of the Church of Scotland* (*ed. cit.*), p. 120. Cf. Clem. Alex., *Strom.*, v, 11: *θυσία ἡ τῷ θεῷ δεκτὴ, σώματός τε καὶ τῶν τούτου παθῶν ἀμετανόητος χωρισμός* St Chrys., Hom. xxxiii in Ioan.: *ὅλον σαυτὸν ἄναθες τῷ θεῷ καὶ ὁλοκαύτωσον. τοῦτο γάρ ἐστι θυσίαν ζῶσαν παραστῆσαι.* St Aug., *De Civ. Dei*, x, 19: 'Sacrificantes non alteri visibile sacrificium offerendum esse noverimus, quam Illi, cujus in cordibus nostris invisibile Sacrificium nos ipsi esse debemus.' St Aug., *op. cit.*, x, 20: 'Cujus rei sacramentum quotidianum voluit esse ecclesiae sacrificium. Quae cum ipsius capitis corpus sit, seipsam per ipsum discit offerre.'

[4] *Westminster Confession*, xxix.

the indubitable need and duty of the Church to participate in the work of its Lord, according to the peculiarly intimate relation in which, at His bidding, it stands to Him. This relation, of which the Church ought ever to be mindful, is better expressed in the abundant *alleluias* of the liturgy of the Columban Church than by the self-conscious exclusion of the sacrificial element that is to be found at a later period. The Church 'does' the Eucharist, however, only in the sense that it is summoned by its Lord to share in what He has done. What we 'do' is not sacrifice according to the common meaning of this term in 'religion', since what we 'do' costs us nothing; what we do is, however, 'the Christian Sacrifice', for we are joined with Christ. Being joined with Christ *means* being surrendered to Him, as the δοῦλος is surrendered to his master. The Christian Sacrifice does not consist in this surrender; the surrender is such as to imply surrender of all pretence to 'do' anything but share in what the Head 'does'. But we 'do' what we are commanded; our Anamnesis, our Eucharist, and our Communion, are our share in the Christian Sacrifice.

If our exposition of the nature of the Church according to the Reformed tradition has demonstrated anything at all, it has demonstrated that the Reformation was essentially an attempt to recover the Headship of Christ in the Body. In the act of doing so, the Reformed Church has discovered an ecclesiology which, grounded on the Chalcedonian christology, is equally with this christology an expression of the Christian faith to which the Scriptures testify. The sixteenth-century Reformation of the Church is by no means unique; it is but a landmark in the process of reform in which the Church is ever engaged as it seeks to unite itself to its Lord and surrender itself to Him; as it seeks, that is, to be what it is called to be, *corpus Christi*. The sixteenth century was, indeed, only the focus of the movement that historians call the Protestant Reformation; but the movement itself extended far beyond that period, as far as the history of the Church itself and so long as the Church cries, as is its bounden duty, *Maranatha!* Though none can predict the course of the future history of the Church, it is likely that there will be other movements, perhaps far more seismic, that will enable the Church more easily to see the sixteenth-century Reformation in better perspective as but one incident in the life of the Body. Outside that Body there is no life in union with Christ: to belong to a group that repudiates the unity of the Church as the Body of Christ is to belong, at the best, to a group of *σκιά*[1] devotees who do not know the *life* of union with Him who is the life of the Body. Within the Church there is schism and heresy that 'crucify Christ afresh'; yet even where the Body of Christ is so afflicted it remains His Body, which He can and does heal, human expectations to the contrary notwithstanding. So Luther could call the Roman Church both holy and Antichrist. Taking up Jerome's question, how Paul could have written of the erring Galatians as though they belonged to the Church of God, Luther says: 'Even today we call the Roman Church and her episcopate holy, though they are in error. . . . Even though Rome is worse than Sodom and Gomorrah, nevertheless there remains, within her, Baptism, the Sacrament, the Word, the sacred Scriptures, the Ministry, the name of Christ and the name of God. The Roman Church is, therefore, holy, because it has [these things] . . . therefore the Church is holy even among the *Schwärmer*, so long as they do not repudiate Word and Sacrament. Wherever Word and Sacrament, therefore, are present in and for themselves, there is holy Church—even if Antichrist has enthroned himself.'[2]

To Word and Sacrament the Reformed Church added, however, Discipline, not because the union of Word and Sacrament is not enough in itself, but because without Discipline it becomes a mockery. It may be that it is in the recovery of the ministry of Discipline, which flows from the mystery of the divine *agape* itself, that the Church will more fully express and so make more visible its wholeness as *corpus Christi*. For the Body of Christ does not exist for itself alone, or only for the benefit of those who are called by Christ and incorporated into it. It exists no less to do

[1] *Supra.*
[2] Luther, *ad Gal.*, i, 2.

Christ's will in the world, for it is His Body, His δοῦλος, which He has called to be, in the picturesque language of the Spanish Teresa, His hands, His feet, to do His bidding, that they who know only His σκιὰν may behold Him exalted and living in His Church. *Et ego si exaltatus fuero a terra, omnia traham ad meipsum.*[1]

[1] John xii. 32.

APPENDIX I

ST AUGUSTINE

THE following passages illustrate the teaching of St Augustine on Christ as the Head and the Church as the Body.

1. *The Whole Christ is Head and Body*

Et quoniam totus Christus caput est et corpus, quod bene vos nosse non dubito: caput est ipse Salvator noster, passus sub Pontio Pilato, qui nunc postea quam resurrexit a mortuis, sedet ad dexteram Patris: corpus autem ejus est Ecclesia; non ista, aut illa, sed toto orbe diffusa; nec ea quae nunc est in hominibus qui praesentem vitam agunt, sed ad eam pertinentibus etiam his qui fuerunt ante nos, et his qui futuri sunt post nos usque in finem saeculi. Tota enim Ecclesia constans ex omnibus fidelibus, quia fideles omnes membra sunt Christi, habet illud caput positum in caelis quod gubernat corpus suum; etsi separatum est visione, sed annectitur charitate. Quia ergo totus Christus caput est et corpus ejus.

In Ps. lvi. 1

2. *The Unity of Christians*

. . . omnis homo in Christo unus homo est, et unitas christianorum unus homo.

In Ps. xxix, En. ii. 5

3. *The Head in Heaven, the Members on Earth*

In Christo autem nos omnes unus homo; quia hujus unius hominis caput est in caelo, et membra adhuc laborant in terra.

In Ps. lx. 1

4. *One Church, because Christ is One*

Jam ergo non unus; sed ideo unus, quia Christus unus, cujus

omnes membras sumus. . . . Haec ergo Christi possessio, haec Christi haereditas, hoc Christi corpus, haec una Christi Ecclesia, haec unitas quae nos sumus, clamat a finibus terrae.

In Ps. lx. 2

5. *One Christ, Head and Body*

Ipsi christiani cum capite suo, quod ascendit in caelum, unus est Christus: non ille unus et nos multi, sed et nos multi in illo uno unum. Unus ergo homo Christus, caput et corpus. Quod est corpus ejus? Ecclesia ejus, dicente Apostolo, *Quoniam membra sumus corporis ejus* (*Ephes.* v. 30); et, *Vos autem estis corpus Christi et membra* (*1 Cor.* xii. 27).

In Ps. cxxvii. 3

6. *We are Many, yet One*

Cum plures christianos appello, in uno Christo unum intelligo. Plures ergo estis, et unus estis; plures sumus, et unus sumus. Quomodo plures sumus, et unus sumus? Quia illi inhaeremus cujus membra sumus; et quorum caput in caelo est, ut membra sequantur.

In Ps. cxxvii. 4

7. *How the Church Speaks as One Man*

Saepe enim admonuimus charitatem vestram, non quasi unius hominis cantantis vocem accipi debere, sed omnium qui sunt in Christi corpore. Et quia in illius corpore sunt omnes, tanquam unus homo loquitur: et ipse est unus qui et multi sunt. Multi enim sunt in seipsis, unus sunt in illo qui unus est.

In Ps. cxxx. 1

8. *The Body of Christ from the Beginning*

Dominus enim ipse in corpore suo, quod est Ecclesia, junior fuit primis temporibus, et ecce jam senuit. Nostis, et agnoscitis, et intelligitis, quia in hoc positi estis, et ita credidistis, quia caput nostrum Christus est; corpus capitis illius nos sumus (*1 Cor.* xii. 27; *Ephes.* iv. 15). Numquid soli nos, et non etiam illi qui fuerunt ante nos? Omnes qui ab initio saeculi fuerunt justi, caput Christum habent. Illum enim venturum esse crediderunt, quem nos venisse jam credimus; et in ejus fide et ipsi sanati sunt, in cujus et nos: ut esset et ipse totius caput civitatis Jerusalem, omnibus connumeratis fidelibus ab initio usque in finem, adjunctis etiam legionibus et exercitibus Angelorum, ut fiat illa una civitas sub uno rege, et una quaedam provincia sub uno imperatore, felix in perpetua pace et salute, laudans Deum sine fine, beata sine fine. Corpus autem Christi, quod est Ecclesia (*Coloss.* i. 18, 24), tanquam unus quidam homo, primo junior fuit, et ecce jam in fine saeculi est in senecta pingui; quoniam de illa dictum est: *Adhuc multiplicabitur in senecta pingui* (*Ps.* xci. 15). Multiplicata est per omnes gentes, et ipsius vox est attendentis quasi unius hominis primam aetatem suam, et istam novissimam respexit per omnia, quia omnes aetates notas habet per Scripturas; et ait exsultans et monens: *Junior fui*, primis temporibus saeculi; *et ecce senui*, sum etiam novissimis temporibus saeculi; *et nunquam vidi justum derelictum, nec semen ejus quaerens panem.*

In Ps. xxxvi, Serm. iii. 4

9. *The Extent of the Body*

Corpus hujus capitis Ecclesia est, non quae hoc loco est, sed et quae hoc loco et per totum orbem terrarum: nec illa quae hoc tempore, sed ab ipso Abel usque ad eos qui nascituri sunt usque in finem et credituri in Christum, totus populus sanctorum ad unam civitatem pertinentium; quae civitas corpus est Christi, cui caput est Christus.

In Ps. xc, Serm. ii. 1

10. *Speaking with Tongues in the Body of Christ*

Crescit enim Ecclesia, donec occupet omnes linguas. Quod vos deseruistis, quosque crevit! Tenete nobiscum quousque accessit.... Loquor omnium linguis, audio tibi dicere. In corpore Christi sum, in Ecclesia Christi sum: si corpus Christi jam omnium linguis loquitur, et ego in omnibus linguis sum; mea est graeca, mea est syra, mea est hebraea, mea est omnium gentium, quia in unitate sum omnium gentium.

In Ps. cxlvii. 19

11. *We Pray to Christ who Prays for us and in us*

Nullum majus donum praestare posset Deus hominibus, quam ut Verbum suum per quod condidit omnia, faceret illis caput, et illos ei tanquam membra coaptaret; ut esset filius Dei et filius hominis, unus Deus cum Patre, unus homo cum hominibus: ut et quando loquimur ad Deum deprecantes, non inde Filium separemus; et quando precatur corpus Filii, non a se separet caput suum; sitque ipse unus salvator corporis sui Dominus noster Jesus Christus Filius Dei, qui et oret pro nobis, et oret in nobis, et oretur a nobis. Orat pro nobis, ut sacerdos noster; orat in nobis, ut caput nostrum; oratur a nobis, ut Deus noster.

In Ps. lxxxv. 1

12. *To that which you are, you Answer Amen*

Corpus ergo Christi si vis intelligere, Apostolum audi dicentem fidelibus, *Vos autem estis corpus Christi, et membra* (*1 Cor.* xii. 27). Si ergo vos estis corpus Christi et membra, mysterium vestrum in mensa Dominica positum est: mysterium vestrum accipitis, Ad id quod estis, Amen respondetis, et respondendo subscribitis. Audis enim, Corpus Christi; et respondes, Amen. Esto membrum corporis Christi, ut verum sit Amen. Quare ergo in pane? Nihil hic de nostro afferamus, ipsum Apostolum identidem audiamus, qui cum de isto Sacramento loqueretur, ait, *Unus panis, unum corpus multi sumus* (*1 Cor.* x. 17): intelligite et gaudete; unitas, veritas, pietas, charitas. *Unus panis:* quis est iste unus panis? *Unum corpus multi.* Recolite quia panis non fit de uno grano, sed de multis. Quando exorcizabamini, quasi molebamini. Quando baptizati estis, quasi conspersi estis. Quando Spiritus sancti ignem accepistis, quasi cocti estis. Estote quod videtis, et accipite quod estis. Hoc Apostolus de pane dixit. Jam de calice quid intelligerimus, etiam non dictum, satis ostendit. Sicut enim ut sit species visibilis panis, multa grana in unum consperguntur, tanquam illud fiat, quod de fidelibus ait Scriptura sancta, *Erat illis anima una, et cor unum in Deum* (*Act.* iv. 32): sic et de vino. Fratres, recolite unde fit vinum. Grana multa pendent ad botrum, sed liquor granorum in unitate confunditur. Ita et Dominus Christus nos significavit, nos ad se pertinere voluit, mysterium pacis et unitatis nostrae in sua mensa consecravit. Qui accipit mysterium unitatis, et non tenet vinculum pacis, non mysterium accipit pro se, sed testimonium contra se. Conversi ad Dominum Deum Patrem omnipotentem, puro corde ei, quantum potest parvitas nostra, maximas atque veras gratias agamus; precantes toto animo singularem mansuetudinem ejus, ut preces nostras in beneplacito suo exaudire dignetur; inimicum quoque a nostris actibus et cogitationibus sua virtute expellat, nobis multiplicet fidem, mentem gubernet, spirituales cogitationes concedat, et ad beatitudinem suam perducat.

Serm. cclxxii

13. *You are what you Receive* (*a Sermon to Children*)

Debetis scire quid accepistis, quid accepturi estis, quid quotidie accipere debeatis. Panis ille quem videtis in altari, sanctificatus per verbum Dei, corpus est Christi. Calix ille, imo quod habet calix, sanctificatum per verbum Dei, sanguis est Christi. Per ista voluit Dominus Christus commendare corpus et sanguinem suum, quem pro nobis fudit in remissionem peccatorum. Si bene accepistis, vos estis quod accepistis.

Serm. ccxxvii

14. *Our Sacrifice, Visible and Invisible*

Qui autem putant haec visibilia sacrificia diis aliis congruere, illi vero tanquam invisibili invisibilia, et majora majori, melioribus meliora, qualia sunt purae mentis et bonae voluntatis officia; profecto nesciunt, haec ita esse signa illorum, sicut verba sonantia signa sunt rerum. Quocrica, sicut orantes atque laudantes ad eum dirigimus significantes voces, cui res ipsas in corde quas significamus offerimus: ita sacrificantes non alteri visibile sacrificium offerendum esse noverimus, quam illi cujus in cordibus nostris invisibile sacrificium nos ipsi esse debemus.

De Civ. Dei, x. 19

15. *Christ and the Church Distinguished*

Tenete hoc, et fixum omnino commendate memoriae, tanquam filii ecclesiasticae eruditionis et fidei catholicae, ut agnoscatis Christum caput et corpus, eumdemque Christum Verbum Dei unigenitum aequalem Patri; et inde videatis quanta gratia pertingatis ad Deum, ut ipse voluerit esse nobiscum unus, qui est cum Patre unus. . . . Christus et Ecclesia, duo in carne una. Refer ad distantiam majestatis duo. Duo plane. Non enim et nos Verbum, non enim et nos in principio Deus apud Deum, non enim et nos ille per quem facta sunt omnia (*Joan.* i, 1, 3).

In Ps. cxlii. 3

16. *The Holy Spirit the Soul of the Body of Christ*

Si vultis habere Spiritum sanctum, intendite, fratres mei: spiritus noster quo vivit omnis homo, anima vocatur; spiritus noster quo vivit singulus quisque homo, anima vocatur: et videtis quid faciat anima in corpore. Omnia membra vegetat; per oculos videt, per aures audit, per nares olfacit, per linguam loquitur, per manus operatur, per pedes ambulat: omnibus simul adest membris, ut vivant; vitam dat omnibus, officium singulis. Non audit oculus . . . sed tamen vivit: vivit auris vivit lingua; officia diversa sunt, vita communis. Sic est Ecclesia Dei: in aliis sanctis facit miracula, in aliis sanctis loquitur veritatem, in aliis sanctis custodit virginitatem, in aliis sanctis custodit pudicitiam conjugalem, in aliis hoc, in aliis illud: singuli proprii operantur, sed pariter vivunt. Quod autem est anima corpori hominis, hoc est Spiritus sanctus corpori Christi, quod est Ecclesia: hoc agit Spiritus sanctus in tota Ecclesia, quod agit anima in omnibus membris unius corporis. . . . Sic et homo christianus catholicus est, dum in corpore vivit; praecisus haereticus factus est, membrum amputatum non sequitur spiritus. Si ergo vultus vivere de Spiritu sancto, tenete charitatem, amate veritatem, desiderate unitatem, ut perveniatis ad aeternitatem.

Serm. cclxvii. 4

17. *How the Body of Christ is Held Together*

Aliquando et dives invenitur pauper, et a paupere praestatur illi aliquid. Venit nescio quis ad flumen, tanto delicatior quanto ditior; transire non potest: si nudatis membris transiret, frigesceret, aegrotaret, moreretur: accedit pauper exercitatior corpore; trajicit divitem; eleemosynam facit in divitem. Ergo nolite eos tantum putare pauperes, qui non habent pecuniam. In quo quisque pauper est, ibi illum vide; quia forte tu in eo dives es, in quo ille pauper est, et habes unde accommodes. Forte membra tua accommodas, et plus est quam si pecuniam accomodares. Consilio indiget, tu plenus es consilio; in consilio ille pauper, tu dives es. Ecce nec laboras, nec aliquid perdis; das consilium, et praesitisti eleemosynam. Modo, fratres mei, cum loquimur, quasi pauperes ad nos estis; et quia nobis Deus dignatus est dare, damus inde vobis; et omnes ab illo accipimus, qui solus est dives. Sic se ergo tenet corpus Christi, membra socia sic compinguntur et adunantur in charitate et in vinculo pacis, cum quisque id quod habet, praestat ei qui non habet: in eo quod habet, dives est; in eo quod ille non habet, pauper est. Sic vos diligite, sic vos amate.

In Ps. cxxv. 13

18. *Our Unity in Christ does not make us Divine*

Non dixit, Ego et ipsi unum; quamvis per id quod Ecclesiae caput est et corpus ejus Ecclesia (*Ephes.* i. 22, 23), posset dicere, Ego et ipsi, non unum, sed unus, quia caput et corpus unus est Christus: sed divinitatem suam consubstantialem Patri ostendens . . . in suo genere, hoc est, in ejusdem naturae consubstantiali parilitate, vult esse suos unum, sed in ipso; quia in se ipsis non possent, dissociati ab invicem per diversas voluptates et cupiditates et immunditias peccatorum: unde mundantur per

Mediatorem, ut sint in illo unum; non tantum per eamdem naturam qua omnes ex hominibus mortalibus aequales Angelis fiunt, sed etiam per eamdem in eamdem beatitudinem conspirantem concordissimam voluntatem, in unum spiritum quodam modo igne charitatis conflatam. Ad hoc enim valet quod ait, *Ut sint unum sicut et nos unum sumus*: ut quemadmodum Pater et Filius, non tantum aequalitate substantiae, sed etiam voluntate unum sunt; ita et ii inter quos et Deum Mediator est Filius, non tantum per id quod ejusdem naturae sunt, sed etiam per eamdem dilectionis societatem unum sint. Deinde idipsum quod Mediator est, per quem reconciliamur Deo, sic indicat, *Ego*, inquit, *in eis et tu in me, ut sint consummati in unum.*

De Trin., *iv.* 9

19. *Christ is Head and Body; the Church the Body*

Non enim Christus in capite et non in corpore, sed Christus totus in capite et in corpore. Quod ergo membra ejus, ipse: quod autem ipse, non continuo membra ejus.

In Joan. Evang., *xxviii. 1*

20. *They know the Body who are the Body*

Norunt fideles corpus Christi, si corpus Christi esse non negligant. Fiant corpus Christi, si volunt vivere de Spiritu Christi. De spiritu Christi non vivit, nisi corpus Christi. . . . O Sacramentum pietatis! o signum unitatis! o vinculum charitatis! Qui vult vivere, habet ubi vivat, habet unde vivat. Accedat, credat; incorporetur, ut vivificetur. Non abhoreat a compage membrorum, non sit patre membrum quod resecari mereatur, non sit distortum de quo erubescatur: sit pulchrum, sit aptum, sit sanum; haereat corpori, vivat Deo de Deo: nunc laboret in terra, ut postea regnet in caelo.

In Joan. Evang., *xxvi. 13*

APPENDIX II

CONFESSIONAL DOCUMENTS

Confessio Augustana (a.d. 1530)

VII. *De Ecclesia*

Item docent, quod una Sancta Ecclesia perpetuo mansura sit. Est autem Ecclesia congregatio Sanctorum,[1] in qua Evangelium recte docetur, et recte adminstrantur Sacramenta.

Et ad veram unitatem Ecclesiae satis est consentire de Doctrina Evangelii et adminstratione Sacramentorum. Nec necesse est ubique esse similes traditiones humanas, seu ritus aut ceremonias, ab hominibus institutas. Sicut inquit Paulus (Eph. iv. 5, 6): Una fides, unum Baptisma, unus Deus et Pater omnium, etc.

VIII. *Quid sit Ecclesia*

Quanquam Ecclesia proprie sit congregatio Sanctorum et vere credentium: tamen, cum in hac vita multi hypocritae et mali admixti sint, licet uti Sacramentis, quae per malos administrantur, juxta vocem Christi (Matt. xxiii. 2): Sedent Scribae et Pharisaei in Cathedra Mosi, etc. Et Sacramenta et verbum propter ordinationem et mandatum Christi sunt efficacia, etiamsi per malos exhibeantur.

Damnant Donatistas et similes, qui negabant licere uti ministerio malorum in Ecclesia, et sentiebant ministerium malorum inutile et inefficax esse.

Theses Bernenses (a.d. 1528)

I. Die heilige christliche Kirche, deren einiges Haupt Christus, ist aus dem Worte Gottes geboren; in demselben bleibt sie, und hört nicht die Stimme eines Fremden.

[1] 1540 edit.: Congregatio membrorum Christi, hoc est, Sanctorum, qui vere credunt et obediunt Christo; etsi in hac vita huic congregationi multi mali et hypocritae admixti sunt usque ad novissimum judicium.

II. Die Kirche Christi macht nicht Gesetze und Gebote ohne Gottes Wort; desshalb alle Menschensatzungen, die man Kirchengebote nennt, uns nicht weiter binden, als sie in Gottes Wort gegründet und geboten sind.

Confessio Helvetica Prior (a.d. 1536)

XV. *Ecclesia*

Et ex talibus lapidibus super vivam hanc petram, hoc pacto, inedificatis, ecclesiam construi, sanctamque sanctorum omnium collectionem et immaculatam Christi sponsam esse tenemus, quam Christus sanguine suo lavet et purificet, et tandem Patri suo eam sine macula et ruga statuat et tradat.

Quae quidem quum solius sit Dei oculis nota, externis tamen quibusdam ritibus, ab ipso Christo institutis, et Verbi Dei velut publica legitimaque disciplina, non solum cernitur cognosciturque, sed ita constituitur, ut in hanc sine his nemo (nisi singulari Dei privilegio) censeatur.

XVII. *Potestas Ecclesiastica*

Ipsa autem verbi, et pascendi gregis Dominici auctoritas, quae proprie *clavium potestas* est, cunctis, summis aeque et imis praescribens, sacrosancta inviolabilisque esse, et vel divino Dei, vel certo et consulto ecclesiae suffragio, electis tantum ad ministrandum committi debet.

XIX. *Pastor Quis*

Christus ipse verum suae ecclesiae caput ac pastor solus est is ecclesiae suae pastores dat et doctores, qui in ecclesia externa hac clavium potestate legitime sic concredita recte et legitime utantur. Unde illos titulotenus tantum pastores, caputque romanum minime agnoscimus.

Confessio Helvetica Posterior (a.d. 1566)

XVII. *De Catholica et Sancta Dei Ecclesia, et Unico Capite Ecclesiae*

1. Quando autem Deus ab initio salvos voluit fieri homines, et ad agnitionem veritatis venire, oportet omnino semper fuisse,

nunc esse, et ad finem usque seculi futuram esse Ecclesiam, id est, e mundo evocatum vel collectum coetum fidelium, sanctorum, inquam, omnium communionem, eorum videlicet, qui Deum verum, in Christo Servatore, per verbum et Spiritum Sanctum vere cognoscunt et rite colunt, denique omnibus bonis per Christum gratuito oblatis fide participant. Sunt isti omnes unius civitatis cives, viventes sub eodem Domino, sub iisdem legibus, in eadem omnium bonorum participatione. Sic enim hos *concives sanctorum et domesticos Dei* appellavit Apostolus (Eph. ii. 19): Sanctos appelans fideles in terris, sanguine Filii Dei sanctificatos (1 Cor. vi. 11). De quibus omnino intelligendus est Symboli articulus: Credo sanctam Ecclesiam Catholicam, sanctorum communionem.

2. Et cum semper unus modo sit Deus, unus Mediator Dei et hominum Jesus Messias, unus item gregis universi pastor, unum hujus corporis caput, unus denique Spiritus, una salus, una fides, unum testamentum vel foedus; necessario consequitur unam duntaxat esse Ecclesiam: quam propterea Catholicam nuncupamus, quod sit universalis, et diffundatur per omnes mundi partes, et ad omnia se tempora extendat, nullis vel locis inclusa vel temporibus. Damnamus ergo Donatistas, qui Ecclesiam in nescio quos Africae coarctabant angulos. Nec Romanensem adprobamus clerum, qui solam prope Romanam Ecclesiam venditat pro Catholica.

3. Diducitur quidem Ecclesia in partes vel species varias, non quod divisa aut divulsa sit in semetipsa, sed magis propter membrorum in ipsa diversitatem distincta. Aliam enim faciunt Ecclesiam militantem, aliam vero triumphantem. Militat illa adhuc in terris, et certat cum carne, cum mundo, et principe mundi hujus, diabolo, cum peccato atque morte. Haec vero rude jam donata, in coelo triumphat de istis devictis omnibus, et exultat coram Domino: nihilominus habent illae inter sese communionem, vel conjunctionem.

4. Et militans in terris Ecclesia semper plurimas habuit particulares ecclesias, quae tamen omnes ad unitatem Catholicae Ecclesiae referuntur. Haec aliter fuit instituta ante legem inter

patriarchas, aliter sub Mose per legem, aliter a Christo per Evangelium. Vulgo numerantur fere duo populi, Israelitarum videlicet et gentium, vel eorum, qui ex Judaeis et gentibus collecti sunt in Ecclesiam, testamenta item duo, vetus et novum. Omnium tamen horum populorum una fuit et est societas, una salus in uno Messia, in quo ceu membra unius corporis sub unum caput connectuntur omnes, in eadem fide, etiam de eodem cibo et potu spirituali participantes. Agnoscimus hic tamen diversa fuisse tempora, diversa symbola promissi et exhibiti Messiae, sublatisque caerimonialibus, lucem nobis illustriorem lucere, et dona auctiora donari, et libertatem esse pleniorem.

5. Haec Ecclesia Dei sancta vocatur domus Dei viventis, exstructa ex lapidibus vivis et spiritualibus, et imposita super petram immotam, super fundamentum, quo aliud collocari non potest: et ideo nuncupatur etiam columna et basis veritatis (1 Tim. iii. 15). Non errat illa, quamdiu innititur petrae Christo et fundamento Prophetarum et Apostolorum. Nec mirum, si erret, quoties deserit illum, qui solus est veritas. Vocatur Ecclesia etiam virgo ac sponsa Christi, et quidem unica et dilecta. Apostolus enim: *Adjunxi vos*, inquit, *uni viro*, *ut virginem castam exhiberetis Christo* (2 Cor. xi. 2). Vocatur Ecclesia grex ovium sub uno pastore Christo, idque apud Ezechielem in Cap. xxxiv, et apud Joannem in Cap. x. Vocatur item corpus Christi, quia fideles sunt viva Christi membra, sub capite Christo.

6. Caput est, quod in corpore eminentiam habet, et unde corpus vitam haurit, cujus spiritu regitur in omnibus, unde et incrementa et, ut crescat, habet. Unicum item est corporis caput, et cum corpore habet congruentiam. Ergo Ecclesia non potest ullum aliud habere caput, quam Christum. Nam ut Ecclesia est corpus spirituale, ita caput habeat sibi congruens spirituale, utique oportet. Nec alio potest regi spiritu, quam Christi. Paulus quoque: *Ipse est caput*, inquit, *corporis ecclesiae*, *qui est principium*, *primogenitus ex mortuis*, *ut sit ipse in omnibus primas tenens* (Col. i. 18). Et idem iterum: *Christus est*, inquit, *caput ecclesiae*, *qui idem salutem dat corpori* (Eph. v. 23). Et rursus: *Qui est caput ecclesiae*, ait, *quae corpus illius*, *complementum ejus*, *qui omnia*

in omnibus adimplet (Eph. i. 22, 23). Item: *Adolescamus in illum per omnia, qui est caput, nempe Christus, in quo totum corpus, si compingatur, incrementum capit* (Eph. iv. 15, 16).

7. Non probamus ergo doctrinam cleri Romani, facientis suum illum Romanum Pontificem Catholicae in terris ecclesiae militantis pastorem universalem et caput summum, adeoque verum Christi vicarium, qui habeat in Ecclesia plenitudinem, ut vocant, potestatis, et dominium supremum.

8. Docemus enim, Christum Dominum esse et manere unicum pastorem universalem, summum item pontificem coram Deo Patre, ac in Ecclesia ipsum omnia pontificis vel pastoris obire munia, ad finem usque saeculi, ideoque nullo indigere vicario, qui absentis est. Christus vero praesens est ecclesiae, et caput vivificum. Hic Apostolis suis Apostolorumque successoribus primatum et dominium in Ecclesia severissime prohibuit. [Quicunque ergo huic illustri veritati contradicentes reluctantur, et in Ecclesiam Christi diversam inducunt gubernationem, quis non videat, eos illis potius esse adcensendos, de quibus Apostoli Christi vaticinantur, Petrus (2 Pet. ii), et Paulus (Act. xx., 2 Cor. xi., et 2 Thess. ii.), et aliis quoque in locis?][1]

9. Sublato autem capite Romano; nullam inducimus in Ecclesiam Christi ἀταξίαν, vel perturbationem: cum doceamus, gubernationem Ecclesiae, ab Apostolis traditem, nobis sufficere ad retinendam in justo ordine Ecclesiam, quae ab initio, dum hujusmodi capite Romano, quale hodie dicitur Ecclesiam conservare in ordine, caruit, atactica vel inordinata non fuit. Servat quidem caput Romanum tyrannidem suam, et corruptelam inductam in Ecclesiam: sed impedit interim, oppugnat, et, quantis potest viribus, exscindit justam ecclesiae reformationem.

10. Objicitur nobis, varia esse in ecclesiis nostris certamina atque dissidia, posteaquam se a Romana separarunt Ecclesia, proinde non esse eas Ecclesias veras. Quasi vero nullae unquam

[1] The bracketed passage was substituted by Bullinger for the following: *Quae vero Romanenses fingunt de ministeriali capite et titulo servi servorum Dei, minime recipimus. Experimur enim voces illas inanes jactari, et papam sese constituere adversarium Christi et efferre se adversus Deum, adeo ut in templo Dei sedeat ostentans se ipsum esse Deum, 2 Thess.* ii.

fuerint in Ecclesia Romana sectae, nulla unquam dissidia atque certamina, et quidem de religione, non tam in scholis, quam in cathedris sacris, in medio populi instituta. Agnoscimus sane, dixisse Apostolum: *Deus non est Deus dissensionis, sed pacis* (1 Cor. xiv, 33). Et: *Cum sit in vobis æmulatio et contentio, an non carnales estis?* (1 Cor. iii, 3). Negari tamen non potest, Deum fuisse in Ecclesia Apostolica, et Apostolicam Ecclesiam fuisse Ecclesiam veram, in qua tamen fuerunt concertationes et dissidia. Reprehendit enim Petrum Apostolum Apostolus Paulus, ab hoc dissidet Barnabas (Gal. ii.). Certamen grave exoritur in Ecclesia Antiochena inter eos, qui unum Christum praedicabant: sicut commemorat Lucas in Actis Apost., Cap. xv. Gravia semper fuerunt in Ecclesia certamina, et dissenserunt inter sese de rebus non levibus doctores ecclesiae praeclarissimi, ut ex his contentionibus interim Ecclesia non id esse desineret, quod erat. Ita enim placet Deo, dissidiis ecclesiasticis uti, ad gloriam nominis sui, ad illustrandam denique veritatem, et ut qui probati sunt, manifesti fiant.

11. Ceterum ut non agnoscimus aliud caput Ecclesiae quam Christum, ita non agnoscimus quamlibet Ecclesiam, quae se venditat pro vera, veram esse Ecclesiam; sed illam docemus veram esse Ecclesiam, in qua signa vel notae inveniuntur Ecclesiae verae, imprimis vero Verbi Dei legitima vel sincera praedicatio, prout nobis est tradita in libris Prophetarum et Apostolorum, qui omnes ad Christum deducunt, qui in Evangelio dixit: *Oves meae vocem meam audiunt, et ego cognosco eas, et sequuntur me, et ego vitam aeternam do eis. Alienum autem non sequuntur, sed fugiunt, ab eo, quia non noverunt vocem alienorum* (Joh. x. 4, 5, 27, 28).

12. Et qui tales sunt in Ecclesia, hi unam habent fidem, unum spiritum, et idcirco unum solum Deum adorant, solum hunc in spiritu et veritate colunt, hunc ex toto corde et omnibus viribus solum diligunt, solum per Christum mediatorem et intercessorem unicum invocant, extra Christum fidemque in ipsum nullam quaerunt justitiam et vitam; quia Christum solum caput et fundamentum Ecclesiae agnoscunt, ac super hoc impositi

quotidie se poenitentia reparant, patientia impositam ipsis crucem ferunt, sed et caritate non ficta cum omnibus Christi membris connexi, hac se declarant discipulos esse Christi, perseverando in vinculo pacis atque unitatis sanctae; simul et participant sacramentis a Christo institutis, et ab Apostolis traditis: neque his aliter utuntur, quam uti acceperunt a Domino. Notum est enim omnibus illud Apostoli: *Ego enim accepi a Domino, quod et tradidi vobis* (1 Cor. xi. 23). Proinde damnamus illas ecclesias, ut alienas a vera Christi Ecclesia, quae tales non sunt, quales esse debere audivimus, utcunque interim jactent successionem episcoporum, unitatem, et antiquitatem. Quinimo praecipiunt nobis Apostoli, ut fugiamus idololatriam et Babylonem, et ne participemus cum hac, nisi et plagarum Dei participes esse velimus (1 Cor. x. 14, 21; 1 Joh. v. 21; Apoc. xviii. 4; 1 Cor. vi. 9).

13. Communionem vero cum Ecclesia Christi vera tanti facimus, ut negemus eos coram Deo vivere posse, qui cum vera Dei Ecclesia non communicant, sed ab ea se separant. Nam ut extra arcam Noë non erat ulla salus, pereunte mundo in diluvio, ita credimus, extra Christum, qui se electis in Ecclesia fruendum praebet, nullam esse salutem certam: et proinde docemus, vivere volentes non oportere separari a vera Christi Ecclesia.

14. Signis tamen commemoratis non ita arcte includimus Ecclesiam, ut omnes illos extra Ecclesiam esse doceamus, qui vel sacramentis non participant, non quidem volentes, neque per contemtum, sed necessitate potius inevitabili coacti, nolentes ab iis abstinent, aut iis carent: vel in quibus aliquando deficit fides, non tamen penitus exstinguitur, aut prorsus desinit: vel in quibus infirmitatis vitia atque errores inveniuntur. Scimus enim, Deum aliquot habuisse in mundo amicos, extra Israelis rempublicam. Scimus, quid populo Dei evenerit in captivitate Babylonica, in qua sacrificiis suis caruerunt annis septuaginta; scimus, quid evenerit S. Petro negatori, et quid quotidie evenire soleat electis Dei fidelibus, errantibus et infirmis. Scimus praeterea, quales Apostolorum temporibus fuerint Galatarum et Corinthiorum ecclesiae, in quibus multa et gravia accusat

Apostolus scelera, et tamen nuncupat easdem sanctas Christi ecclesias.

15. Quinimo fit aliquando, ut Deus justo judicio veritatem verbi sui, fidemque Catholicam, et cultum Dei legitimum sic obscurari et convelli sinat, ut prope videatur exstincta, et nulla amplius superesse Ecclesia: sicuti factum videmus Eliae et aliis temporibus. Interim habet Deus in hoc mundo et in hisce tenebris suos illos veros adoratores, nec paucos, sed septem millia ac plures (1 Reg. xix. 18; Apoc. vii. 4, 9). Nam et Apostolus clamat: *Solidum fundamentum Dei stat, habens signaculum hoc, novit Dominus, qui sunt sui!* etc. (2 Tim. ii. 19). Unde et Ecclesia invisibilis appellari potest, non, quod homines sint invisibiles, ex quibus Ecclesia colligitur, sed quod oculis nostris absconsa, Deo autem soli nota, judicium humanum saepe subterfugiat.

16. Rursus non omnes, qui numerantur in Ecclesia, sancti et viva atque vera sunt ecclesiae membra. Sunt enim hypocritae multi, qui foris Verbum Dei audiunt, et sacramenta palam percipiunt, Deum quoque per Christum invocare solum, Christum confiteri, justitiam suam unicam, Deum item colere, et caritatis officia exercere, patientiaque in calamitatibus ad tempus perdurare videntur; sed intus vera Spiritus illuminatione, et fide animique sinceritate, et finali perseverantia destituuntur. Qui etiam, quales sint, tandem deteguntur fere. Joannes enim Apostolus: *Exierunt ex nobis*, inquit, *sed non erant ex nobis. Nam si fuissent ex nobis, permansissent utique nobiscum* (1 Joh. ii. 19). Et tamen, dum hi simulant pietatem, licet ex Ecclesia non sint, numerantur tamen in Ecclesia: sicuti proditores in republica, priusquam detegantur, numerantur et ipsi inter cives, et quemadmodum lolium vel zizania et palea inveniuntur in tritico, aut sicut strumae et tumores inveniuntur in integro corpore, cum revera morbi et deformitates sint verius corporis, quam membra vera. Proinde Ecclesia Dei recte comparatur sagenae, quae omnis generis pisces attrahit, et agro, in quo inveniuntur et zizania et triticum. Ubi maxime cavere oportet, ne ante tempus judicemus, et excludere abjicereque, aut excindere conemur eos, quos Dominus excludi abjicique non vult, aut

quos sine jactura Ecclesiae separare non possumus. Rursus vigilandum est, ne, stertentibus piis, impii proficiendo damnum dent Ecclesiae (Matt. xiii. 25).

17. Observandum praeterea diligenter docemus, in quo potissimum sit sita veritas et unitas Ecclesiae, ne temere schismata, excitemus, et in Ecclesia foveamus. Sita est illa non in caerimoniis et ritibus externis, sed magis in veritate et unitate fidei Catholicae. Fides Catholica non est nobis tradita humanis legibus, sed Scriptura divina, cujus compendium est Symbolum Apostolicum. Unde legimus, apud veteres rituum fuisse diversitatem variam, sed eam liberam, qua nemo unquam existimavit dissolvi unitatem ecclesiasticam. In dogmatibus itaque et in vera concordique praedicatione Evangelii Christi, et in ritibus a Domino diserte traditis, dicimus veram Ecclesiae constare concordiam; ubi illam maxime Apostoli sententiam urgemus. *Quotquot itaque perfecti sumus, hoc sentiamus. Quod si quid aliter sentitis, hoc quoque vobis Deus revelabit. Attamen in eo, ad quod pervenimus, eadem incedamus regula, et itidem simus affecti* (Phil. iii. 15, 16).

Confessio Fidei Gallicana (A.D. 1559)[1]

XXV. Or, parce que nous ne jouissons de Jésus-Christ que par l'Évangile, nous croyons que l'ordre de l'Église, qui a été établi en son autorité, doit être sacré et inviolable, et partant que l'Église ne peut subsister sinon qu'il y ait des pasteurs qui aient la charge d'enseigner, lesquels on doit honorer et écouter en révérence quand ils sont dûment appelés, et exercent fidèlement leur office. Non pas que Dieu soit attaché à telles aides ou moyens inférieurs, mais parce qu'il lui plaît nous entretenir sous telle bride. En quoi nous détestons tous Fantastiques qui voudraient bien, en tant qu'en eux est, anéantir le ministère et prédication de la parole de Dieu et des sacrements.

XXVI. Nous croyons donc que nul ne se doit retirer à part, et se contenter de sa personne, mais que tous ensemble doivent

[1] The spelling is modernized as in the authorized text published at Toulouse, 1864, by the *Société des livres religieux*.

garder et entretenir l'union de l'Église, se soumettant à l'instruction commune et au joug de Jésus-Christ; et ce en quelque lieu où Dieu aura établi un vrai ordre de l'Église encore que les magistrats et leurs édits y soient contraires, que tous ceux qui ne s'y rangent, ou s'en séparent, contrarient à l'ordonnance de Dieu.

XXVII. Toutefois, nous croyons qu'il convient discerner soigneusement, et avec prudence, quelle est la vraie Église, parce que par trop on abuse de ce titre. Nous disons donc, suivant la parole de Dieu, que c'est la compagnie des fidèles qui s'accordent à suivre cette Parole et la pure religion qui en dépend, et qui profitent en elle tout le temps de leur vie, croissant et se confirmant en la crainte de Dieu, selon qu'ils ont besoin de s'avancer et de marcher toujours plus outre. Même quoiqu'ils s'efforcent, qu'il leur convient avoir incessamment recours à la rémission de leurs péchés, néanmoins nous ne nions point que parmi les fidèles il n'y ait des hypocrites et réprouvés, desquels la malice ne peut effacer le titre de l'Église.

XXVIII. Sous cette créance nous protestons que là où la parole de Dieu n'est point reçue, et où on ne fait nulle profession de s'assujettir à elle, et où il n'y a nul usage des sacrements, à parler proprement, on ne peut juger qu'il y ait aucune Église. Partant, nous condamnons les assemblées de la papauté, vu que la pure vérité de Dieu en est bannie, esquelles les sacrements sont corrompus, abâtardis, falsifiés ou anéantis du tout; et esquelles toutes superstitions et idolâtries ont la vogue. Nous tenons donc que tous ceux qui se mêlent en tels actes, et y communiquent, se séparent et se retranchent du corps de Jésus-Christ. Toutefois, parce qu'il reste encore quelque petite trace de l'Église en la papauté, et même que la vertu et substance du baptême y est demeurée, joint que l'efficace du baptême ne dépend pas de celui qui l'administre, nous confessons ceux qui y sont baptisés n'avoir besoin d'un second baptême. Cependant à cause des corruptions qui y sont, on n'y peut présenter les enfants sans se polluer.

XXIX. Quant est da la vraie Église, nous croyons qu'elle doit être gouvernée selon la police que notre Seigneur Jésus-Christ à établie. C'est qu'il y ait des pasteurs, des surveillants et des diacres, afin que la pure doctrine ait son cours, que les vices soient corrigés et réprimés, et que les pauvres et tous autres affligés soient secourus en leurs nécessités; et que les assemblées se fassent au nom de Dieu, esquelles grands et petits soient édifiés.

XXX. Nous croyons tous vrais pasteurs, en quelque lieu qu'ils soient, avoir même autorité et égale puissance sous un seul chef, seul souverain et seul universel évêque, Jésus-Christ; et pour cette cause, que nulle Église ne doit prétendre aucune domination ou seigneurie sur l'autre.

XXXI. Nous croyons que nul ne se doit ingérer de son autorité propre pour gouverner l'Église, mais que cela se doit faire par élection, en tant qu'il est possible et que Dieu le permet. Laquelle exception nous y ajoutons notamment, parce qu'il a fallu quelquefois, et même de notre temps (auquel l'état de l'Église était interrompu), que Dieu ait suscité des gens d'une façon extraordinaire pour dresser l'Église de nouveau, qui était en ruine et désolation. Mais, quoi qu'il en soit, nous croyons qu'il se faut toujours conformer à cette règle. Que tous pasteurs, surveillants et diacres aient témoignage d'être appelés à leur office.

XXXII. Nous croyons aussi qu'il est bon et utile que ceux qui sont élus pour être superintendants, avisent entre eux quel moyen ils devront tenir pour le régime de tout le corps, et toutefois qu'ils ne déclinent nullement de ce qui nous en a été donné par notre Seigneur Jésus-Christ. Ce qui n'empêche point qu'il n'y ait quelques ordonnances particulières en chacun lieu, selon que la commodité le requerra.

XXXIII. Cependant nous excluons toutes inventions humaines, et toutes lois qu'on voudrait introduire sous ombre du service de Dieu, par lesquelles on voudrait lier les consciences; mais seulement recevons ce qui fait et est propre pour nourir la concorde, et tenir chacun depuis le premier jusqu'au dernier en obéissance. En quoi nous avons à suivre ce que notre Seigneur Jésus a déclaré quant à l'excommunication; laquelle nous approuvons et confessons être nécessaire avec toutes ses appartenances.

Confessio Belgica (A.D. 1561)[1]

XXVII. *De Ecclesia Catholica*

Nous croyons et confessons une seule Église catholique ou universelle, laquelle est une sainte congrégation et assemblée des vrais fidèles Chrétiens, attendant tout leur salut en Jésus-Christ, étant lavés par son sang, et sanctifiés et scellés par le Saint-Esprit.

Cette Église a été dès le commencement du monde, et sera ainsi jusqu'à la fin, comme il appert en ce que Christ est Roi éternel, qui ne peut être sans sujets. Et cette sainte Église est maintenue de Dieu contre la rage de tout le monde, encore que pour quelque temps elle soit bien petite en apparence, aux yeux des hommes, et comme éteinte; comme le Seigneur pendant un temps si dangereux qu'était celui d'Achab, s'est réservé sept mille hommes, qui n'ont pas ployé le genou devant Baal.

Aussi cette sainte Église n'est point située, attachée ni limitée en un certain lieu, ou à certains personnages; mais elle est répandue et dispersée par tout le monde, étant toutefois jointe et unie de cœur et de volonté, en un même esprit par la vertu de la foi.

XXVIII. *De Communione Sanctorum cum Vera Ecclesia*

Nous croyons que puisque cette sainte assemblée et congrégation, est l'assemblée des sauvés, et qu'il n'y a point de salut hors d'elle, que nul, de quelque état et qualité qu'il soit, ne se doit retirer à part pour se contenter de sa personne, mais tous ensemble s'y doivent ranger et unir, entretenant l'unité de l'Église, en se soumettant à son instruction et discipline, ployant le col sous le joug de Jésus-Christ, et servant à l'édification des frères, selon les dons que Dieu a mis en eux, comme membres communs d'un même corps; et, afin que cela se puisse mieux

[1] The spelling is modernized as in the authorized text published at Brussels, 1850, by the *Société evangélique belge*. Text as revised by Synod of Dort, 1619.

garder, c'est le devoir de tous fidèles, selon la Parole de Dieu, de se séparer de ceux qui ne sont point de l'Église pour se ranger à cette assemblée, en quelque lieu que Dieu l'ait mise, encore que les magistrats, et les édits des Princes fussent contraires, et que la mort et punition corporelle en dépendît.

Ainsi tous ceux qui s'en retirent, ou ne s'y rangent, contrarient à l'ordonnance de Dieu.

XXIX. *De Notis Verae Ecclesiae*

Nous croyons qu'il faut bien diligemment discerner, et avec bonne prudence par la Parole de Dieu, quelle est la vraie Église, à cause que toutes les sectes qui sont aujourd'hui au monde se couvrent de ce nom d'Église.

Nous ne parlons pas ici de la compagnie des hypocrites qui sont mêlés parmi les bons en l'Église, et cependant n'en sont point, bien qu'ils y soient présents quant au corps; mais nous parlons de distinguer le corps et la communion de la vraie Église d'avec toutes autres sectes qui se disent être l'Église.

Les marques pour connaître la vraie Église sont telles: Si l'Église use de la pure prédication de l'Évangile; si elle use de la pure administration des sacrements, comme Christ les a ordonnés; si la discipline ecclésiastique est en usage pour corriger les vices. Bref, si on se règle selon la pure Parole de Dieu, rejetant toutes choses contraires à elle, tenant Jésus-Christ pour le seul chef. Par cela on peut être assuré de connaître la vraie Église, et n'est le devoir d'aucun d'en être séparé. Et quant à ceux qui sont de l'Église, on les peut connaître par les marques des Chrétiens; savoir par la foi; et quand, ayant reçu un seul sauveur Jésus-Christ, ils fuient le péché et suivent justice, aimant le vrai Dieu et leurs prochains, sans se détourner à droite ou à gauche, crucifiant leur chair avec ses faits; non pas toutefois qu'il n'y ait une grande infirmité en eux, mais ils combattent contre par l'Esprit, tous les jours de leur vie, ayant continuellement recours au sang, à la mort, passion et obéissance du Seigneur Jésus, par lequel ils ont rémission de leurs péchés en la foi en lui.

Quant à la fausse Église, elle s'attribue à elle et à ses ordonnances plus d'autorité qu'à la Parole de Dieu. Elle ne veut pas s'assujettir au joug de Christ. Elle n'administre point les sacrements selon que Christ a ordonné par sa Parole; mais elle y ajoute et diminue, comme il lui plaît; elle se fonde sur les hommes plus que sur Jésus-Christ; elle persécute ceux qui vivent saintement selon la Parole de Dieu, et qui la reprennent de ses vices, de ses avarices, de ses idolâtries. Ces deux Églises sont aisées à connaître pour les distinguer l'une de l'autre.

CONFESSIO SCOTICANA[1] (A.D. 1560)

XVIII. *Of the Notis, be the quhilk the Trewe Kirk is Decernit fra the False, and quha sall be Judge of the Doctrine*

Because that *Sathan* from the beginning hes laboured to deck his pestilent Synagoge with the title of the Kirk of God, and hes inflamed the hertes of cruell murtherers to persecute, trouble, and molest the trewe Kirk and members thereof, as *Cain* did *Abell*, *Ismael Isaac*, *Esau Jacob*, and the haill Priesthead of the Jewes Christ Jesus himselfe, and his Apostles after him. It is ane thing maist requisite, that the true Kirk be decerned fra the filthie Synagogues, be cleare and perfite notes, least we being deceived, receive and imbrace, to our awin condemnatioun, the ane for the uther. The notes, signes, and assured takens whereby the immaculate Spouse of *Christ Jesus* is knawen fra the horrible harlot, the Kirk malignant, we affirme, are nouther Antiquitie, Title usurpit, lineal Descence, Place appointed, nor multitude of men approving ane error. For *Cain*, in age and title, was preferred to *Abel* and *Seth*. *Jerusalem* had prerogative above all places of the eird, where alswa were the Priests lineally descended fra Aaron, and greater number followed the Scribes, Pharisies, and Priestes, then unfainedly beleeved and approved Christ Jesus and his doctrine: And zit, as we suppose, no man of sound judgment will grant, that ony of the forenamed were

[1] A Latin version, attributed to Patrick Adamson, was published at St Andrews, 1572.

the Kirk of God. The notes therefore of the trew Kirk of God we beleeve, confesse, and avow to be, first, the trew preaching of the Worde of God, into the quhilk God hes revealed himselfe unto us, as the writings of the Prophets and Apostles dois declair. Secundly, the right administration of the Sacraments of *Christ Jesus*, quhilk man be annexed unto the word and promise of God, to seale and confirme the same in our hearts. Last, Ecclesiastical discipline uprightlie ministred, as Goddis Worde prescribes, whereby vice is repressed, and vertew nurished. Wheresoever then thir former notes are seene, and of ony time continue (be the number never so fewe, about two or three), there, without all doubt, is the trew Kirk of *Christ*: Who, according unto his promise, is in the middis of them. Not that universall, of quhilk we have before spoken, bot particular, sik as wes in *Corinthus*, *Galatia*, *Ephesus*, and uther places in quhilk the ministrie wes planted be *Paull*, and were of himselfe named the kirks of God. And sik kirks, we the inhabitantis of the Realme of *Scotland*, professoris of *Christ Jesus*, professis our selfis to have in our citties, townes, and places reformed, for the doctrine taucht in our Kirkis, conteined in the writen Worde of God, to wit, in the buiks of the Auld and New Testamentis, in those buikis we meane quhilk of the ancient have been reputed canonicall. In the quhilk we affirme, that all thingis necessary to be beleeved for the salvation of mankinde is sufficiently expressed. The interpretation quhairof, we confesse, neither appertaines to private nor publick persone, nether zit to ony Kirk, for ony preheminence or prerogative, personallie or locallie, quhilk ane hes above ane uther, bot apperteines to the Spirite of God, be the quhilk also the Scripture was written. When controversie then happines, for the right understanding of ony place or sentence of Scripture, or for the reformation of ony abuse within the Kirk of God, we ought not sa meikle to luke what men before us have said or done, as unto that quhilk the haly Ghaist uniformelie speakes within the body of the Scriptures, and unto that quhilk Christ Jesus himselfe did, and commanded to be done. For this is ane thing universallie granted, that the Spirite of God, quhilk is the Spirite of unitie, is in nathing contrarious unto himselfe. Gif then the interpretation, determination, or sentence of ony Doctor, Kirk, or Councell, repugne to the plaine Worde of God, written in ony uther place of the Scripture, it is a thing maist certaine, that there is not the true understanding and meaning of the haly Ghaist, although that Councels, Realmes, and Nations have approved and received the same. For we dare non receive or admit ony interpretation quhilk repugnes to ony principall point of our faith, or to ony uther plaine text of Scripture, or zit unto the rule of charitie.

Articuli xxxix Ecclesiae Anglicanae[1] (A.D. 1562)

XIX. *De Ecclesia*

Ecclesia Christi uisibilis est cœtus fidelium, in quo uerbum Dei purum prædicatur, et sacramenta, quoad ea quae necessario exiguntur, iuxta Christi institutum recte administrantur.

Sicut errauit ecclesia Hierosolymitana, Alexandrina et Antiochena: ita et errauit Ecclesia Romana, non solum quoad agenda et cæremoniarum ritus, uerum in hijs etiam quae credenda sunt.

The Irish Articles of Religion (A.D. 1615)

68. There is but one Catholic Church (out of which there is no salvation), containing the universal company of all the saints that ever were, are, or shall be, gathered together in one body, under one head, Christ Jesus: part whereof is already in heaven *triumphant*, part as yet *militant* here upon earth. And because this Church consisteth of all those, and those alone, which are elected by God unto salvation, and regenerated by the power of his Spirit, the number of whom is known only unto God himself: therefore it is called the *Catholic* or universal, and the *Invisible* Church.

[1] The English text was published at London in 1571 by John Cawood, and published with the Latin by royal authority in the same year; thereafter subscription to the English text was required. Nevertheless, it is the Latin text that is to be preferred in case of doubt. (Cf. Charles Hardwick, *History of the Articles of Religion* (Cambridge, edit. 1859), p. 277 ff.).

69. But particular and visible Churches (consisting of those who make profession of the faith of Christ, and live under the outward means of salvation) be many in number: wherein the more or less sincerely, according to Christ's institution, the Word of God is taught, the Sacraments are administered, and the authority of the Keys is used, the more or less pure are such Churches to be accounted.

70. Although in the visible Church the evil be ever mingled with the good, and sometimes the evil have chief authority in the ministration of the Word and Sacraments: yet, forasmuch as they do not the same in their own name, but in Christ's, and minister by his commission and authority, we may use their ministry both in hearing the Word and in receiving the Sacraments. Neither is the effect of Christ's ordinance taken away by their wickedness, nor the grace of God's gifts diminished from such as by faith and rightly do receive the Sacraments ministered unto them; which are effectual, because of Christ's institution and promise, although they be ministered by evil men. Nevertheless it appertaineth to the discipline of the Church that inquiry be made of evil ministers, and that they be accused by those that have knowledge of their offences, and finally, being found guilty, by just judgment be deposed.

The Westminster Confession of Faith (A.D. 1647)

XXV. *Of the Church*

I. The catholic or universal Church, which is invisible, consists of the whole number of the elect, that have been, are, or shall be gathered into one, under Christ the head thereof; and is the spouse, the body, the fullness of him that filleth all in all.

II. The visible Church, which is also catholic or universal under the gospel (not confined to one nation as before under the law) consists of all those, throughout the world, that profess the true religion, and of their children; and is the kingdom of the Lord Jesus Christ, the house and family of God, out of which there is no ordinary possibility of salvation.

III. Unto this catholic visible Church Christ hath given the ministry, oracles, and ordinances of God, for the gathering and perfecting of the saints, in this life, to the end of the world: and doth by his own presence and Spirit, according to his promise, make them effectual thereunto.

IV. This catholic Church hath been sometimes more, sometimes less visible. And particular churches, which are members thereof, are more or less pure, according as the doctrine of the gospel is taught and embraced, ordinances administered, and public worship performed more or less purely in them.

V. The purest churches under heaven are subject both to mixture and error; and some have so degenerated as to become no churches of Christ, but synagogues of Satan. Nevertheless, there shall be always a Church on earth to worship God according to his will.

VI. There is no other head of the Church but the Lord Jesus Christ: nor can the Pope of Rome, in any sense be head thereof; but is that Antichrist, that man of sin and son of perdition, that exalteth himself in the Church against Christ, and all that is called God.

BIBLIOGRAPHY

The following is a list of some modern works relating to the nature of the Church

Abbott, T. K., *Commentary on Ephesians* (International Critical Commentary), 1897.

Adam, K., 'Das Problem des Geschichtlichen im Leben der Kirche' in *Theol. Quartalsch.*, 1948.

Ainslie, J. L., *Doctrines of Ministerial Order in the Reformed Churches*, 1940.

Alivisatos, H., 'The Greek Orthodox Church's Unbroken Continuity with the Undivided Church' in *Church Quarterly Review*, July 1934.

Allis, O. T., *Prophecy and the Church*, 1945.

Allo, E. B., *Première épître aux Corinthiens*, 1934.

Althaus, P., *Communio sanctorum*, 1929; *Die christliche Wahrheit*, 1948.

Amiot, F., *L'Enseignement de Saint Paul* (4th ed.), 1946.

Anderson, W. K. (ed.), *Protestantism, a Symposium* (3rd ed.), 1946.

Asmussen, H., 'Kirche augsburgischer Konfession' in *Theologische Existenz Heute* (xvi), 1934; *Die Kirche und das Amt*, 1939.

Ashworth, R. A., 'The Witness of the Churches of the Congregational Order' in *Christendom* (v, 4), 1940.

Aubrey, E. E., 'The Church and the Holy Spirit' in *J. T. S.* (xli), 1940.

Aulén, G., 'The Church in the Light of the New Testament' in *The Universal Church in God's Design*, 1948; *The Faith of the Christian Church*, 1948; 'The "Errors" of Lutheranism' in *Theology*, March 1949.

Bacon, B. W., *The Founding of the Church*, 1925.

Baillie, D. M., *God Was in Christ*, 1948; *The Theology of the Sacraments*, 1956.

Bainton, R. H., 'The Sectarian Theory of the Church' in *Christendom* (xi, 3), 1946.

Bainvel, J. 'Apostolicité' in *Dict. de Théologie Catholique.*

Barrett, C. K., *The Holy Spirit and the Gospel Tradition*, 1947.

Barry, F. R., *The Relevance of the Church*, 1935.

Barth, K., *Die kirchliche Dogmatik*, 1932 ff.; 'Die Kirche und die Kultur' in *Zwischen den Zeiten*, 1926; *Die Theologie und die Kirche*,

1928; *Credo*, 1936; *The Teaching of the Church regarding Baptism*, 1948; *The Church and the Churches*, 1937; 'The Church—the Living Congregation of the Living Lord Jesus Christ' in *The Universal Church in God's Design*, 1948; 'Gottes Wille und unsere Wünsche' in *Theologische Existenz Heute* (vii), 1934.

Barth, Markus, *Die Taufe ein Sakrament?* 1951.

Barthélemy, D., and Milik, J. T., *Discoveries in the Judean Desert, Qumran Cave I*, 1955.

Bartlet, J. V., *Church Life and Church Order during the First Four Centuries*, 1941.

Bate, H. N., *Faith and Order*, 1927.

Batiffol, P., *L'Église naissante et le catholicisme*, 1909.

Baxter, R., *Gildas Salvianus: The Reformed Pastor* (ed. J. T. Williams), 1950.

Behm, J., *Die Handauflegung im Urchristentum*, 1911.

Bell, G. K. A., and Deissmann, A. (edd.), *Mysterium Christi*, 1930.

Belser, J. E., *Der Epheserbrief*, 1908.

Bernardin, J. B., 'The Church in the New Testament' in *Anglican Theological Review*, xxi (1939).

Bésobrasoff, C., *La Pentecôte johannique*, 1939; *The Approach to Christian Unity*, 1951.

Best, E., *One Body in Christ*, 1955.

Bettenson, H., *The Early Christian Fathers*, 1956.

Bévenot, M., 'Membership of the Church' in *The Month*, June 1950.

Boegner, M., *Qu'est ce que l'Église?* 1931.

Birkbeck, J., *Russia and the English Church During the last Fifty Years*, 1895.

Bohatec, *Calvins Lehre von Staat und Kirche*, 1937.

Bolshakoff, S., *The Doctrine of the Unity of the Church*, 1946.

Bonhoeffer, D., *Sanctorum communio*, 1930; 'Zur Frage nach der Kirchengemeinschaft' in *Evangelische Theologie*, 1936; *The Cost of Discipleship*, 1949.

Bonnard, P., *Jésus-Christ édifiant son Église*, 1928.

Bousset, W., *Kyrios Christos* (3rd ed.) 1926; *Die Religion des Judentums im späthellenistischen Zeitalter* (3rd ed.), 1926.

Bowman, J. W., *The Intention of Jesus*, 1943.

Brandon, S. G. F., *The Fall of Jerusalem and the Christian Church*, 1951.

Braun, F. M., *Neues Licht auf der Kirche*, 1946; *Aspects nouveaux du problème de l'Église*, 1942.

Brilioth, Y., *Eucharistic Faith and Practice, Evangelical and Catholic*, 1930.

Bronkhorst, A. J., *Op Weeg naar een nieuwe Kerkorde*, 1945; *Schrift en Kerkorde*, 1947.

Broutin, P., *L'Evêque dans la tradition pastorale du XVIème siècle*, 1953.
Bruce, F. F., *The Acts of the Apostles*, 1951.
Brunner, E., *Revelation and Reason*, 1946; *The Misunderstanding of the Church*, 1952; *The Divine Imperative*, 1937.
Bultmann, R., 'Die Frage nach der Echtheit von Matthäus 16: 17–19' in *Theol. Blatter* (xx), 1941, 265ff; *Theology of the New Testament*, 1951, 1955; *Primitive Christianity in its Contemporary Setting*, 1956; 'The Transformation of the Idea of the Church in Early Christianity' in *Can. Journ. of Theol.* (i, 2), July 1955.
Burkhardt, B. L., 'The Rise of the Christian Priesthood' in *Journal of Religion* (xxii), 1942.
Burn-Murdoch, H., *Church, Continuity and Unity*, 1945.
Burrows, M., *An Outline of Biblical Theology*, 1946; *The Dead Sea Scrolls from St Mark's Monastery* (ii, fasc. 2) 1951; *The Dead Sea Scrolls*, 1955.

Caird, G. B., *The Apostolic Age*, 1955.
Campbell, J. Y., '*Koinonia* and its Cognates in the New Testament' in *J. B. L.* (li), 1932; 'The Origin and Meaning of the Christian Use of the Word *Ekklesia*' in *J. T. S.* (xlix), 1948.
Campbell, T., *A Declaration and Address*, 1809.
Campenhausen, H. von, *Der urchristliche Apostelbegriff*, 1948; *Kirchliches Amt und Geistliche Vollmacht in den ersten Jahrhunterten*, 1953.
Carrington, P., *The Early Christian Church*, 1957.
Casel, O., 'Die Kirchenordnung Hippolyts von Rom' in *Archiv für Liturgiewissenschaft* (ii), 1952.
Cave, S., *The Doctrines of the Christian Faith*, 1931.
Cerfaux, L., *La Théologie de l'Église suivant Saint Paul* (2nd ed.) 1948.
Chavasse, C., *The Bride of Christ*, 1940.
Clark, E. T., *The Small Sects in America*, 1949.
Congar, Y., *Vraie et Fausse réforme dans l'Église*, 1950; *Divided Christendom*, 1939.
Congar et Long-Hasselmans: 'Sur la sacerdoce' in *Revue des sciences relig.* (xxv), 1951.
Coppens, J., *L'imposition des mains*, 1925; *Les documents du désert de Juda et les origines du Christianısme* (Analecta Lovaniensa 39), 1953.
Courvoisier, *La notion de l'Église chez Bucer*, 1933.
Couturier, P., 'Chaque chrétien est responsable de l'Église' in *Amıtié*, Jan. 1947.
Craig, C. T., 'The Church of the New Testament' in *The Universal Church in God's Design*, 1948; *The One Church*, 1951.
Cullmann, O., *Köningsherrschaft Christi und Kirche im Neuen Testament*

(3rd ed.), 1950; *Urchristentum und Gottesdienst*, 1950; *Christ and Time*, 1951; *Peter, Disciple, Apostle, Martyr*, 1951; 'The Significance of the Qumran Texts for Research into the Beginnings of Christianity' in *J. B. L.* (lxxiv), December 1955.

Dahl, N. A., *Das Volk Gottes*, 1941; 'Christ, Creation and the Church' in *The Background of the New Testament and its Eschatology* (C. H. Dodd *Festschrift*, edd. Davies, W. D., and Daube, D.), 1955.

Darquennes, A., 'La définition de l'Église d'après saint Thomas d'Aquin' in *L'Organisation corporative du Moyen-Âge à la fin de l'Ancien Régime*, 1943.

Davies, J. G., *He Ascended into Heaven* (Bampton Lectures), 1958.

Davies, R. E., *The Problem of Authority in the Continental Reformers*, 1946.

Davies, W. D., *Paul and Rabbinic Judaism* (2nd ed.), 1948.

Deissmann, A., *Die neutestamentliche Formel 'in Christo Jesu'*, 1892.

Dhorme, P., *L'emploi métaphorique des noms de parties du corps en hebreu et en accidien*, 1923.

Dibelius, M., *Pastoralbriefe*, 1931; *Kolosser, Epheser, und Philemon* (3rd ed., Greeven), 1953.

Dieckmann. H., *De Ecclesia*, 1925; *Die Verfassung der Urkirche*, 1923.

Dillistone, F. W., 'How is the Church Christ's Body?' in *Theology Today* (ii, 1), 1945; *The Word of God and the People of God*, 1948; *The Structure of the Divine Society*, 1951; 'Augustine's Anti-Donatist Writings' in *A Companion to the Study of St Augustine* (ed. Battenhouse, R. W.), 1955.

Dix, G., *The Shape of the Liturgy*, 1945; 'The Ministry in the Early Church' in *The Apostolic Ministry* (ed. Kirk, K. E.), 1946.

Dobschütz, E. von, *Christian Life in the Primitive Church*, 1904; 'Die Kirche im Urchristentum' in *Z. N. T. W.* (xxviii), 1929.

Dodd, C. H., *Commentary on Ephesians* (Abingdon Commentary), 1928; *The Apostolic Preaching and its Developments*, 1936; *According to the Scriptures*, 1952.

Dorner, J. A., *Kirche und Reich Gottes*, 1883; 'Das Prinzip unserer Kirche nach dem inneren Verhaltnis der materialen und formalen Seite desselben zu einander' in *Gesam. Schriften*, 1883.

Dun, A., *Prospecting for a United Church*, 1946.

Dunkerley, R., (ed.), *The Ministry and the Sacraments*, 1937.

Dupont, J., *ΣΥΝ ΧΡΙΣΤΩΙ, L'Union avec le Christ suivant Saint Paul*, 1952.

Easton, B. S., 'The Church in the New Testament' in *Anglican Theological Review* (xxii), 1940; *The Pastoral Epistles*, 1947.

Ehrenberg, H., (ed.), *Credo Ecclesiam*, 1930.

Ehrhardt, A., 'The Beginnings of Monepiscopacy' in *C. Q. R.* (cxl), 1945; *The Apostolic Succession in the First Two Centuries of the Church*, 1953; 'Jewish and Christian Ordination' in *Journal of Ecclesiastical History* (v), 1954.

Elderenbosch, P., *De Oplegging der Handen*, 1953.

Ewald, P., *Epheser, Kolosser, u. Philemon* (Zahn Comm.), 1910.

Fagley, F., *The Congregational Churches*, 1938.

Fascher, E., *ΠΡΟΦΗΤΗΣ*, 1927.

Feckes, C., *Die Kirche als Herrenlieb*, 1949.

Feuerer, G., *Der Kirchenbegriff der dialektischen Theologie*, 1933.

Field, R., *Of the Church*, 1850.

Flemington, W. F., *The New Testament Doctrine of Baptism*, 1948.

Flew, R. N., (ed.), *The Nature of the Church*, 1952; (ed.), *The Nature of the Christian Church according to the Teaching of the Methodists*, 1937; *Jesus and His Church* (2nd ed.), 1943.

Florovsky, G., 'The Church: Her Nature and Task' in *The Universal Church in God's Design* (W. C. C.), 1948.

Foerster, E., 'Fragen zu Luthers Kirchenbegriff aus dem Gedankenwelt seines Alters' in *Festgabe Kaftan*, 1930; 'Kirche wider Kirche' in *Theol. Rundschau*, 1932.

Forsyth, P. T., *The Church and the Sacraments*, 1917.

Fraeymann, M., *La spiritualisation de l'idée du temple dans les épîtres paulines*, 1948.

Frick, H., *Das Reich Gottes*, 1926.

Fridrichsen, A., 'Église et sacrement dans le Nouveau Testament' in *Revue d'hist. et de philos. relig.* (xvii), 1937.

Gall, A. von, *ΒΑΣΙΛΕΙΑ ΤΟΥ ΘΕΟΥ*, 1926.

Galtier, *L'Unité du Christ*, 1939; 'La religion du Fils' in *Rev. d'Ascétique et de Mystique* (xix), 1938.

Garvie, A. E., *The Holy Catholic Church from the Congregationalist Point of View*, 1920.

Gaugler, E., 'Die Bedeutung der Kirche in den johannischen Schriften' in *Intern. kirchl. Z.* (xiv, xv), 1924, 1925.

George, R., *Communion with God*, 1953.

Gilmour, S. M , 'The Church in the Letter to the Ephesians' in *Christendom* (vi, 3), 1941.

Ginzberg, L., *Eine unbekannte judische Secte*.

Gloege, G., *Reich Gottes und Kirche im Neuen Testament*, 1929.

Goguel, M., *Trois Etudes sur la pensée religieuse du christianisme primitif*,

1931; (ed.), *Le Problème de l'Église*, 1947; *L'Église primitive*, 1947; *La naissance du christianisme*, 1953.
Goosens, W., *L'Église corps du Christ d'après saint Paul*, 1949.
Gore, C., *The Church and the Ministry*, 1936 (ed. Turner, C. H.).
Görres, I. Fr., 'Briefe über die Kirche' in *Frankfurter Hefte*, 1946.
Goudge, H. L., *The Church of England and Reunion*, 1938.
Grabmann, M., *Die Lehre des hl. Thomas von der Kirche als Gotteswerk*, 1903.
Grant, F. C., 'The Nature of the Church in the N.T.' in *Anglican Theol. Review* (xxi), 1939; *An Introduction to New Testament Thought*, 1950.
Grützmacher, R. D., 'Die alt- und neuprotestantische Auffassung von der Kirche' in *Neue kirchliche Zeitschrift* (xxvii), 1916.
Gutbrod, W., *Die paulinische Anthropologie*, 1934.

Hahn, W. T., *Das Mitsterben und Mitauferstehen mit Christus bei Paulus*, 1937.
Hamel, A., *Die Kirche bei Hippolyt*, 1951.
Hamilton, H. F., *The People of God*, 1912.
Hanson, S., *The Unity of the Church in the New Testament: Colossians and Ephesians*, 1946.
Harnack, A. von, *Sources of the Apostolic Canons*, 1895; *The Constitution and Law of the Church*, 1910; 'Der Spruch über Petrus als den Felsen der Kirche, Matt, 16:17f.' in *Sitz. Akad. Wiss.*, 1918, pp. 637–54.
Hastie, W., *Theology of the Reformed Churches*, 1904.
Hatch, E., *The Organization of the Early Christian Churches* (4th ed.), 1892.
Hauck, F., '*KOINΩNIA*' in Kittel's *T. W. N. T.*
Haupt, E., *Die Gefangenschaftsbriefe* (Meyer), 1902.
Havet, J., 'Christ collectif ou Christ individuel en I Cor. xii. 12?' in *Ephem. Theol. Lovan*, (xxiii), 1947.
Headlam, A. C., *The Doctrine of the Church and Christian Reunion* (2nd ed.), 1921.
Hebert, A. G., *The Throne of David*, 1941; *The Form of the Church*, 1944.
Heiler, F., *Im Ringen um die Kirche*, 1931; *Der Katholizismus*, 1923.
Heim, K., *Spirit and Truth*, 1935.
Henderson, G. D., *The Nature of the Church*, 1948.
Hendry, G. S., 'The Exposition of Holy Scripture' in *Scot. J. Theol.* (i, 1), 1948.
Hettlinger, R., and Fairweather, E. G., *Episcopacy*, 1952.
Heussi, K., *War Petrus im Rom?* 1936.
Hill, G., *Lectures in Divinity*, 1821.

Hodgson, L., (ed.), *The Second World Conference on Faith and Order*, 1937; *The Doctrine of the Church as held and taught in the Church of England*, 1946; *The Doctrine of the Trinity*. 1943,

Holk, J. van, 'The Nature of the Church' in *Christendom* (v, 1) 1940.

Holl, K., 'Der Kirchenbegriff des Paulus in seinem Verhältnis zur dem der Urgemeinde' in *Sitz. der preuss. Akad. der Wissenschaft*, 1921; *Gesammelte Aufsätze zur Kirchengeschichte*, II, 1–2, Der Osten, 1927–8.

Holtzmann, H. J., *Lehrbuch der NTliche Theologie* (2nd ed.), 1911.

Hopwood, P. G. S., *The Religious Experience of the Primitive Church*, 1936.

Hort, F. J. A., *The Christian Ecclesia*, 1897.

Horton, W. M., *Toward a Reborn Church*, 1948.

Howat, J., *Concerning Christ and the Church*, 1943.

Howard, G. B., *The Canons of the Primitive Church*, 1897.

Hromadka, J., [Principles of the Evangelical Church of Czech Brethren] (in Czech), 1932.

Huby, J., *Saint Paul, Les épîtres de la captivité*, 1947.

Huls, G., *De dienst der vrouw in de Kerk*, 1951.

Issel, E., *Der prot. Begriff der Kirche und s. Verhältnis zum Reiche Gottes*, 1889.

Jalland, T. G., *The Origin and Evolution of the Christian Church*, 1948.

Jenkins, C., and Mackenzie, K. D. (edd.), *Episcopacy, Ancient and Modern*, 1930.

Jenkins, D. T., *The Nature of Catholicity*, 1942; *The Gift of the Ministry*, 1947.

Jeremias, J., *Pastoralbriefe*, 1934; *The Eucharistic Words of Jesus*, 1955; *The Servant of God* (with Zimmerli, W.), 1957.

Johnson, S. E., *Commentary on Matthew* (The Interpreter's Bible), 1951; 'The Dead Sea Manual and the Jerusalem Church of Acts' in *Z. A. W.* (lxvi), 1954.

Johnston, G., *The Doctrine of the Church in the New Testament*, 1943; 'The Continuity of the Church' in *The Congregational Quarterly*, 1946; 'Spirit' in *A Theological Word Book of the Bible*, (ed. Richardson), 1950; 'The Church and Israel; Continuity and Discontinuity' in *Journal of Religion* (xxxiv), 1954; 'The Constitution of the Church in Early Christianity' in *Twentieth-Century Encyclopaedia of Religious Knowledge*, (ed. Loetscher), 1955; 'The Doctrine of the Church in the New Testament' in the *New Peake Commentary* (forthcoming); 'The Constitution of the Church in the NT' in the *New Peake Commentary* (forthcoming); 'Colossians' and 'Ephesians' in *The Interpreter's Dictionary of the Bible* (forthcoming).

Jungmann, J., *Die Stellung Christi in liturgischen Gebet*, 1925.

Juster, J., *Les Juifs dans l'empire romain*, 1914.

Käsemann, E., *Leib und Leib Christi* (Beitr. zur hist. Theol. 9), 1933; 'Anliegen und Eigenart der paulinischen Abendmahlslehre' in *Evangelische Theologie*, 1947–8.

Kattenbusch, F., 'Der Quellort der Kirchenidee' in *Festgabe für Harnack*, 1921; 'Der Spruch über Petrus und die Kirche bei Matthäus' in *Theologische Studien und Kritiken* (xciv), 1922; *Die Doppelschichtigkeit in Luthers Kirchenbegriff*, 1928.

Kennedy, H. A. A., *The Theology of the Epistles*, 1934.

Khomyakov, A. S., *The Church is One*, 1948.

Kirk, K. E. (ed.), *The Apostolic Ministry*, 1946 (new ed. 1957).

Knox, J., *Chapters in a Life of Paul*, 1950; 'The Ministry in the Primitive Church' in *The Advancement of Theological Education* (ed. Niebuhr, H. R., Williams, and Gustafson), 1956.

Knox, W. L., *St Paul and the Church of Jerusalem*, 1925; *St Paul and the Church of the Gentiles*, 1939.

Kohler, K., *The Origins of the Synagogue and the Church*, 1929.

Köhnlein, H., 'La notion de l'Église chez l'Apôtre Paul' in *Revue d'hist. et philos. relig.* (xvii), 1937.

Köstlin, J., *Das Wesen der Kirche nach der Lehre u. Gesch. des n. Testaments*, 1872.

Köster, J., *Die Idee der Kirche beim Apostel Paulus*, 1928.

Krauss, A., *Das protestantische Dogma von der unsichtbaren Kirche*, 1876.

Kümmel, W. G., *Der Kirchenbegriff und Geschichtsbewusstsein in der Urgemeinde und bei Jesus*, 1943.

Lacey, T. A., *The One Body and the One Spirit*, 1925.

Lauerer, H., 'Sichtbarkeit der Kirche' in *Luthertum* (xx), 1939.

Lecerf, A., 'La doctrine de l'Église dans Calvin' in *Revue de théol. et de philos.*, 1929; *An Introduction to Reformed Dogmatics*, 1949.

Leenhardt, F. J., 'Réalité et caractères de l'Église' in *La Sainte Eglise Universelle*, 1948.

Leuba, J. L. 'Le Problème de l'Église chez K. Barth' in *Verbum caro*, 1947; *New Testament Pattern*, 1953.

Leeuw, G. van der, *Religion in Essence and Manifestation*, 1938.

Leeuen, P. A. van, *Het Kerkbegrip in de Theologie van A. Kuyper*, 1946.

Lewis, E., *A Philosophy of the Christian Revelation*, 1940.

Lietzmann, H., *Messe und Herrenmahl*, 1926; *Petrus und Paulus in Rom.* 1927; *The Beginnings of the Christian Church*, 1949; *An die Korinther* (4th ed.), 1949.

Lilje, H., 'Die reformatorische Lehre von der Kirche' in *Allgemeine evangelisch-lutherische Kirchenzeitung*, 1935.

Lindsay, T. M., *The Church and the Ministry in the Early Centuries* (3rd ed.), 1907.

Linton, O., *Das Problem der Urkirche in der neueren Forschung*, 1932.

Lock, W., *The Epistle to the Ephesians*, 1929.

Lohmeyer, E., *Vom Begriff der religiösen Gemeinschaft* (Wiss. Grundfragen. Phil. Abhandl. iii), 1925; *ΣΥΝ ΧΡΙΣΤΩΙ* in *Festgabe für A. Deissmann*, 1927; *Grundlagen paulinischer Theologie* (Beitr. zur hist. Theol. i), 1929; 'Vom urchristlichen Abendmahl' in *Theologische Rundschau*, 1937.

Loisy, A., *La naissance du Christianisme*, 1933.

Lowber, *Struggles and Triumphs of the Truth*, 1888.

Lowrie, W., *The Church and its Organization*, 1904; *Problems of Church Unity*, 1924.

Lubac, H., *Catholicisme*, 1947.

MacGregor, Janet, *Scottish Presbyterian Polity*, 1926.

Mackenzie, K., *The Union of Christendom*, 1938.

Macpherson, J., *The Doctrine of the Church in Scottish Theology*, 1903.

Malevez, L., 'L'Église, corps du Christ' in *Science relig.* (27–94), 1944.

Manson, T. W., *The Teaching of Jesus* (2nd ed.), 1943; *The Church's Ministry*, 1948.

Mascall, E. L., *Christ, the Christian, and the Church*, 1946.

Masson, Ch., *Colossians*, (edd. Bonnard, Cullmann &c), 1950; *Ephesians*, 1953.

Mathews, S., *The Church and the Christian*, 1938.

Meinertz, M., *Die Gefangenschaftsbriefe des hl. Paulus* (4th ed., Tillmann), 1931; Theologie des Neuen Testaments, 1950.

Menoud, P.-H., *L'Église et les ministères selon le Nouveau Test.*, 1949.

Mersch, E., *Le corps mystique du Christ*, 1933 (2nd ed. 1936); *The Whole Christ*, 1949; *La théologie du Corps Mystique*, 1944.

Messenger, E. C., *Rome and Reunion*, 1934.

Metzger, B. M., 'Paul's Vision of the Church' in *Theology Today*, (vi), 1949.

Meyer, E., *Die Gemeinde des Neuen Bundes im Lande Damaskus*, 1919.

Michaelis, W., *Täufer, Jesus, Urgemeinde*, 1928.

Michel, O., *Das Zeugnis des N.Ts. von der Gemeinde*, 1941.

Micklem, N., *Congregationalism and the Church Catholic*, 1943.

Mirbt, C., *Quellen zur Geschichte des Papsttums und des römischen Katholizismus*, (4th ed.), 1924.

Mitton, C. L., *The Epistle to the Ephesians*, 1951.

Mittring, K., *Heilswirklichkeit bei Paulus*, 1929.

Moberly, G., *The Administration of the Holy Spirit in the Body of Christ*, 1868.

Moffatt, J., *The First Epistle of Paul to the Corinthians*, 1938.

Morrison, C. C., *What is Christianity?* 1940; *The Unfinished Reformation*, 1953.

Moore, G. F., 'The Covenanters of Damascus' in *Harvard Theol. Review*, (iv), 1911.

Morgan, W., *The Religion and Theology of Paul*, 1927.

Moule, C. F. D., 'Deacons in the N.T.' in *Theology* (lviii), 1950; *The Office of a Bishop*, 1948; *Colossians and Philemon* (C.G.T.C.), 1957; '"Fulness" and "Fill" in the N.T.' in *Scot. J. Theol.*, March 1951.

Mulert, H., *Congregatio sanctorum*, 1921.

Munck, J., 'Paul, the Apostles, and the Twelve' in *Studia Theologica* (iii), 1950.

Mundle, W., 'Das Apostelbild der Apostelgeschichte' in *Z.N.W.*, 1928.

Mussner, F., 'Christus, das All, und die Kirche' in *Studien zur Theol. des Epheserbriefes*, 1955.

Nautin, P., *Je crois à l'Esprit-Saint dans la sainte Église pour la Résurrection de la chair* (Unam sanctam, xvii), 1947.

Neeser, M., *L'Église qui sauve*, 1934.

Neill, S. (ed.), *The Ministry of the Church*, 1947.

Nelson, J. R., *The Realm of Redemption*, 1949.

Newbigin, L., *The Reunion of the Church*, 1948; *The Household of God*, 1953.

Niebuhr, H. R., *The Purpose of the Church and its Ministry*, 1956.

Niesel, W., 'Wesen und Gestalt der Kirche nach Calvin' in *Evangel. Theol.* (iii), 1936.

Nock, A. D., *St Paul*, 1938

Nygren, A., 'Corpus Christi', in *En bok om kyrken av svenska teologer*, 1943; *Agape and Eros* (rev. E. T. by Watson, P.S.), 1953; *Christ and His Church* (tr. Carlesten, A.), 1957.

Oepke, A., 'Der Herrenspruch über die Kirche Mt 16^{17-19} in der neuesten Forschung' in *Studia Theol.* (ii, 2), 1948.

Oldham, J. H., (ed.), *Church, Community and State*, (iii), 1938.

Otterbein, A., *The Diaconate according to the Apostolic Tradition of Hippolytus and Derived Documents*, 1945.

Oxnam, G. B., *On this Rock*, 1949.

Pannier, *Calvin et l'épiscopat*, 1926.

Parkes, J. W., *The Conflict of the Church and the Synagogue*, 1934.

Peel, A., (ed.), *Essays Congregational and Catholic*, 1933.

Percy, E., *Der Leib Christi*, 1942; *Die Probleme der Kolosser- und Epheserbriefe*, 1946.

Perels, O., 'Kirche und Welt nach dem Epheser- und Kolosserbriefe' in *Theol. Lit. Zeitung* (lxxvi), 1951.

Peterson, E., Die Kirche, 1929.

Pfatschbacher, H., 'Römische Recht und Katholische Kirche', in *Theologie und Glaube* (xxii), 1930.

Phythian-Adams, W. J., *The Call of Israel*, 1934; *The Way of At-onement*, 1944; *The Fulness of Israel*, 1938.

Pittenger, W. N., 'The Church as the Body of Christ' in *Christendom* (ix, 2), 1944; *His Body the Church*, 1945.

Prenter, R., *L'Église d'après le témoinage de la Confession d'Augsburg. La Sainte Église Universelle*, 1948.

Poland, F., *Geschichte des griechischens Vereinswesens*, 1909.

Prat, F., *La Théologie de Saint Paul*: I (8th ed.), 1920; II (7th ed.), 1923.

Quick, O. C., *The Christian Sacraments*, 1927

Radermacher, A., *Die Kirche als Gemeinschaft und Gesellschaft*, 1931.

Rall, H. F., 'The Church, Given or Gathered?' in *Christendom* (iv, 2), 1939.

Ramsey, A. M., *The Gospel and the Catholic Church*, 1936.

Raven, C. E., *The Gospel and the Church*, 1939.

Rawlinson, A. E. J., *The Church of England and the Church of Christ*, 1930; 'Corpus Christi' in *Mysterium Christi* (ed. Bell and Deissmann), 1930.

Reicke, B., 'Constitution of the Early Church in the Light of the Dead Sea Scrolls' in *The Scroll and the New Testament* (ed. Stendahl, K.), 1957.

Rengstorf, K. H., *Apostleship* (Bible Key Words from Kittel, tr. J. R. Coates) 1950.

Réville, J., *Les Origines de l'épiscopat*, 1894.

Richardson, A., *Une interprétation anglicane de l'Église: La Sainte Église Universelle*, 1948.

Richardson, C. C., *The Church through the Centuries*, 1938.

Richel, P. J., *Het Kerkbegrip van Calvijn*, 1942.

Riedel, W. (ed.), *Die Kirchenrechtsquellen des Patriarchats Alexandrien*, 1900.

Rietschel, E., 'Luthers Anschauung von der Unsichtbarkeit und Sichtbarkeit der Kirche' in *Theol. Studien und Kritiken*, 1900.

Robinson, J. A., *Ephesians* (3rd ed.), 1922.

Robinson, J. A. T., *The Body: A Study in Pauline Theology*, 1952.

Robinson, W., *Essays on Christian Unity*, 1922; *The Biblical Doctrine of the Church.*

Rothe, R., Die Anfänge der Christlichen Kirche und ihrer Verfassung, 1837.

Salin, E., *Civitas Dei*, 1926.

Saussure, J. de, 'Les signes de l'Église' in *Études théol. et relig.*, 1933.

Schechter, S., *Documents of Jewish Sectaries*, 1910.

Scheel, O., *Die Kirche im Urchristentum*, 1912.

Schlatter, A., *Die Geschichte der ersten Christenheit*, 1926; 'Die Grenzen der kirchl. Gemeinschaft' in *Deutsche Theologie*, 1935; *Theologie des Neuen Testaments.*

Schlier, H., *Christus und die Kirche im Epheserbrief* (Beitr. zur hist. Theol. 6), 1930.

Schmauch, W., *In Christus: Eine Untersuchung zur Sprache und Theologie des Paulus*, 1935.

Schmid, J., *Der Epheserbrief des Apostels Paulus*, 1928.

Schmidt, K. L., 'Die Kirche des Urchristentums' in *Festgabe für A. Deissmann*, 1927; *The Church* (Bible Key Words from Kittel, tr. Coates), 1950; *Le Problème du Christianisme primitif*, 1938.

Schmidt, T., *Der Leib Christi*, 1919.

Schnackenburg, R., *Das Heilsgeschehen bei der Taufe nach dem Apostel Paulus*, 1950; ' "Er hat uns mitauferweckt." Zur Tauflehre des Eph.' in *Liturg. Jahrbuch*, (ii, 2), 1952; *Die Johannesbriefe*, 1953.

Schneider, J., *Die Passionsmystik des Paulus*, 1929.

Schoeps, H. J., *Theologie und Geschichte des Judenschristentums*, 1949.

Schweitzer, A., *The Mysticism of Paul the Apostle*, 1931.

Schweizer, E., *Gemeinde nach dem N.T.*, 1942; *Das Leben des Herrn in der Gemeinde und ihren Diensten*, 1946.

Scott, C. A. A., *Christianity according to St Paul*, 1927; *The Church: Its Worship and Sacraments*, 1927.

Scott, E. F., *The Nature of the Early Church*, 1941.

Seeberg, R., *Studien z. Gesch. d. Begriffes der Kirche*, 1885.

Seesemann, M., *Die Begriff κοινωνία im N.T.*, 1933.

Selwyn, E. G. (ed.), *Essays Catholic and Critical*, 1929.

Sertillanges, A. D., *The Church*, 1922.

Shepherd, M. H., 'The Development of the Early Ministry' in *A. T. R.*, 1944.
Sickenberger, J., *Die Briefe des hl. Paulus an die Korinther und Römer*, 1932.
Simon, P., *Das Menschliche in der Kirche Christi*, 1936.
Simpson, P. Carnegie, *Church Principles*, 1923; *The Evangelical Church Catholic*, 1934.
Sladek, P., 'Göttliches und Menschliches in der Kirche. Ein Betrag zur Frage aus der Sicht des Grenzlandes' in *Theol. Quartalsch.*, 1941.
Sohm, R., *Kirchenrecht*, 1892.
Soivon, Th., *Die Kirche als der Leib Christi nach der Lehre des hl. Paulus*, 1951.
Sommerlath, E., 'Kirche und Reich Gottes' in *Z. für syst. Theol.* (xvi), 1939.
Spicq, C., *Les Epîtres pastorales*, 1947.
Spikowski, L., *La doctrine de l'Église chez S. Irenée*, 1926.
Spòrri, T., *Der Gemeindegedanke im ersten Petrusbrief*, 1925.
Stählin, W., *The Mystery of God*, 1937.
Stauffer, E., 'Jüdische Erbe im urchr. Kirchenrecht' in *Theol. Lit. Z.* (lxxvii), 1952.
Stone, D., *The Christian Church*, 1905; *The Notes of the Church*, 1910.
Streeter, B. H., *The Primitive Church*, 1929.
Strohl, H., 'La notion de l'Église chez les Réformateurs' in *Rev. d'hist. et de philos. relig.* 1936.
Strom, A. V., 'Kyrkan som Kristi kropp' in *Svensk Exegetisk Årsbok* (viii), 1943; *Vetekornet*, 1944; *Kyrkans Vasen*, 1948.
Swete, H. B. (ed.), *Essays in the Early History of the Church and Ministry* (2nd ed.), 1921.
Sykes, N., *Old Priest and New Presbyter*, 1956.

Taylor, F. J., *The Church of God*, 1946.
Taylor, V., *Jesus and His Sacrifice*, 1937; *Forgiveness and Reconciliation*, 1946.
Telfer, W., 'Episcopal Succession in Egypt' in *J. Eccl. Hist.* (iii), 1952.
Temple, W., *Christ in His Church*, 1925; *Christian Unity and Church Reunion*, 1943.
Thornton, L. S., *The Incarnate Lord*, 1928; *The Common Life in the Body of Christ* (2nd ed.), 1944.
Thurneysen, E., 'Kirche und Staat' in *Zwischen den Zeiten*, 1925.
Til, C. van, *The New Modernism*, 1946.

Tomkins, O. S., *The Wholeness of the Church*, 1949.
Torrance, T. F., 'The Nature and Mission of the Church' in *Scot. J. Theol.* (ii, 3), 1949; *Royal Priesthood*, 1956.

Vidler, A. R., *The Orb and the Cross*, 1945.
Vielhauer, Ph., *Oikodome. Das Bild vom Bau in der chr. Literatur vom N.T. bis Clem. Alex.*, 1939.
Visser 't Hooft, W. A., *The Church and its Function in Society*, 1937; *The Wretchedness and Greatness of the Church*, 1944.
Vooght, P. de, 'La part de saint Augustin dans le "De Ecclesia" de Jean Hus' in *Rech. Théol. Anc. et Méd.* (xiii), 1946.
Voste, J. M., *Commentarium in epistolam ad Ephesios* (2nd ed.), 1932.

Wagenführer, M. A., *Die Bedeutung Christi fur Welt und Kirche*, 1941.
Wagner, W., 'Die Kirche als Corpus Christi mysticum beim jungen Luther' in *Z.f. kathol. Theol.*, 1937.
Wahlstrom, E., 'A Book about the Church' in *Christendom* (xiii, 2), 1948.
Walker, J., *Scottish Theology and Theologians* (2nd ed.), 1888.
Warnack, V. and Schlier, H., *Die Kirche im Epheserbrief*, 1949.
Wedel, T. O., *The Coming Great Church*, 1945.
Weinel, H., *Biblische Theologie des N. Ts.* (4th ed.), 1928.
Weiss, J., *Die Predigt Jesu vom Reiche Gottes*, 1893; *Der erste Korintherbrief* (9th ed.), 1910; *Das Urchristentum* (completed by Knopf, R.; E. T. 1937: *The History of Primitive Christianity*), 1917.
Weltin, E. G., 'Origen's "Church" ' in *Studies Presented to David M. Robinson* (ed. Mylonas and Raymond), 1953.
Wendland, H.-D., *Die Eschatologie des Reiches Gottes bei Jesus*, 1931; 'Geistleibliche Gestalt der Kirche' in *Luthertum*, 1939.
Werdermann, H., *Der evangel. Pfarrer in Geschichte und Gegenwart*, 1925.
Werner, M., *Die Entstehung des chr. Dogmas*, 1941.
Whale, J. S., *Christian Doctrine*, 1941; *The Protestant Tradition*, 1955.
Wieland, F., 'Die genetische Entwicklung der sog. Ordines minores' in *Römische Quartalschrift* (supp. 7), 1897.
Wilkenhauser, A., *Die Kirche als der mystische Leib Christi nach dem Apostel Paulus*, 1937.
Will, R., 'La conception protestante de l'Église considerée comme le corpus Christi' in *Rev. de l'hist. et de philos. relig.* (xii), 1932.
Willis, G. G., *Saint Augustine and the Donatist Controversy*, 1950.
Windisch, H., 'Urchristentum' in *Theologische Rundschau*, 1933.
Winkler, R., *Das Wesen der Kirche, mit besonderer Berücksichtigung ihrer Sichtbarkeit*, 1930.

Woodhouse, H. F., *The Doctrine of the Church in Anglican Theology, 1547–1603*, 1954.

Zernov, N., *Three Russian Prophets*, 1944; *The Russians and their Church*, 1946; *The Church of the Eastern Christians* (4th ed.), 1947.

Zöllner and Stählin (edd.), *Die Kirche Jesu Chr. und das Wort Gottes*, 1937.

INDEX